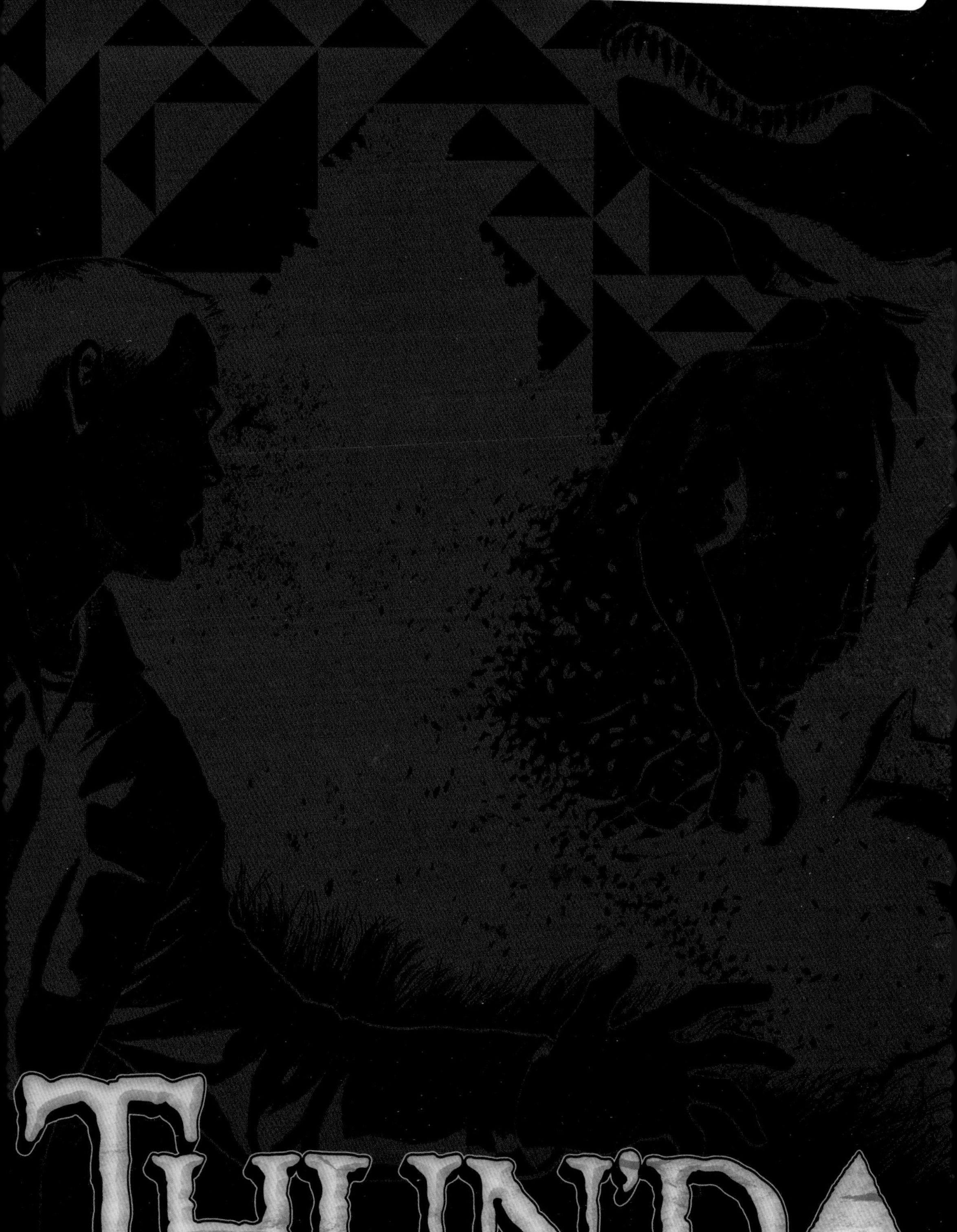

THUN'DA

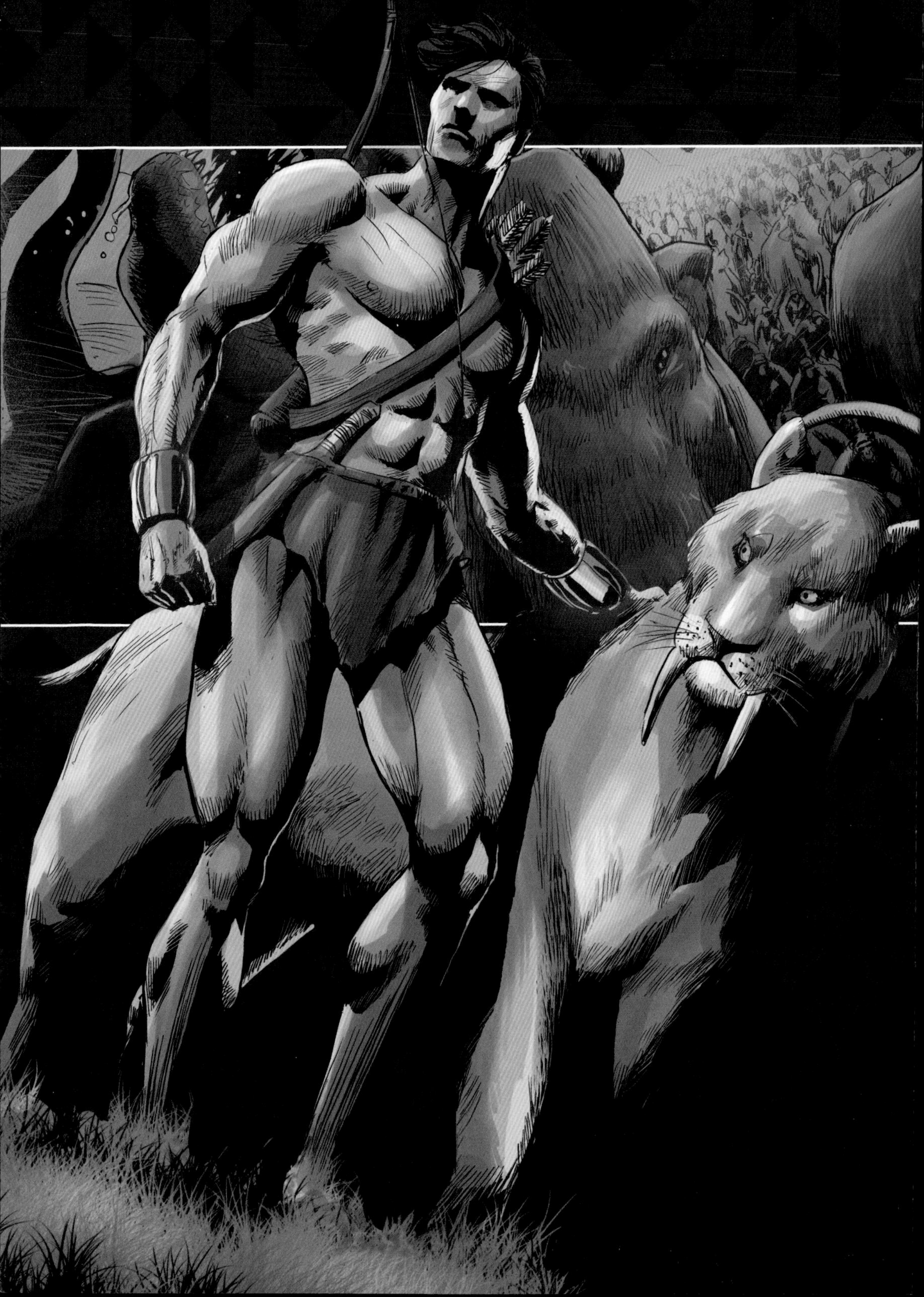

Thun'da

Written By
Robert Place Napton

Illustrated By
Cliff Richards

Colored By
Esther Sanz

Lettered By
Marshall Dillon

Cover By
Jae Lee

Thun'da Created By
Frank Frazetta

Collection By
Alexis Persson

DYNAMITE®

Nick Barrucci, CEO / Publisher
Juan Collado, President / COO

Joe Rybandt, Executive Editor
Matt Idelson, Senior Editor
Rachel Pinnelas, Associate Editor
Anthony Marques, Assistant Editor
Kevin Ketner, Editorial Assistant

Jason Ullmeyer, Art Director
Geoff Harkins, Senior Graphic Designer
Cathleen Heard, Graphic Designer
Alexis Persson, Production Artist

Chris Caniano, Digital Associate
Rachel Kilbury, Digital Assistant

Brandon Dante Primavera, V.P. of IT and Operations
Rich Young, Director of Business Development

Alan Payne, V.P. of Sales & Marketing
Keith Davidsen, Marketing Manager
Pat O'Connell, Sales Manager

Online at www.DYNAMITE.com
On Facebook /Dynamitecomics
Instagram /Dynamitecomics
On Tumblr dynamitecomics.tumblr.com
On Twitter @Dynamitecomics
On YouTube /Dynamitecomics

ISBN-10: 1-5241-0036-6
ISBN-13: 978-1-5241-0036-0

First Printing
10 9 8 7 6 5 4 3 2 1

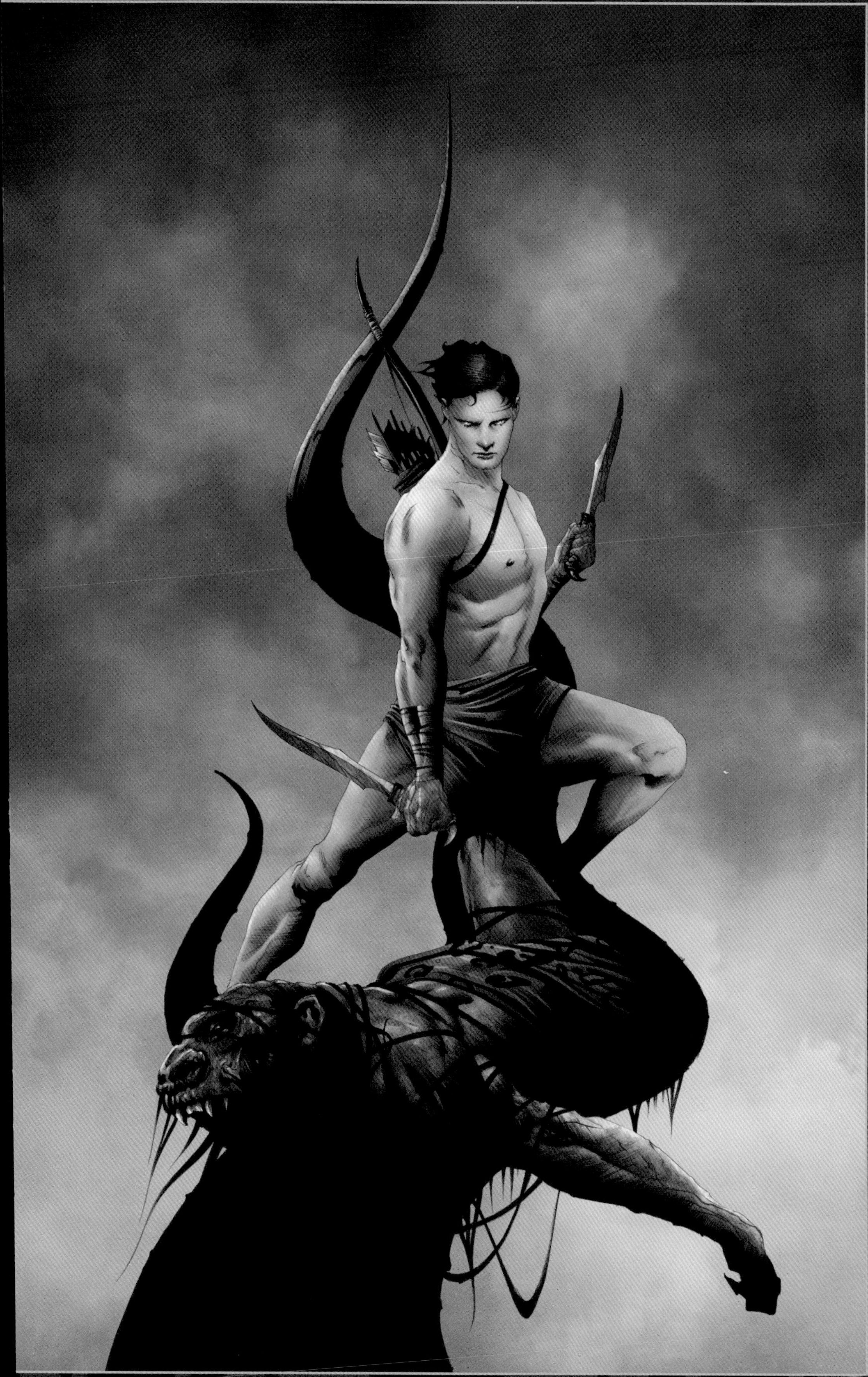

Issue One Cover by Jae Lee

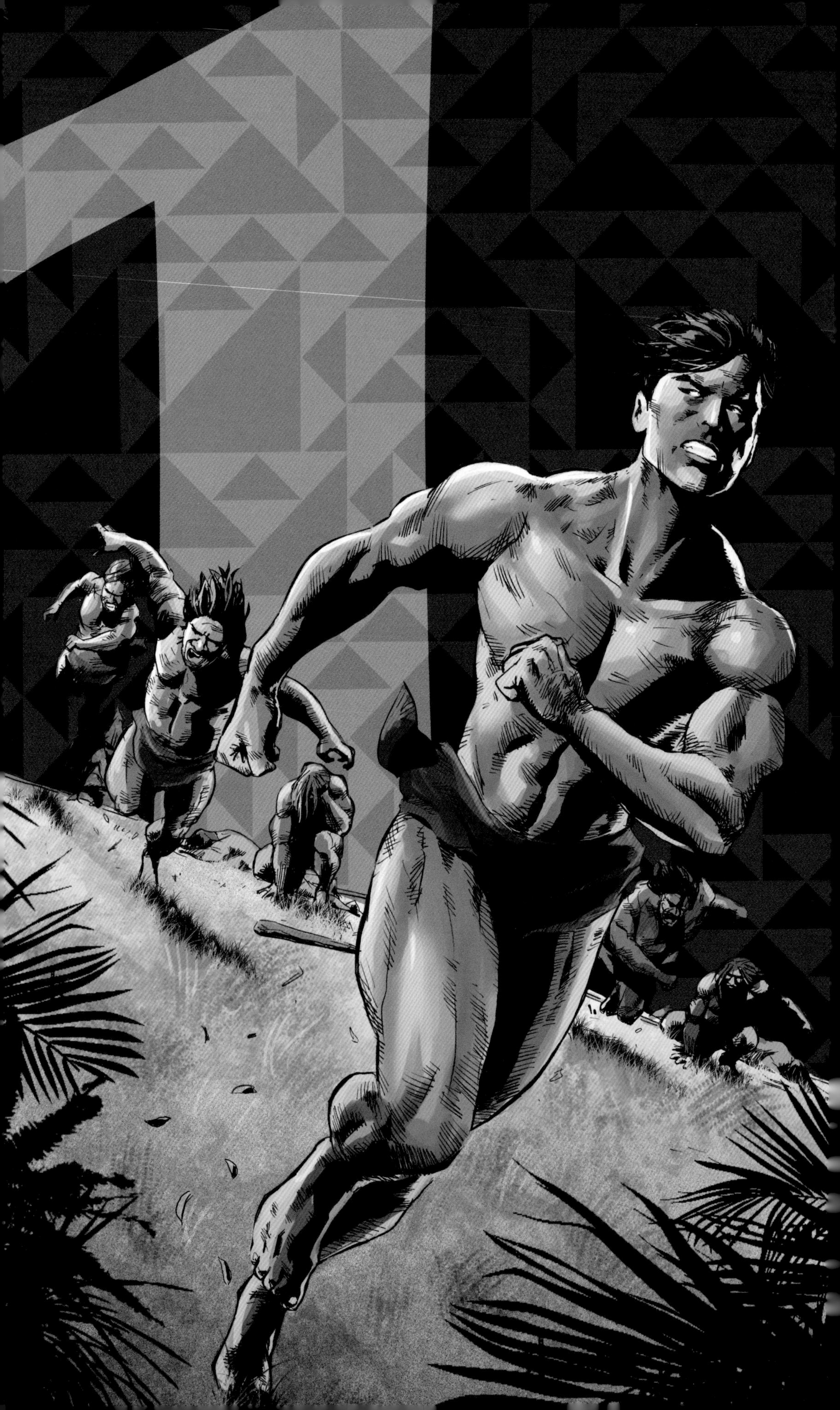

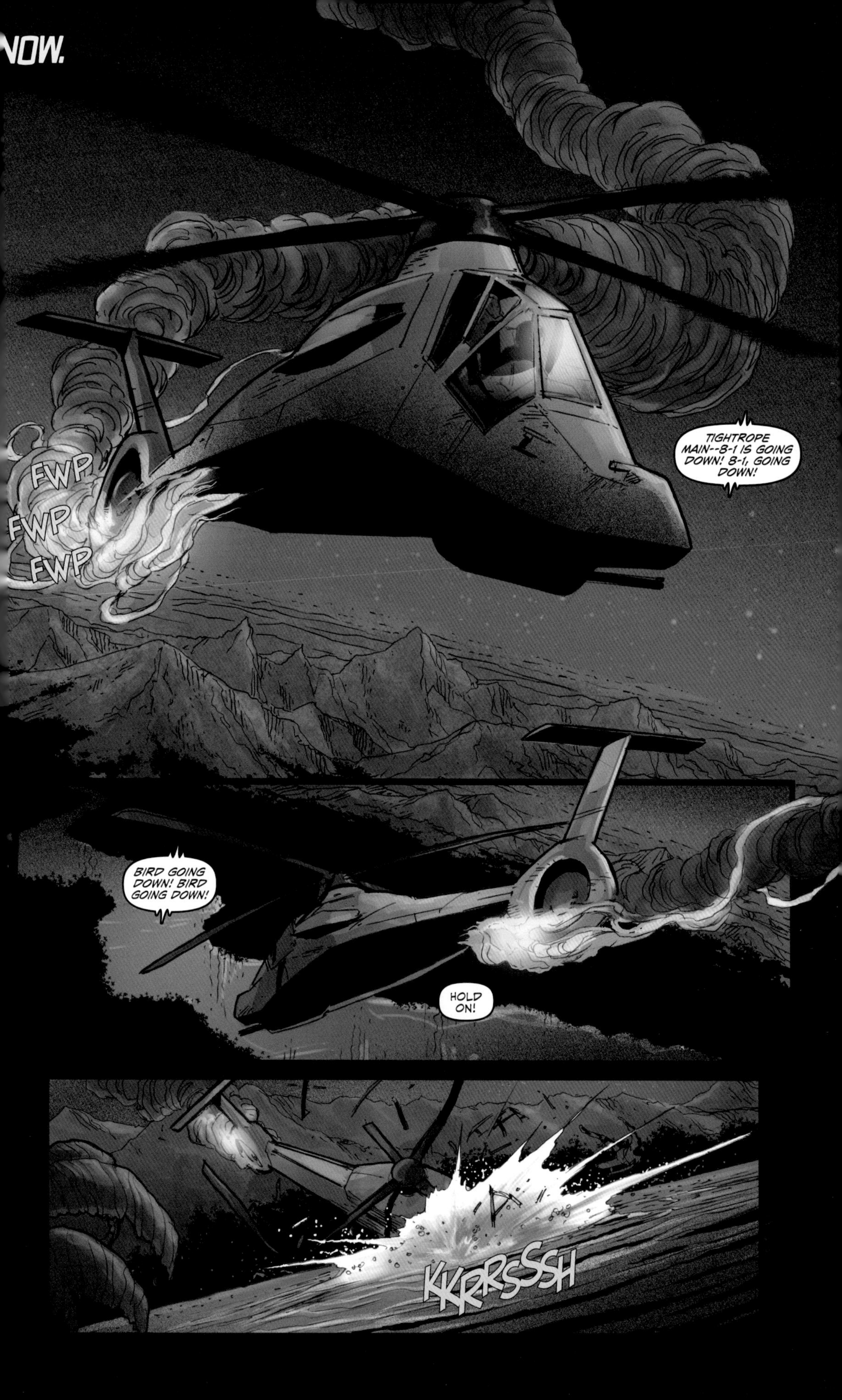
NOW.
TIGHTROPE MAIN--8-1 IS GOING DOWN! 8-1, GOING DOWN!
FWP
FWP
FWP
BIRD GOING DOWN! BIRD GOING DOWN!
HOLD ON!
KKRRSSSH

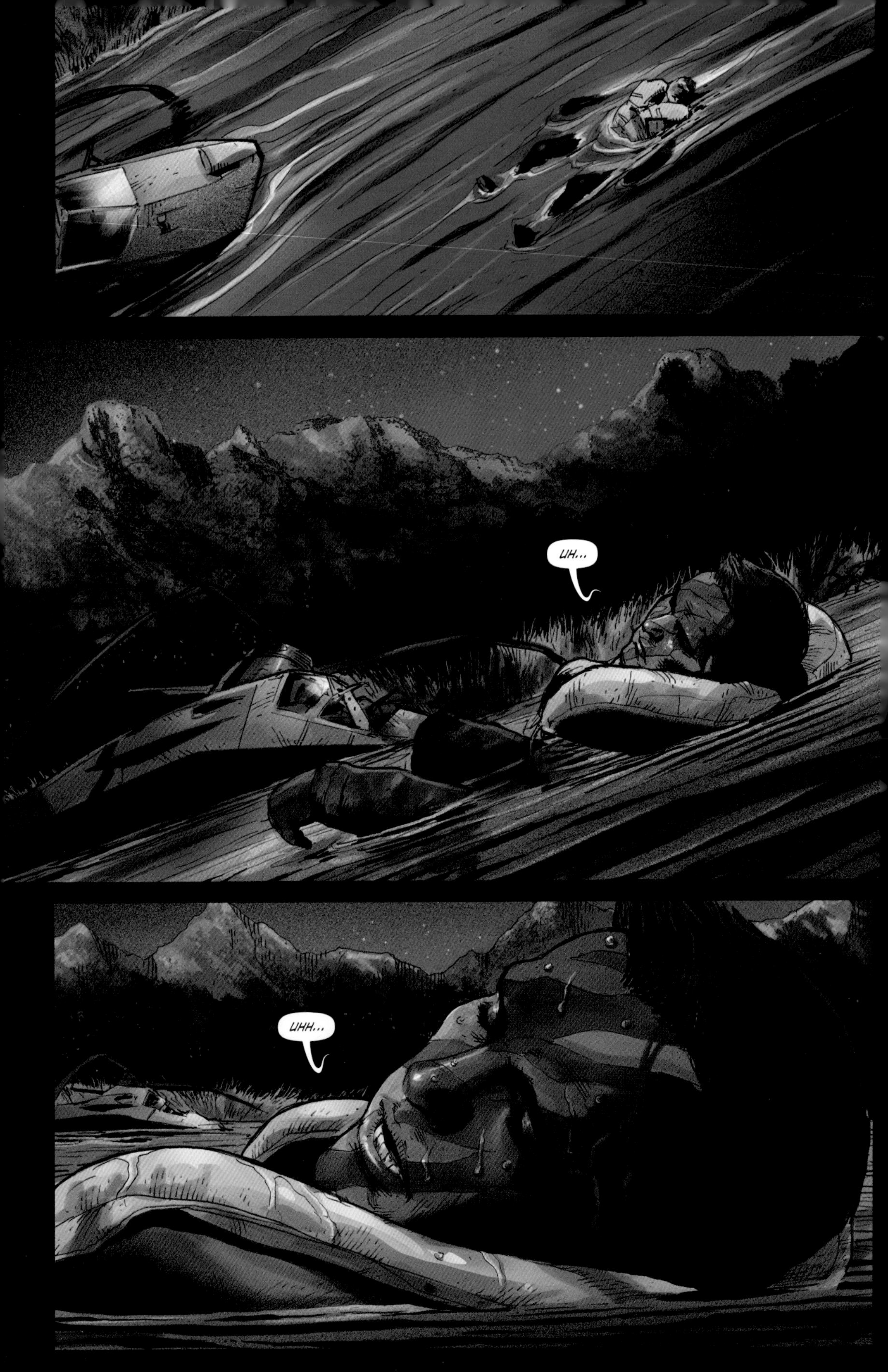
UH...
UHH...

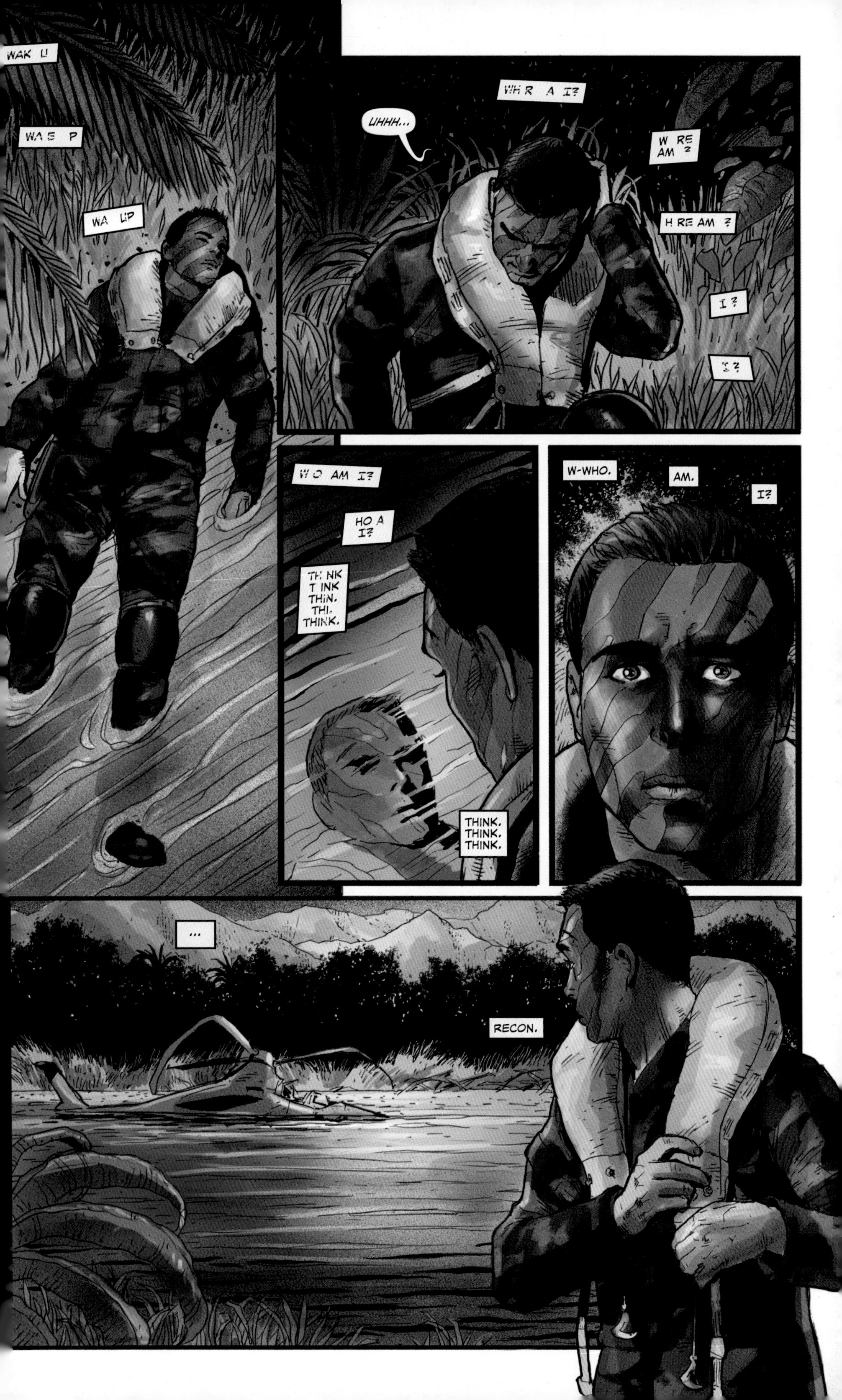
WAK U!
WA E P
WA UP
UHHH...
WH R A I?
W RE AM ?
H RE AM ?
I?
I?
W O AM I?
HO A I?
TH NK
T INK
THIN.
THI.
THINK.
THINK.
THINK.
THINK.
W-WHO.
AM.
I?
...
RECON.

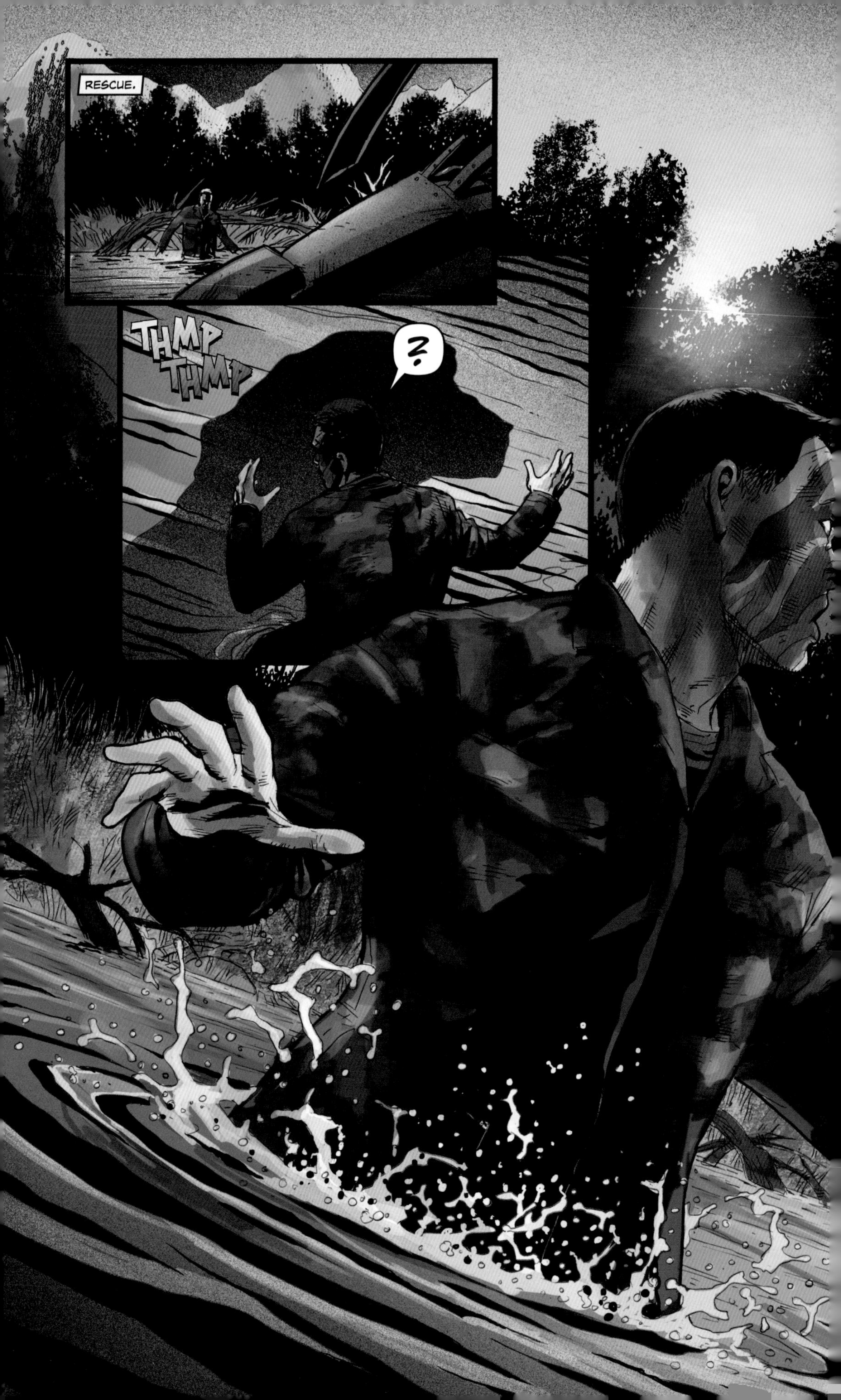
RESCUE.
THMP THMP
?

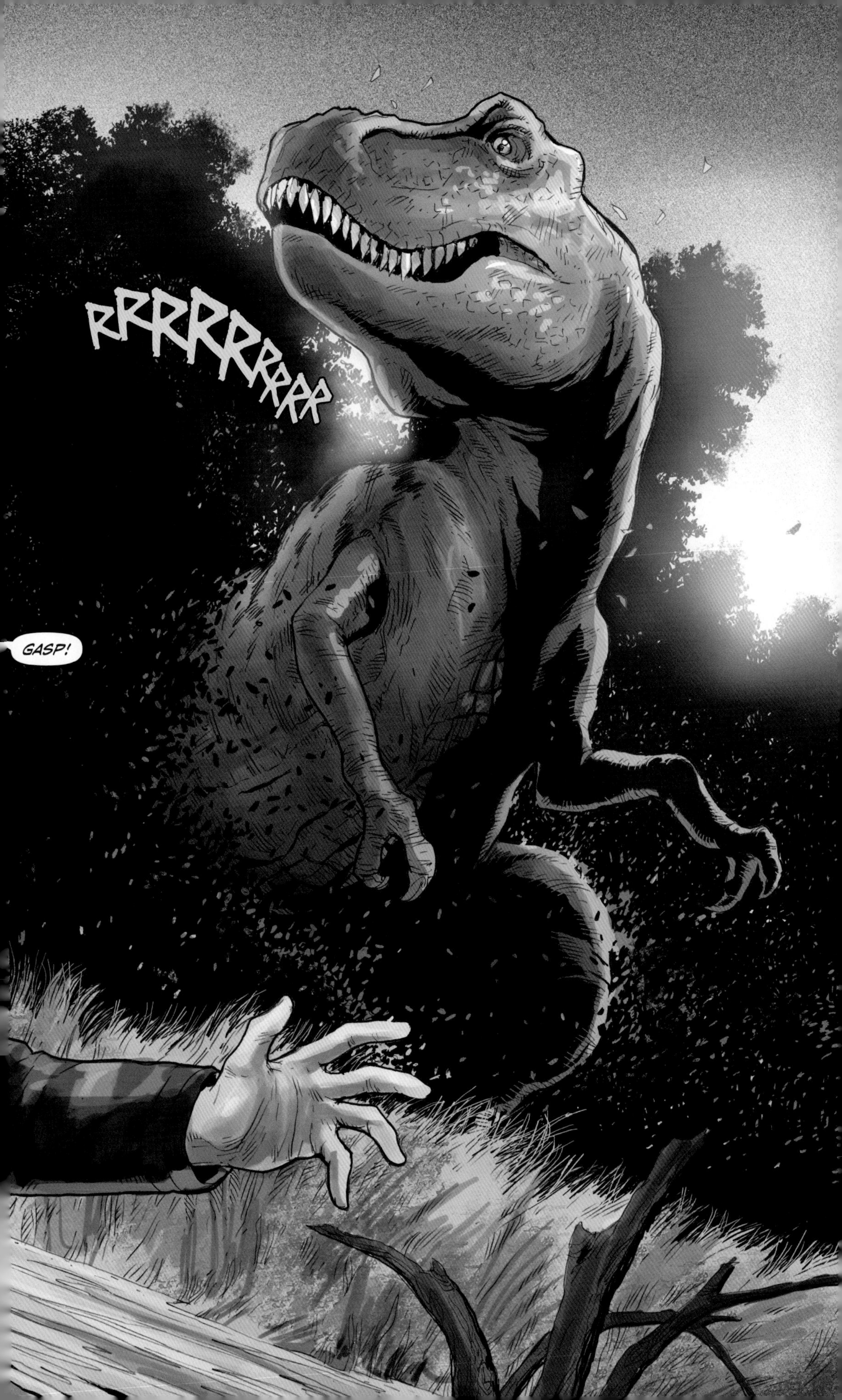
RRRRRRRRRR
GASP!

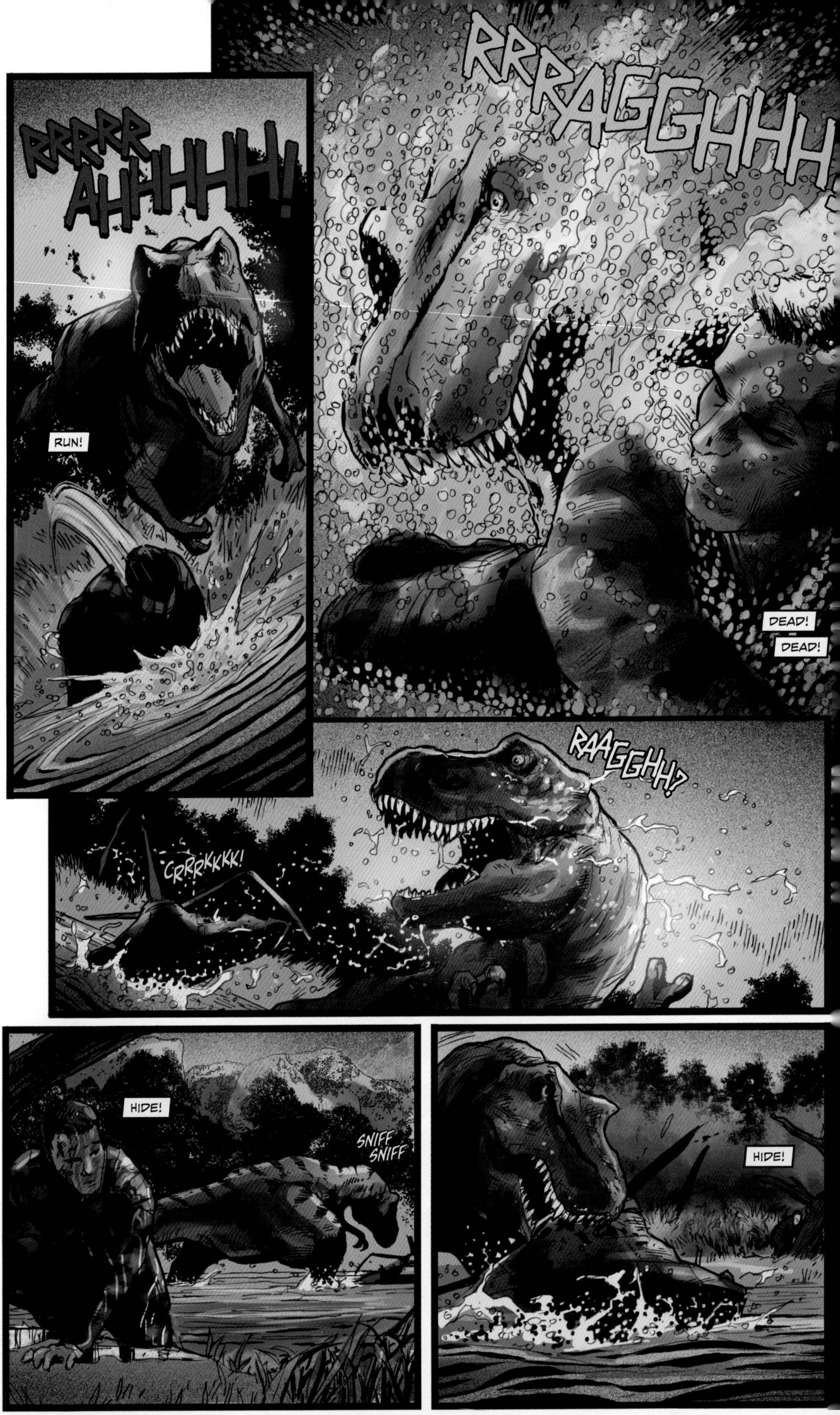
RRRRR AHHHHH!
RUN!
RRRAGGHHH!
DEAD!
DEAD!
RAAGGHH?
CRRRKKKK!
HIDE!
SNIFF SNIFF
HIDE!

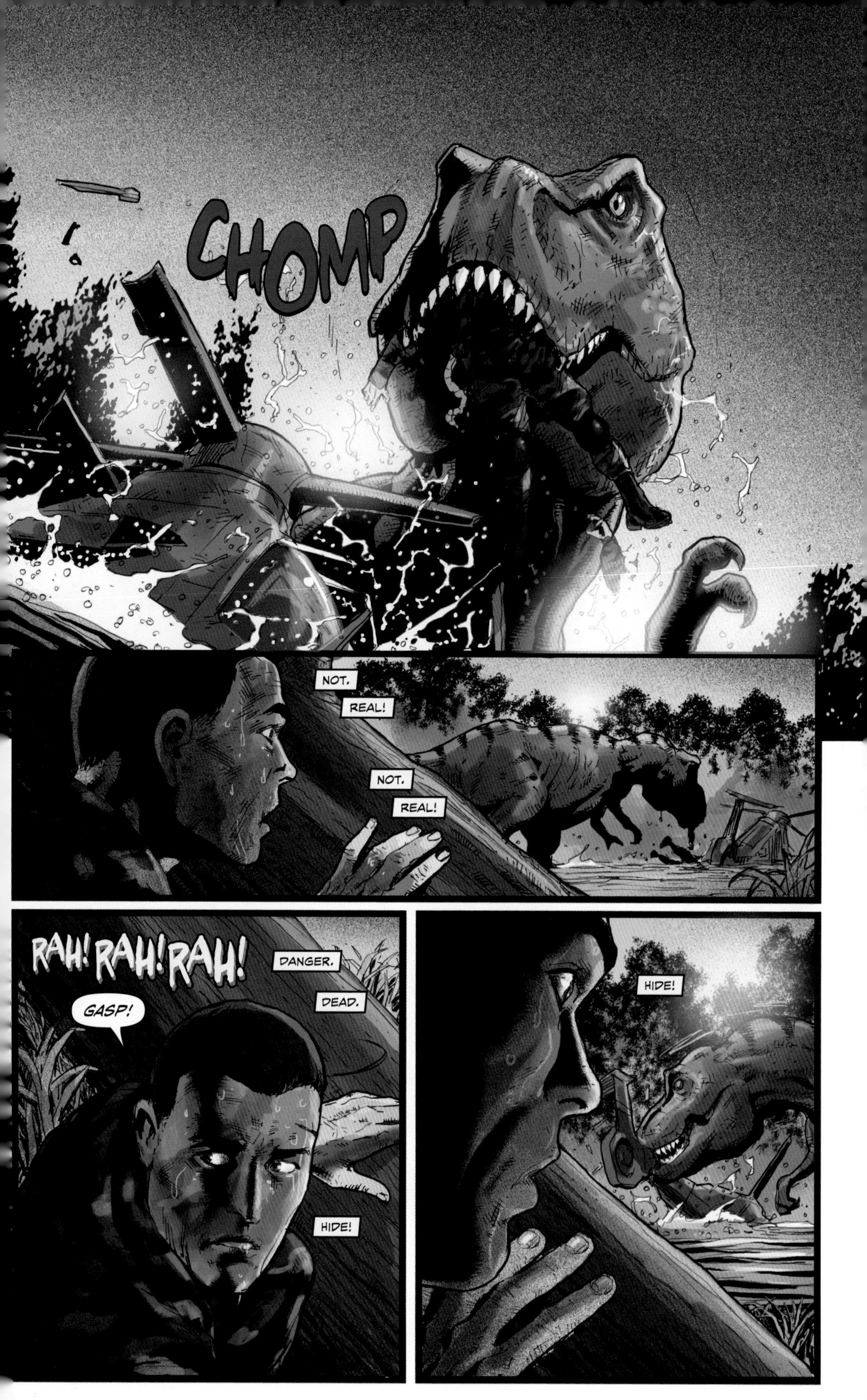
CHOMP
NOT.
REAL!
NOT.
REAL!
RAH! RAH! RAH!
DANGER.
DEAD.
GASP!
HIDE!
HIDE!

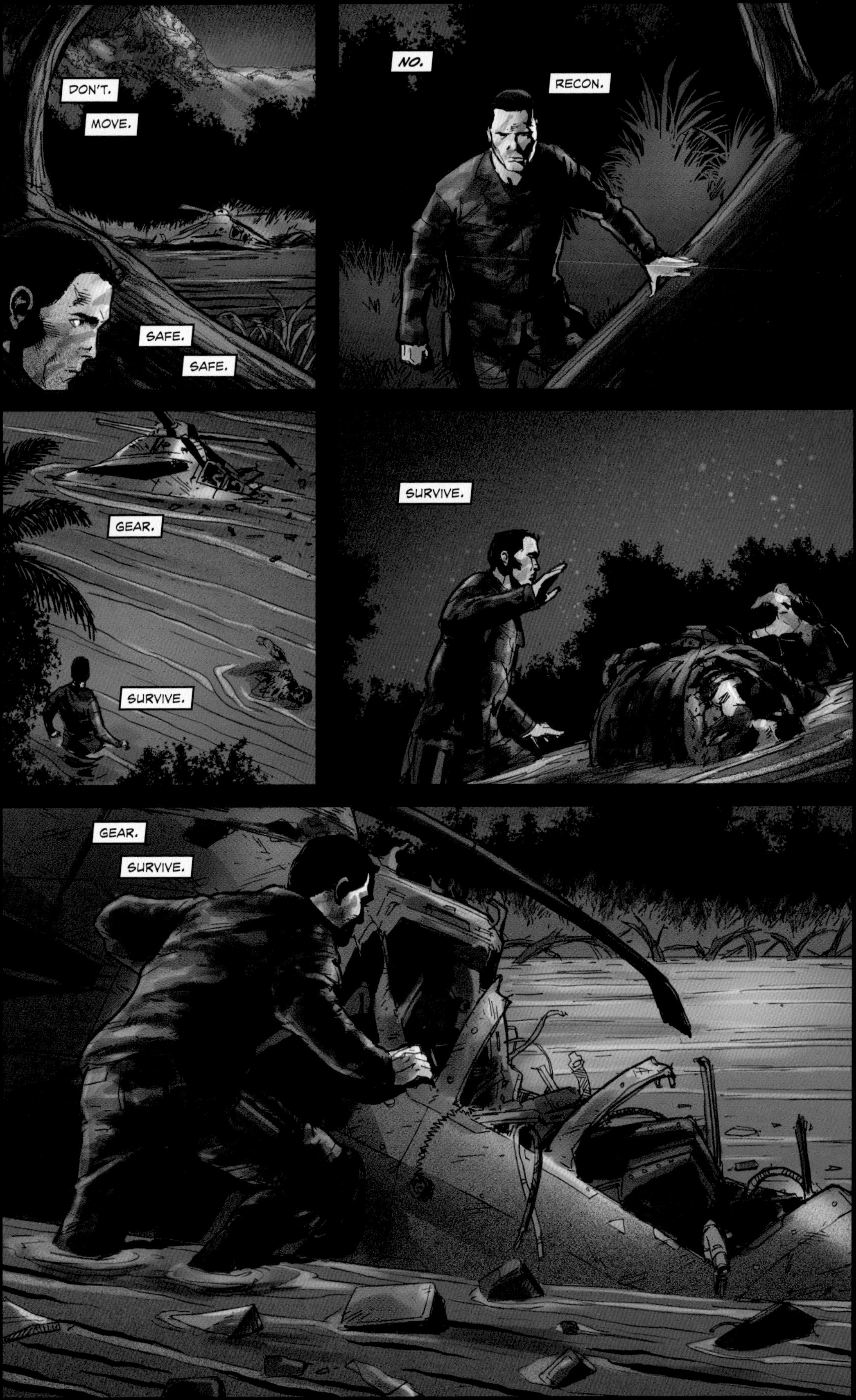
DON'T.
MOVE.
SAFE.
SAFE.
NO.
RECON.
GEAR.
SURVIVE.
SURVIVE.
GEAR.
SURVIVE.

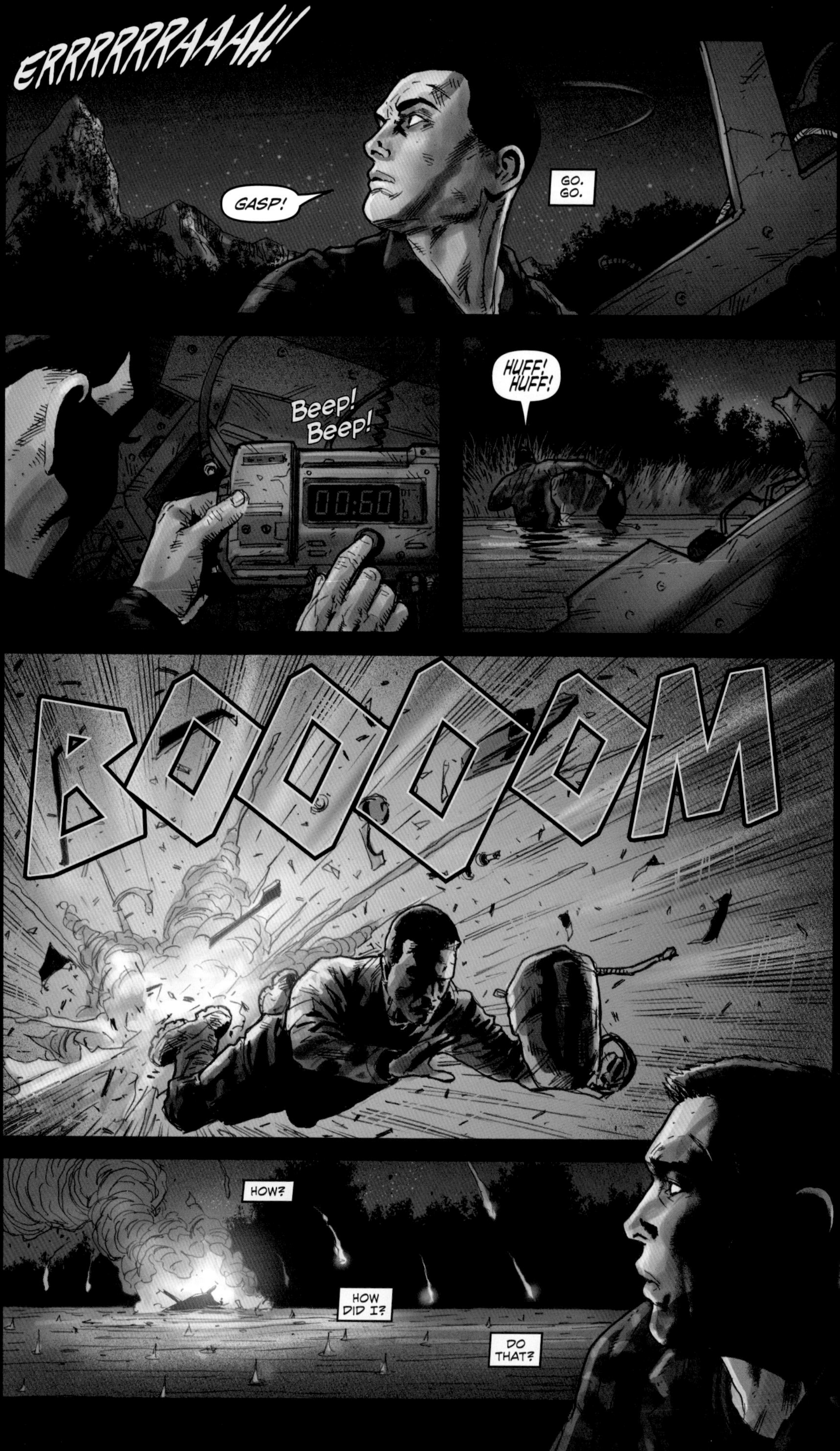
ERRRRRRAAAH!
GASP!
GO.
GO.
Beep!
Beep!
00:60
HUFF!
HUFF!
BOOOOM
HOW?
HOW
DID I?
DO
THAT?

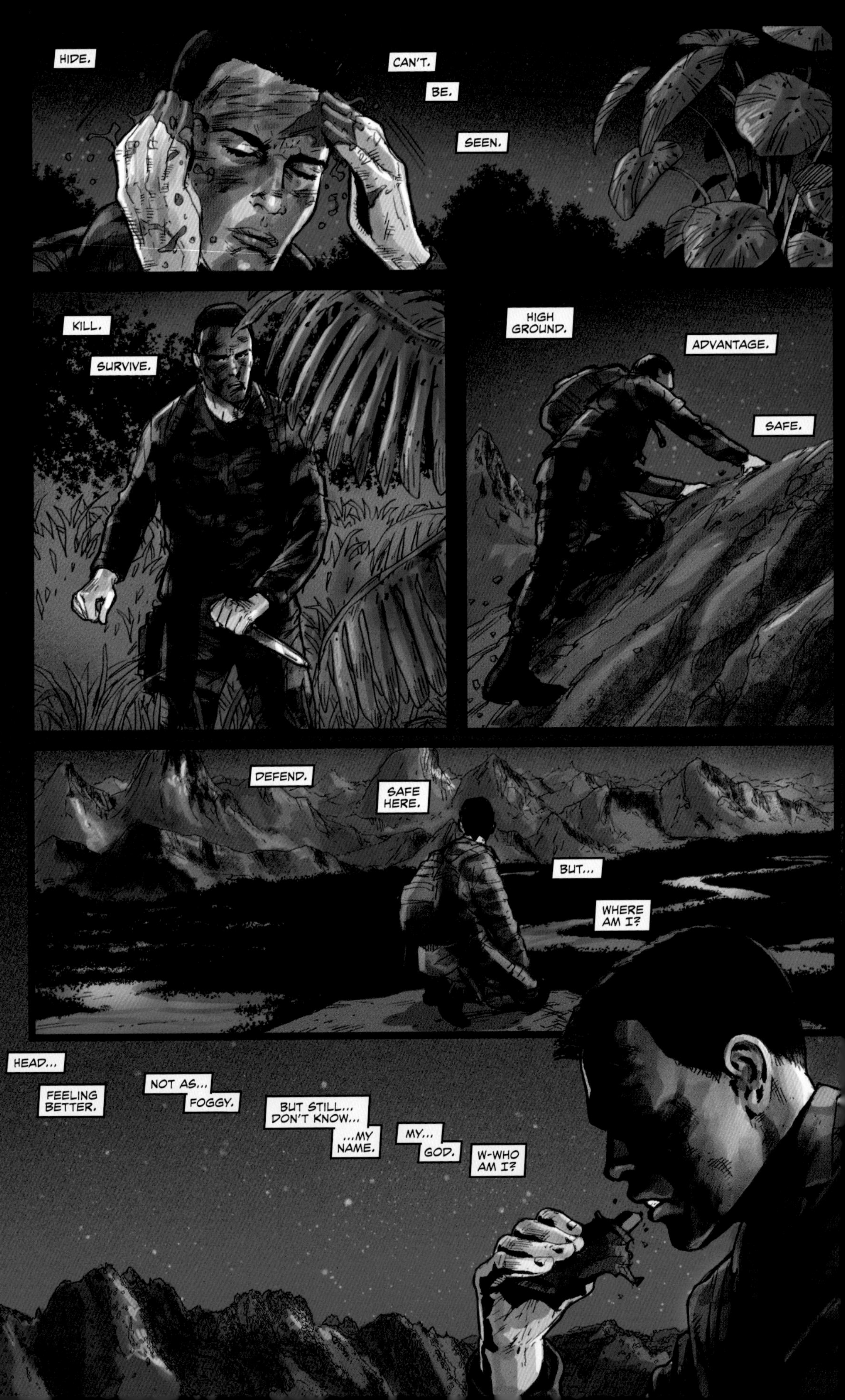
HIDE.
CAN'T.
BE.
SEEN.
KILL.
SURVIVE.
HIGH GROUND.
ADVANTAGE.
SAFE.
DEFEND.
SAFE HERE.
BUT...
WHERE AM I?
HEAD...
FEELING BETTER.
NOT AS...
FOGGY.
BUT STILL... DON'T KNOW...
...MY NAME.
MY...
GOD.
W-WHO AM I?

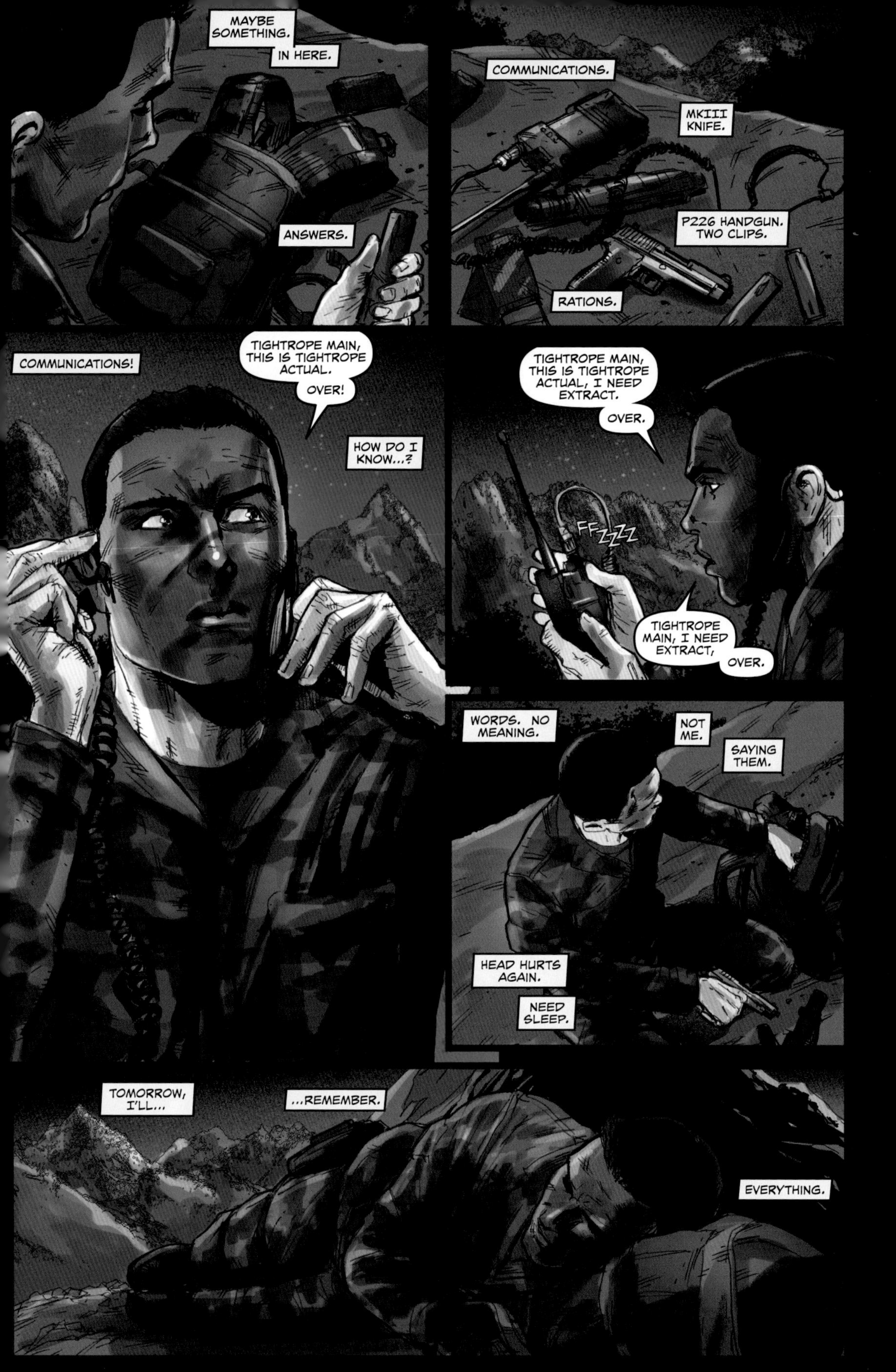
MAYBE SOMETHING.
IN HERE.
ANSWERS.
COMMUNICATIONS.
MKIII KNIFE.
P226 HANDGUN. TWO CLIPS.
RATIONS.
COMMUNICATIONS!
TIGHTROPE MAIN, THIS IS TIGHTROPE ACTUAL.
OVER!
HOW DO I KNOW...?
TIGHTROPE MAIN, THIS IS TIGHTROPE ACTUAL, I NEED EXTRACT.
OVER.
FFZZZZ
TIGHTROPE MAIN, I NEED EXTRACT,
OVER.
WORDS. NO MEANING.
NOT ME.
SAYING THEM.
HEAD HURTS AGAIN.
NEED SLEEP.
TOMORROW, I'LL...
...REMEMBER.
EVERYTHING.

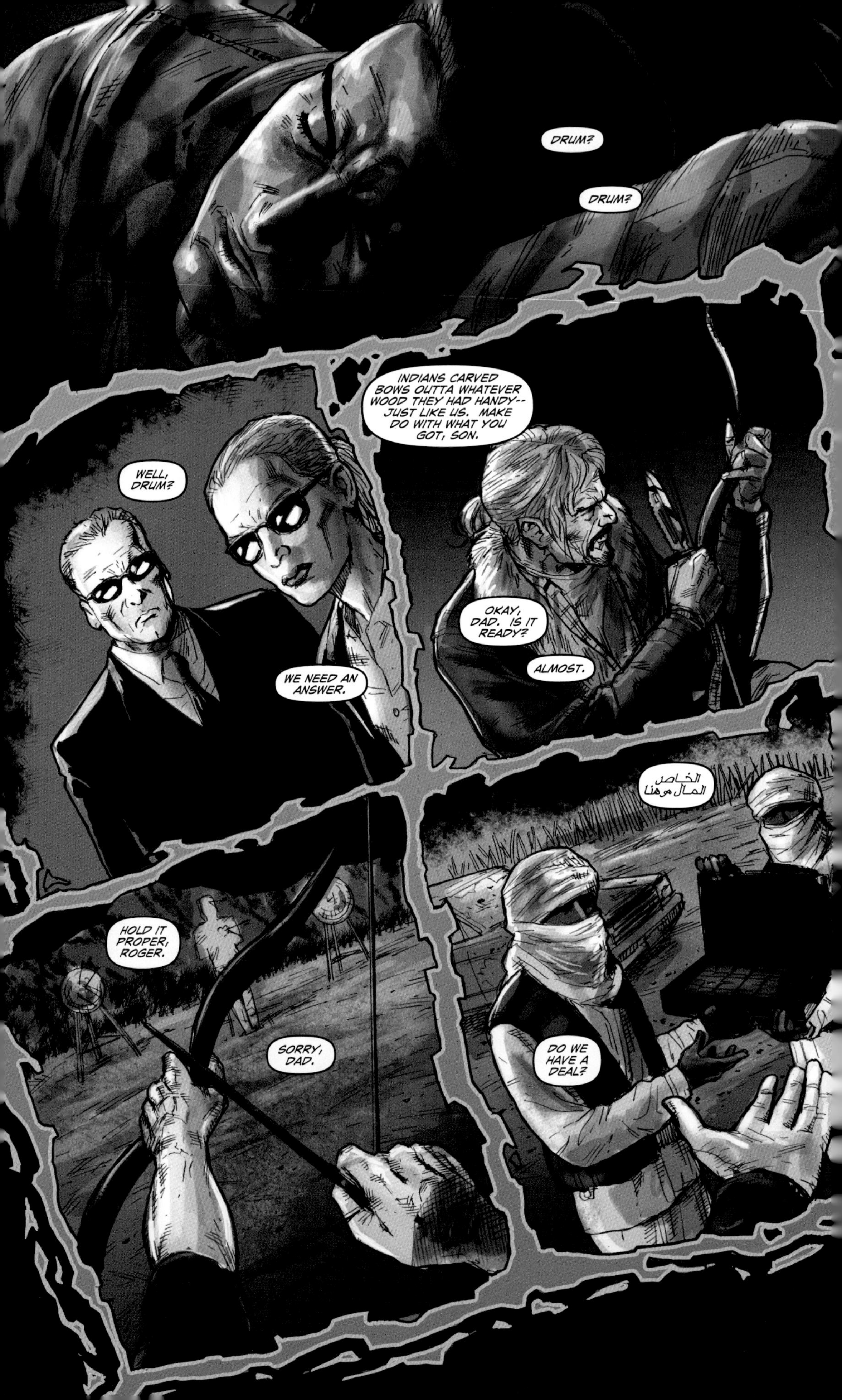
DRUM?
DRUM?
WELL, DRUM?
INDIANS CARVED BOWS OUTTA WHATEVER WOOD THEY HAD HANDY-- JUST LIKE US. MAKE DO WITH WHAT YOU GOT, SON.
OKAY, DAD. IS IT READY?
ALMOST.
WE NEED AN ANSWER.
الخاص
المال موهنا
HOLD IT PROPER, ROGER.
SORRY, DAD.
DO WE HAVE A DEAL?

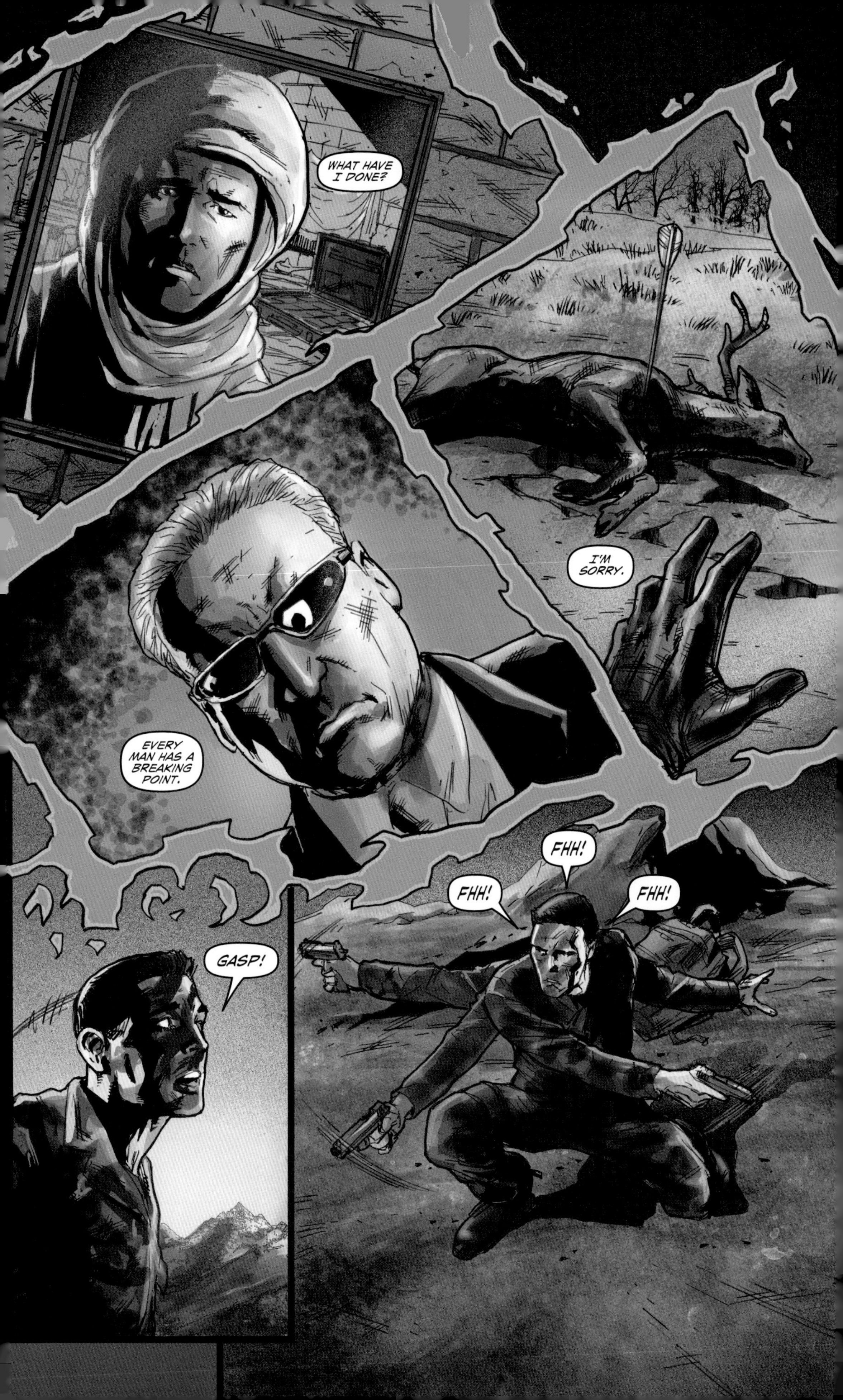
WHAT HAVE I DONE?
I'M SORRY.
EVERY MAN HAS A BREAKING POINT.
GASP!
FHH!
FHH!
FHH!

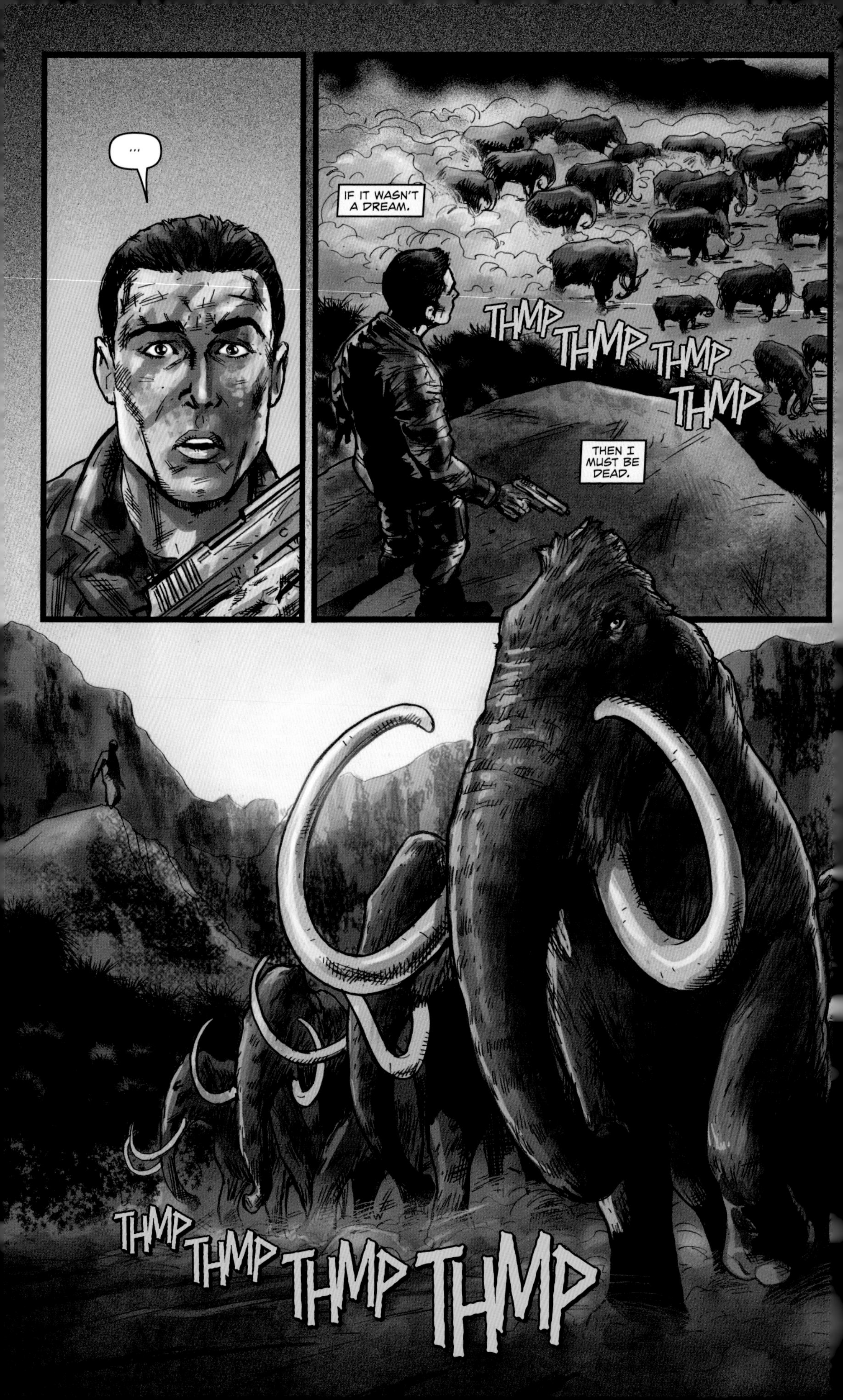
...
IF IT WASN'T A DREAM.
THMP THMP THMP THMP
THEN I MUST BE DEAD.
THMP THMP THMP THMP

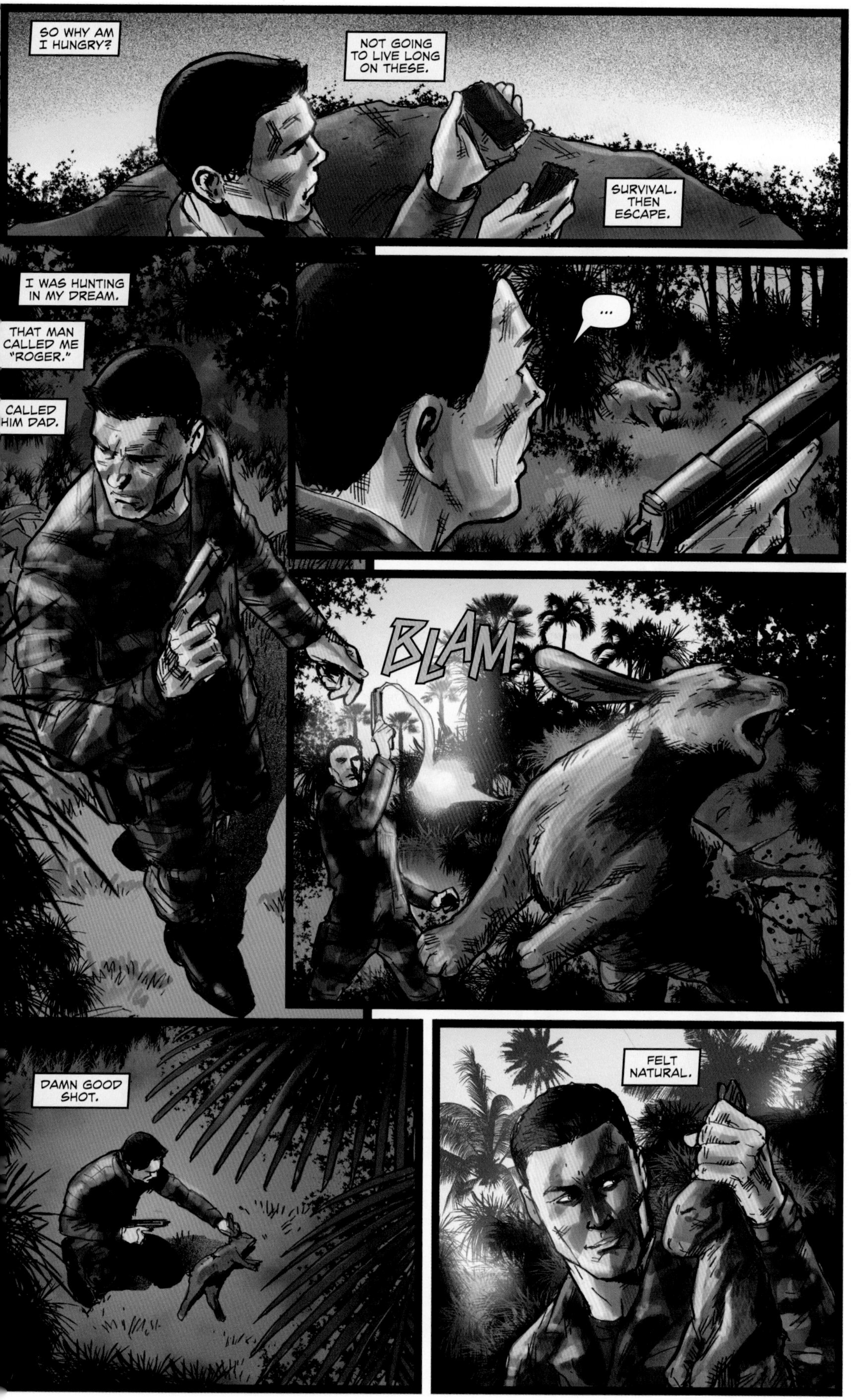
SO WHY AM I HUNGRY?
NOT GOING TO LIVE LONG ON THESE.
SURVIVAL. THEN ESCAPE.
I WAS HUNTING IN MY DREAM.
THAT MAN CALLED ME "ROGER."
CALLED HIM DAD.
...
BLAM
DAMN GOOD SHOT.
FELT NATURAL.

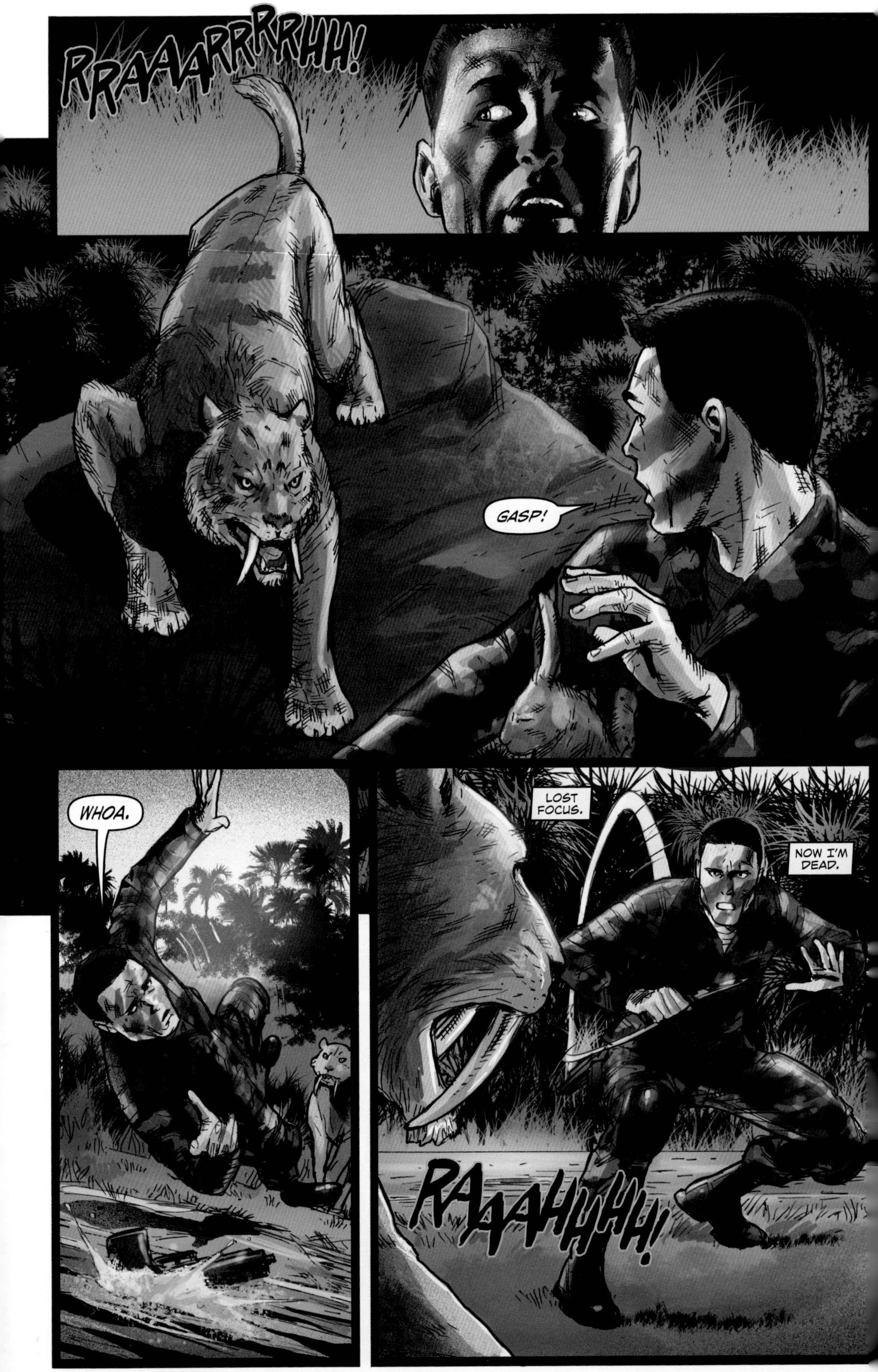
RRAAARRRRHH!
GASP!
WHOA.
LOST FOCUS.
NOW I'M DEAD.
RAAAHHHH!

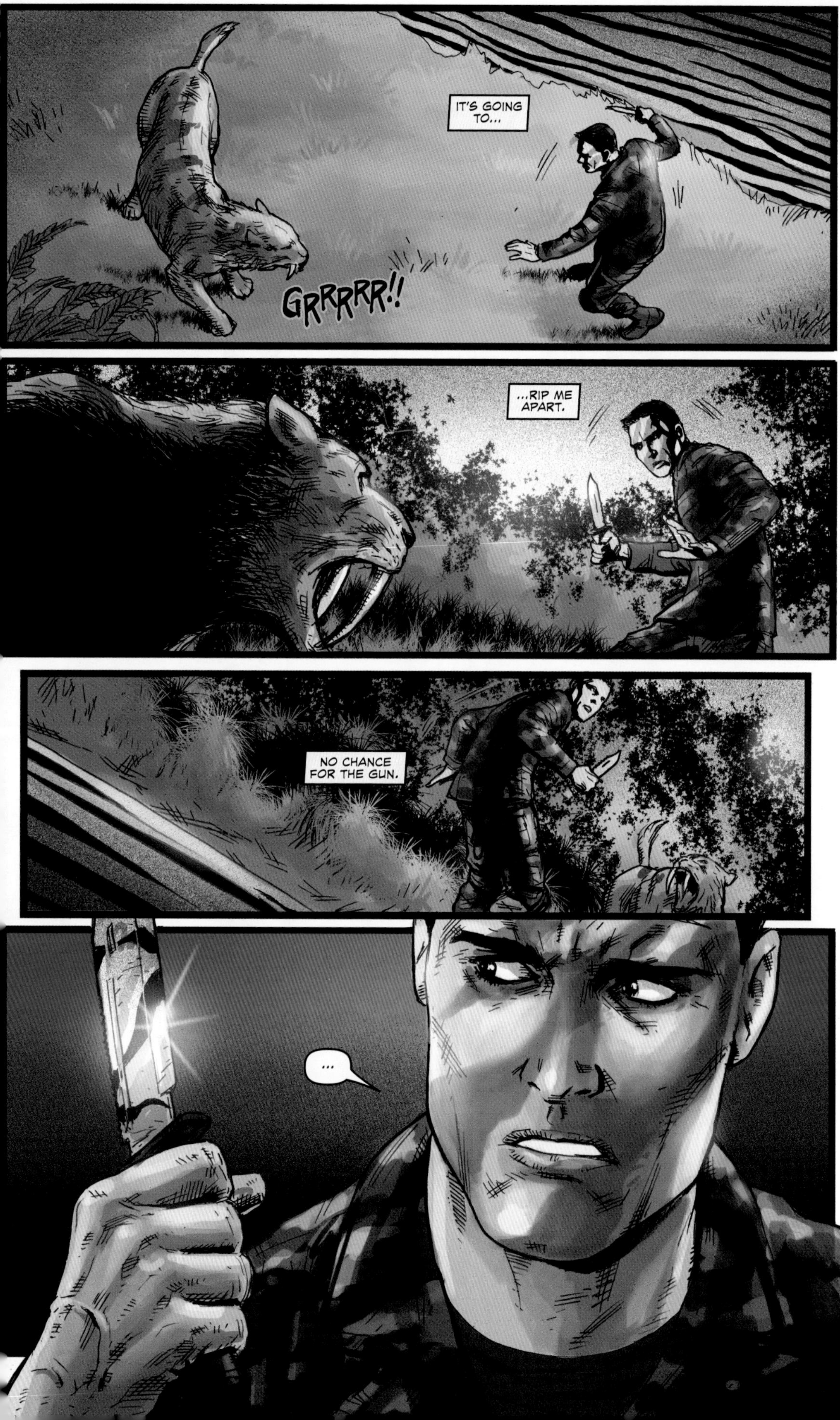
IT'S GOING TO...
GRRRRR!!
...RIP ME APART.
NO CHANCE FOR THE GUN.
...

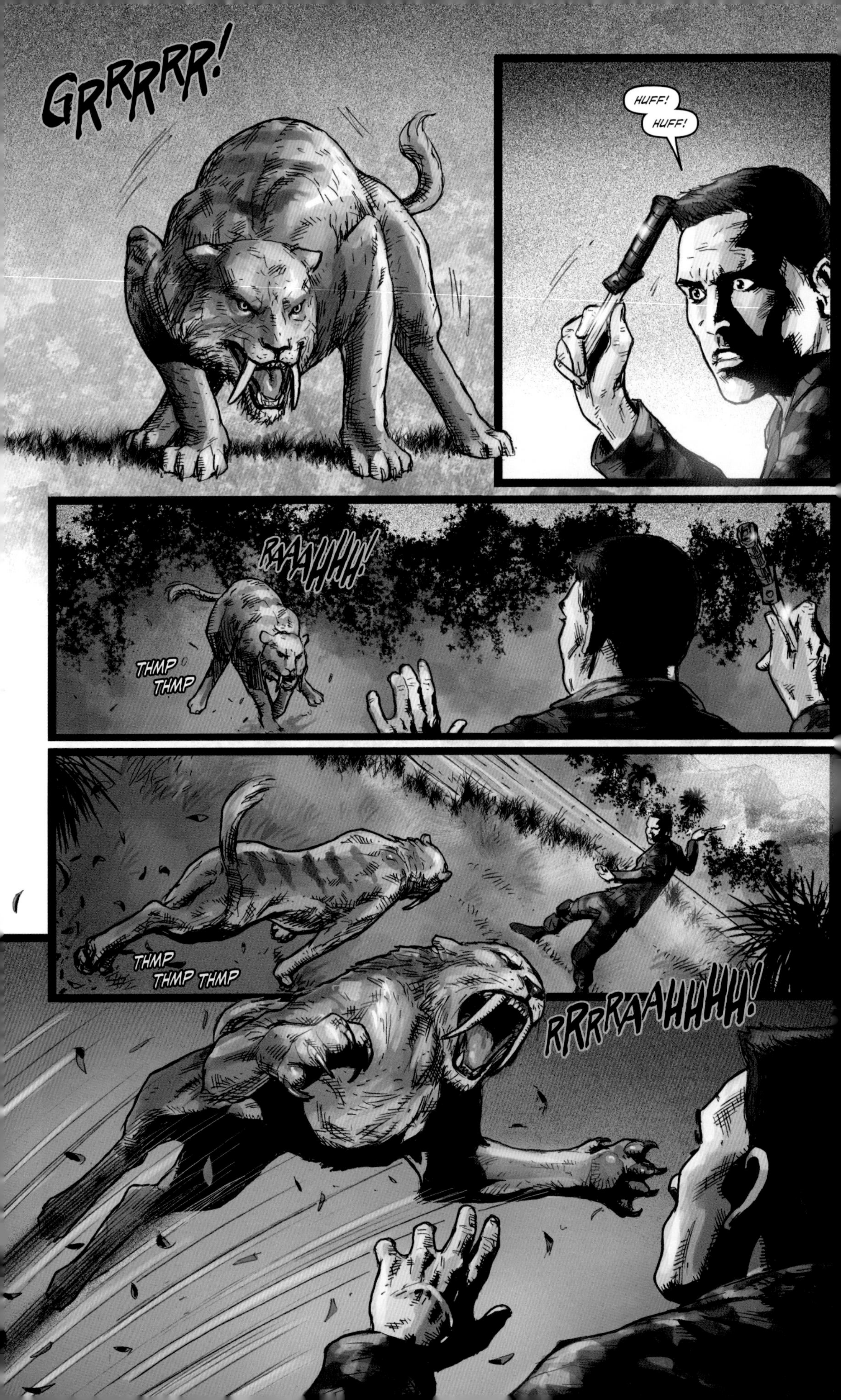
GRRRRR!
HUFF!
HUFF!
RAAAHHH!
THMP
THMP
THMP
THMP THMP
RRRRAAHHHHH!

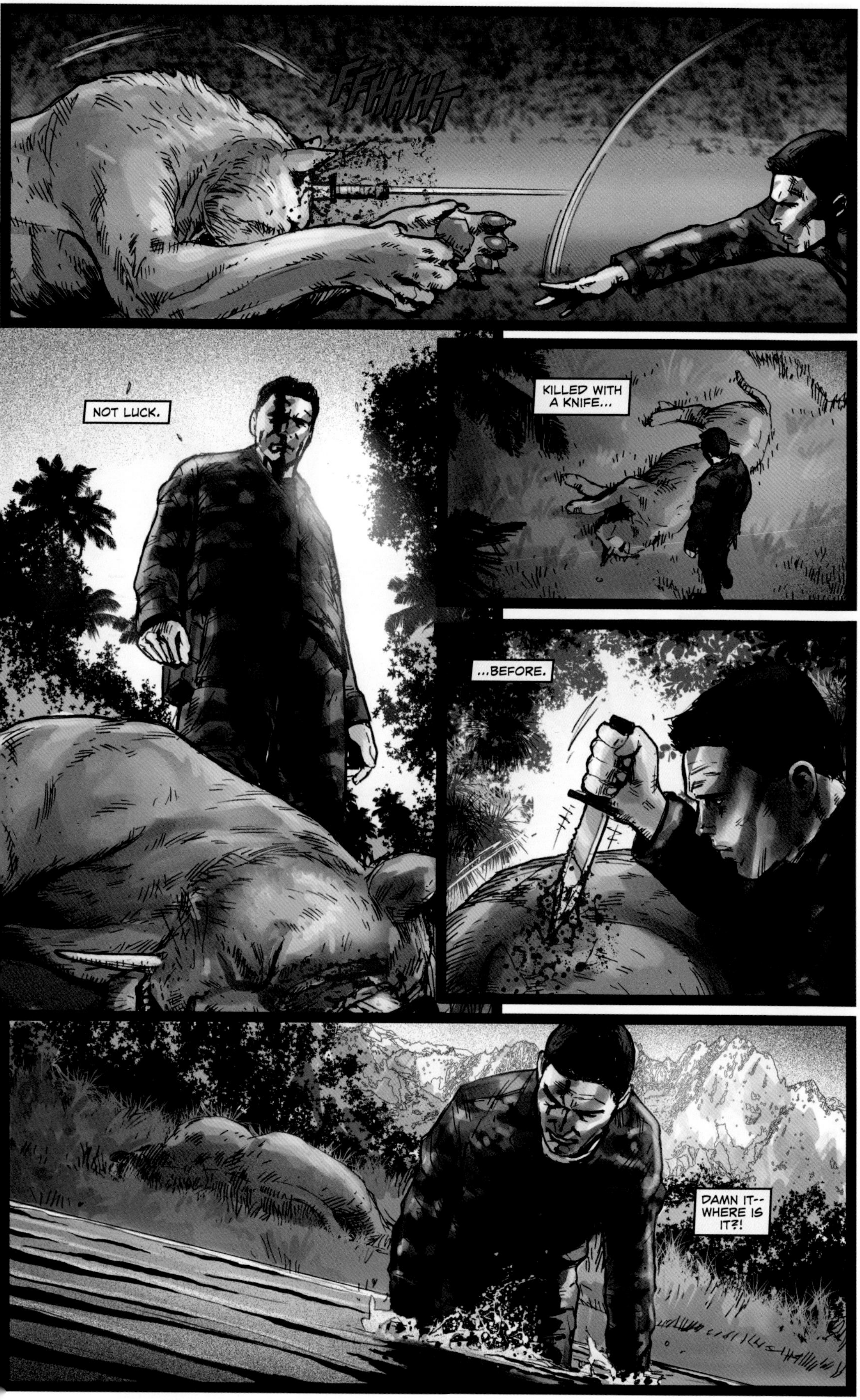

FFFWHHT
NOT LUCK.
KILLED WITH A KNIFE...
...BEFORE.
DAMN IT-- WHERE IS IT?!

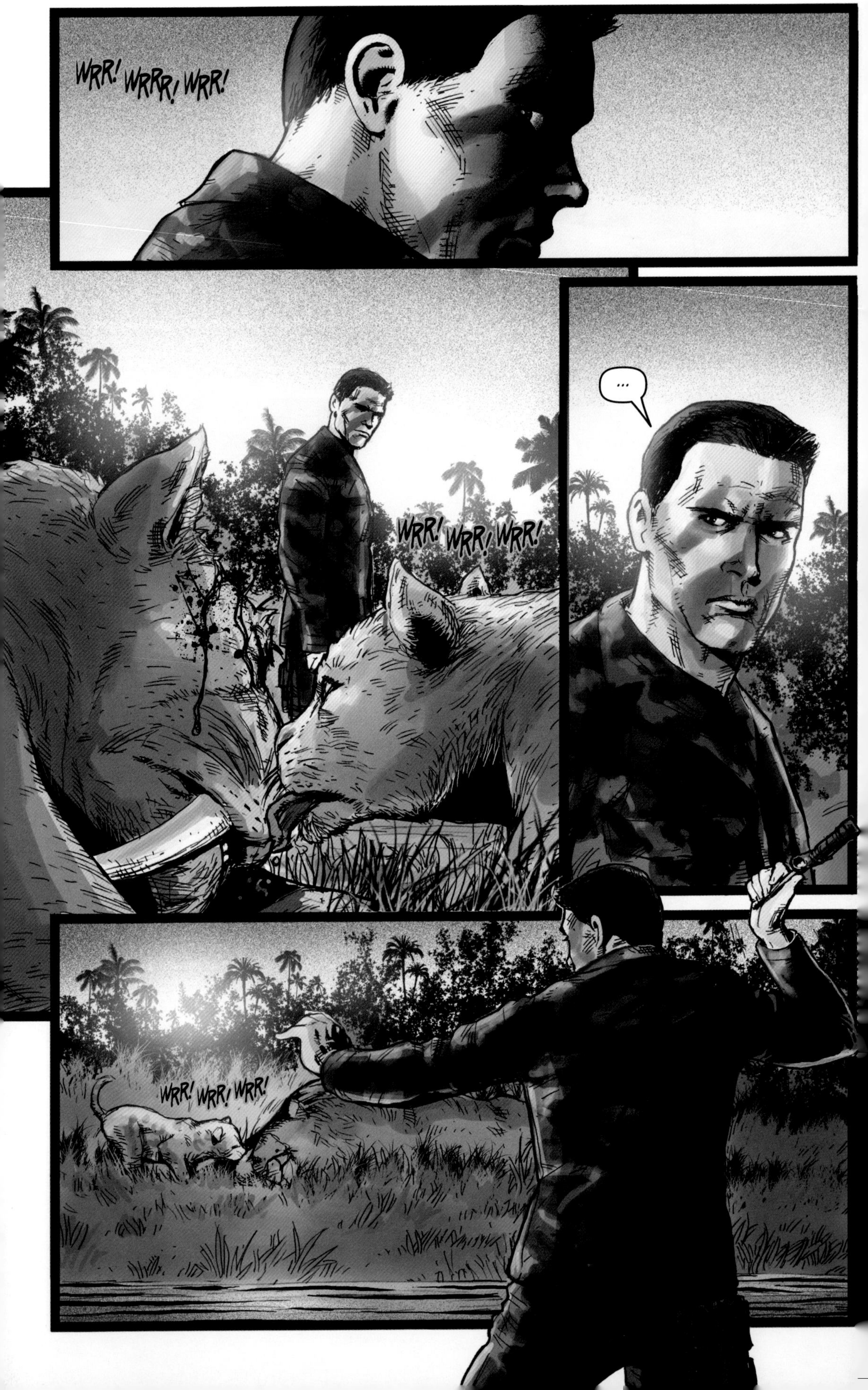
WRR! WRRR! WRR!
WRR! WRR! WRR!
...
WRR! WRR! WRR!

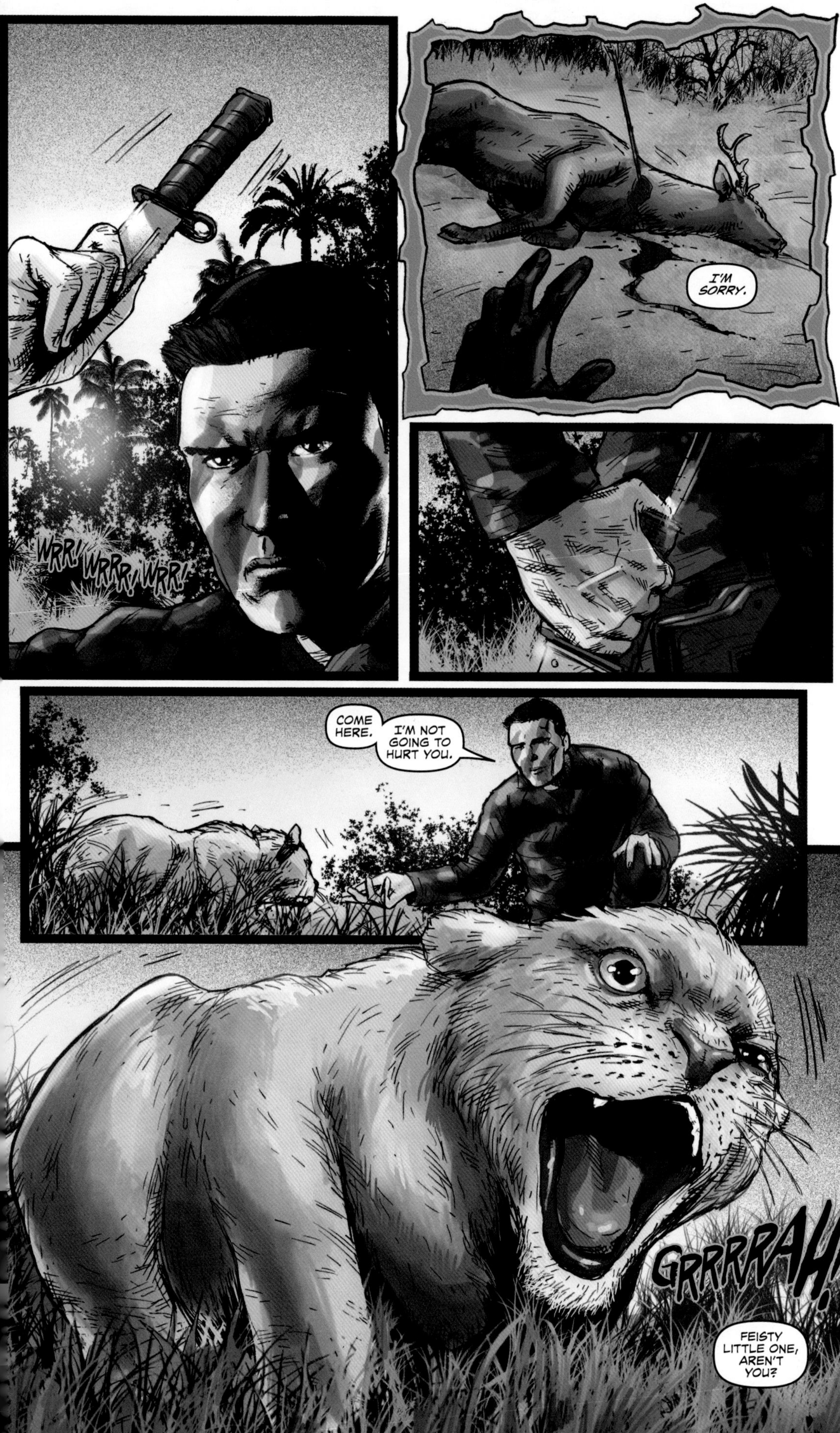
WRR! WRRR! WRR!
I'M SORRY.
COME HERE.
I'M NOT GOING TO HURT YOU.
GRRRRAH!
FEISTY LITTLE ONE, AREN'T YOU?

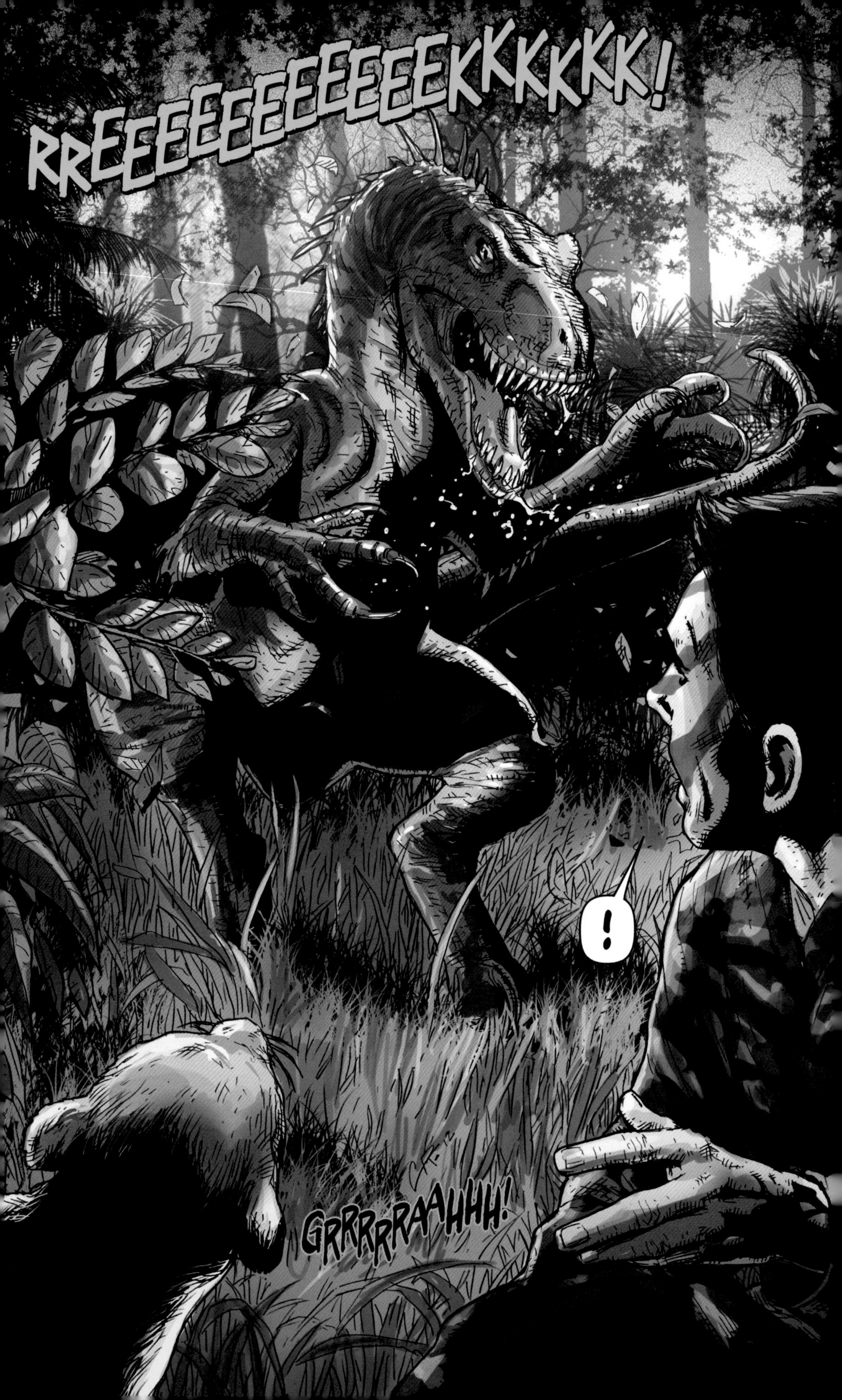
RREEEEEEEEEEEEKKKKKK!
!
GRRRRRAAHHH!

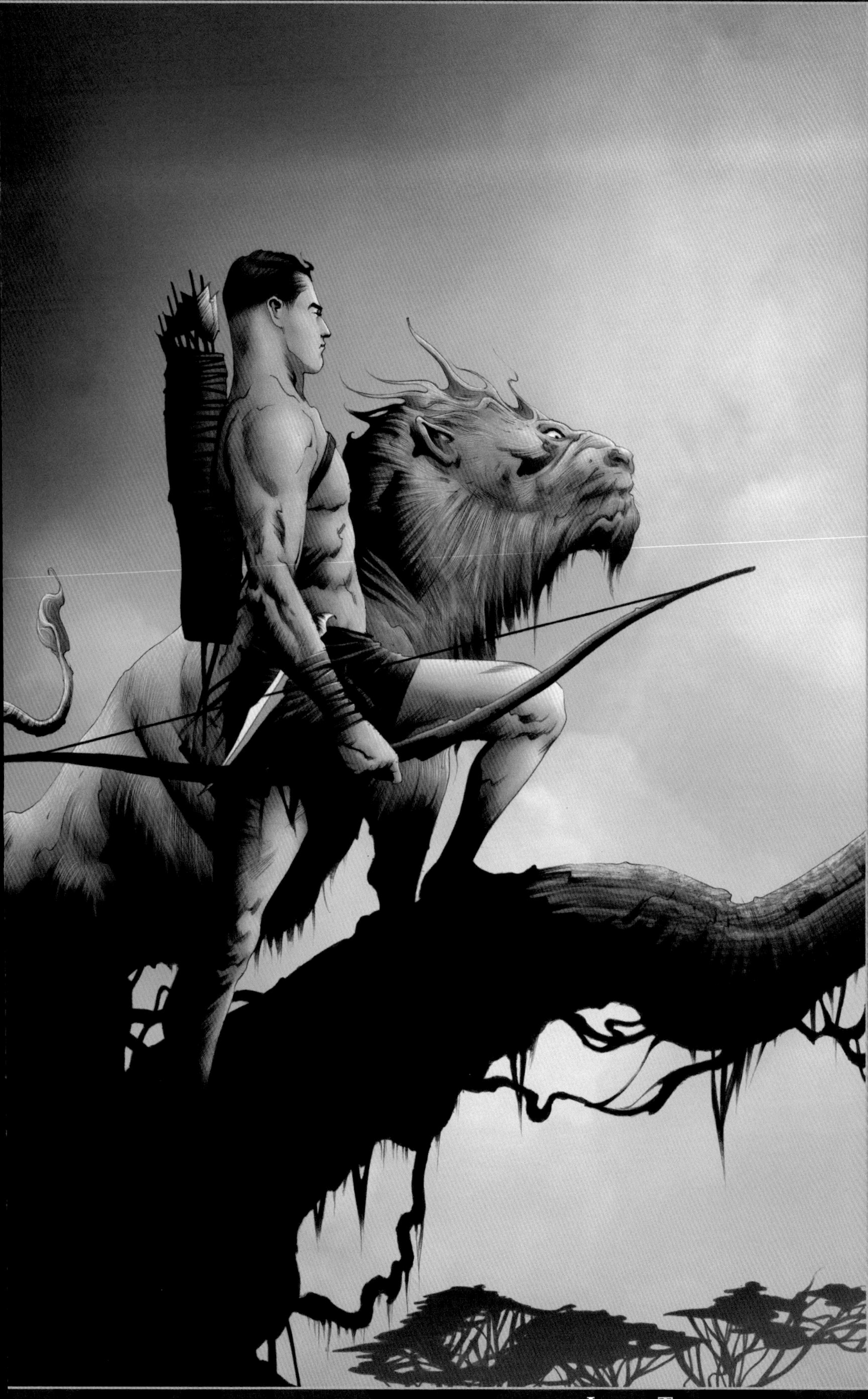

Issue Two Cover by Jae Lee

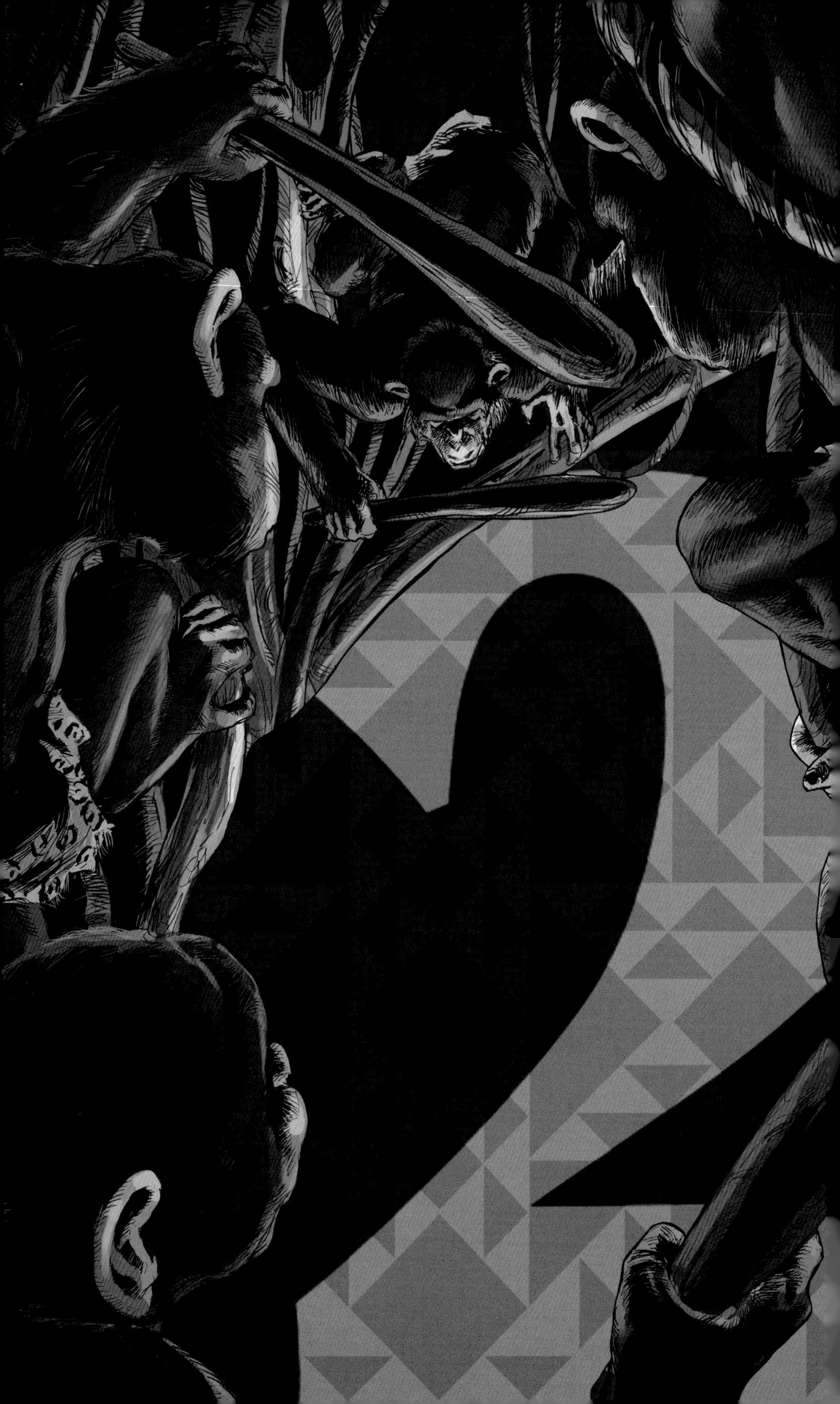

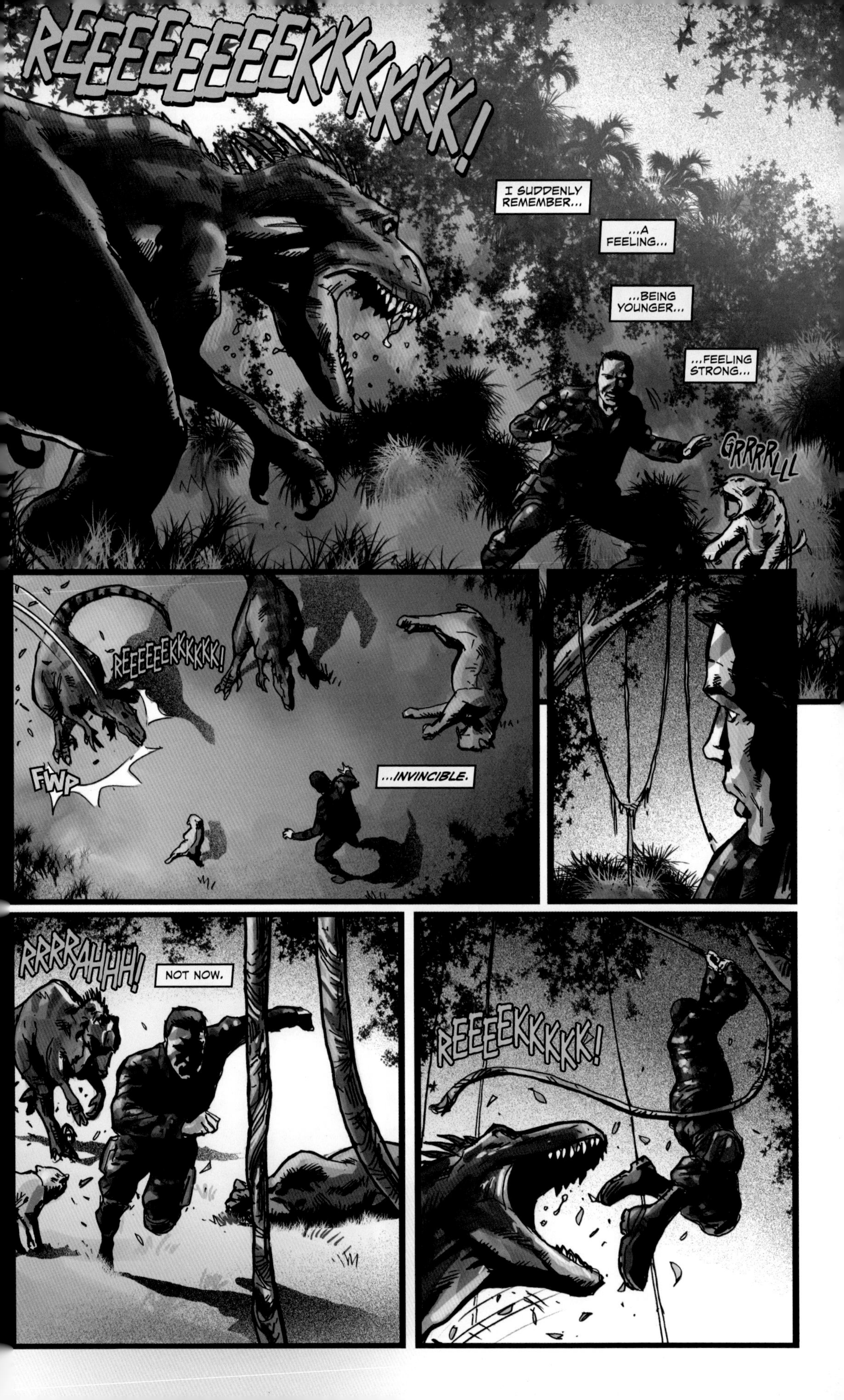

REEEEEEEEEKKKKKK!
I SUDDENLY REMEMBER...
...A FEELING...
...BEING YOUNGER...
...FEELING STRONG...
GRRRRLLL
REEEEEEKKKKK!
FWP
...INVINCIBLE.
RRRRAHHH!
NOT NOW.
REEEEKKKKK!

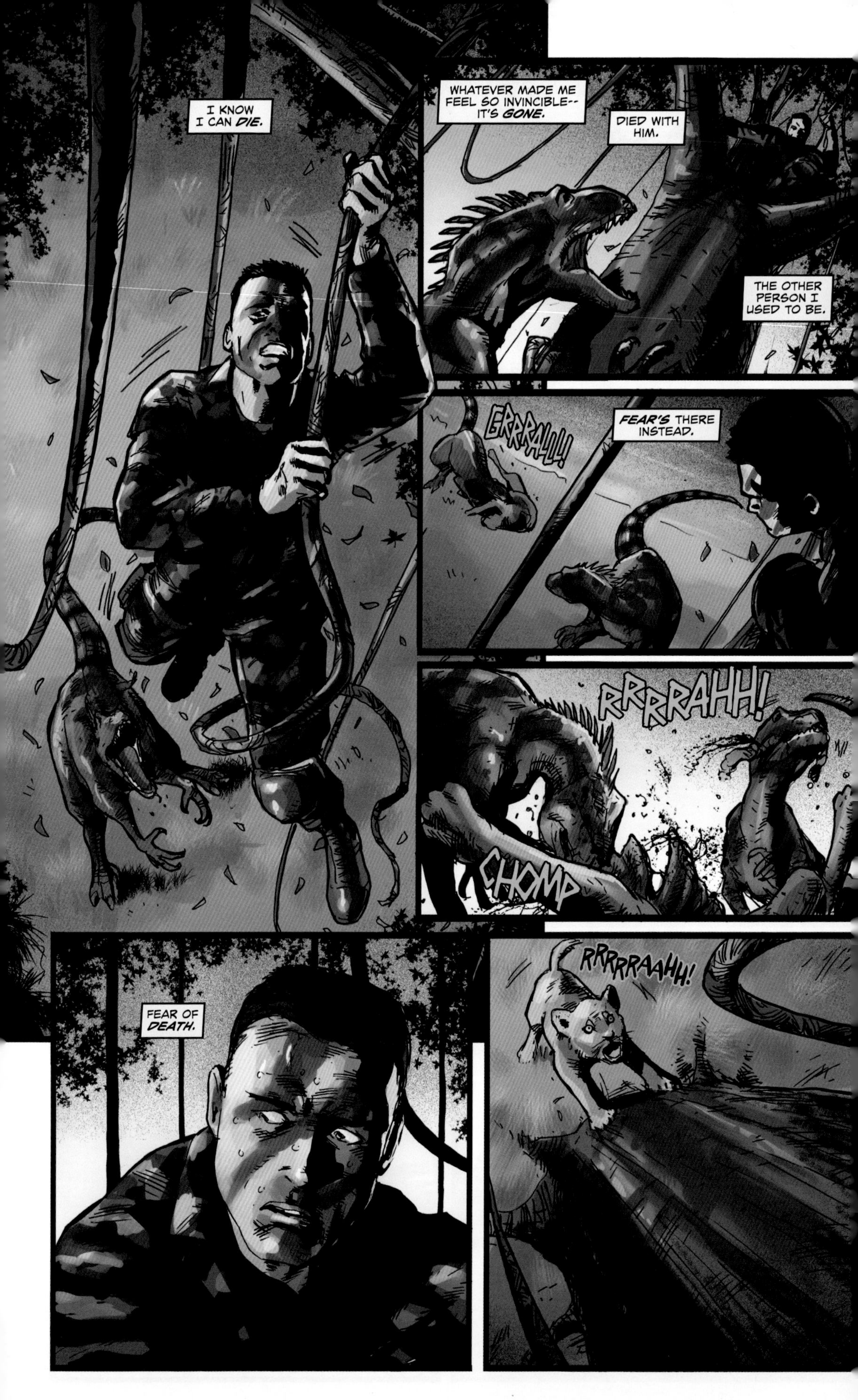
I KNOW I CAN *DIE*.
WHATEVER MADE ME FEEL SO INVINCIBLE-- IT'S *GONE*.
DIED WITH HIM.
THE OTHER PERSON I USED TO BE.
GRRRALLL!
FEAR'S THERE INSTEAD.
RRRRAHH!
CHOMP
FEAR OF *DEATH*.
RRRRRAAHH!

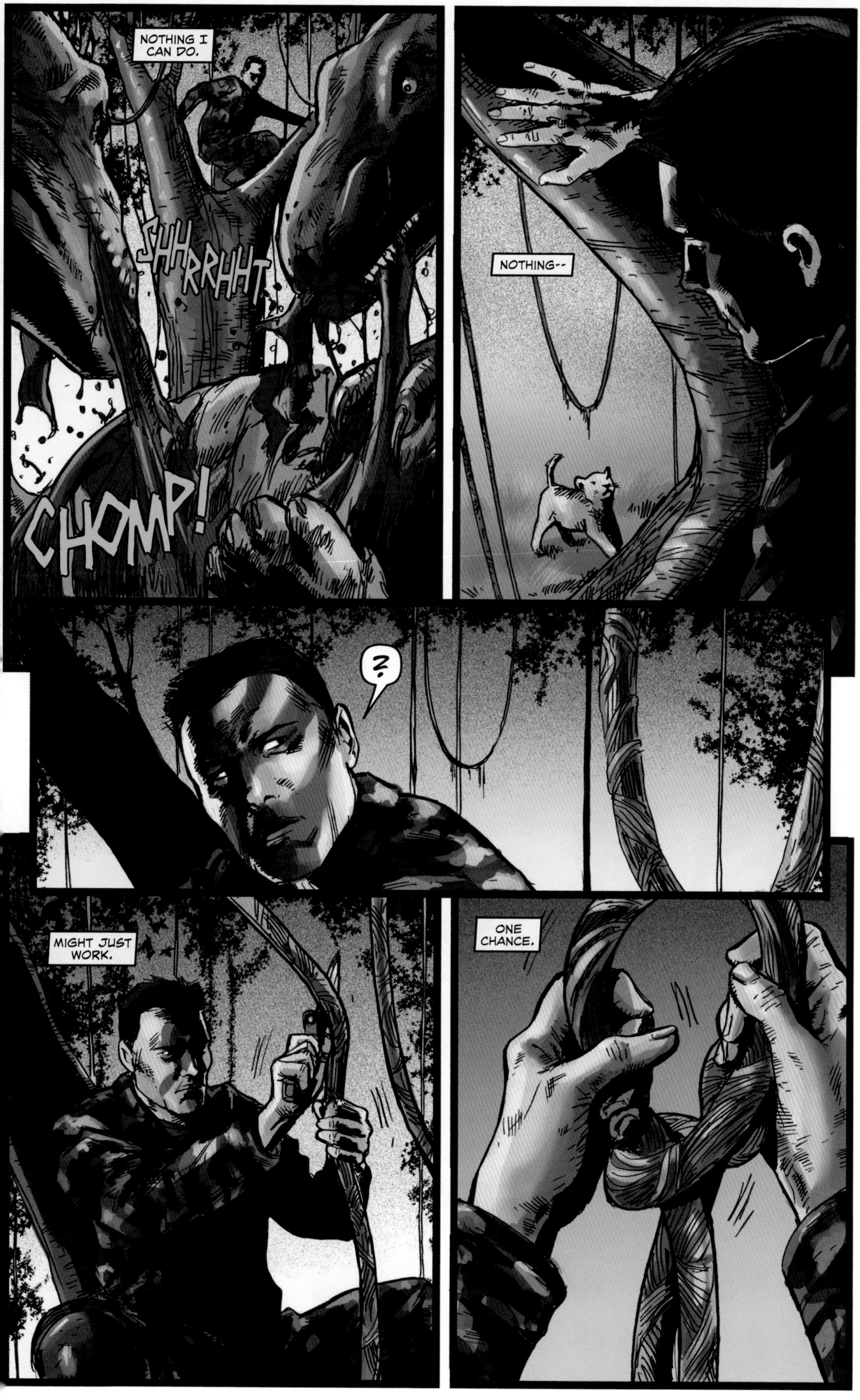
NOTHING I CAN DO.
SHHRRHHT
CHOMP!
NOTHING--
?
MIGHT JUST WORK.
ONE CHANCE.

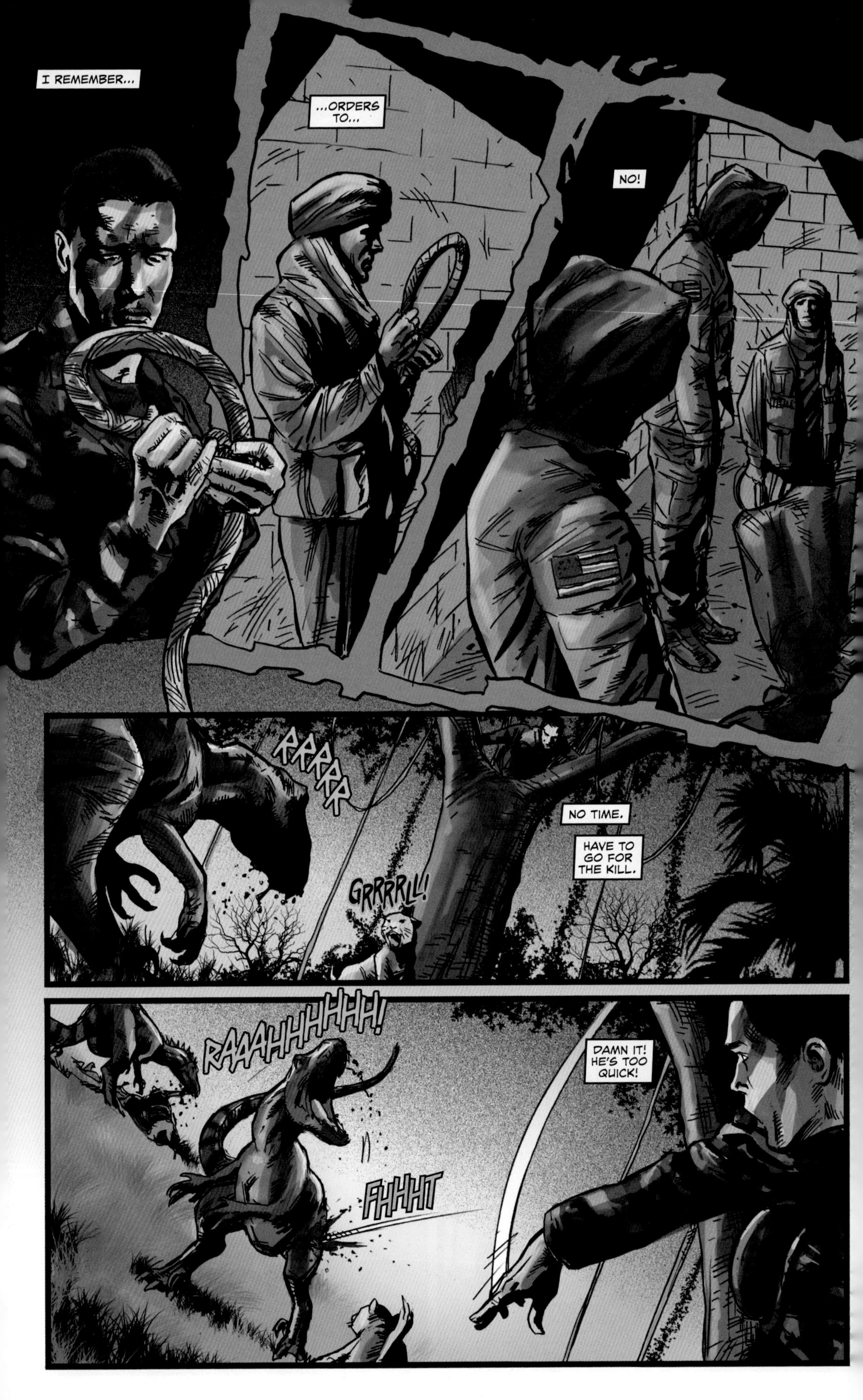
I REMEMBER...
...ORDERS TO...
NO!
RRRRR
NO TIME.
HAVE TO GO FOR THE KILL.
GRRRRLL!
RAAAHHHHHH!
DAMN IT! HE'S TOO QUICK!
FHHHT

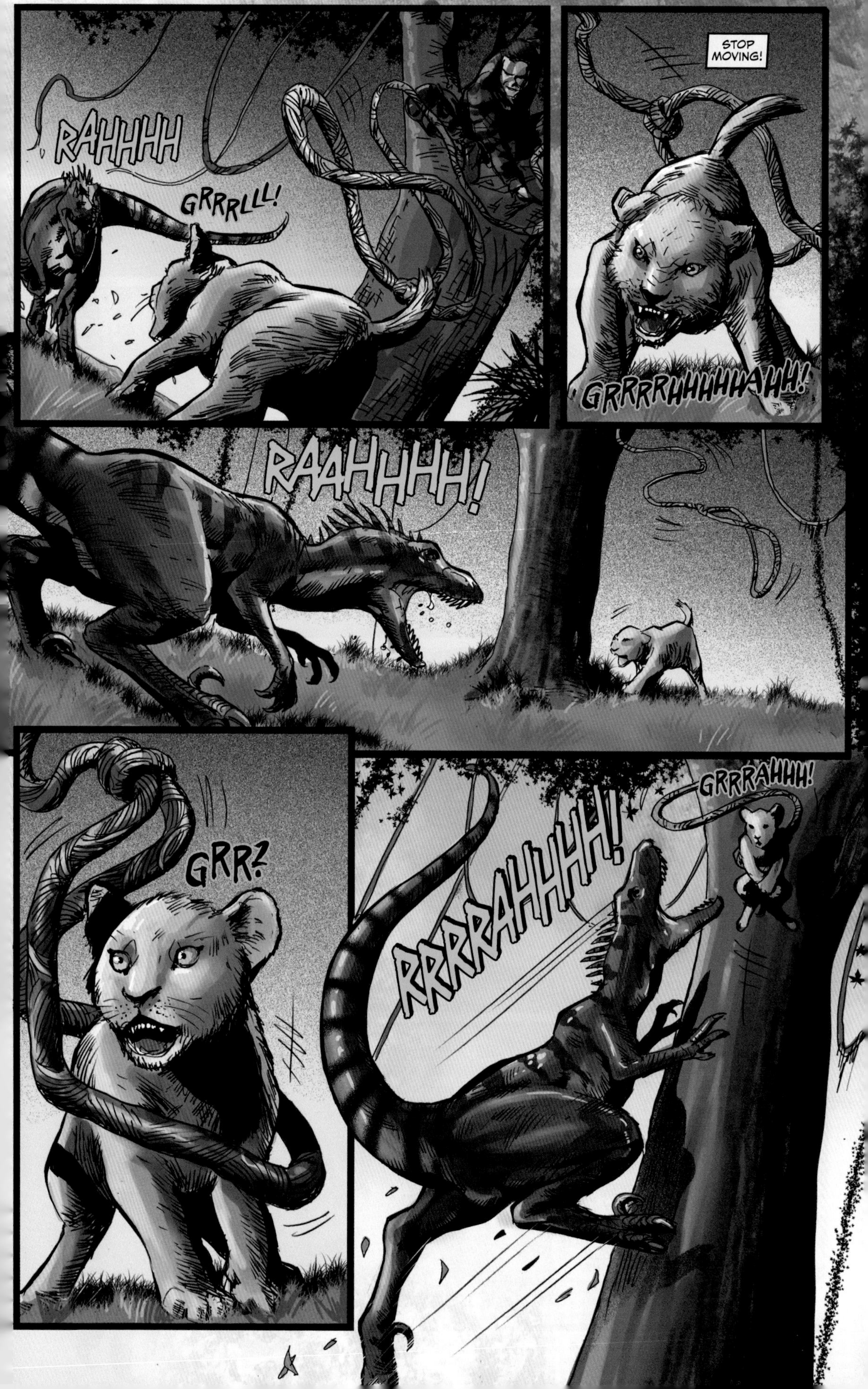
RAHHHH
GRRRLLL!
STOP MOVING!
GRRRRHHHHHAHH!
RAAHHHH!
GRR?
GRRRAHHH!
RRRRAHHHH!

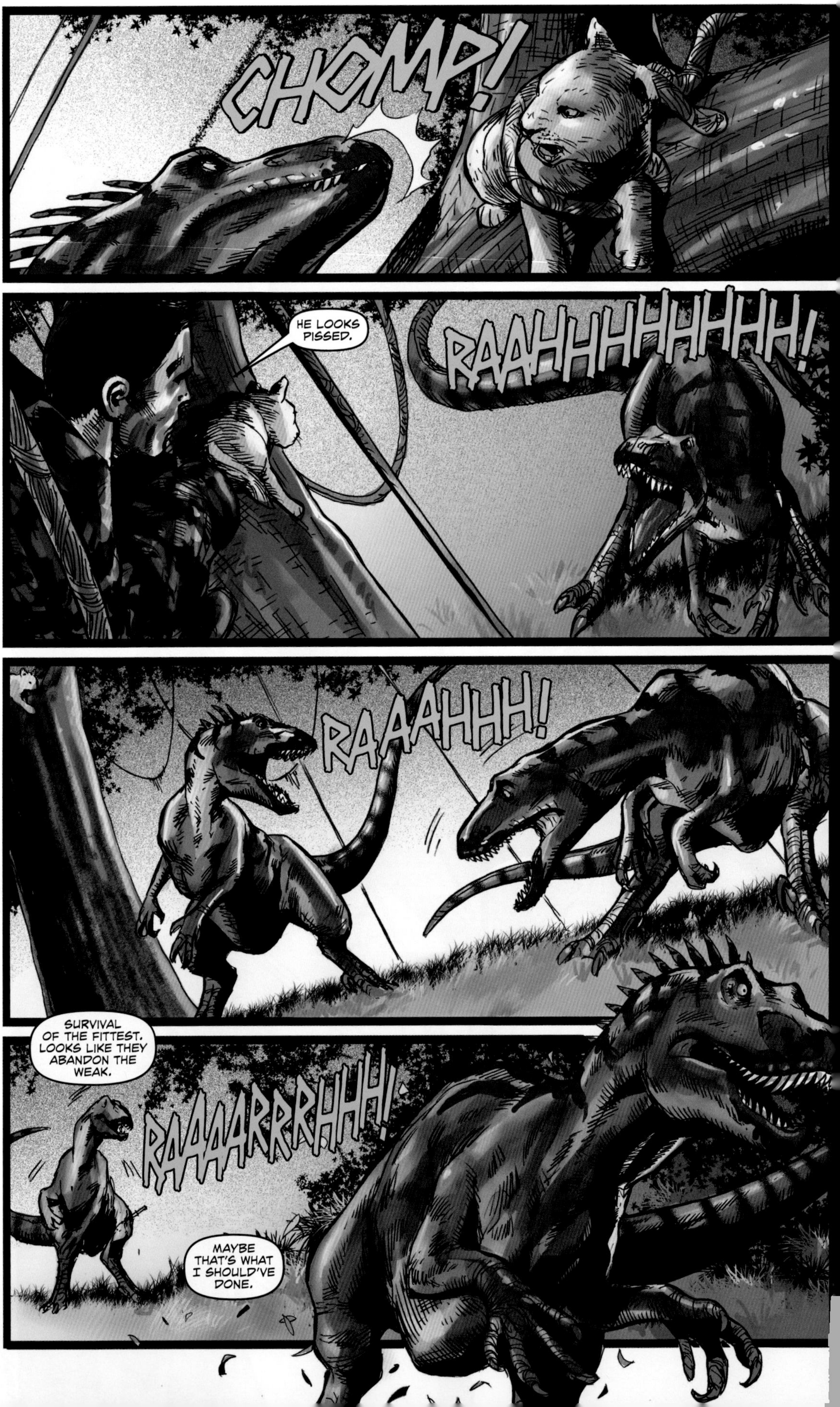
CHOMP!
HE LOOKS PISSED.
RAAHHHHHHHH!
RAAAHHH!
SURVIVAL OF THE FITTEST. LOOKS LIKE THEY ABANDON THE WEAK.
RAAAARRRHHH!
MAYBE THAT'S WHAT I SHOULD'VE DONE.

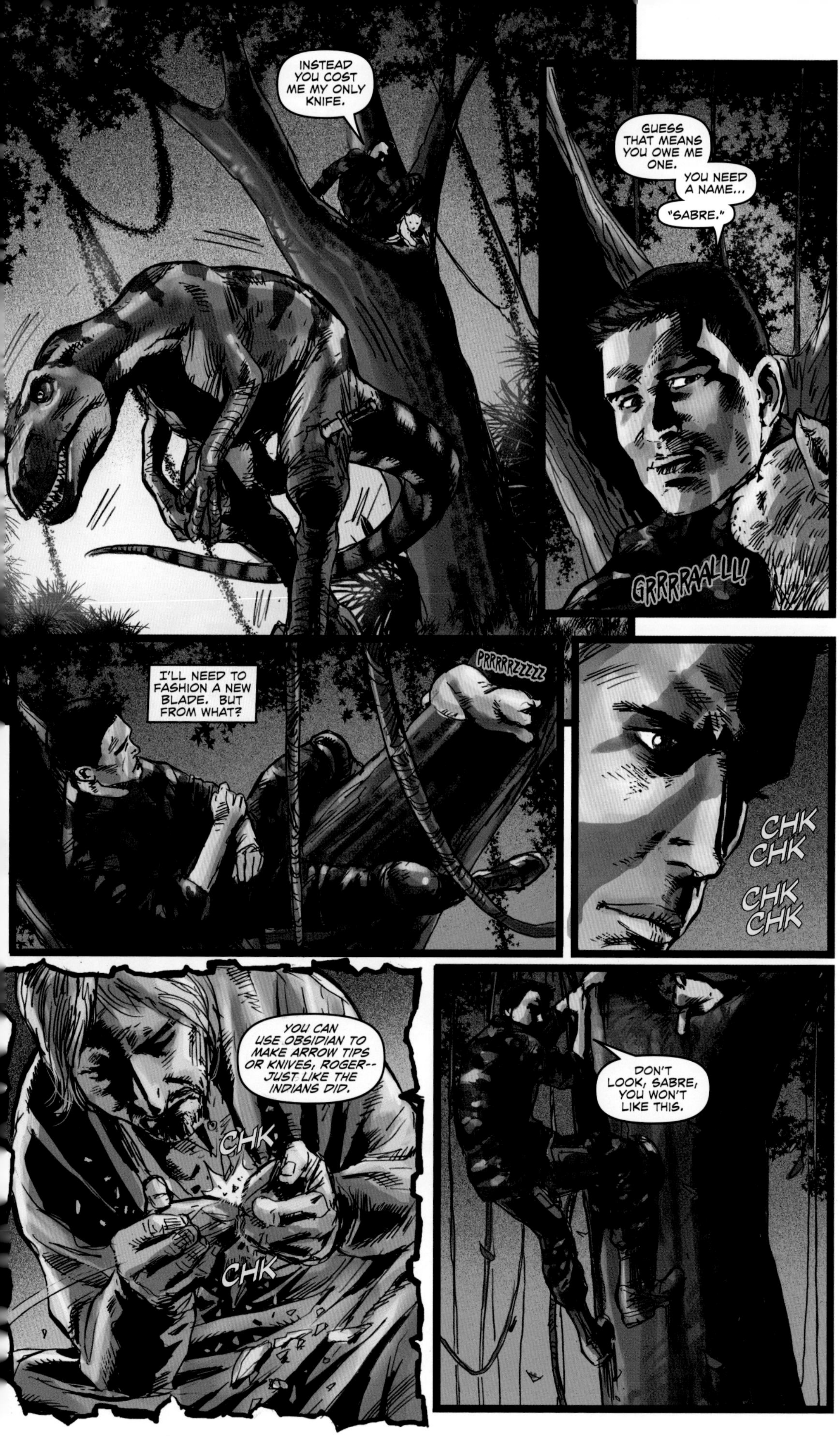
INSTEAD YOU COST ME MY ONLY KNIFE.
GUESS THAT MEANS YOU OWE ME ONE.
YOU NEED A NAME...
"SABRE."
GRRRRAALLL!
I'LL NEED TO FASHION A NEW BLADE. BUT FROM WHAT?
PRRRRRZZZZZ
CHK CHK
CHK CHK
YOU CAN USE OBSIDIAN TO MAKE ARROW TIPS OR KNIVES, ROGER-- JUST LIKE THE INDIANS DID.
CHK
CHK
DON'T LOOK, SABRE, YOU WON'T LIKE THIS.

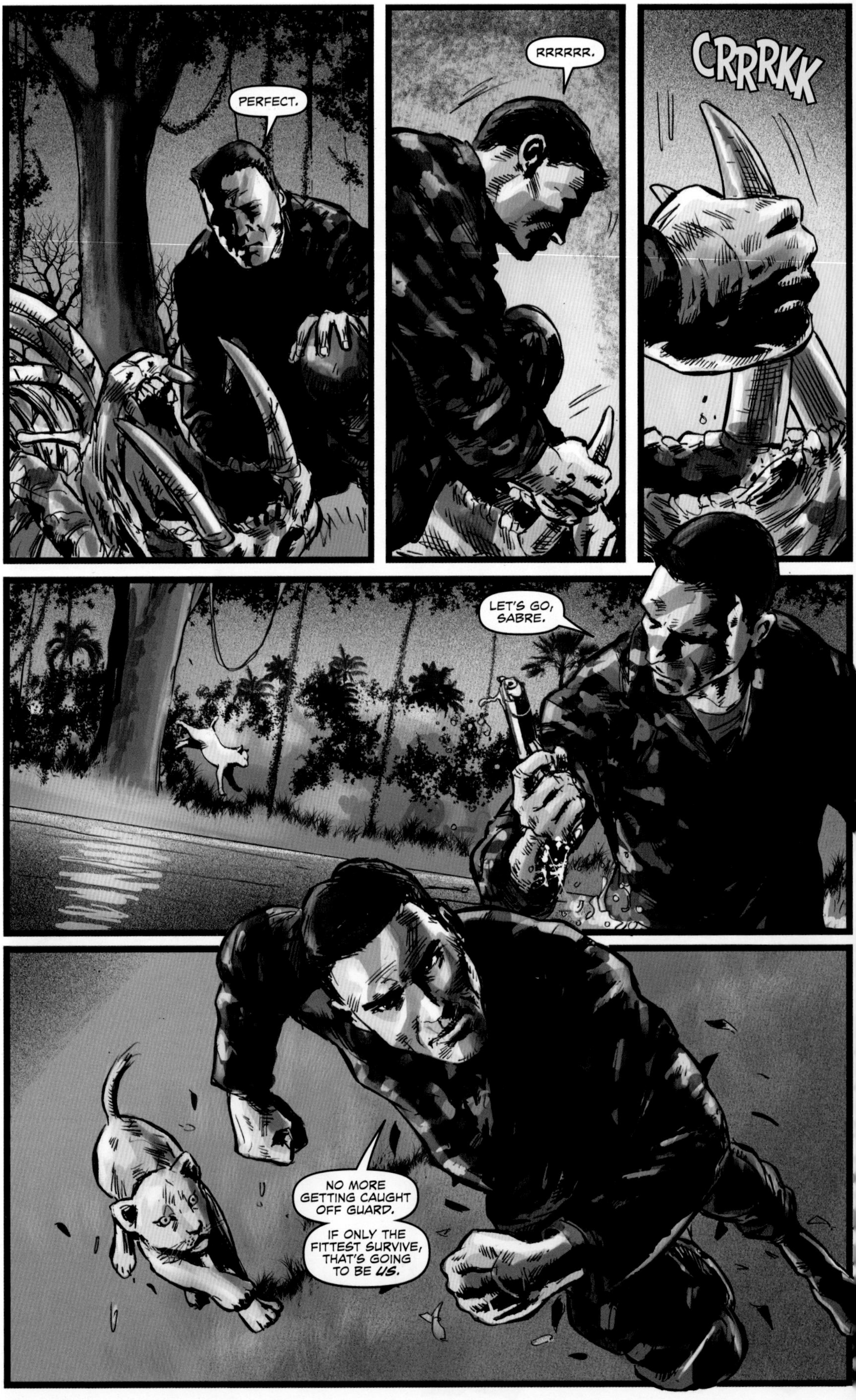
PERFECT.
RRRRRR.
CRRRKK
LET'S GO, SABRE.
NO MORE GETTING CAUGHT OFF GUARD.
IF ONLY THE FITTEST SURVIVE, THAT'S GOING TO BE *US*.

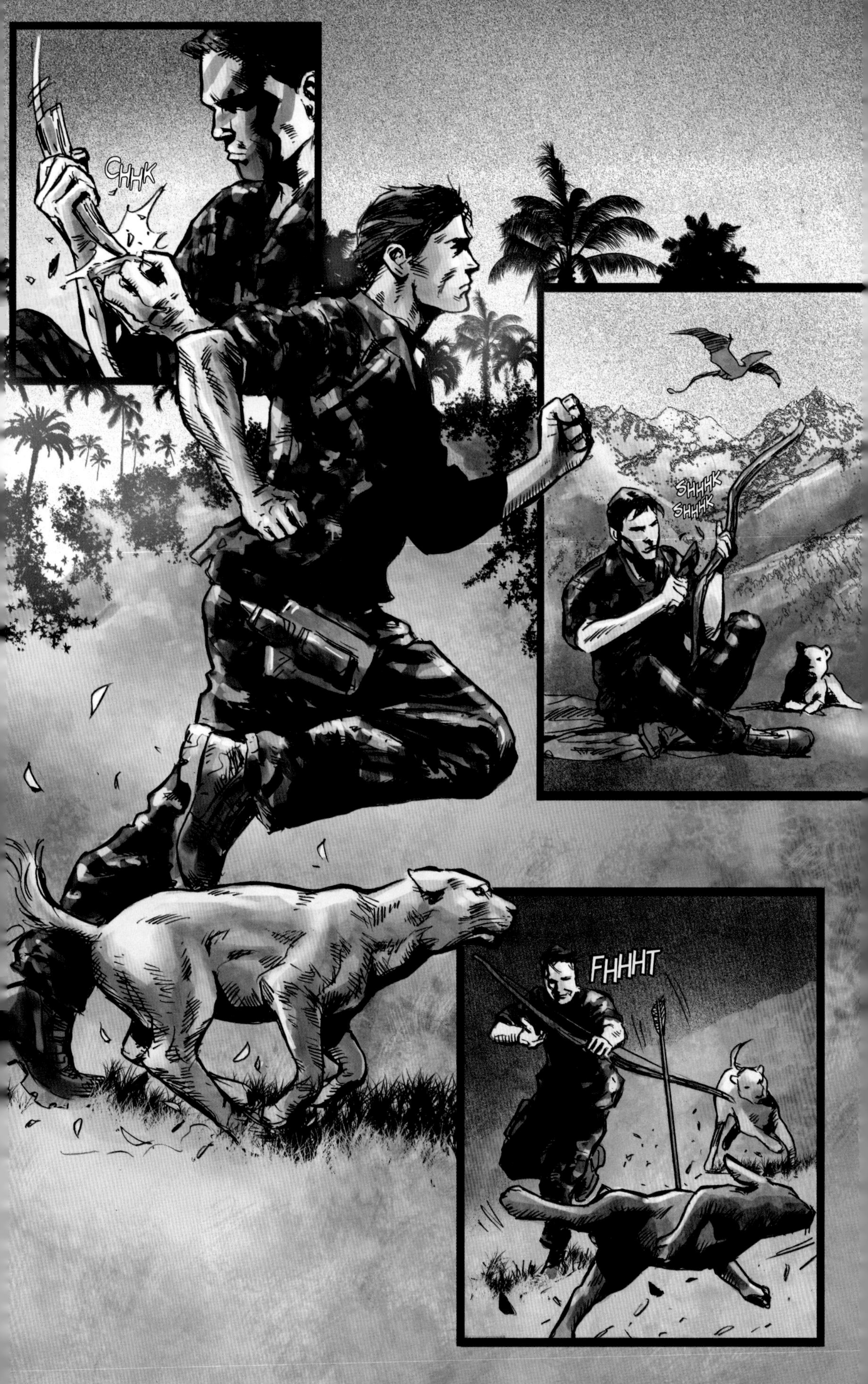
CHHK
SHHHK
SHHHK
FHHHT

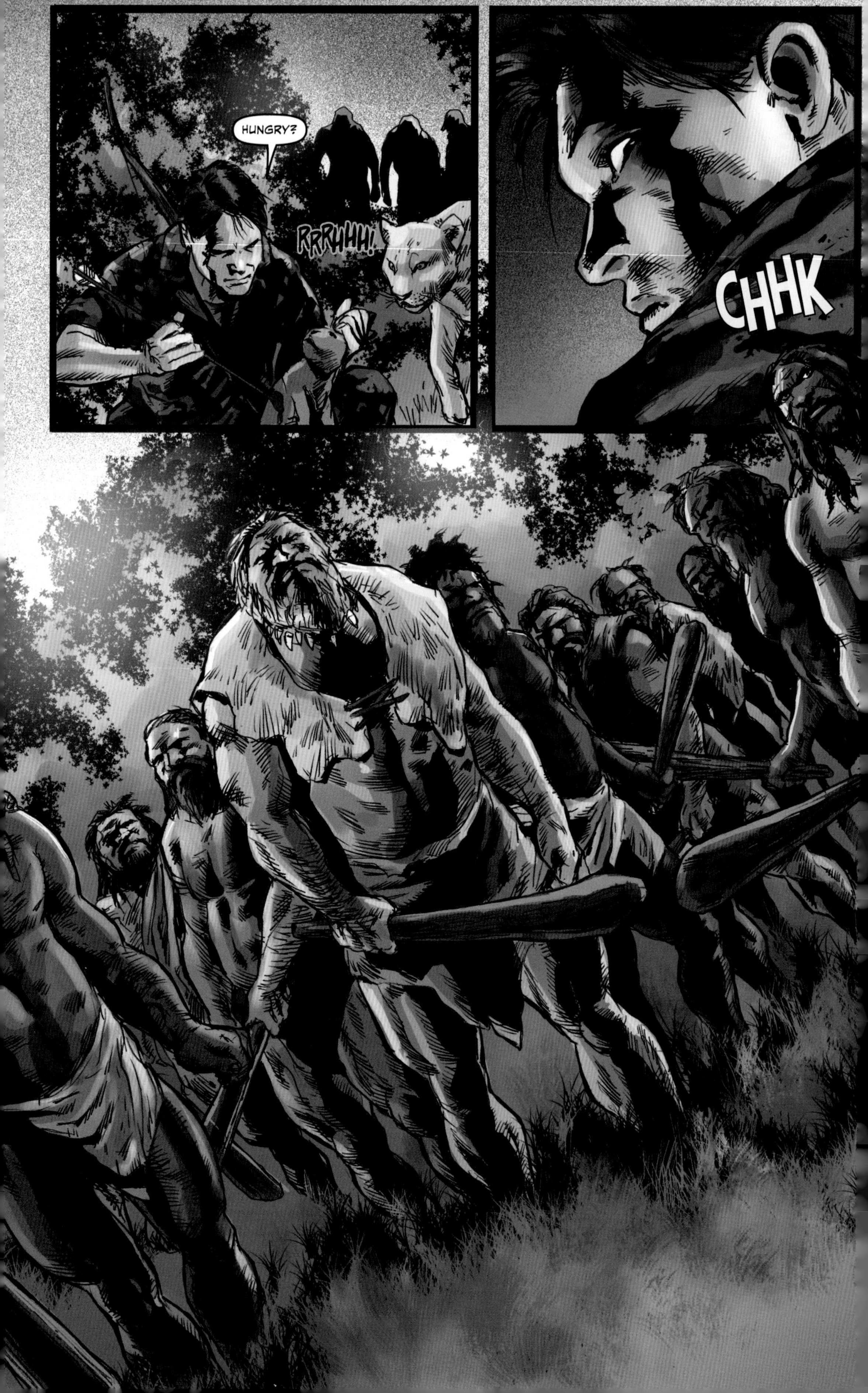
HUNGRY?
RRRUHH!
CHHK

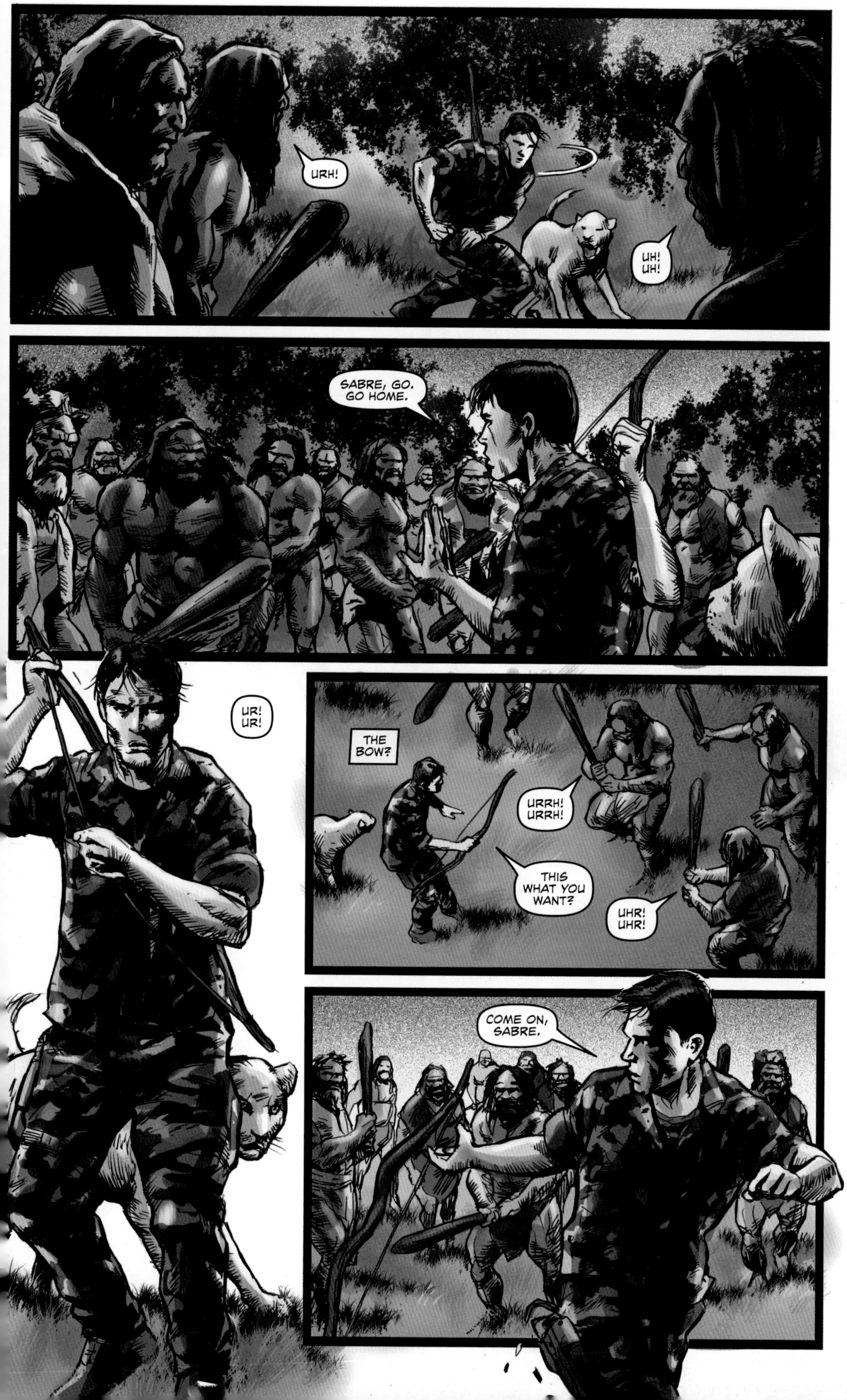
URH!
UH! UH!
SABRE, GO. GO HOME.
UR! UR!
THE BOW?
URRH! URRH!
THIS WHAT YOU WANT?
UHR! UHR!
COME ON, SABRE.

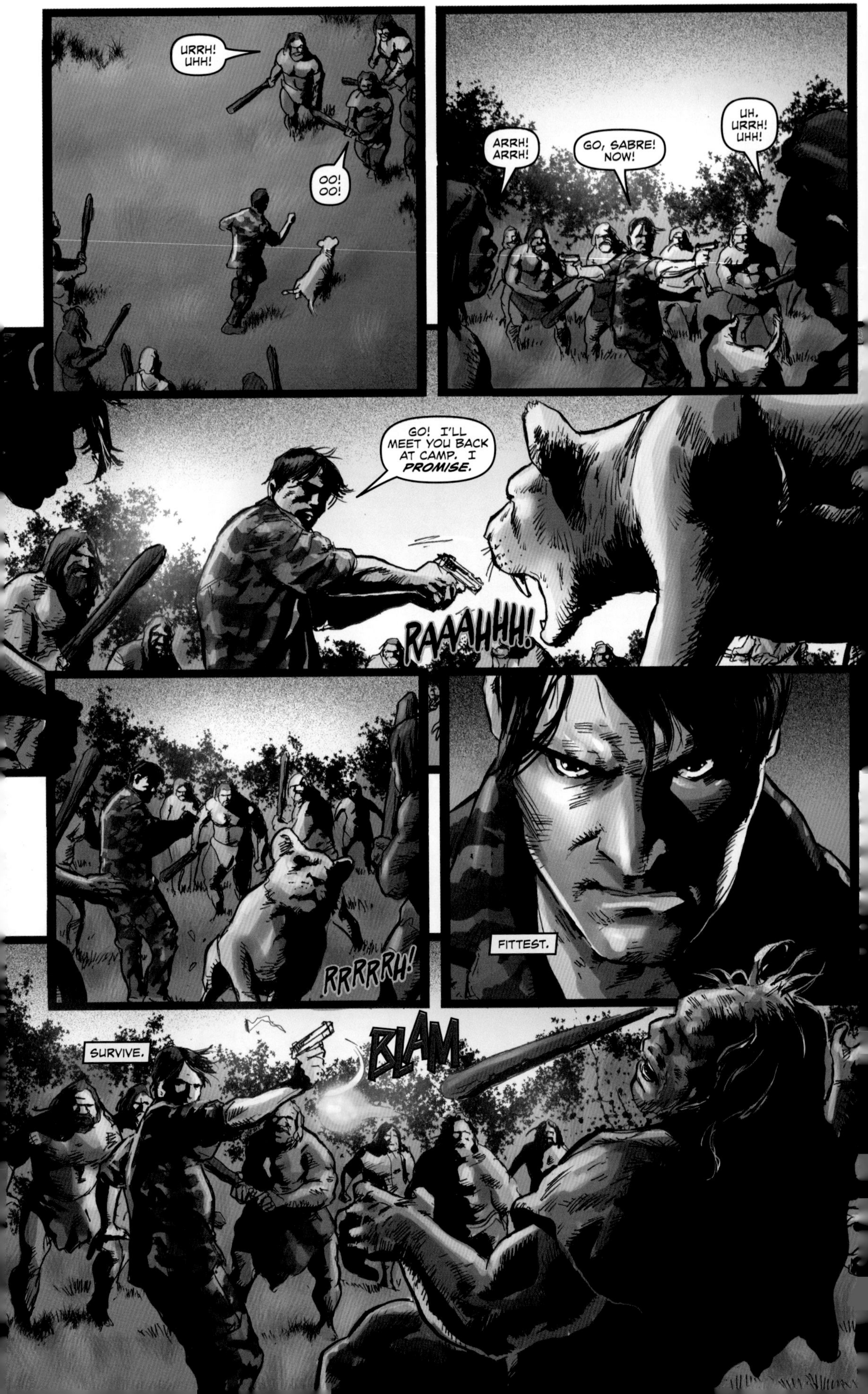
URRH! UHH!
OO! OO!
ARRH! ARRH!
GO, SABRE! NOW!
UH. URRH! UHH!
GO! I'LL MEET YOU BACK AT CAMP. I *PROMISE.*
RAAAHHH!
RRRRRH!
FITTEST.
SURVIVE.
BLAM

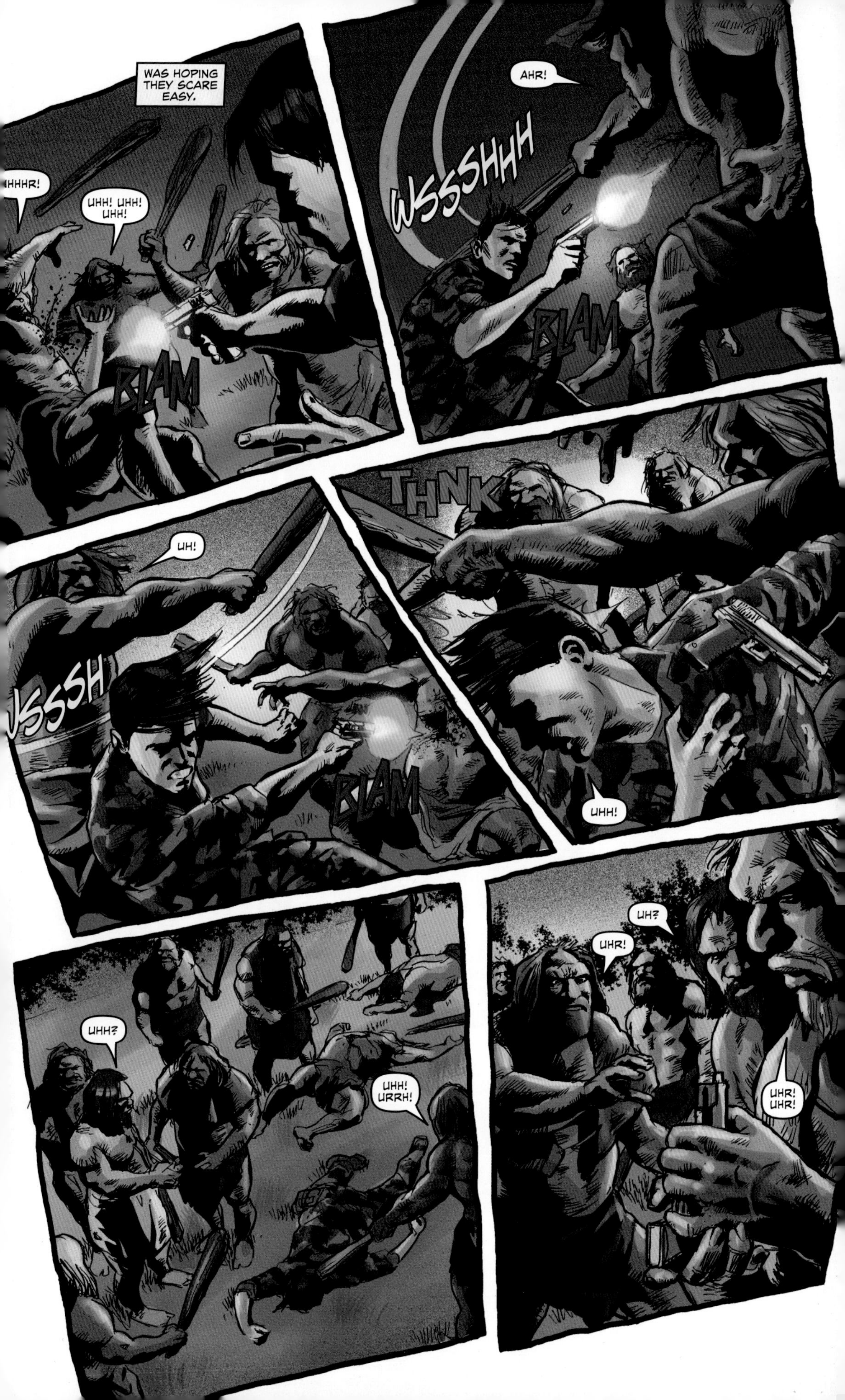
WAS HOPING THEY SCARE EASY.
HHHR!
UHH! UHH! UHH!
BLAM
AHR!
WSSSHHH
BLAM
UH!
WSSSH
BLAM
THNK
UHH!
UHH?
UHH! URRH!
UH?
UHR!
UHR! UHR!

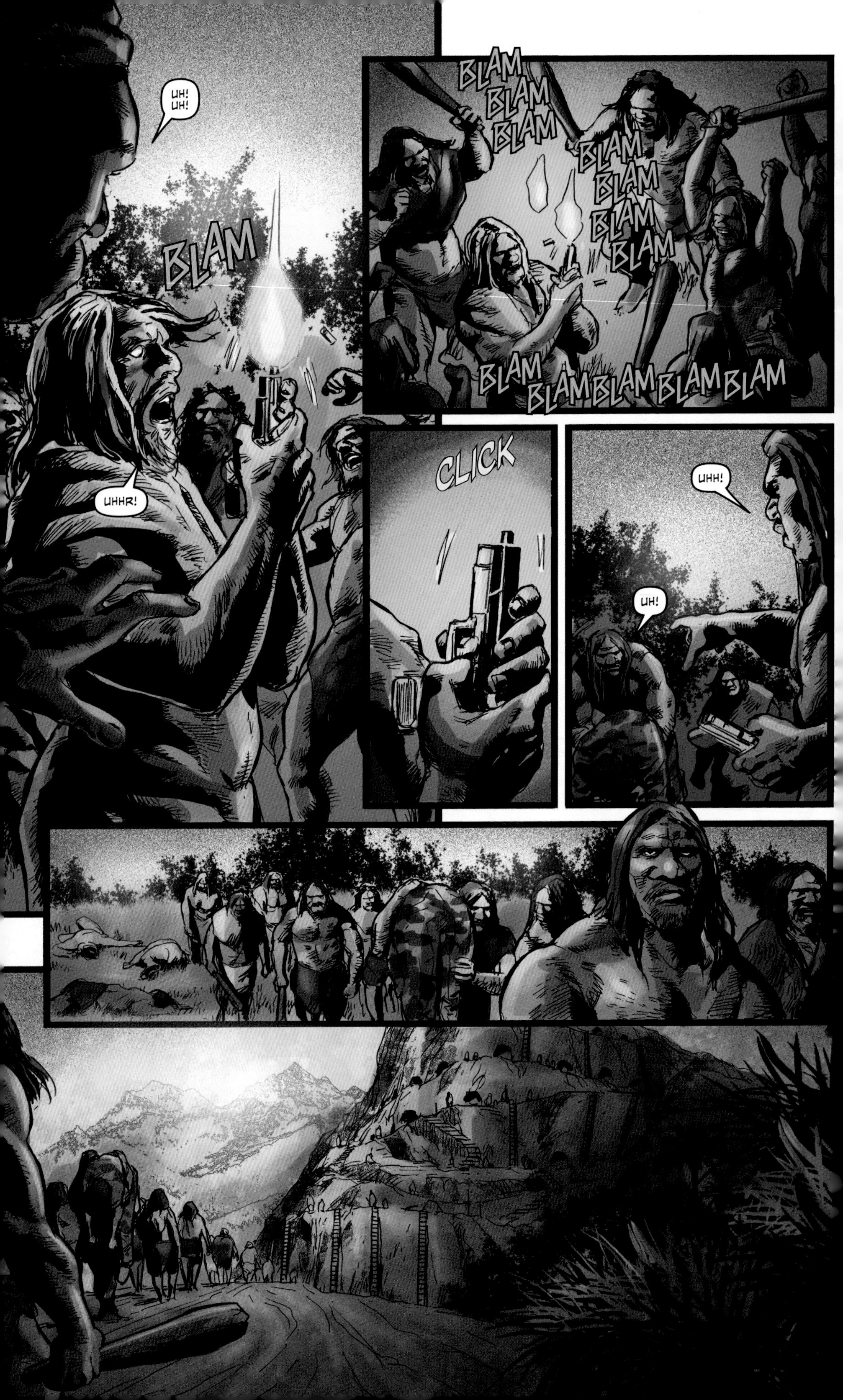
UH! UH!
BLAM
UHHR!
BLAM BLAM BLAM
BLAM BLAM BLAM BLAM
BLAM BLAM BLAM BLAM BLAM BLAM
CLICK
UHH!
UH!

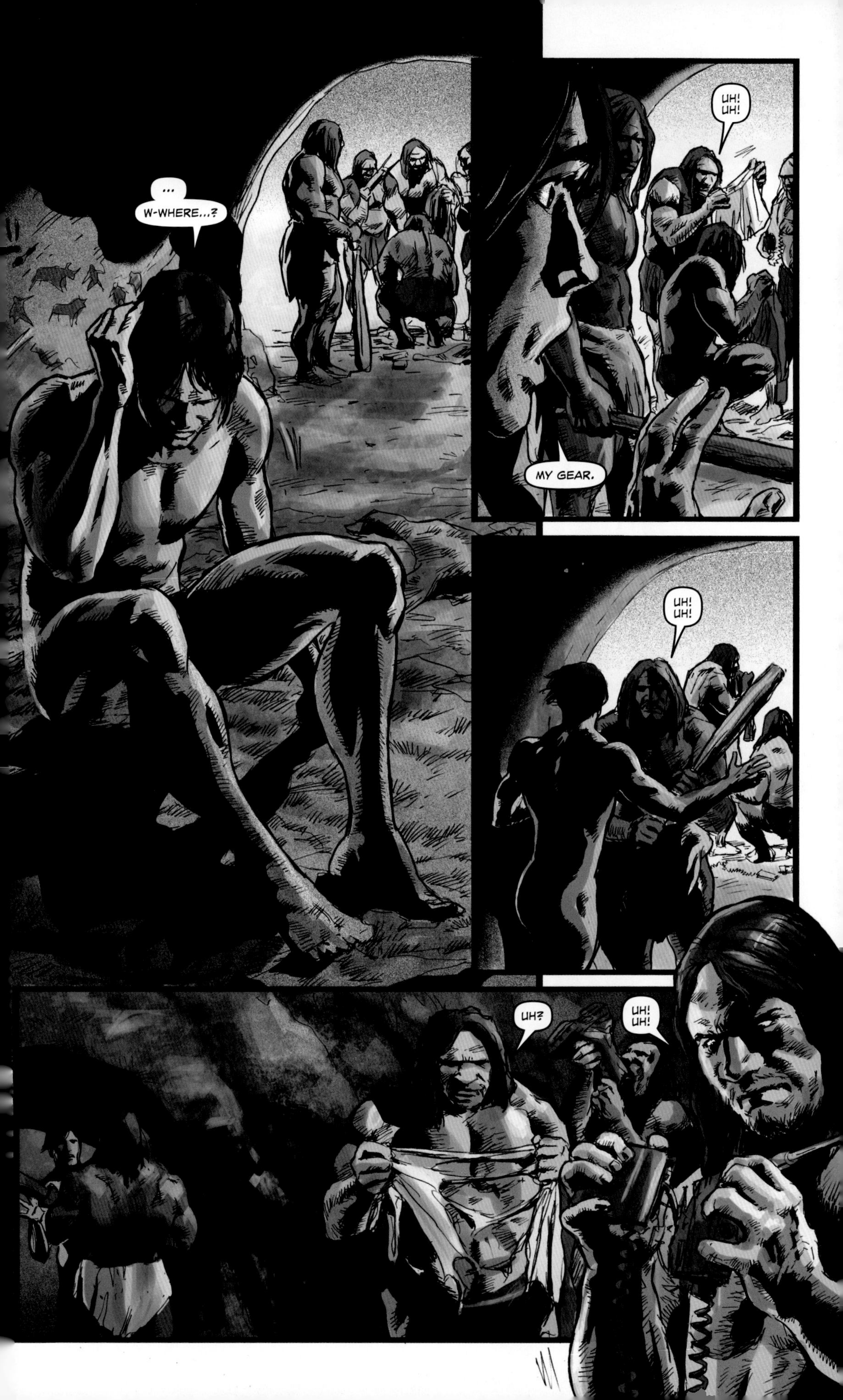
...
W-WHERE...?
UH! UH!
MY GEAR.
UH! UH!
UH?
UH! UH!

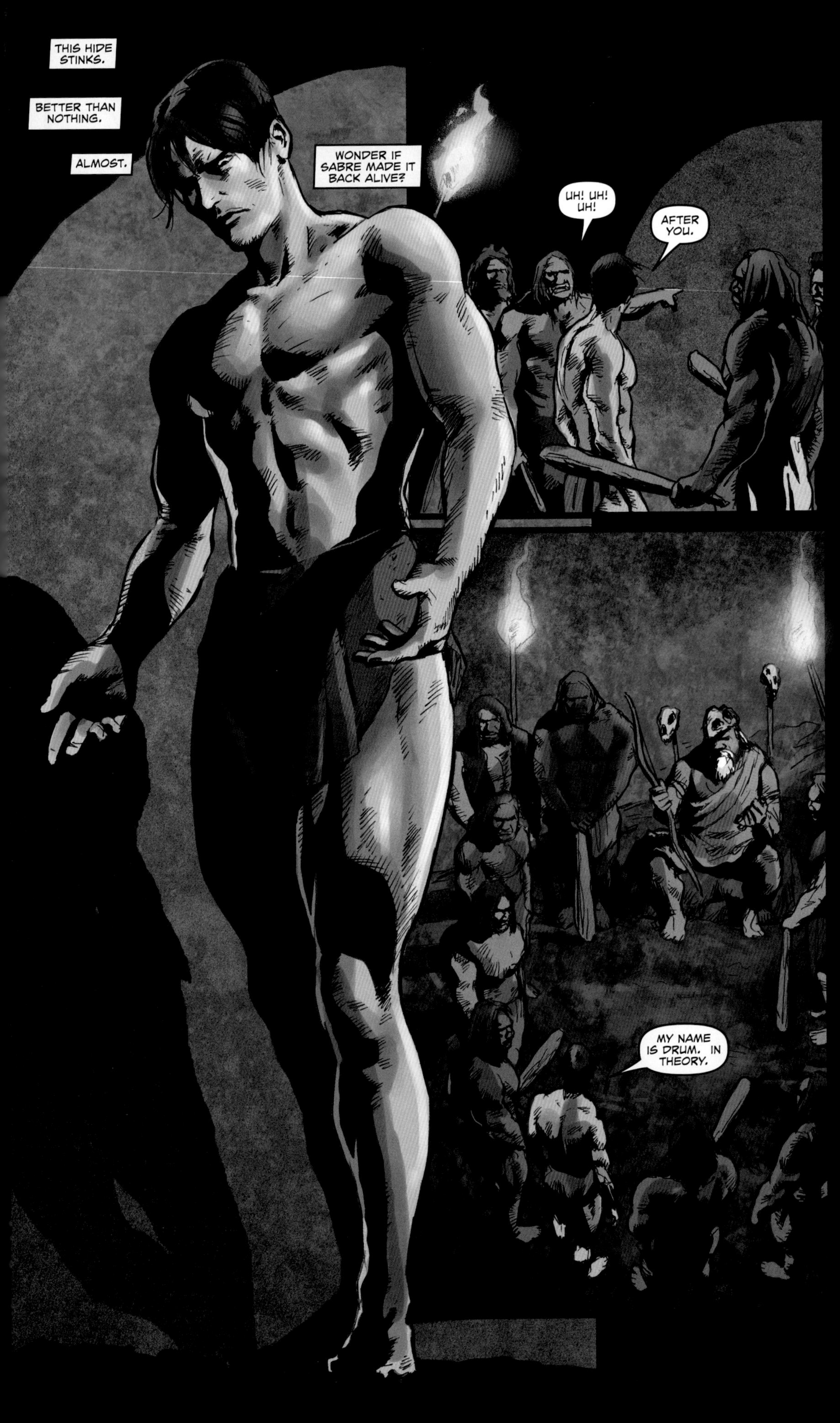
THIS HIDE STINKS.
BETTER THAN NOTHING.
ALMOST.
WONDER IF SABRE MADE IT BACK ALIVE?
UH! UH! UH!
AFTER YOU.
MY NAME IS DRUM. IN THEORY.

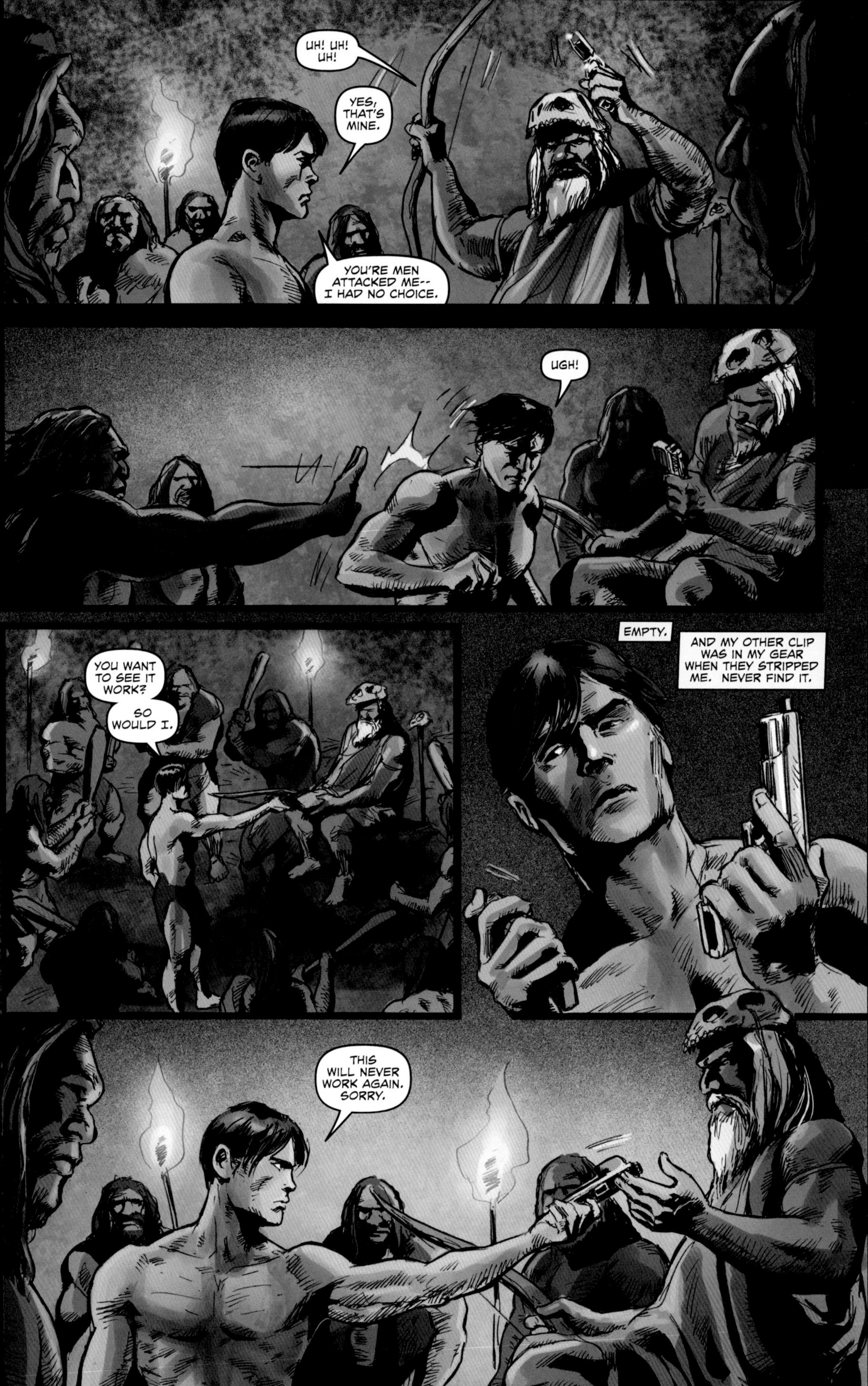
UH! UH! UH!
YES, THAT'S MINE.
YOU'RE MEN ATTACKED ME-- I HAD NO CHOICE.
UGH!
YOU WANT TO SEE IT WORK?
SO WOULD I.
EMPTY.
AND MY OTHER CLIP WAS IN MY GEAR WHEN THEY STRIPPED ME. NEVER FIND IT.
THIS WILL NEVER WORK AGAIN. SORRY.

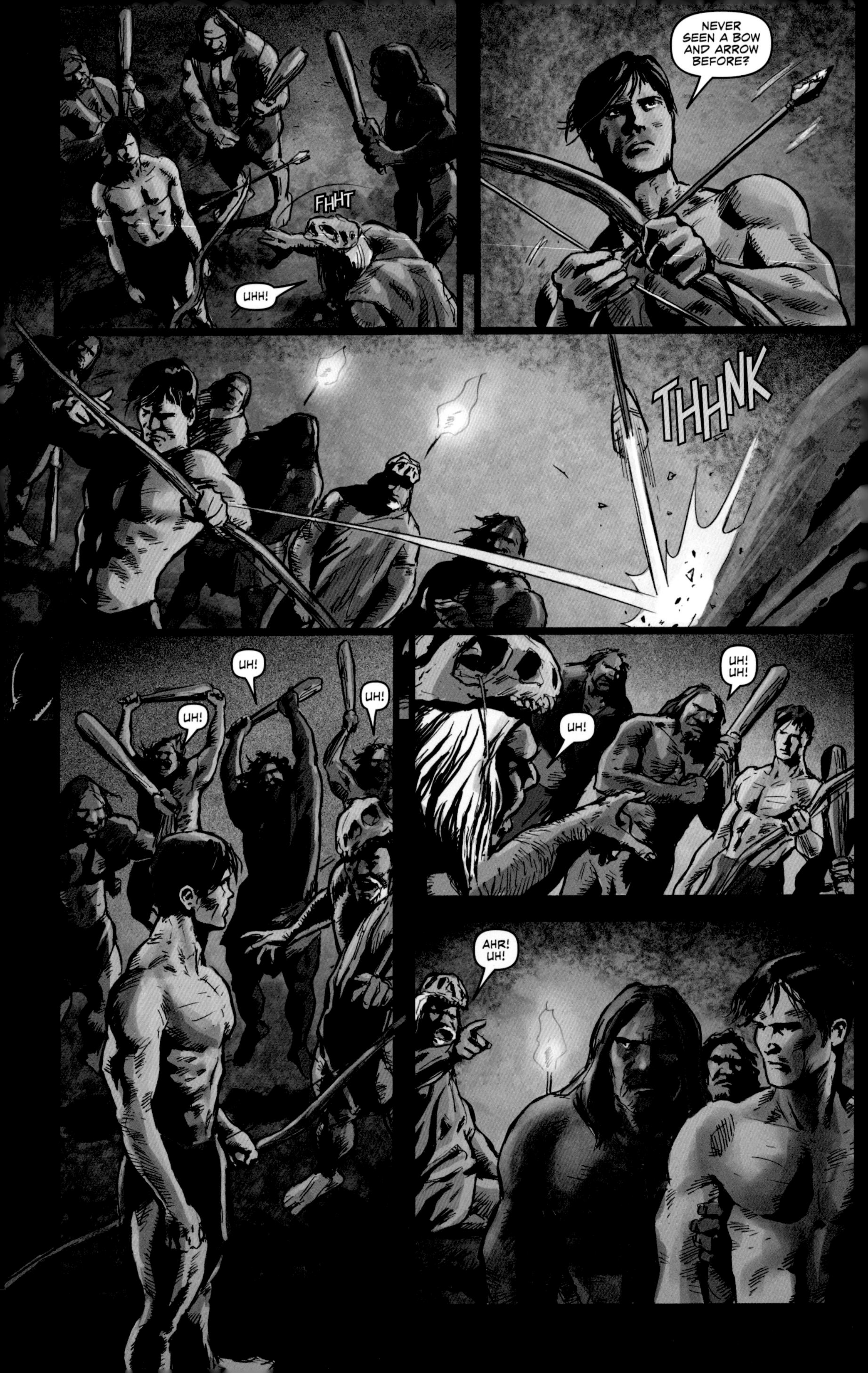
FHHT
UHH!
NEVER SEEN A BOW AND ARROW BEFORE?
THHNK
UH!
UH!
UH!
UH!
UH! UH!
AHR! UH!

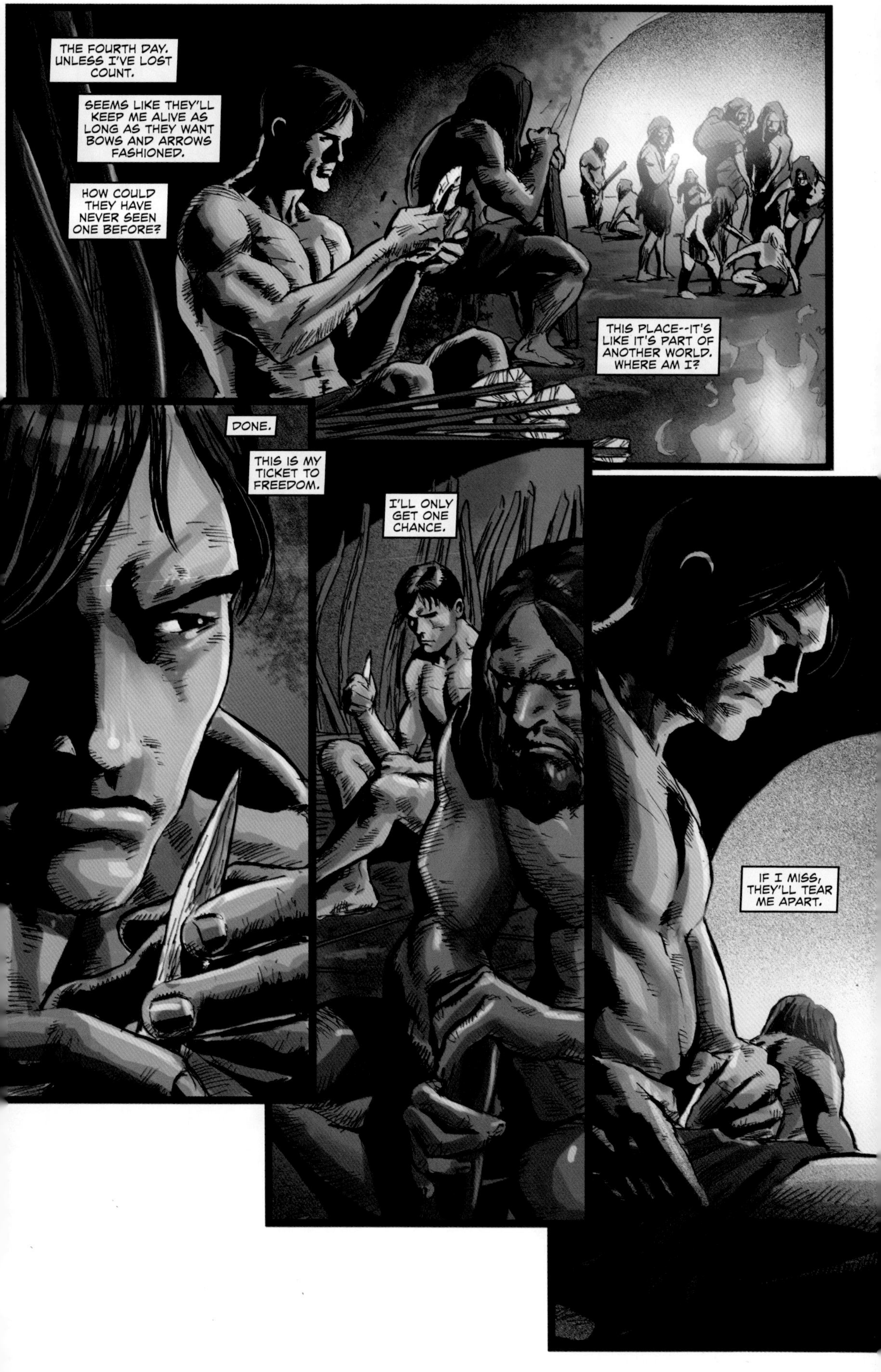
THE FOURTH DAY. UNLESS I'VE LOST COUNT.
SEEMS LIKE THEY'LL KEEP ME ALIVE AS LONG AS THEY WANT BOWS AND ARROWS FASHIONED.
HOW COULD THEY HAVE NEVER SEEN ONE BEFORE?
THIS PLACE--IT'S LIKE IT'S PART OF ANOTHER WORLD. WHERE AM I?
DONE.
THIS IS MY TICKET TO FREEDOM.
I'LL ONLY GET ONE CHANCE.
IF I MISS, THEY'LL TEAR ME APART.

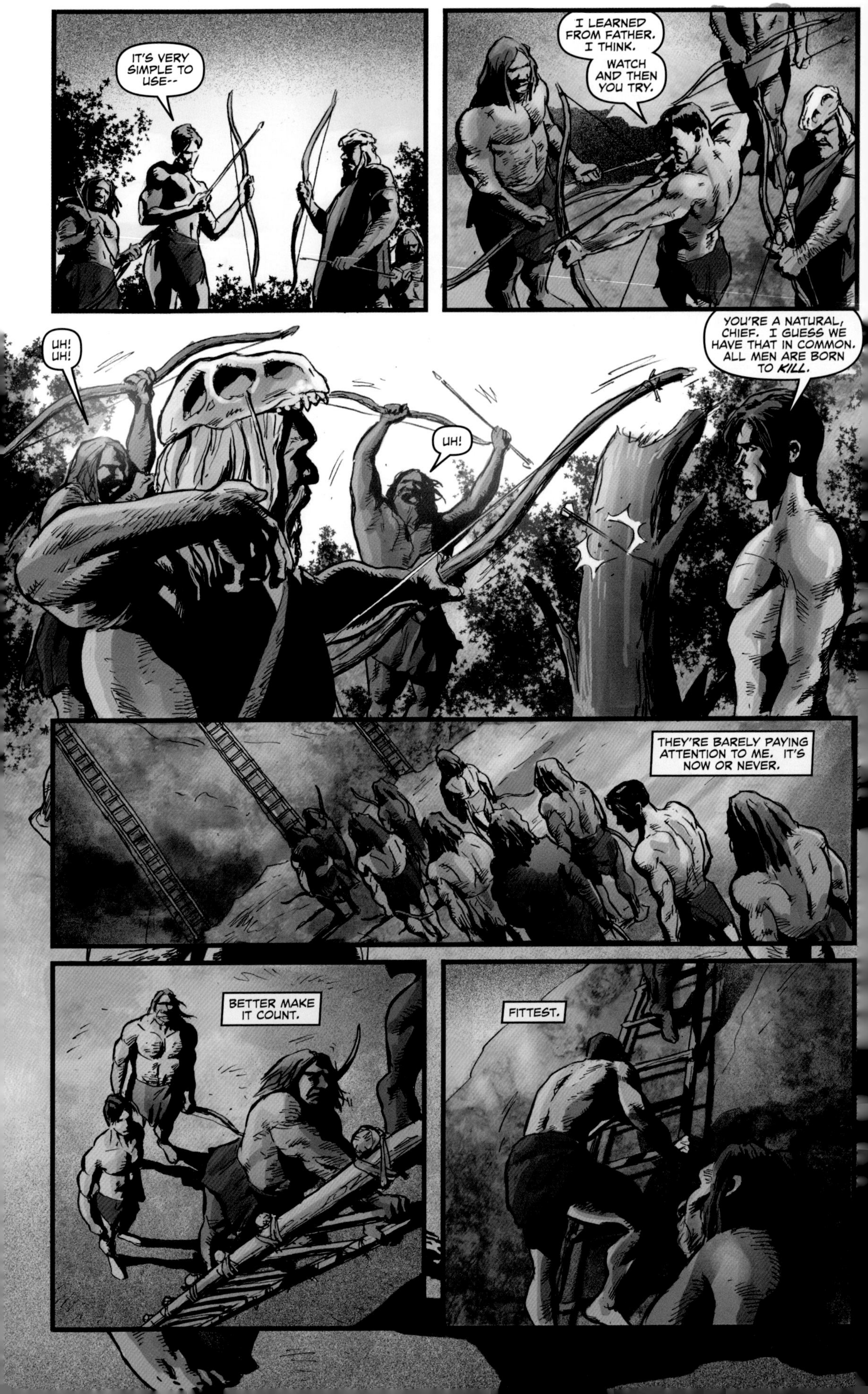
IT'S VERY SIMPLE TO USE--
I LEARNED FROM FATHER. I THINK.
WATCH AND THEN YOU TRY.
UH! UH!
UH!
YOU'RE A NATURAL, CHIEF. I GUESS WE HAVE THAT IN COMMON. ALL MEN ARE BORN TO KILL.
THEY'RE BARELY PAYING ATTENTION TO ME. IT'S NOW OR NEVER.
BETTER MAKE IT COUNT.
FITTEST.

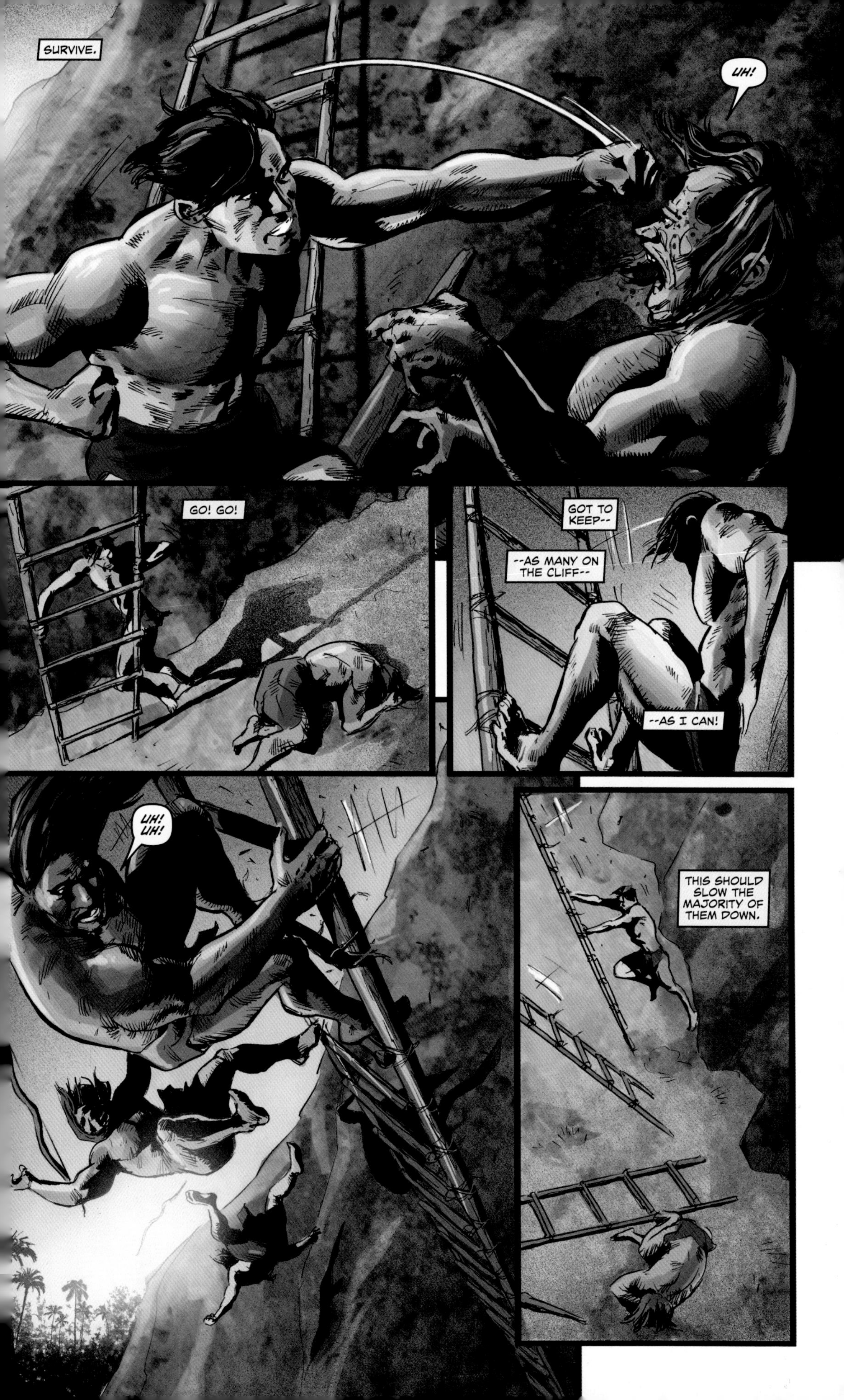
SURVIVE.
UH!
GO! GO!
GOT TO KEEP--
--AS MANY ON THE CLIFF--
--AS I CAN!
UH! UH!
THIS SHOULD SLOW THE MAJORITY OF THEM DOWN.

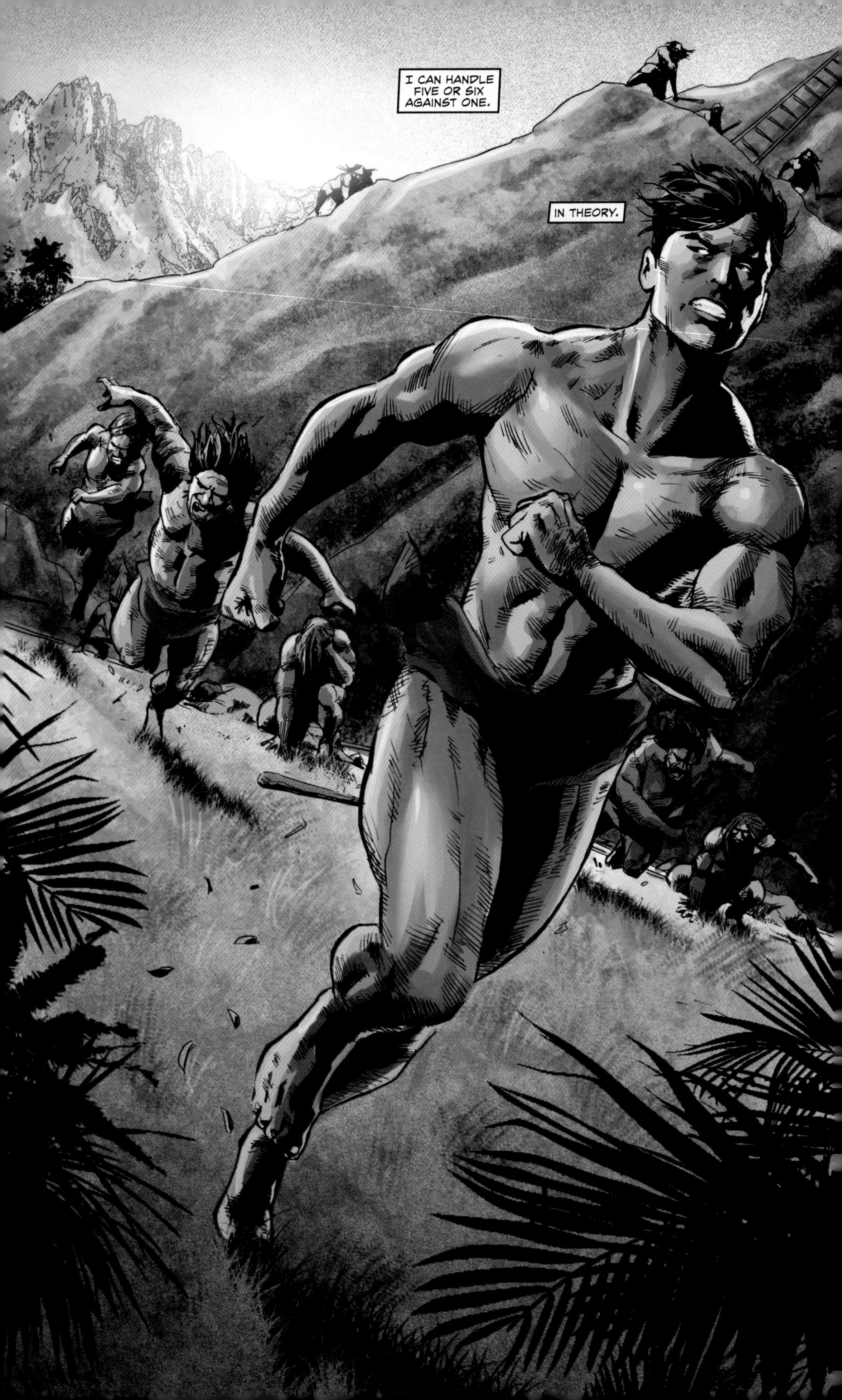
I CAN HANDLE FIVE OR SIX AGAINST ONE.
IN THEORY.

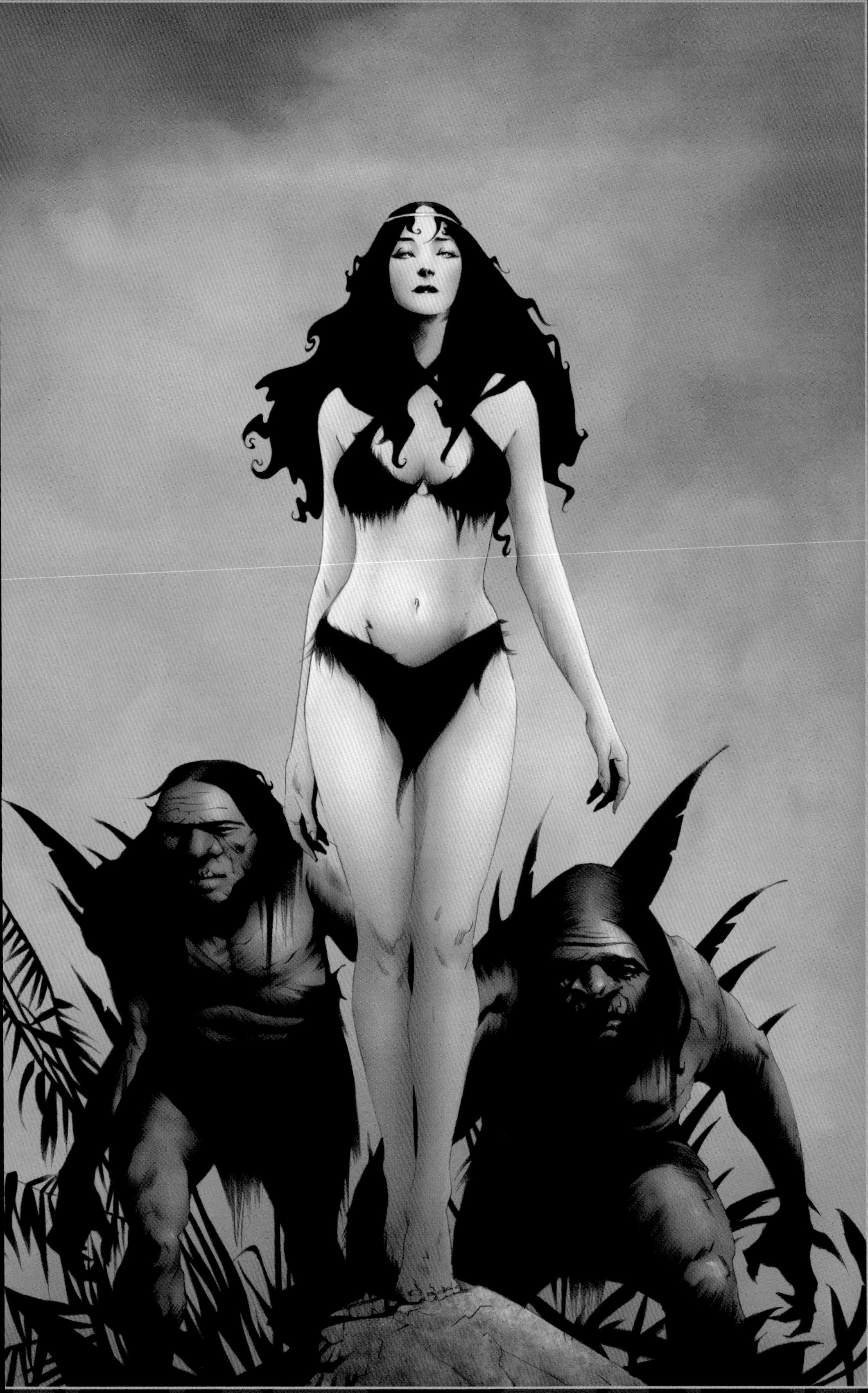

Issue Three Cover by Jae Lee

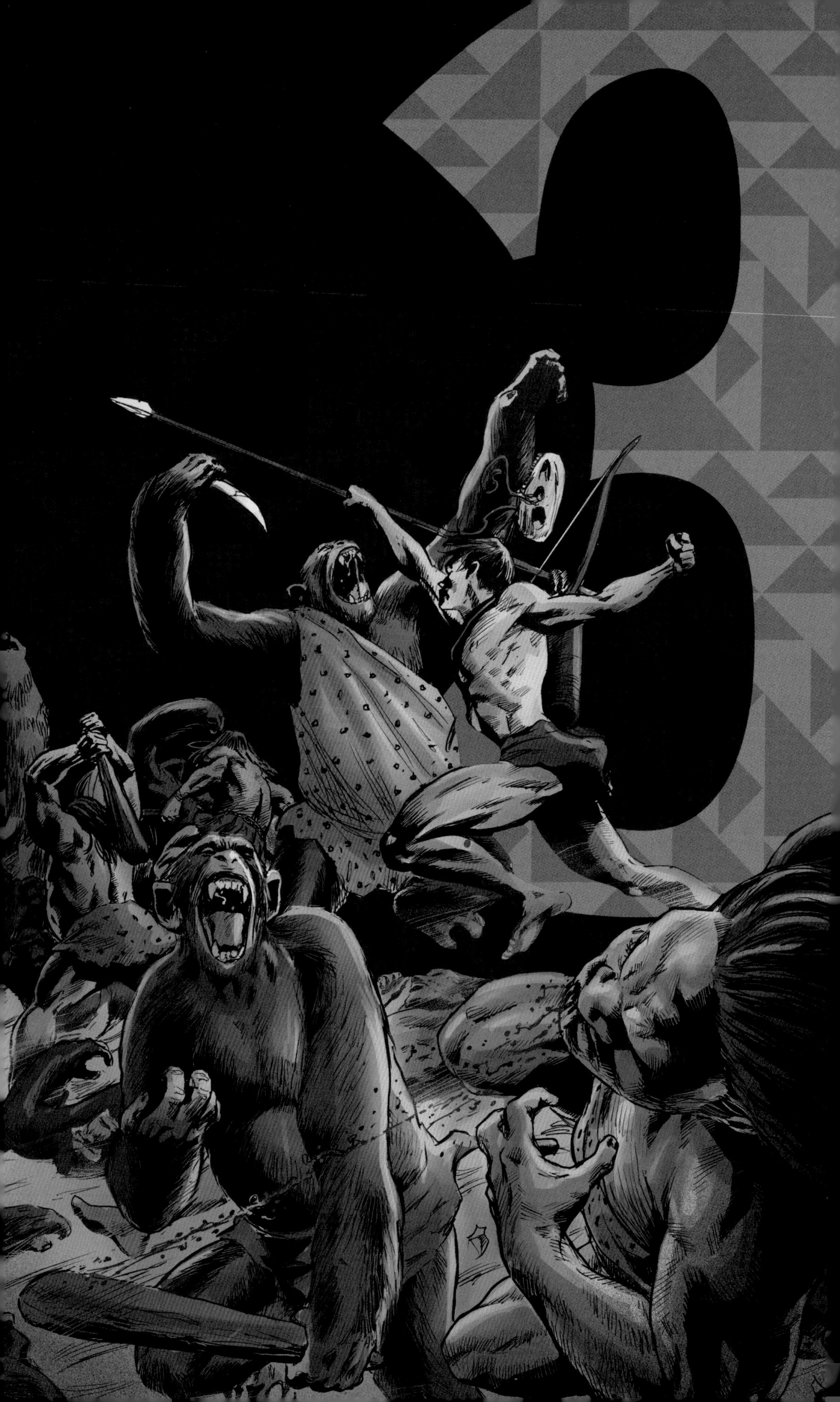

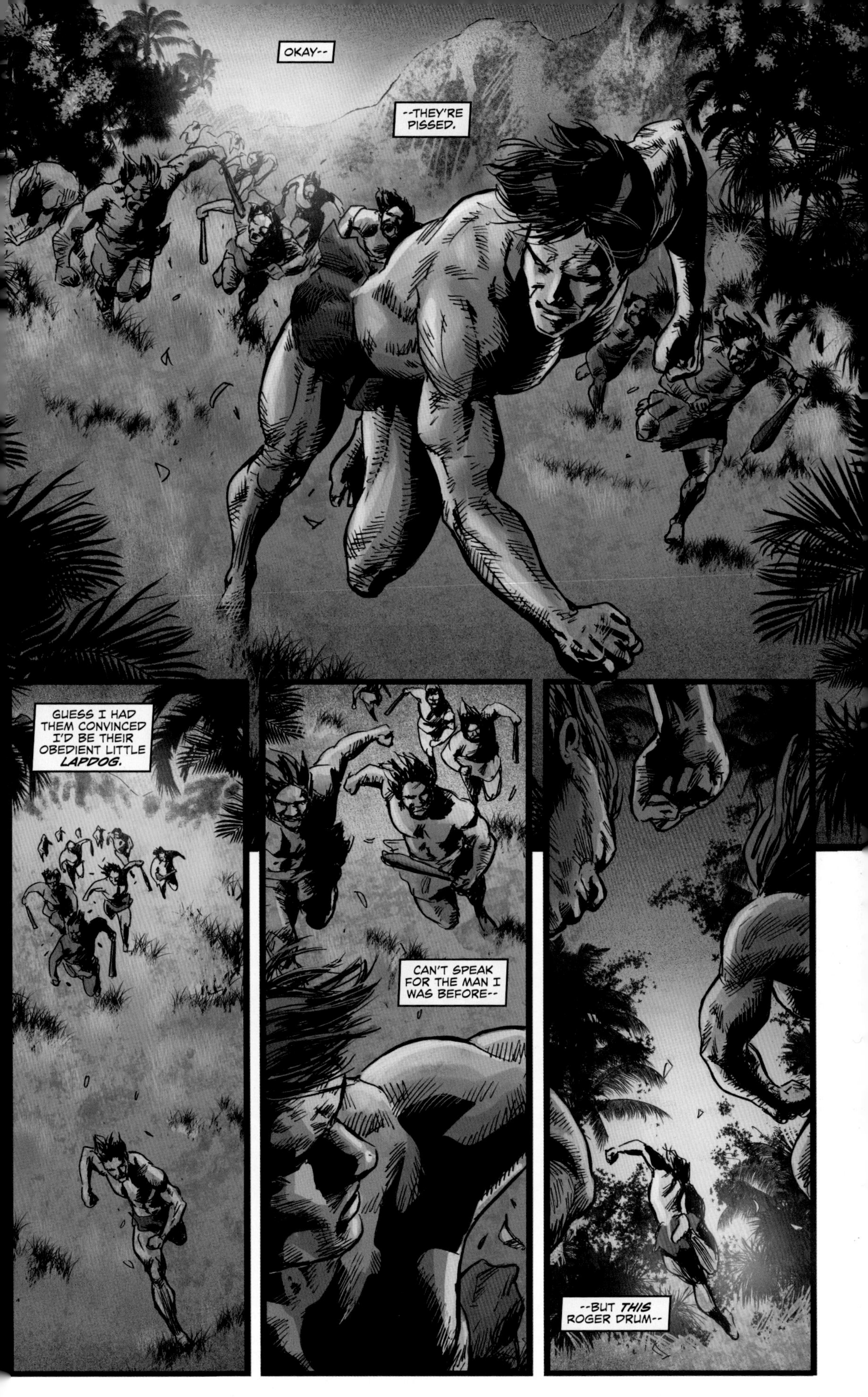
OKAY--
--THEY'RE PISSED.
GUESS I HAD THEM CONVINCED I'D BE THEIR OBEDIENT LITTLE LAPDOG.
CAN'T SPEAK FOR THE MAN I WAS BEFORE--
--BUT THIS ROGER DRUM--

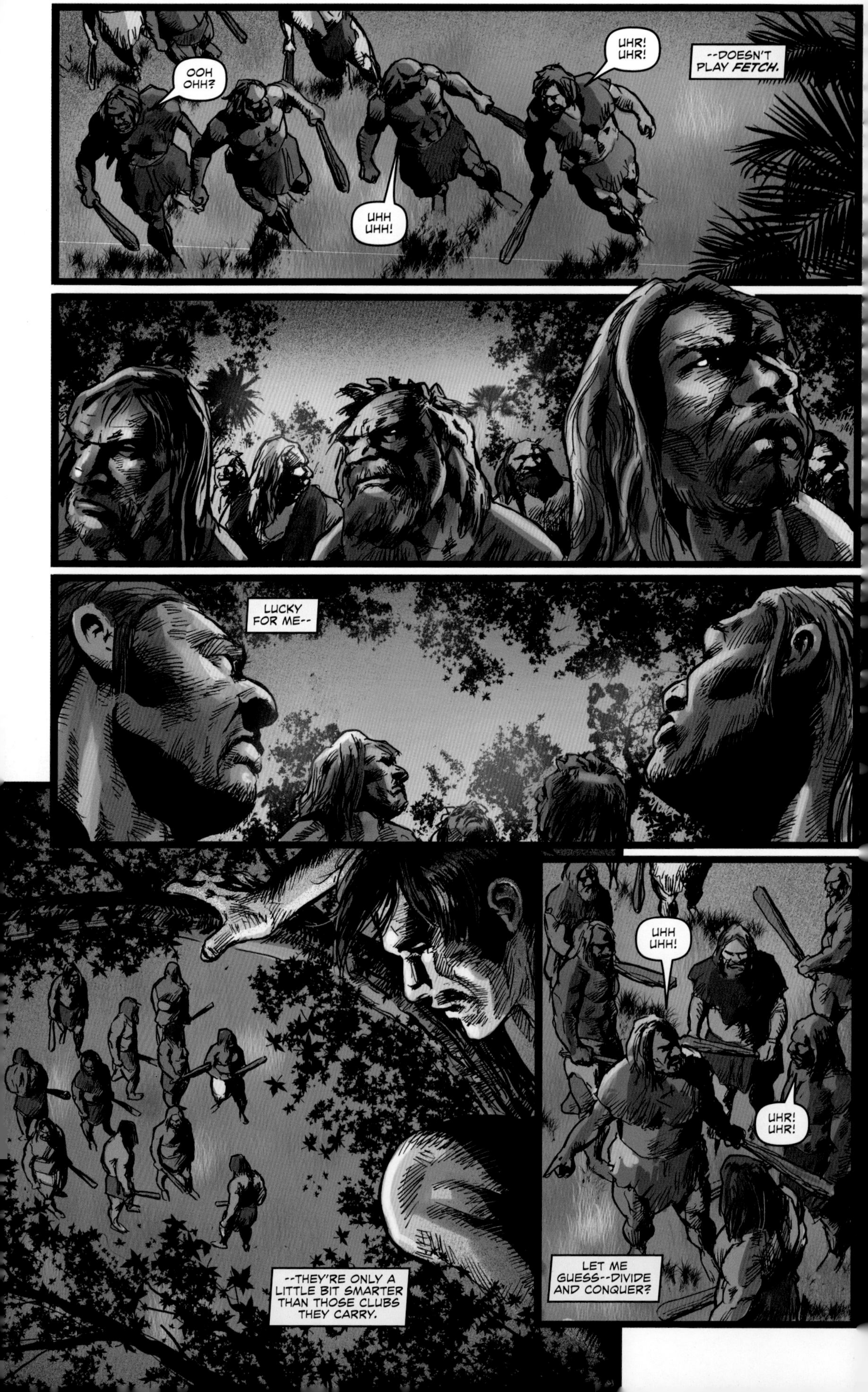
OOH
OHH?
UHH
UHH!
UHR!
UHR!
--DOESN'T
PLAY *FETCH*.
LUCKY
FOR ME--
--THEY'RE ONLY A
LITTLE BIT SMARTER
THAN THOSE CLUBS
THEY CARRY.
UHH
UHH!
UHR!
UHR!
LET ME
GUESS--DIVIDE
AND CONQUER?

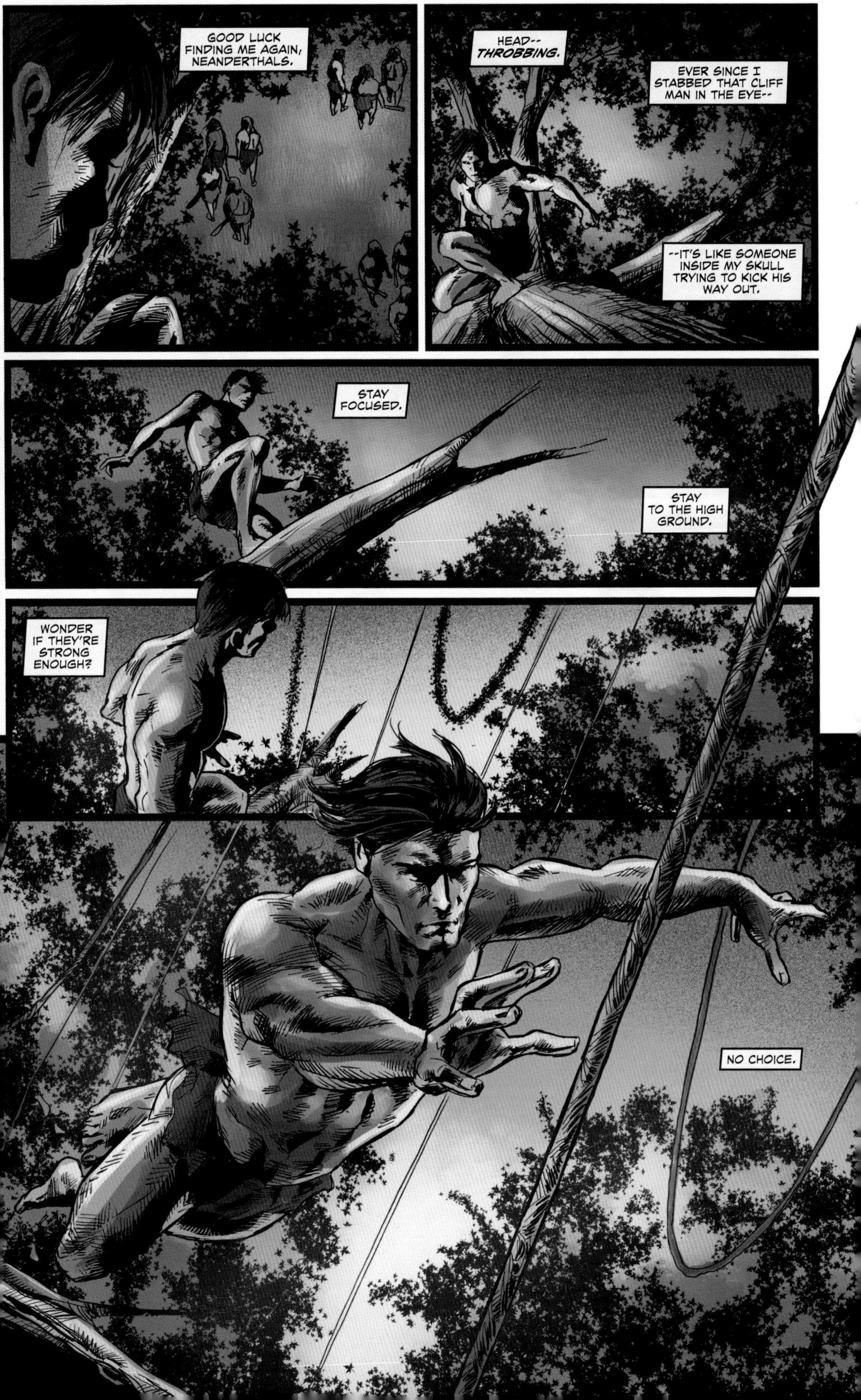
GOOD LUCK FINDING ME AGAIN, NEANDERTHALS.
HEAD-- *THROBBING.*
EVER SINCE I STABBED THAT CLIFF MAN IN THE EYE--
--IT'S LIKE SOMEONE INSIDE MY SKULL TRYING TO KICK HIS WAY OUT.
STAY FOCUSED.
STAY TO THE HIGH GROUND.
WONDER IF THEY'RE STRONG ENOUGH?
NO CHOICE.

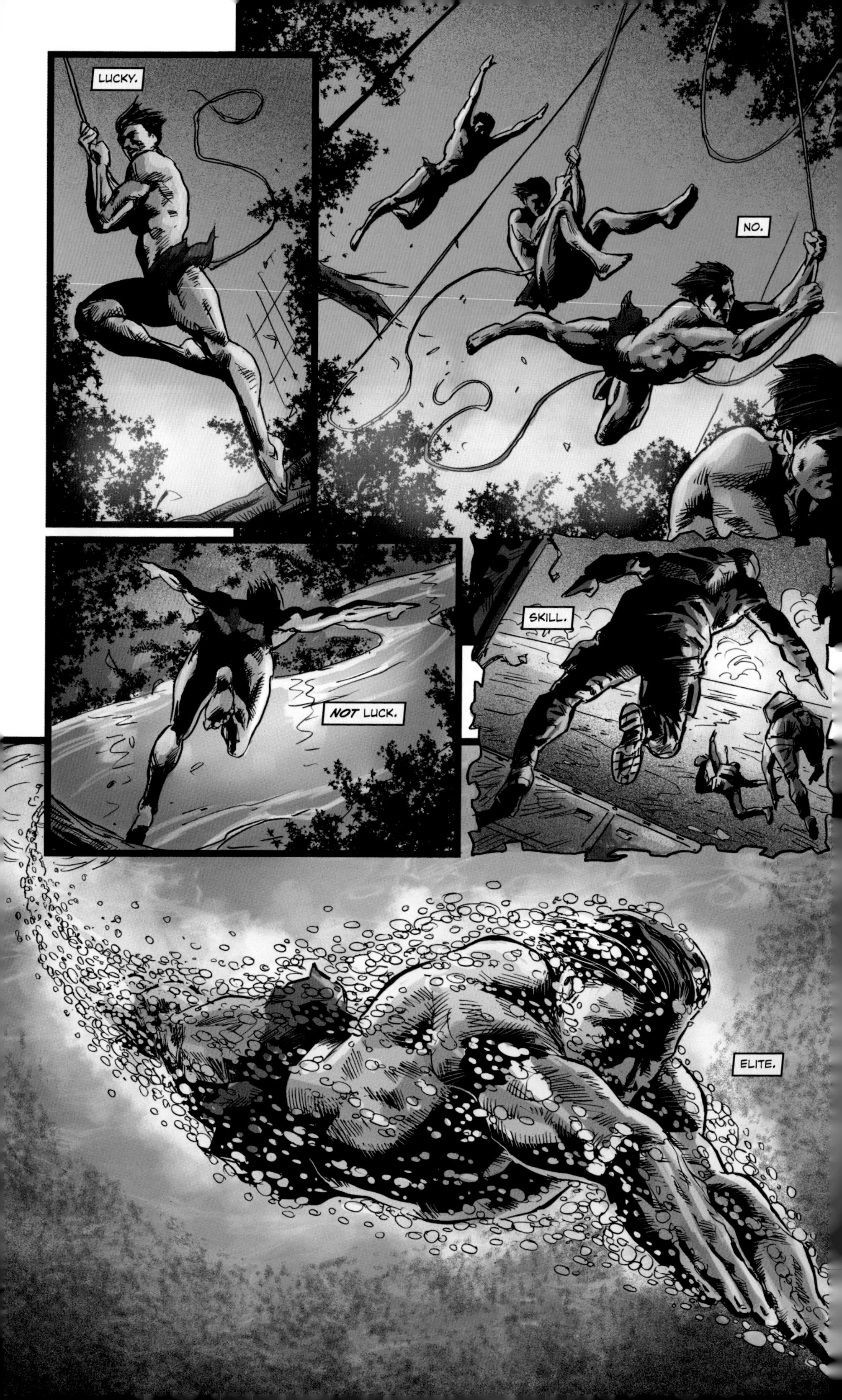
LUCKY.
NO.
NOT LUCK.
SKILL.
ELITE.

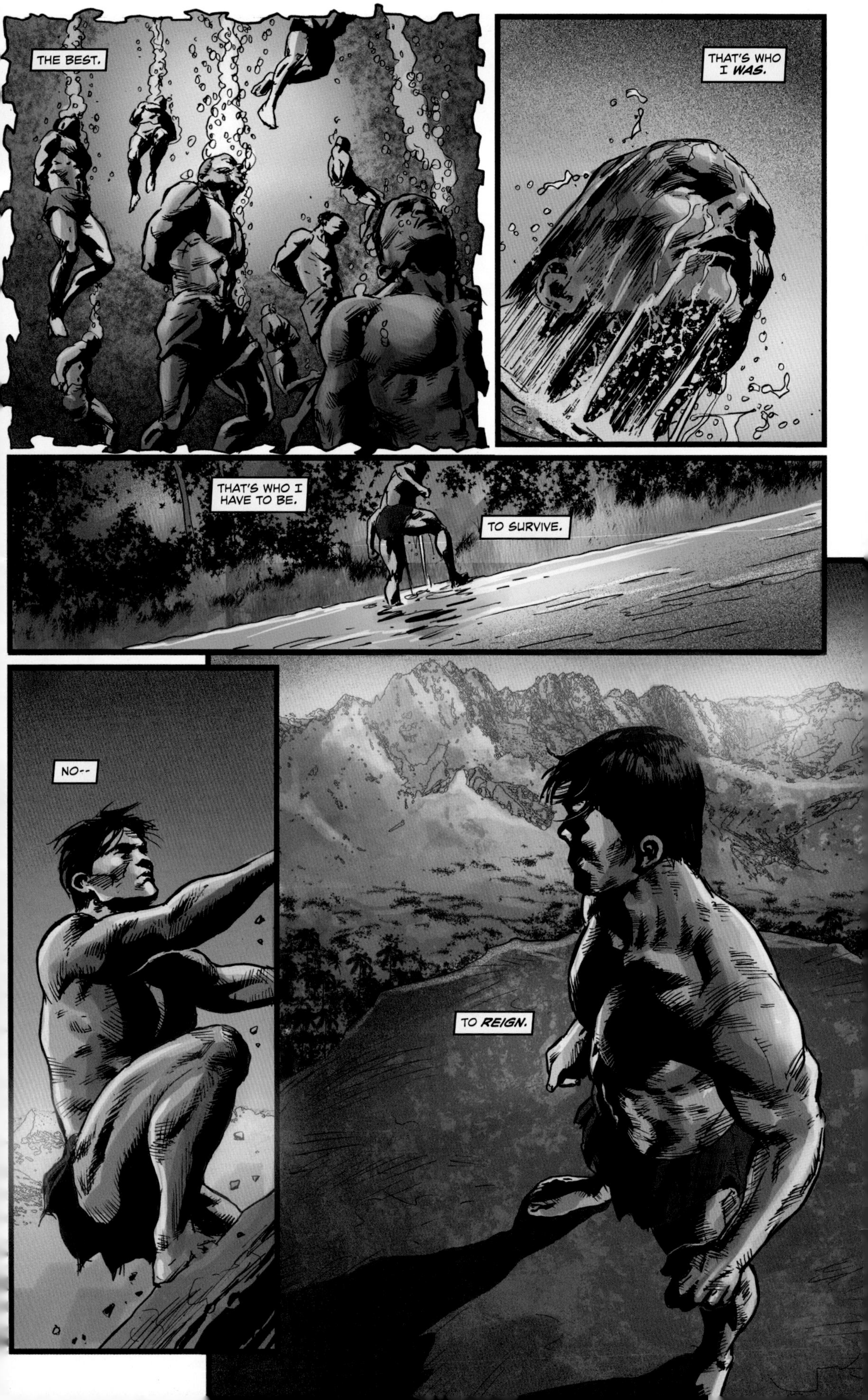
THE BEST.
THAT'S WHO I WAS.
THAT'S WHO I HAVE TO BE.
TO SURVIVE.
NO--
TO REIGN.

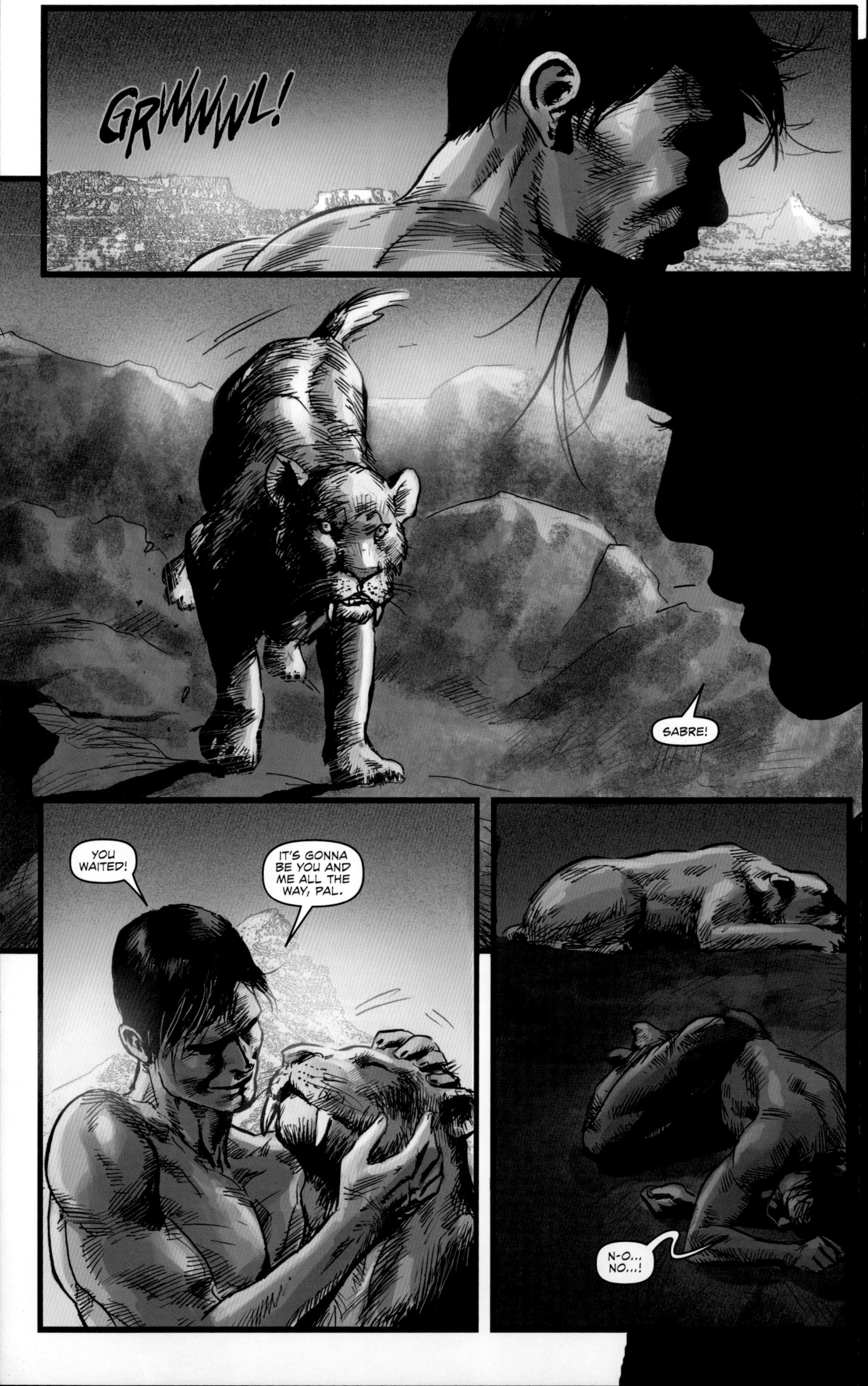
GRWWWL!
SABRE!
YOU WAITED!
IT'S GONNA BE YOU AND ME ALL THE WAY, PAL.
N-O... NO...!

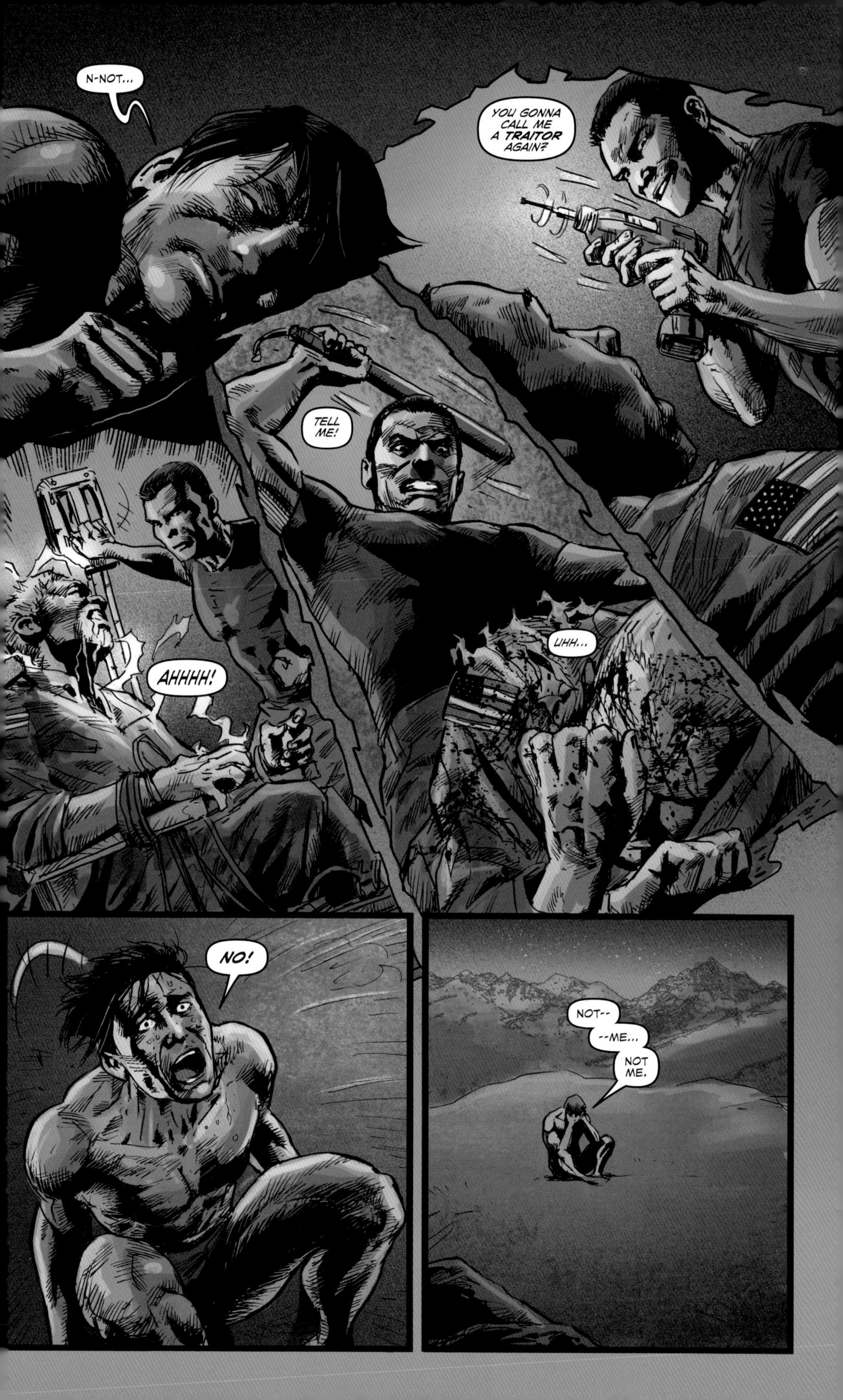
N-NOT...
YOU GONNA CALL ME A TRAITOR AGAIN?
TELL ME!
AHHHH!
UHH...
NO!
NOT--
--ME...
NOT ME.

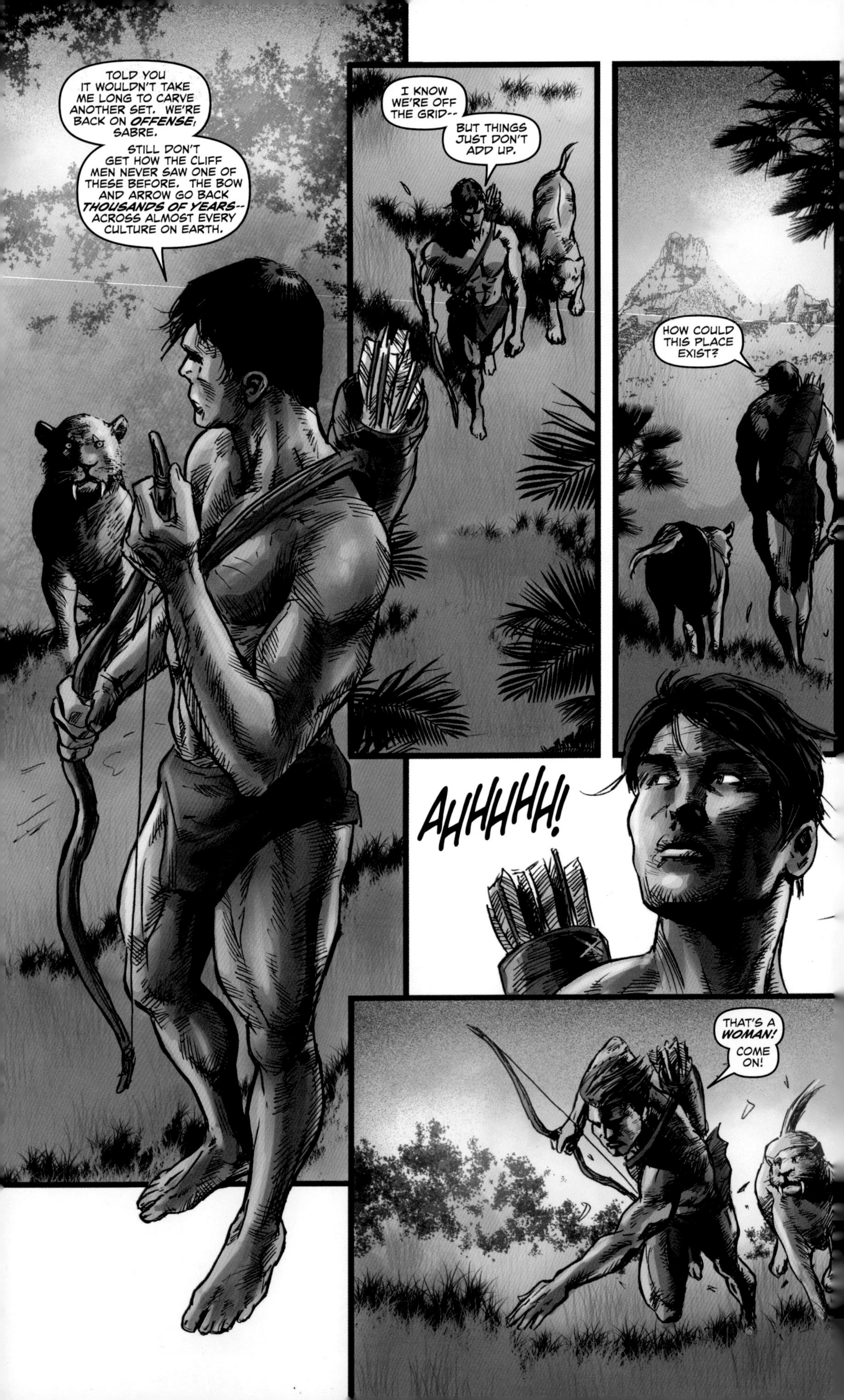
TOLD YOU IT WOULDN'T TAKE ME LONG TO CARVE ANOTHER SET. WE'RE BACK ON OFFENSE, SABRE.
STILL DON'T GET HOW THE CLIFF MEN NEVER SAW ONE OF THESE BEFORE. THE BOW AND ARROW GO BACK THOUSANDS OF YEARS-- ACROSS ALMOST EVERY CULTURE ON EARTH.
I KNOW WE'RE OFF THE GRID--
BUT THINGS JUST DON'T ADD UP.
HOW COULD THIS PLACE EXIST?
AHHHHH!
THAT'S A WOMAN! COME ON!

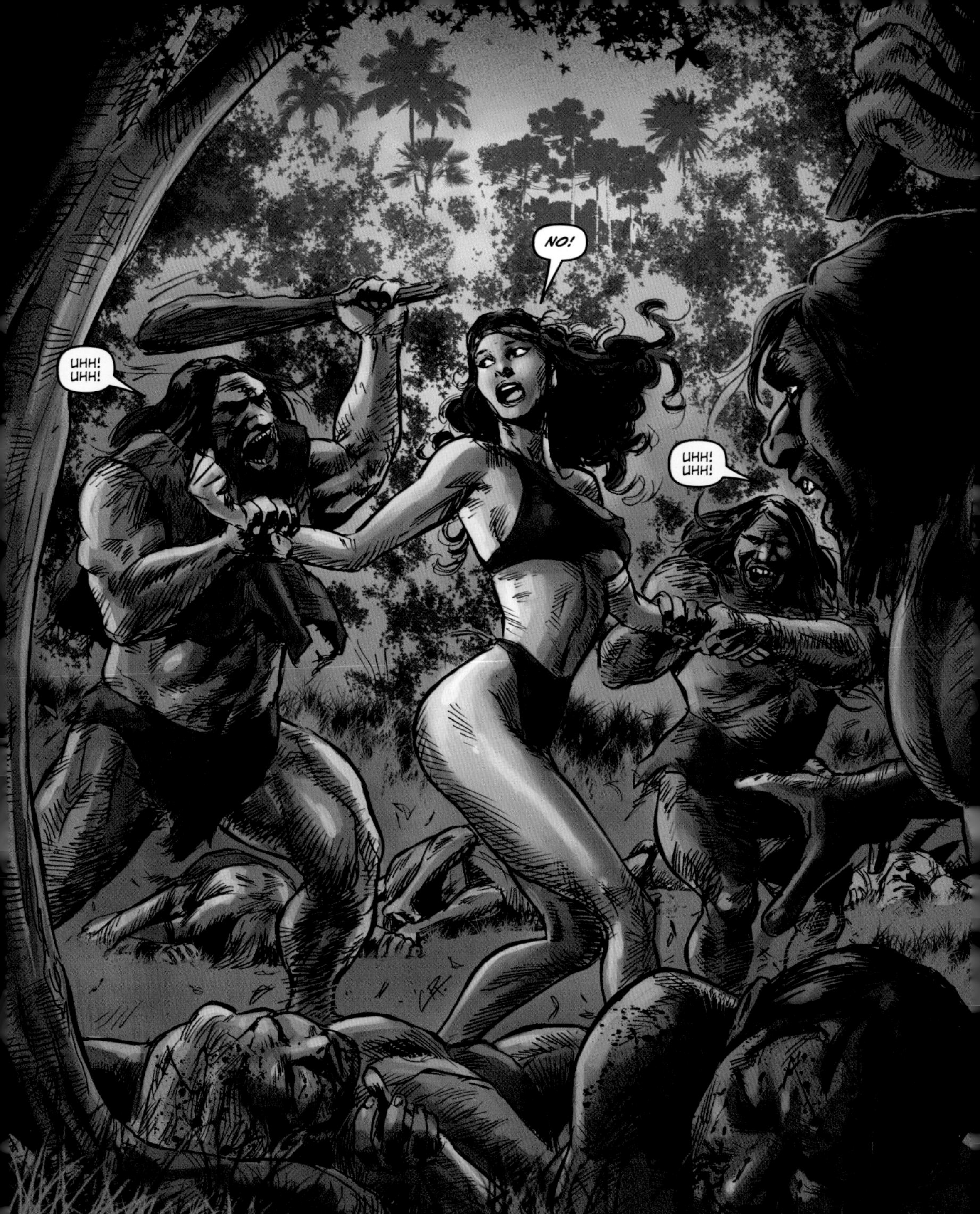
NO!
UHH! UHH!
UHH! UHH!

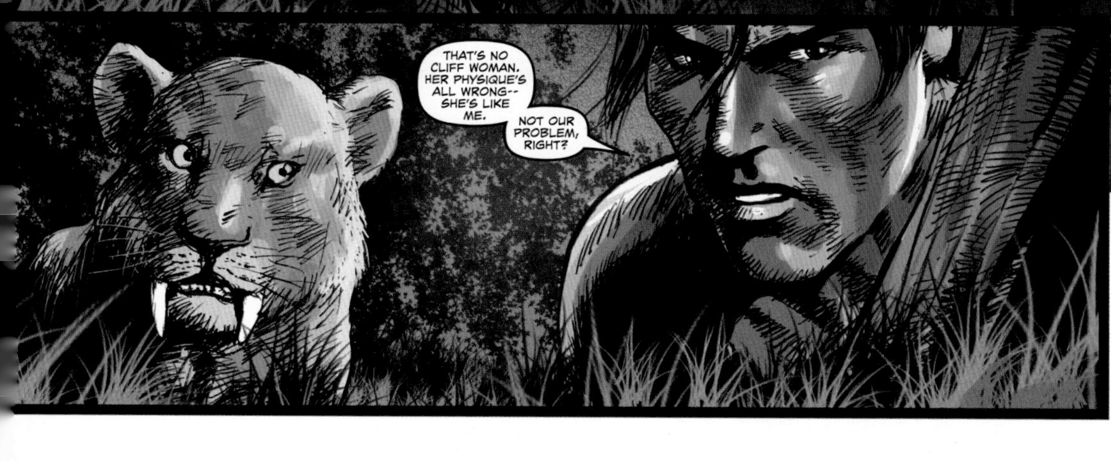
THAT'S NO CLIFF WOMAN. HER PHYSIQUE'S ALL WRONG-- SHE'S LIKE ME.
NOT OUR PROBLEM, RIGHT?

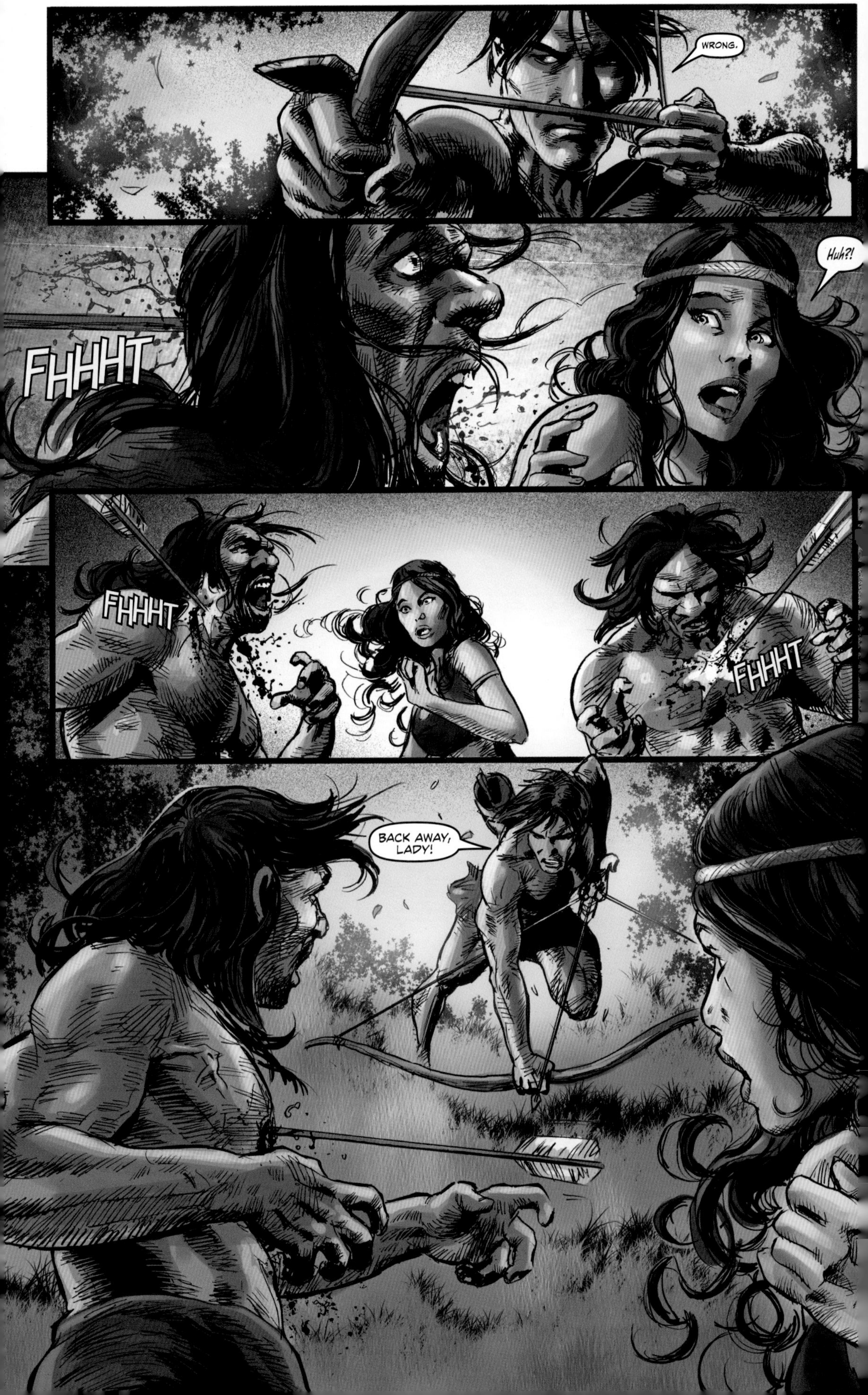
WRONG.
Huh?!
FHHHT
FHHHT
FHHHT
BACK AWAY, LADY!

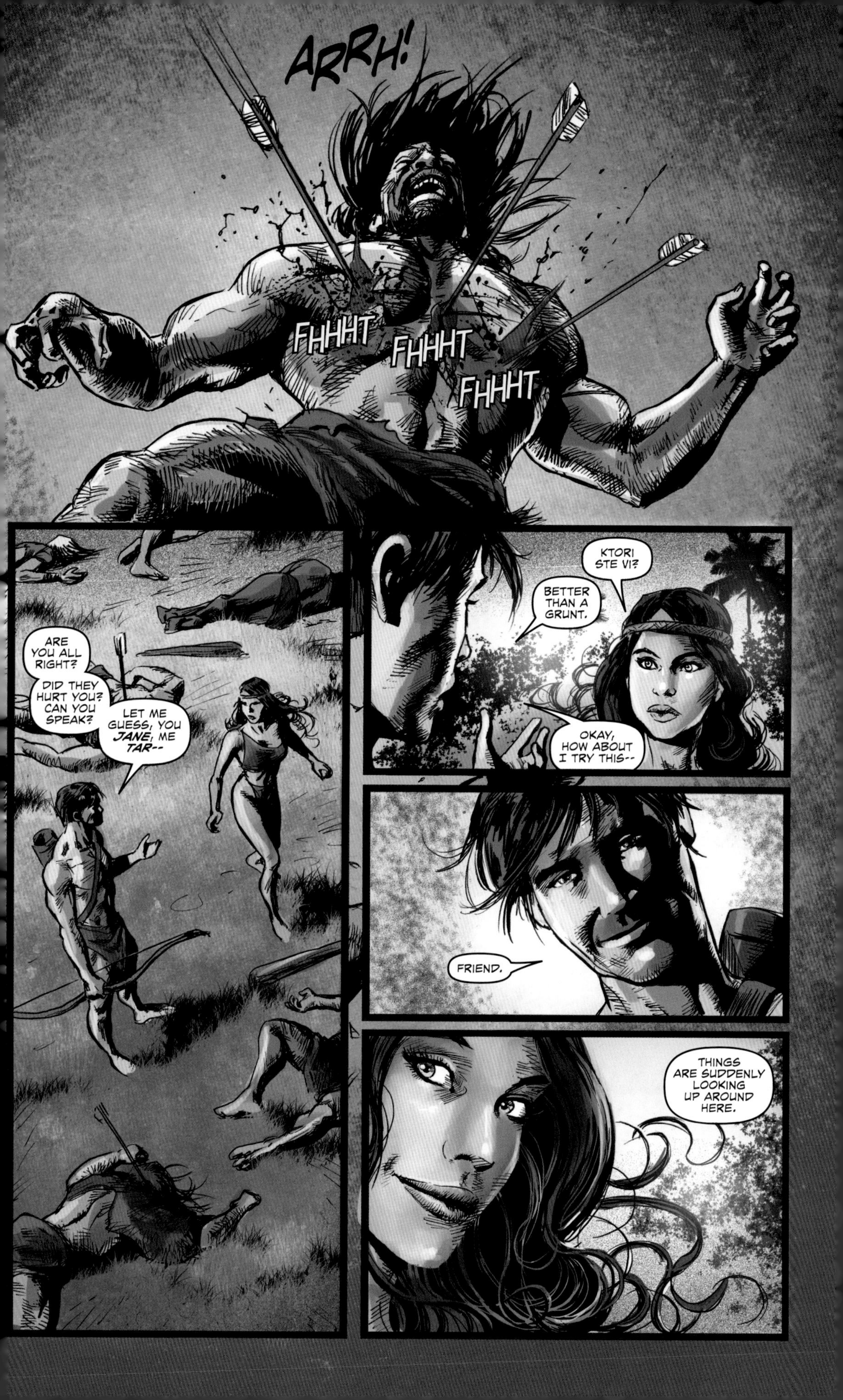
ARRH!
FHHHT
FHHHT
FHHHT
ARE YOU ALL RIGHT?
DID THEY HURT YOU? CAN YOU SPEAK?
LET ME GUESS, YOU *JANE*, ME *TAR--*
KTORI STE VI?
BETTER THAN A GRUNT.
OKAY, HOW ABOUT I TRY THIS--
FRIEND.
THINGS ARE SUDDENLY LOOKING UP AROUND HERE.

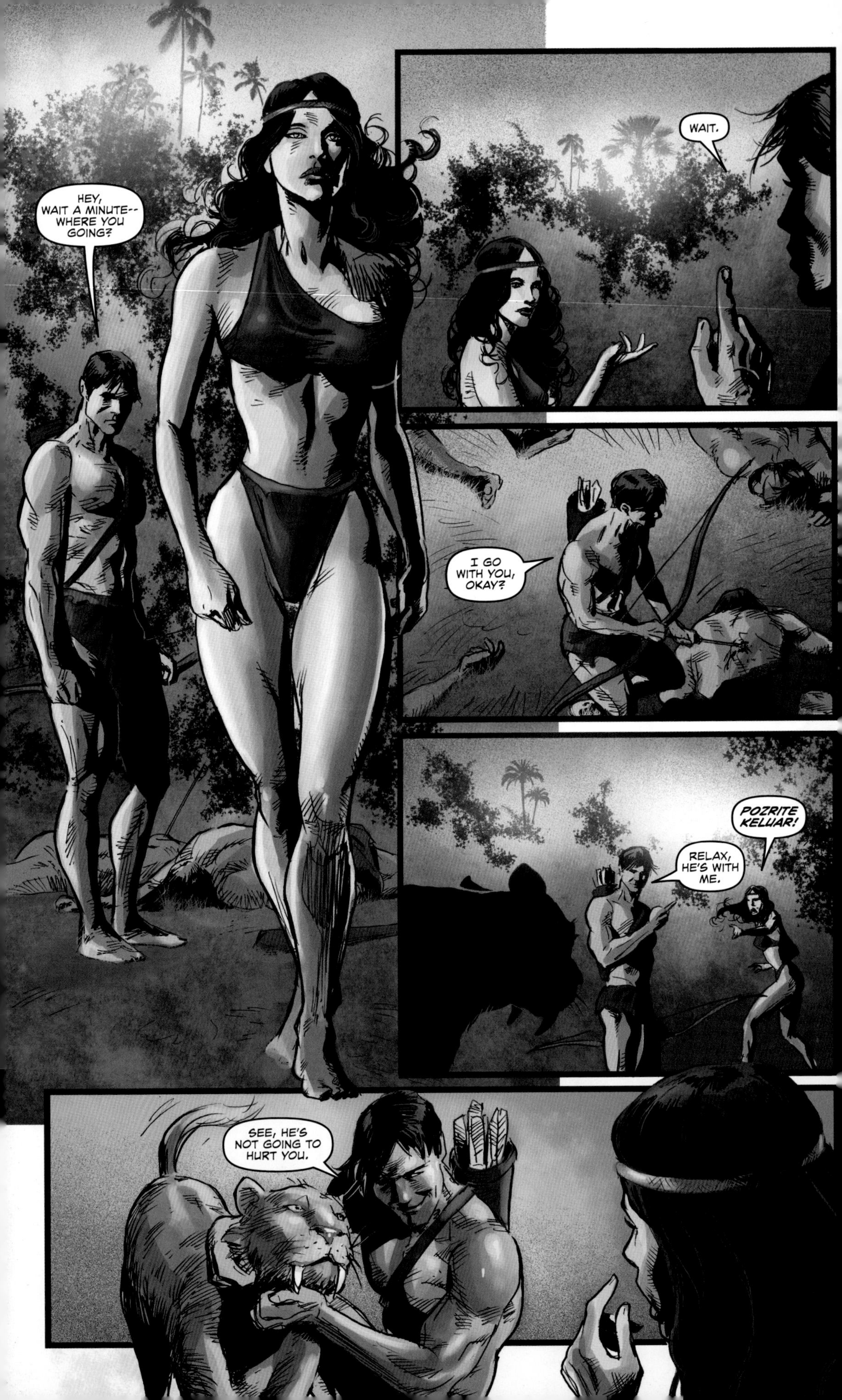
HEY, WAIT A MINUTE-- WHERE YOU GOING?
WAIT.
I GO WITH YOU, OKAY?
POZRITE KELUAR!
RELAX, HE'S WITH ME.
SEE, HE'S NOT GOING TO HURT YOU.

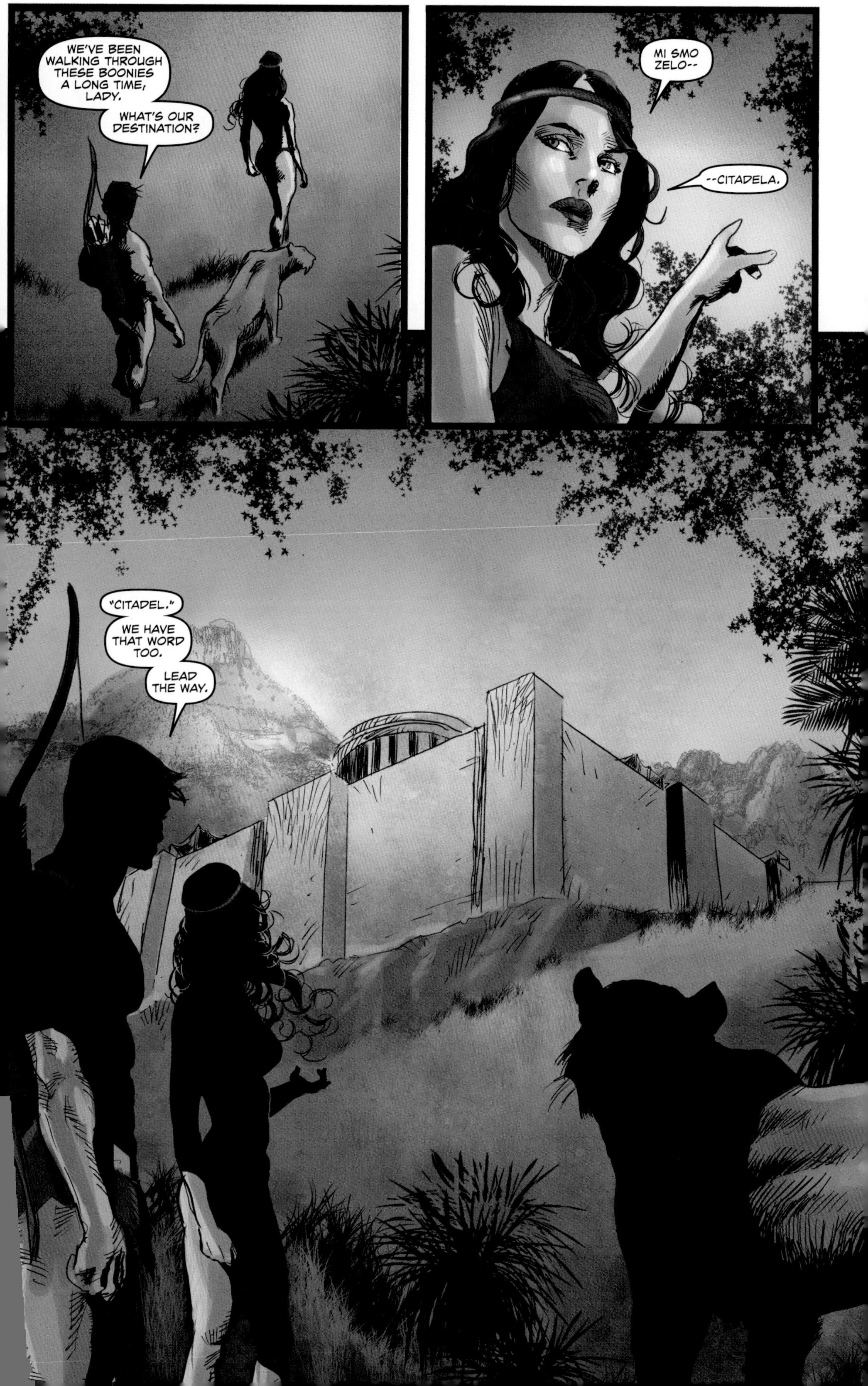
WE'VE BEEN WALKING THROUGH THESE BOONIES A LONG TIME, LADY.
WHAT'S OUR DESTINATION?
MI SMO ZELO--
--CITADELA.
"CITADEL."
WE HAVE THAT WORD TOO.
LEAD THE WAY.

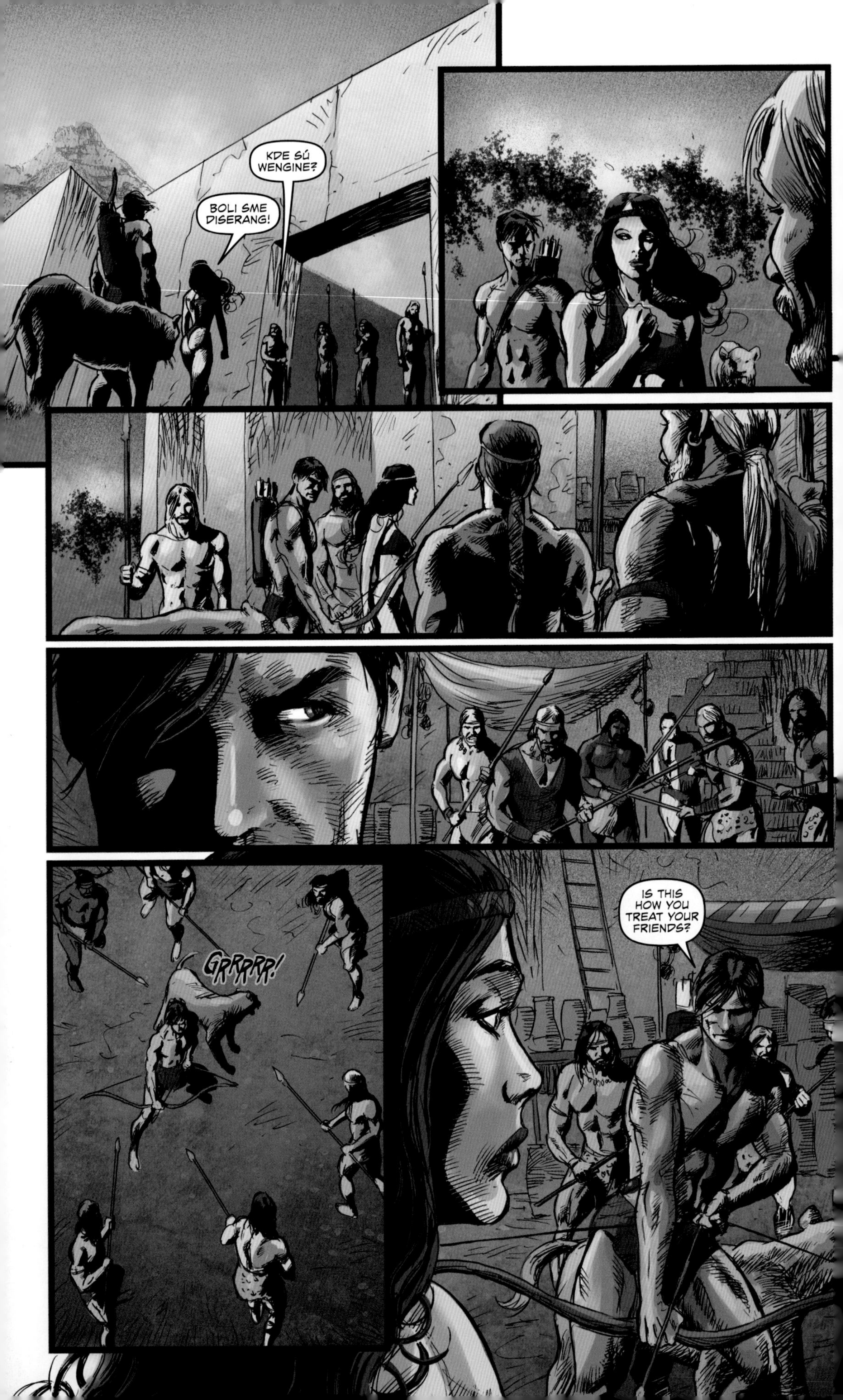
KDE SÚ WENGINE?
BOLI SME DISERANG!
GRRRRR!
IS THIS HOW YOU TREAT YOUR FRIENDS?

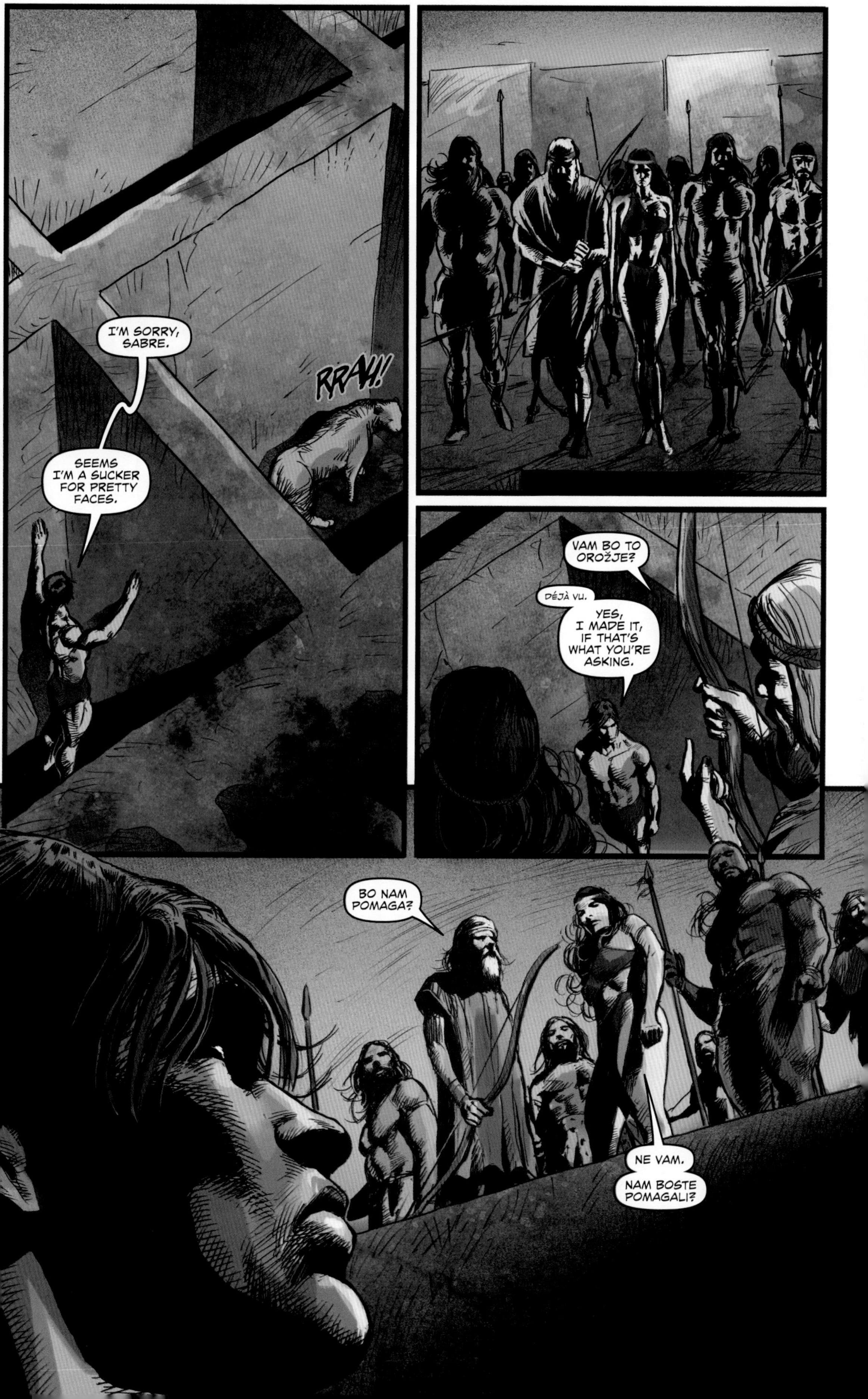
I'M SORRY, SABRE.
SEEMS I'M A SUCKER FOR PRETTY FACES.
RRAH!
VAM BO TO OROŽJE?
DÉJÀ VU.
YES, I MADE IT, IF THAT'S WHAT YOU'RE ASKING.
BO NAM POMAGA?
NE VAM.
NAM BOSTE POMAGALI?

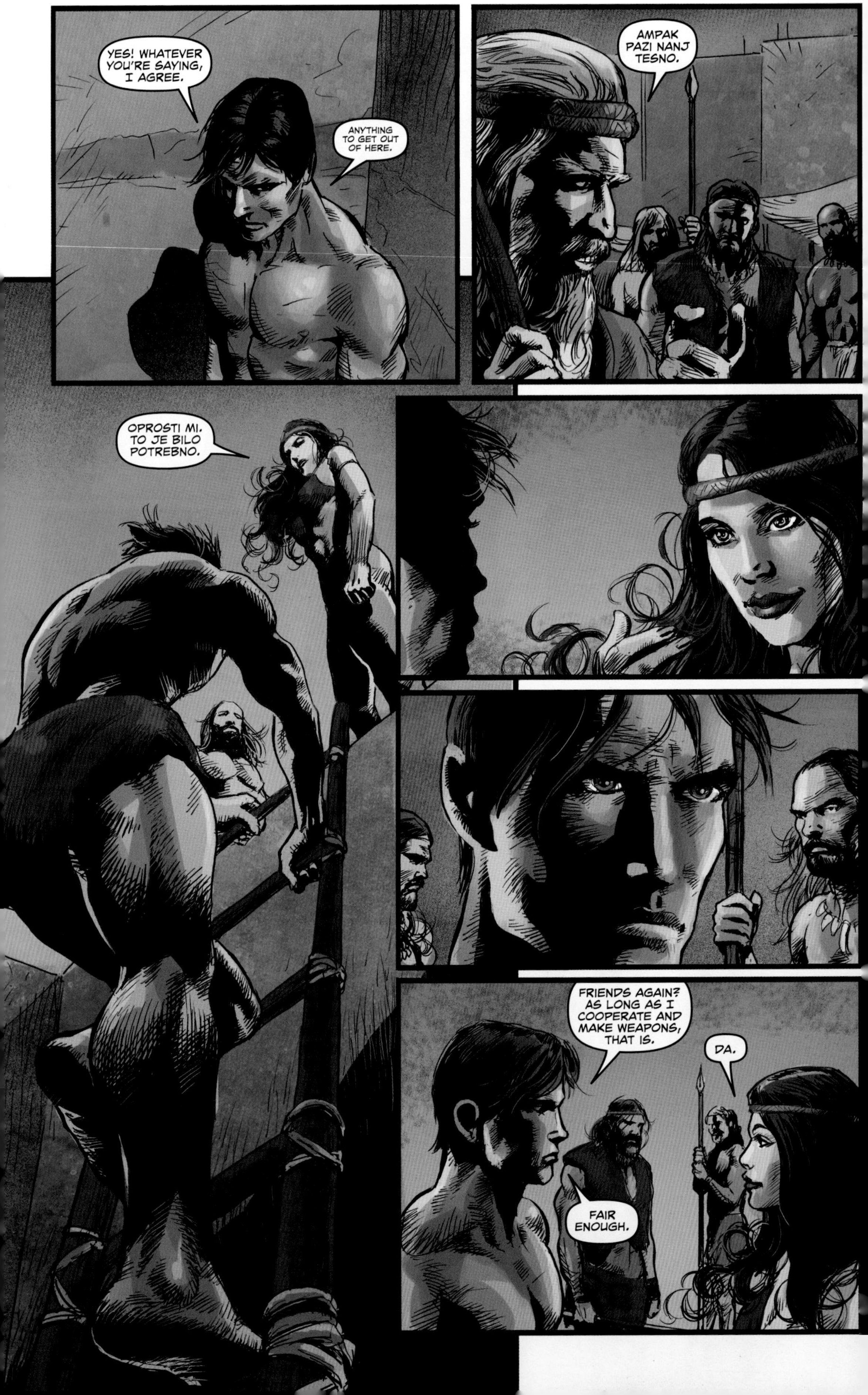
YES! WHATEVER YOU'RE SAYING, I AGREE.
ANYTHING TO GET OUT OF HERE.
AMPAK PAZI NANJ TESNO.
OPROSTI MI. TO JE BILO POTREBNO.
FRIENDS AGAIN? AS LONG AS I COOPERATE AND MAKE WEAPONS, THAT IS.
DA.
FAIR ENOUGH.

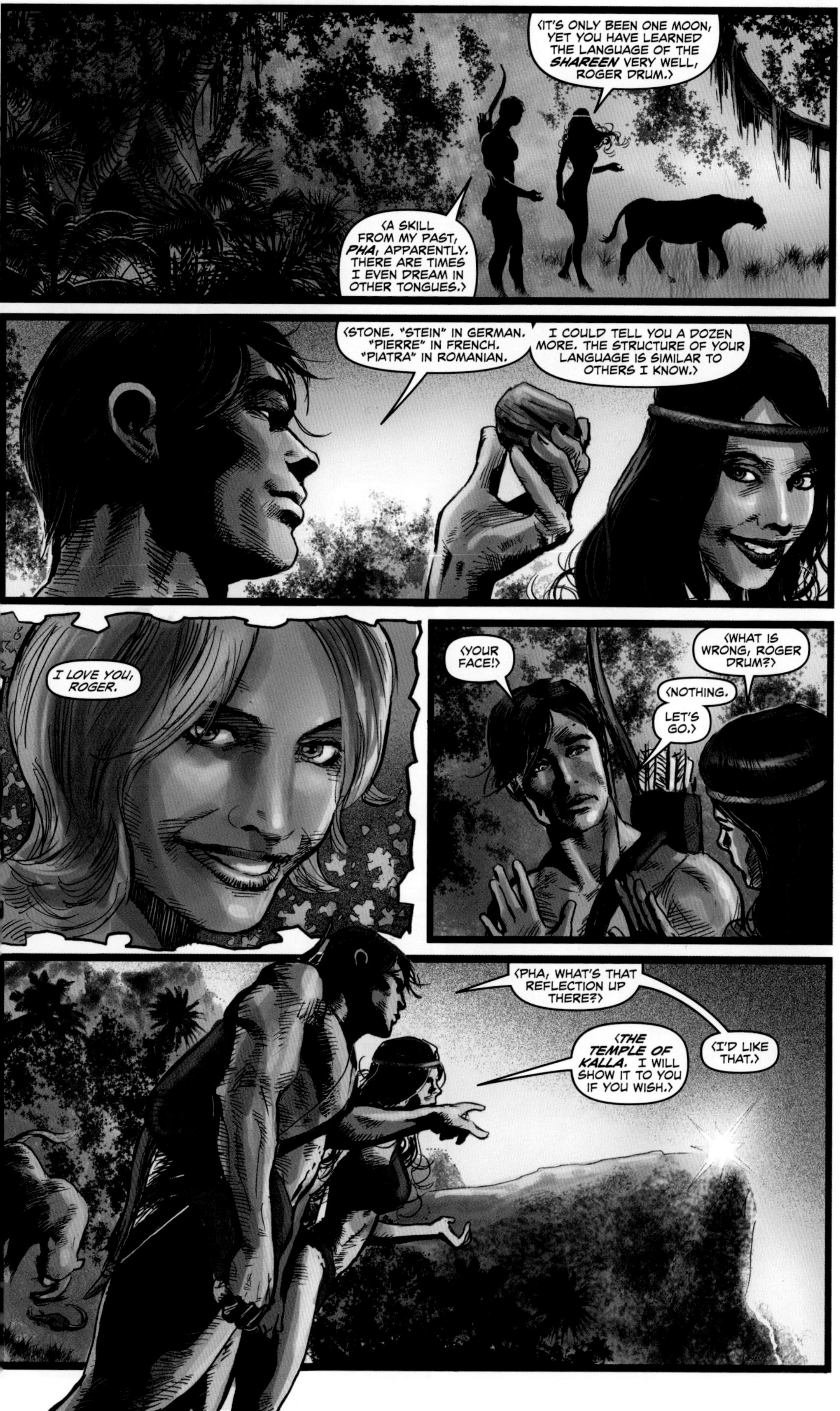

‹IT'S ONLY BEEN ONE MOON, YET YOU HAVE LEARNED THE LANGUAGE OF THE SHAREEN VERY WELL, ROGER DRUM.›
‹A SKILL FROM MY PAST, PHA, APPARENTLY. THERE ARE TIMES I EVEN DREAM IN OTHER TONGUES.›
‹STONE. "STEIN" IN GERMAN. "PIERRE" IN FRENCH. "PIATRA" IN ROMANIAN.
I COULD TELL YOU A DOZEN MORE. THE STRUCTURE OF YOUR LANGUAGE IS SIMILAR TO OTHERS I KNOW.›
I LOVE YOU, ROGER.
‹YOUR FACE!›
‹WHAT IS WRONG, ROGER DRUM?›
‹NOTHING.
LET'S GO.›
‹PHA, WHAT'S THAT REFLECTION UP THERE?›
‹THE TEMPLE OF KALLA. I WILL SHOW IT TO YOU IF YOU WISH.›
‹I'D LIKE THAT.›

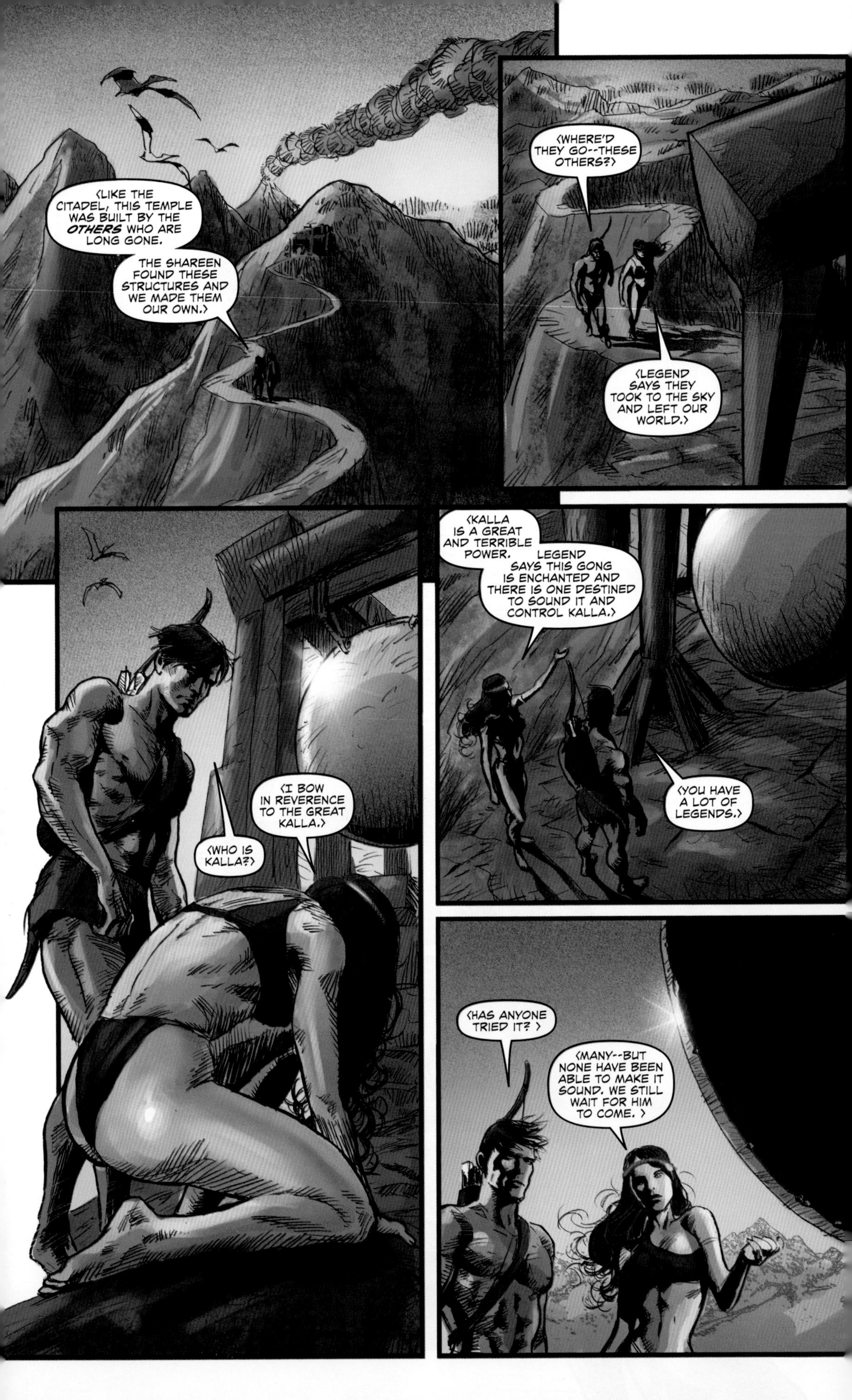

<LIKE THE CITADEL, THIS TEMPLE WAS BUILT BY THE *OTHERS* WHO ARE LONG GONE.
THE SHAREEN FOUND THESE STRUCTURES AND WE MADE THEM OUR OWN.>
<WHERE'D THEY GO--THESE OTHERS?>
<LEGEND SAYS THEY TOOK TO THE SKY AND LEFT OUR WORLD.>
<I BOW IN REVERENCE TO THE GREAT KALLA.>
<WHO IS KALLA?>
<KALLA IS A GREAT AND TERRIBLE POWER.
LEGEND SAYS THIS GONG IS ENCHANTED AND THERE IS ONE DESTINED TO SOUND IT AND CONTROL KALLA.>
<YOU HAVE A LOT OF LEGENDS.>
<HAS ANYONE TRIED IT? >
<MANY--BUT NONE HAVE BEEN ABLE TO MAKE IT SOUND. WE STILL WAIT FOR HIM TO COME. >

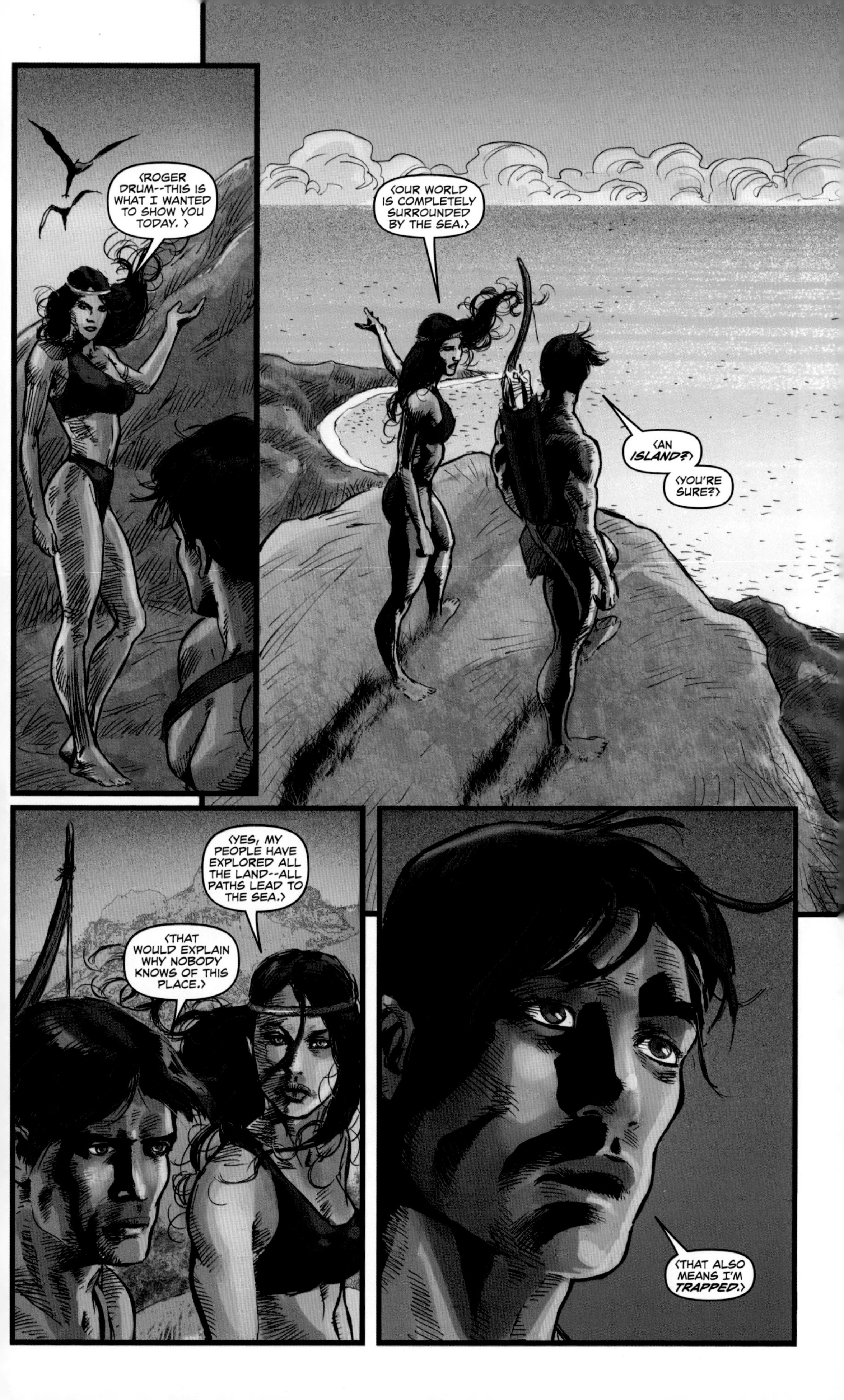
‹ROGER DRUM--THIS IS WHAT I WANTED TO SHOW YOU TODAY.›
‹OUR WORLD IS COMPLETELY SURROUNDED BY THE SEA.›
‹AN *ISLAND?*›
‹YOU'RE SURE?›
‹YES, MY PEOPLE HAVE EXPLORED ALL THE LAND--ALL PATHS LEAD TO THE SEA.›
‹THAT WOULD EXPLAIN WHY NOBODY KNOWS OF THIS PLACE.›
‹THAT ALSO MEANS I'M *TRAPPED.*›

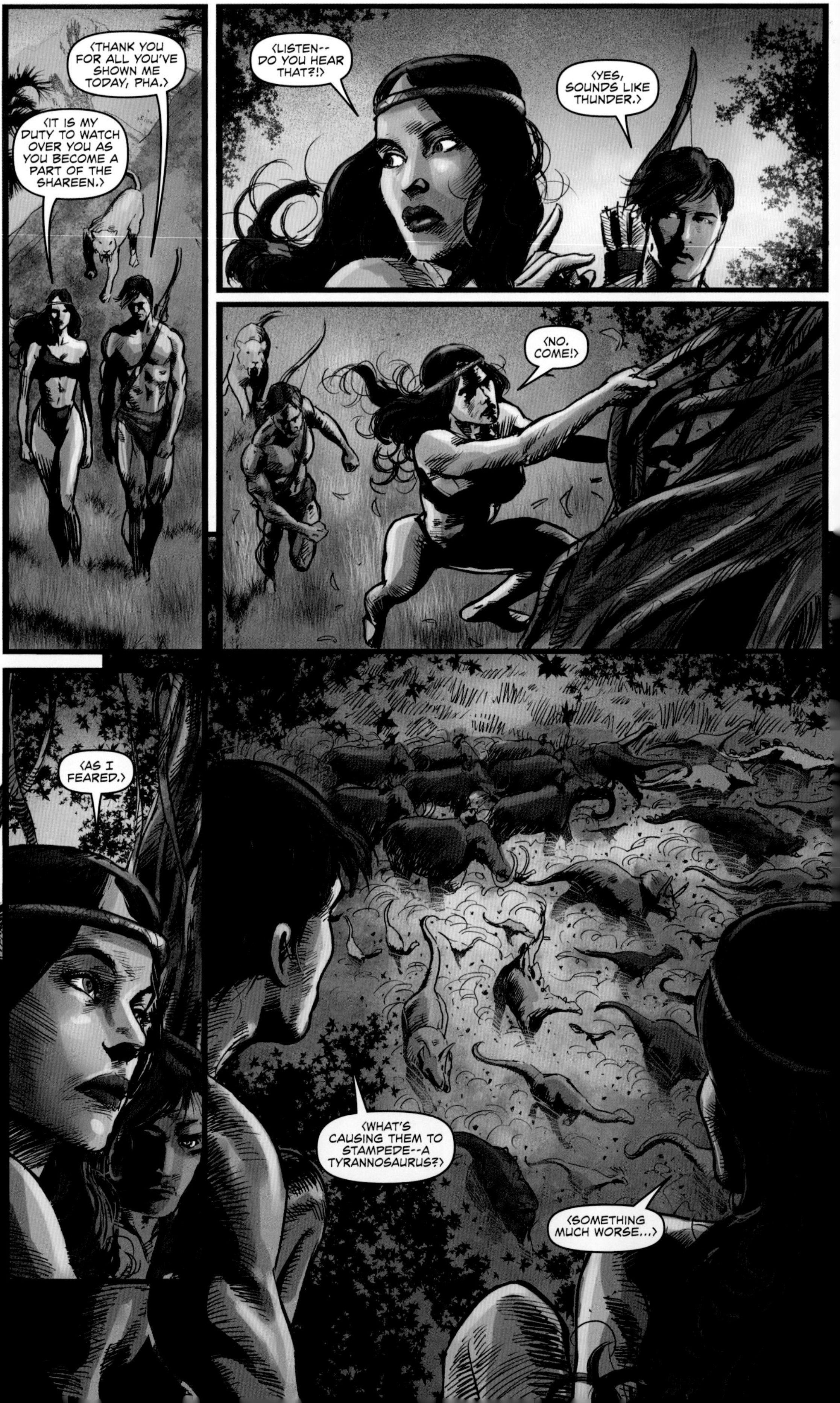
‹THANK YOU FOR ALL YOU'VE SHOWN ME TODAY, PHA.›
‹IT IS MY DUTY TO WATCH OVER YOU AS YOU BECOME A PART OF THE SHAREEN.›
‹LISTEN-- DO YOU HEAR THAT?!›
‹YES, SOUNDS LIKE THUNDER.›
‹NO. COME!›
‹AS I FEARED.›
‹WHAT'S CAUSING THEM TO STAMPEDE--A TYRANNOSAURUS?›
‹SOMETHING MUCH WORSE...›

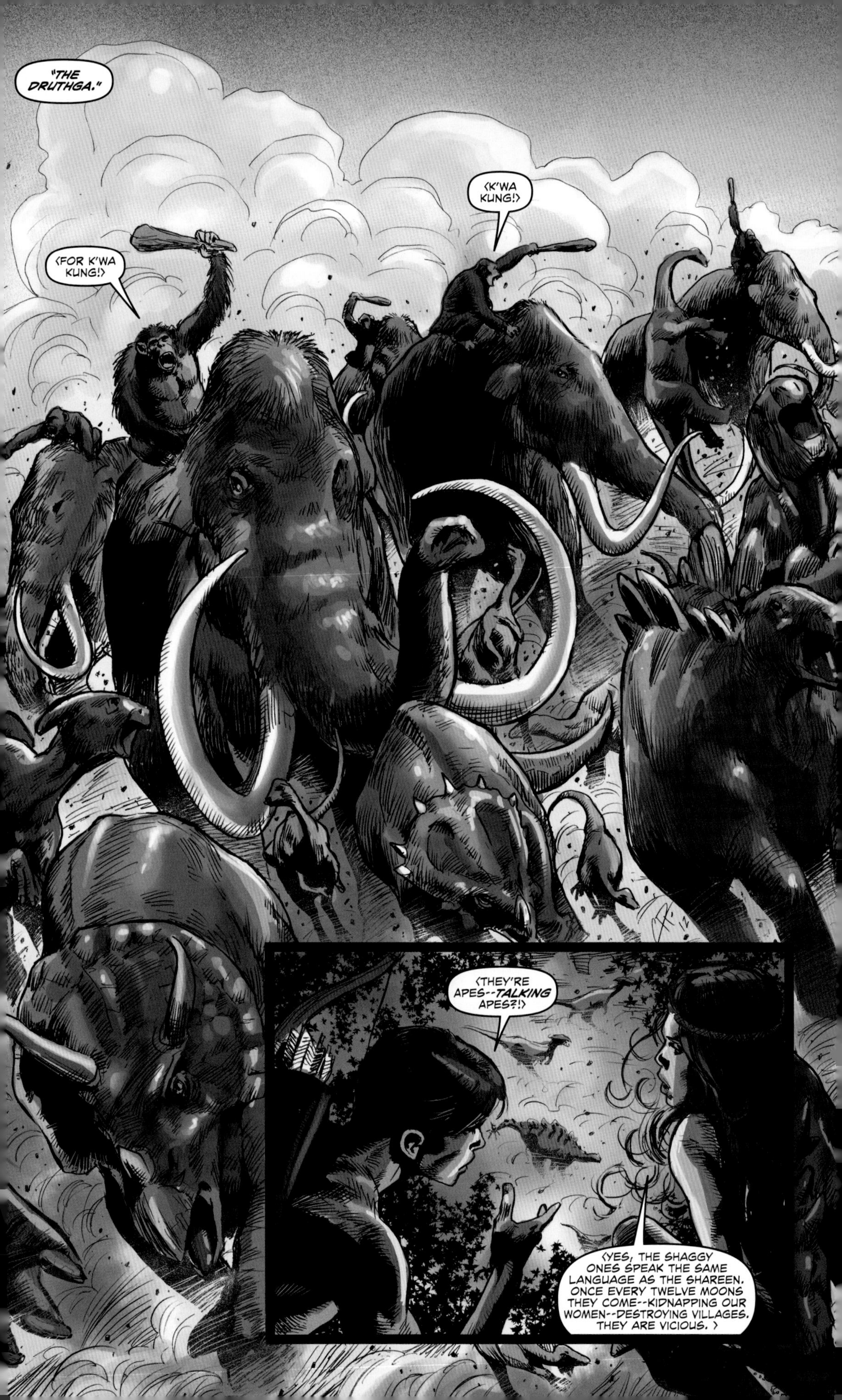
"THE DRUTHGA."
‹FOR K'WA KUNG!›
‹K'WA KUNG!›
‹THEY'RE APES--*TALKING* APES?!›
‹YES, THE SHAGGY ONES SPEAK THE SAME LANGUAGE AS THE SHAREEN. ONCE EVERY TWELVE MOONS THEY COME--KIDNAPPING OUR WOMEN--DESTROYING VILLAGES. THEY ARE VICIOUS.›

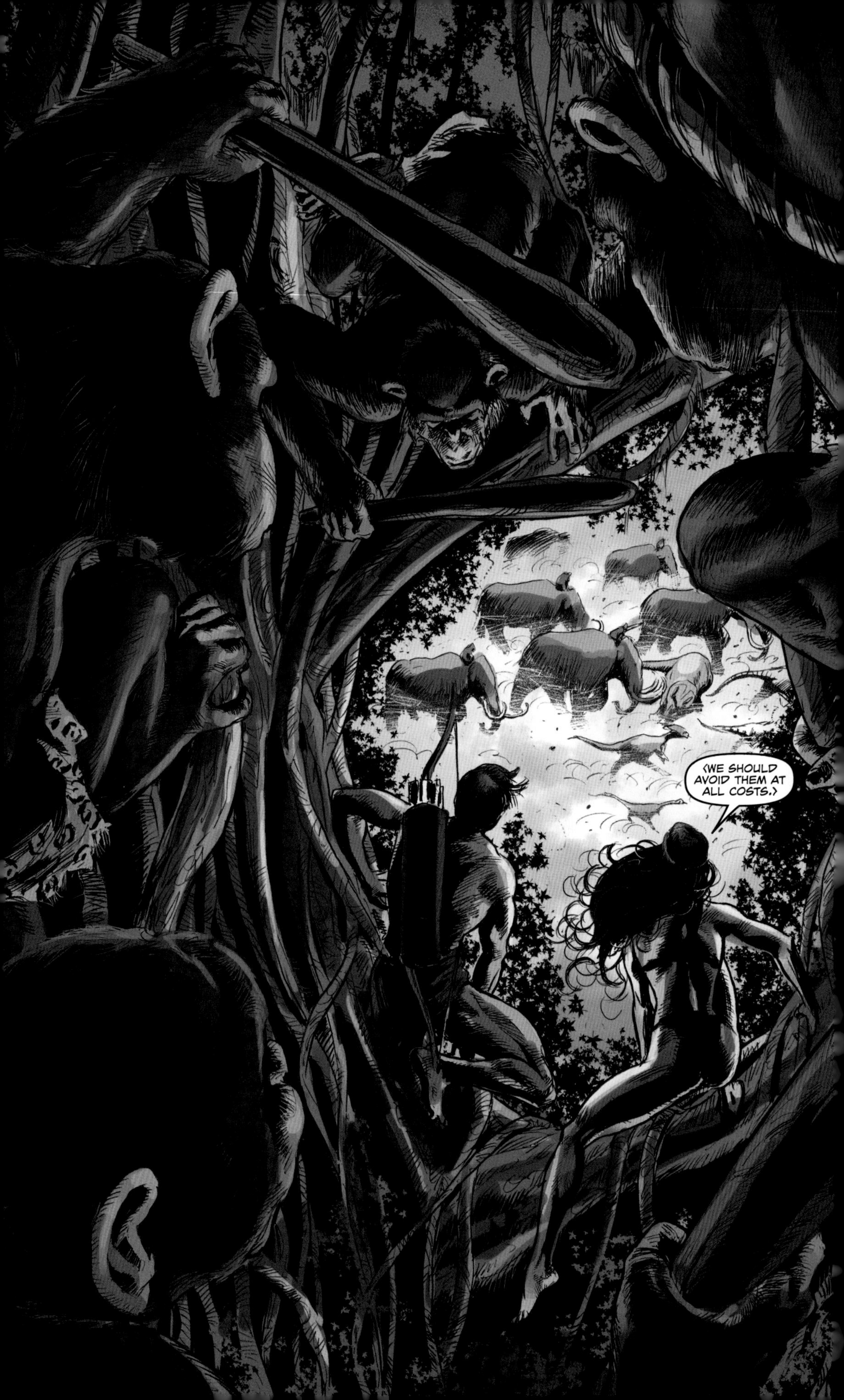
‹WE SHOULD AVOID THEM AT ALL COSTS.›

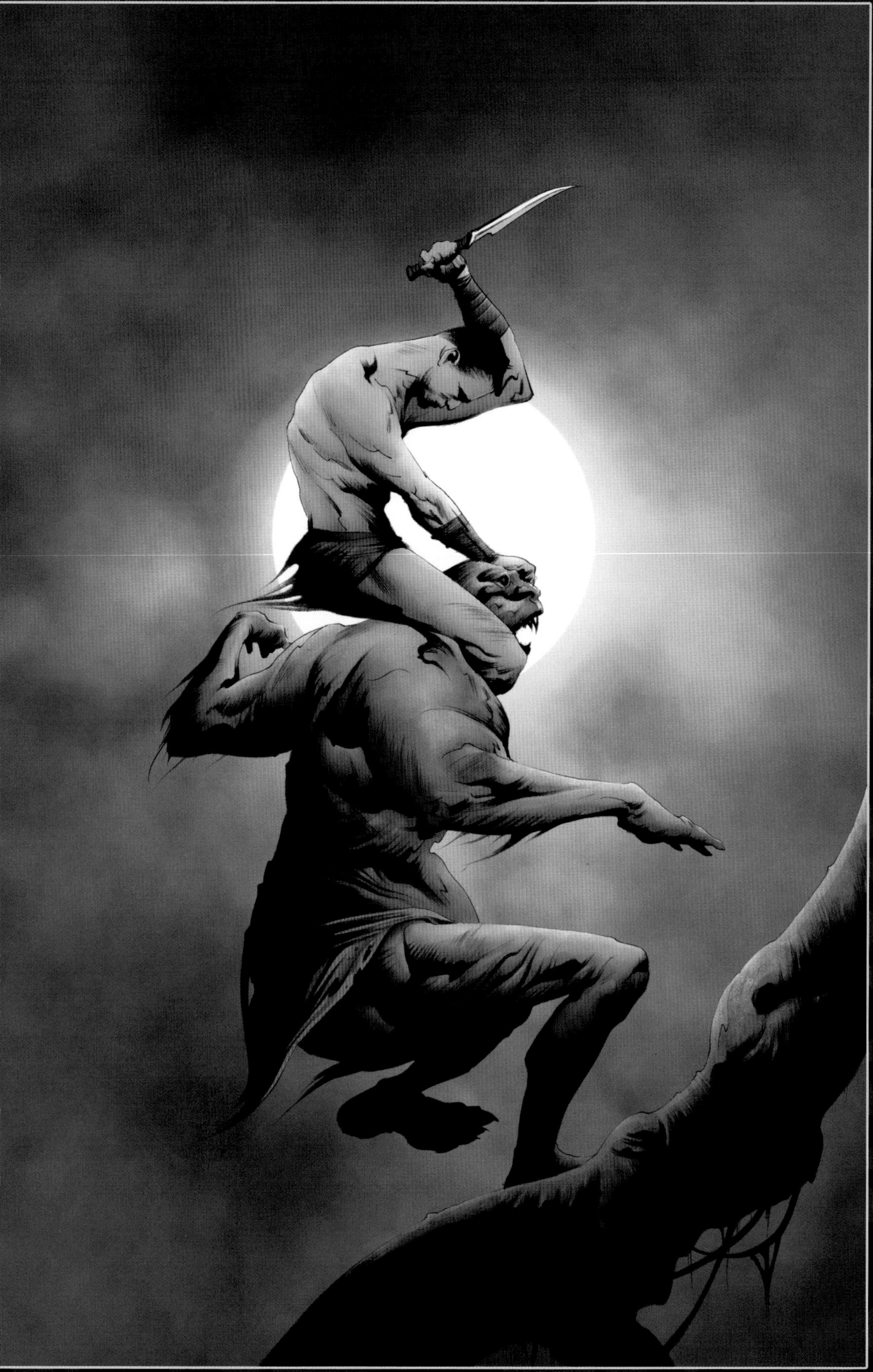

Issue Four Cover by Jae Lee

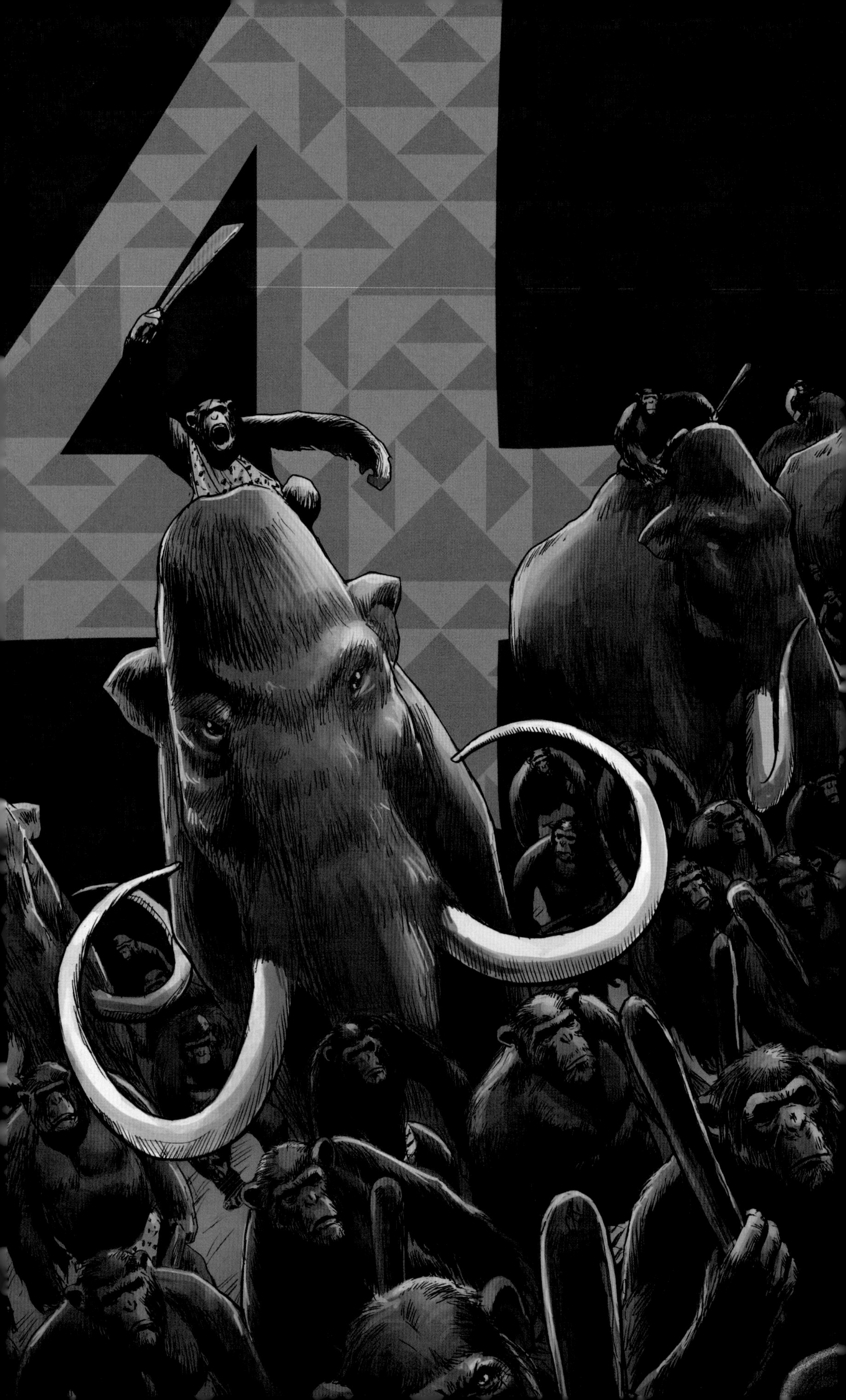

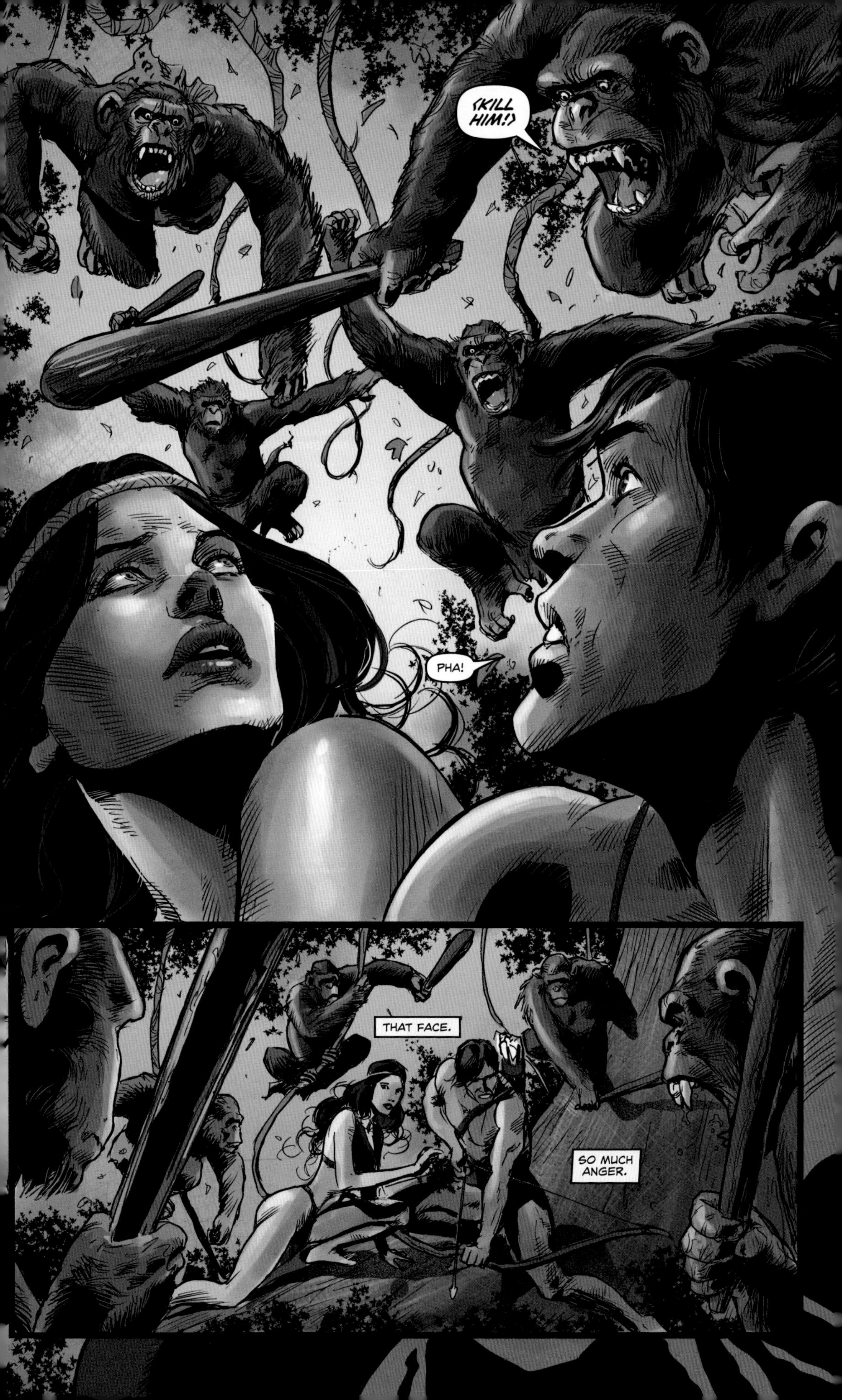
‹KILL HIM!›
PHA!
THAT FACE.
SO MUCH ANGER.

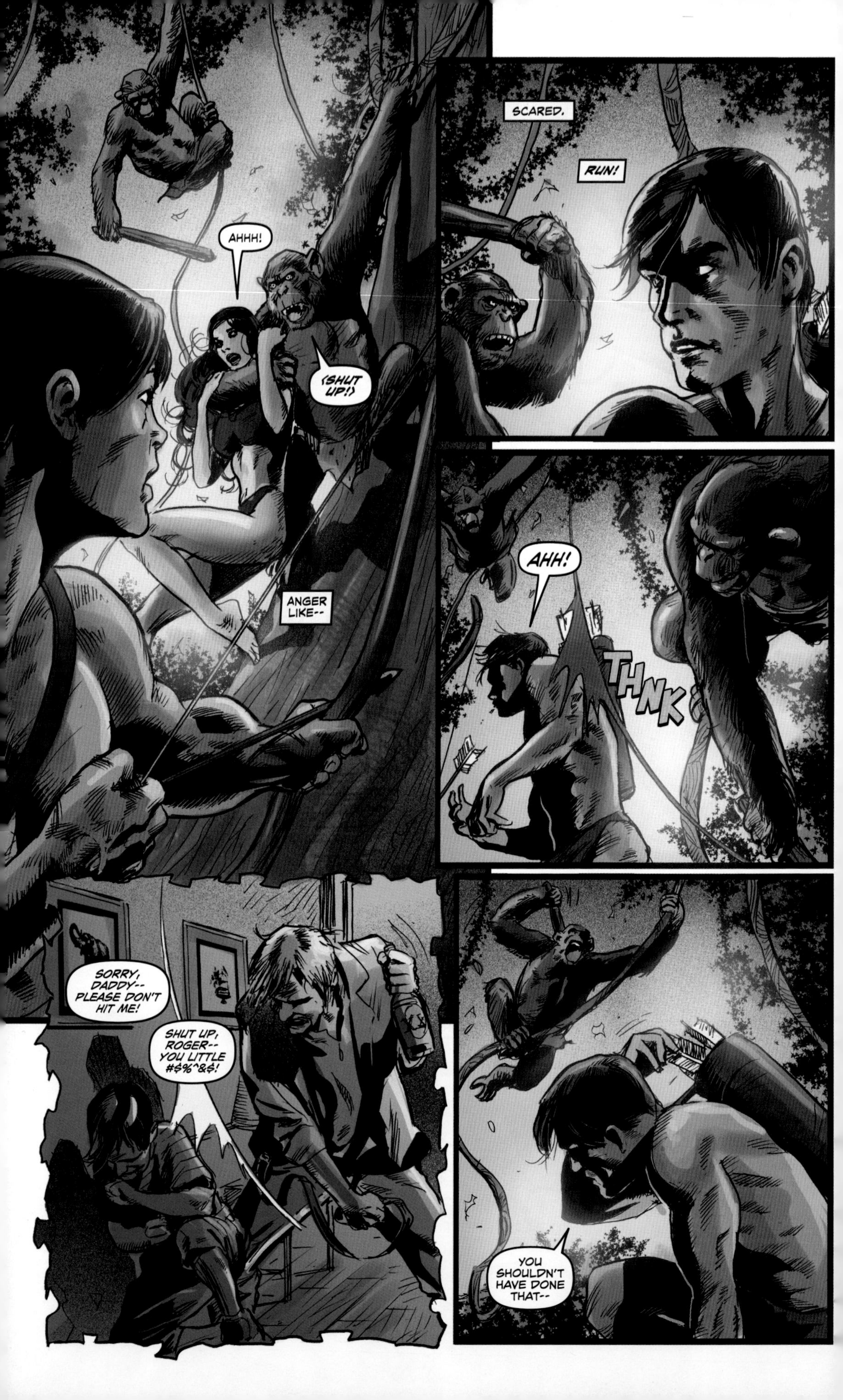
AHHH!
‹SHUT UP!›
ANGER LIKE--
SCARED.
RUN!
AHH!
THNK
SORRY, DADDY-- PLEASE DON'T HIT ME!
SHUT UP, ROGER-- YOU LITTLE #$%^&$!
YOU SHOULDN'T HAVE DONE THAT--

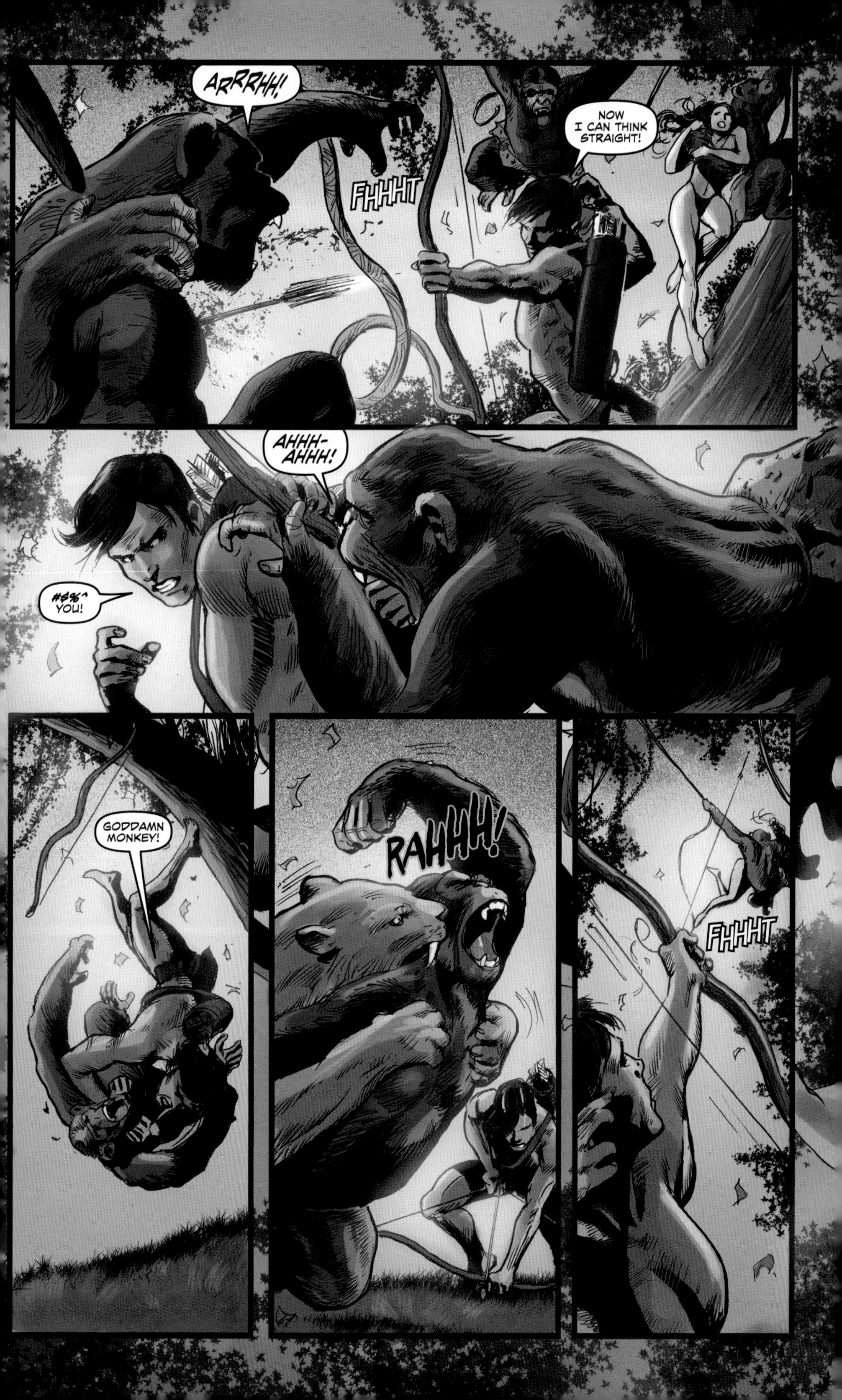

ARRRHH!
NOW I CAN THINK STRAIGHT!
FHHHT
AHHH-AHHH!
#$%^ YOU!
GODDAMN MONKEY!
RAHHH!
FHHHT

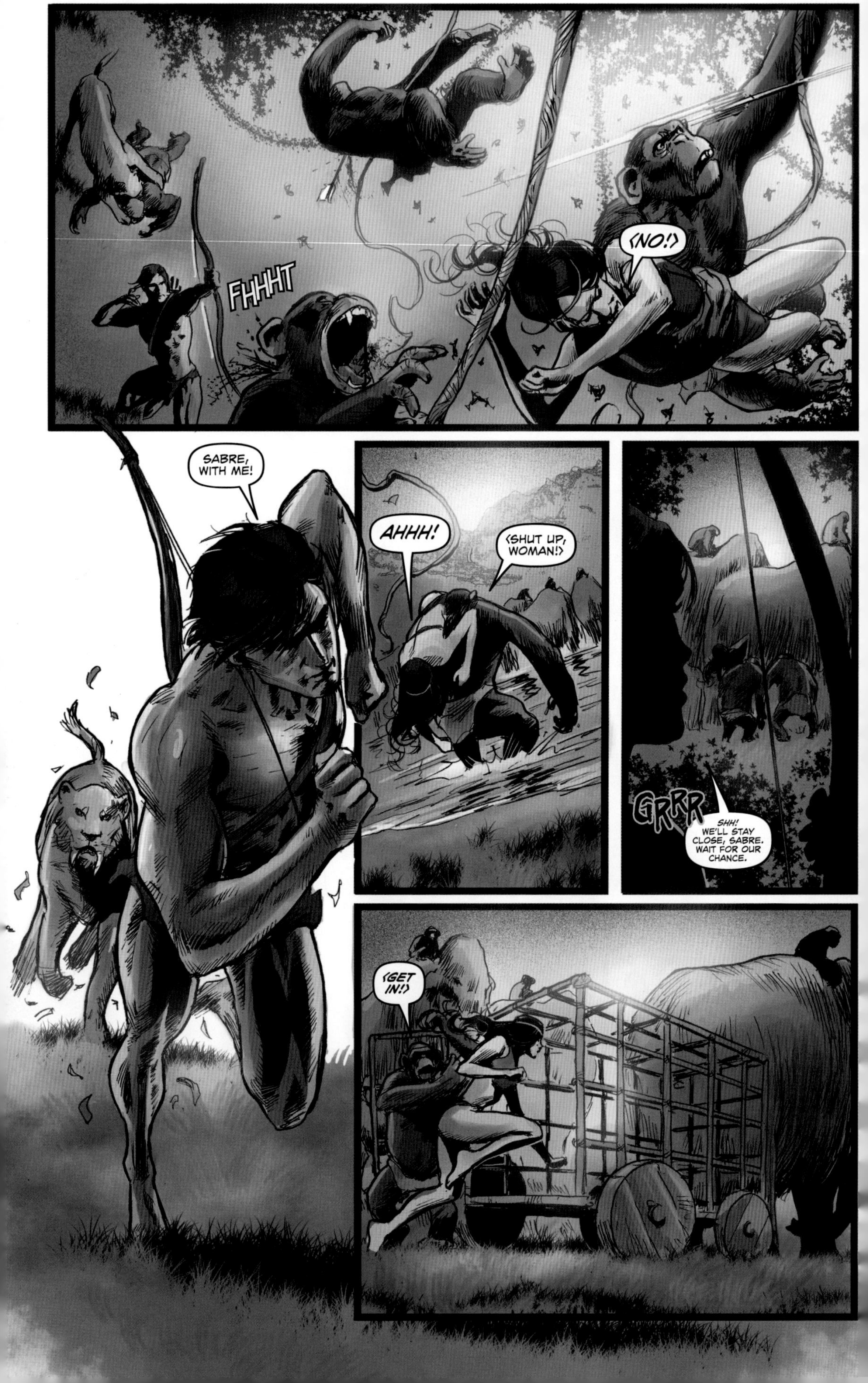

FHHHT
⟨NO!⟩
SABRE, WITH ME!
AHHH!
⟨SHUT UP, WOMAN!⟩
GRRR
SHH! WE'LL STAY CLOSE, SABRE. WAIT FOR OUR CHANCE.
⟨GET IN!⟩

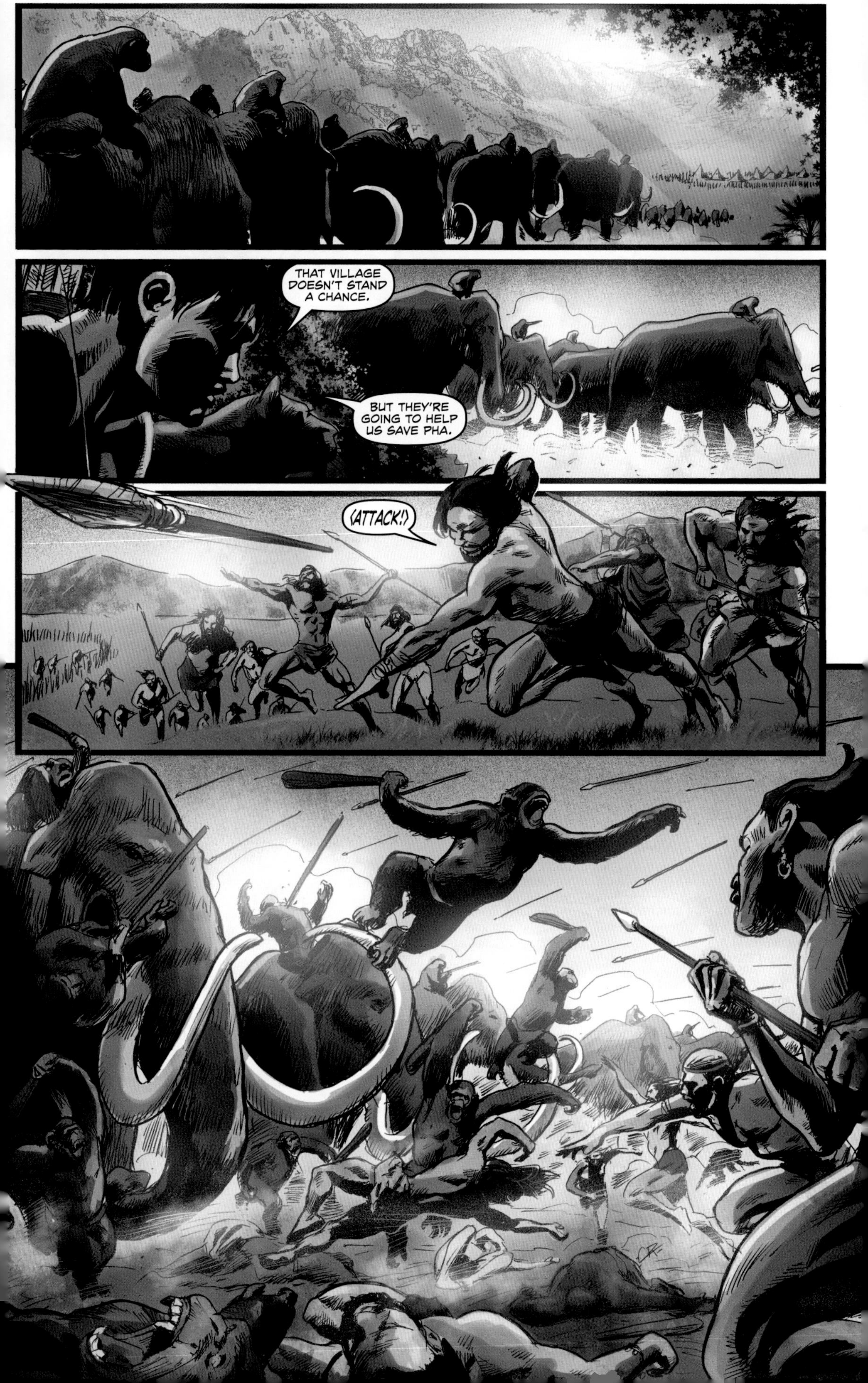
THAT VILLAGE DOESN'T STAND A CHANCE.
BUT THEY'RE GOING TO HELP US SAVE PHA.
(ATTACK!)

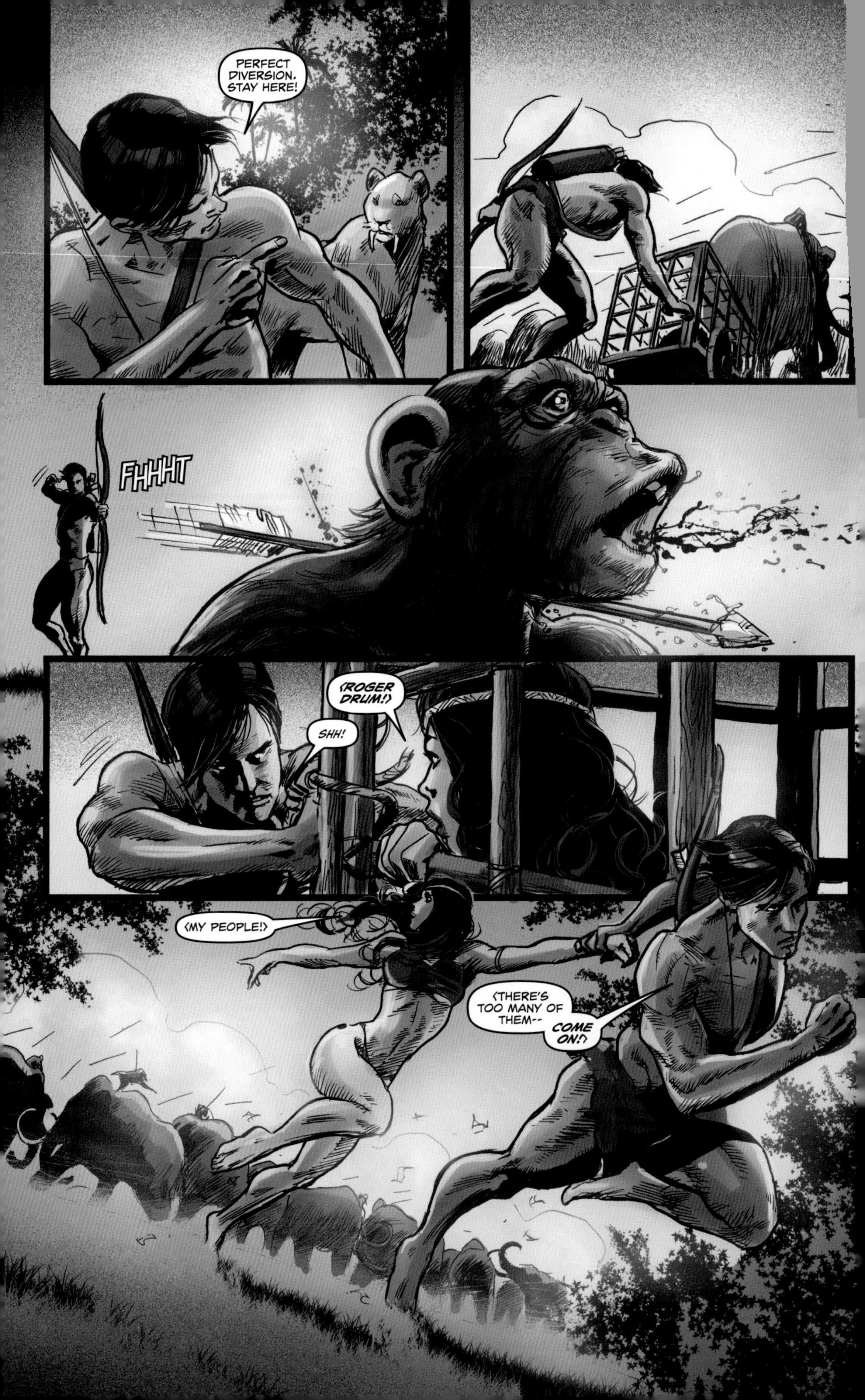
PERFECT DIVERSION. STAY HERE!
FHHHT
‹ROGER DRUM!›
SHH!
‹MY PEOPLE!›
‹THERE'S TOO MANY OF THEM-- COME ON!›

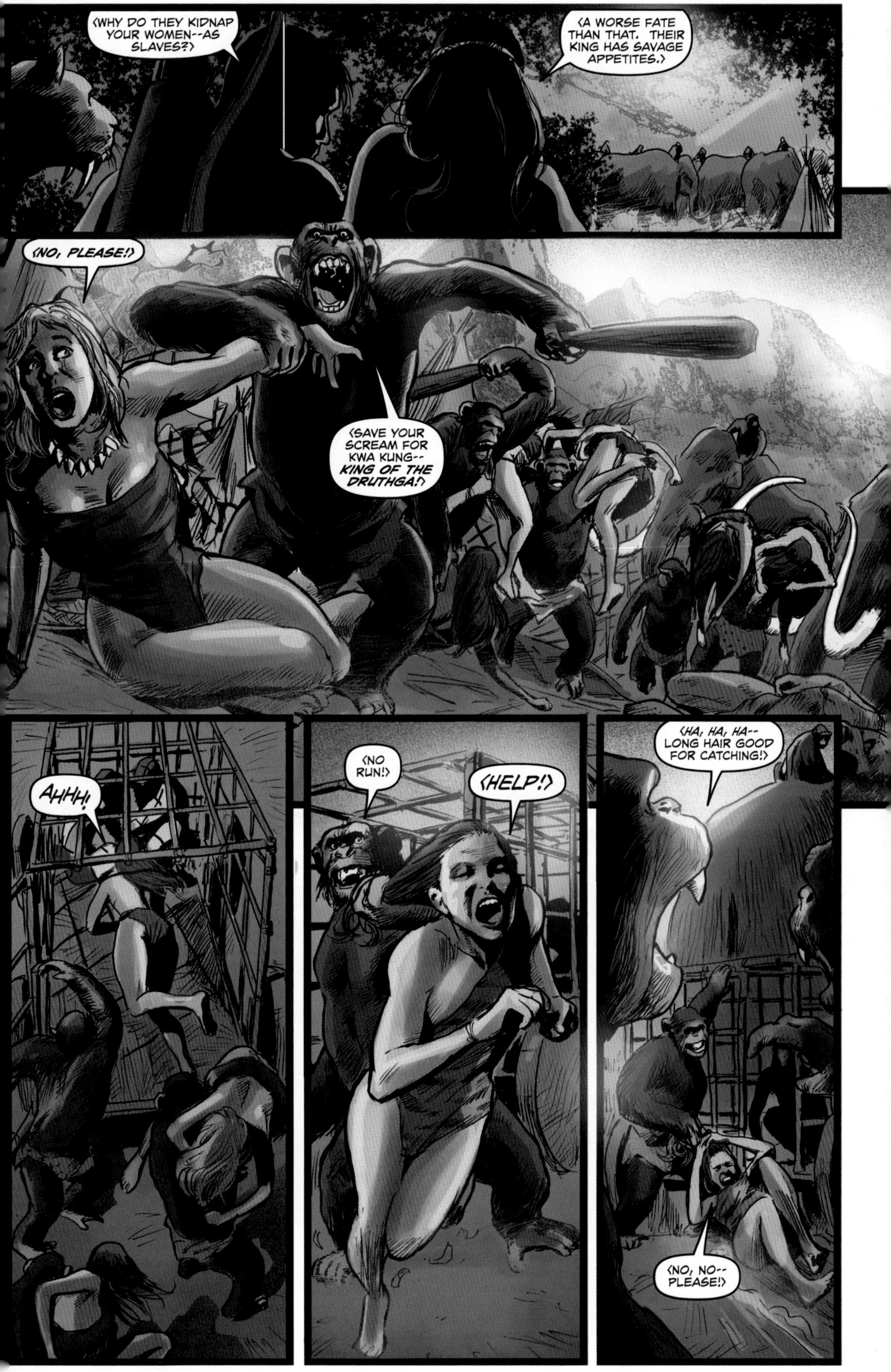
‹WHY DO THEY KIDNAP YOUR WOMEN--AS SLAVES?›
‹A WORSE FATE THAN THAT. THEIR KING HAS SAVAGE APPETITES.›
‹NO, PLEASE!›
‹SAVE YOUR SCREAM FOR KWA KUNG-- KING OF THE DRUTHGA!›
AHHH!
‹NO RUN!›
‹HELP!›
‹HA, HA, HA-- LONG HAIR GOOD FOR CATCHING!›
‹NO, NO-- PLEASE!›

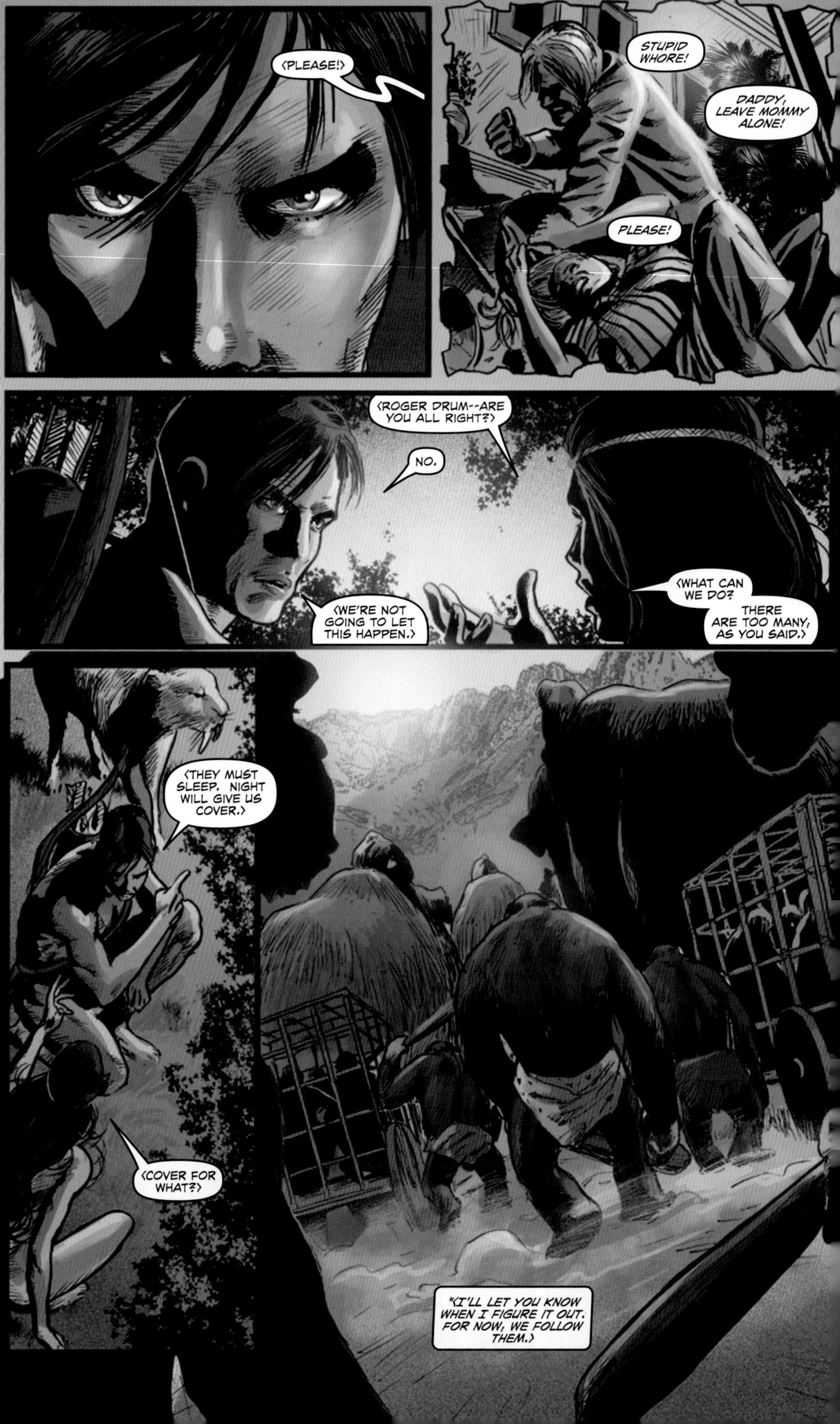

‹PLEASE!›
STUPID WHORE!
DADDY, LEAVE MOMMY ALONE!
PLEASE!
‹ROGER DRUM--ARE YOU ALL RIGHT?›
NO.
‹WE'RE NOT GOING TO LET THIS HAPPEN.›
‹WHAT CAN WE DO? THERE ARE TOO MANY, AS YOU SAID.›
‹THEY MUST SLEEP. NIGHT WILL GIVE US COVER.›
‹COVER FOR WHAT?›
"‹I'LL LET YOU KNOW WHEN I FIGURE IT OUT. FOR NOW, WE FOLLOW THEM.›

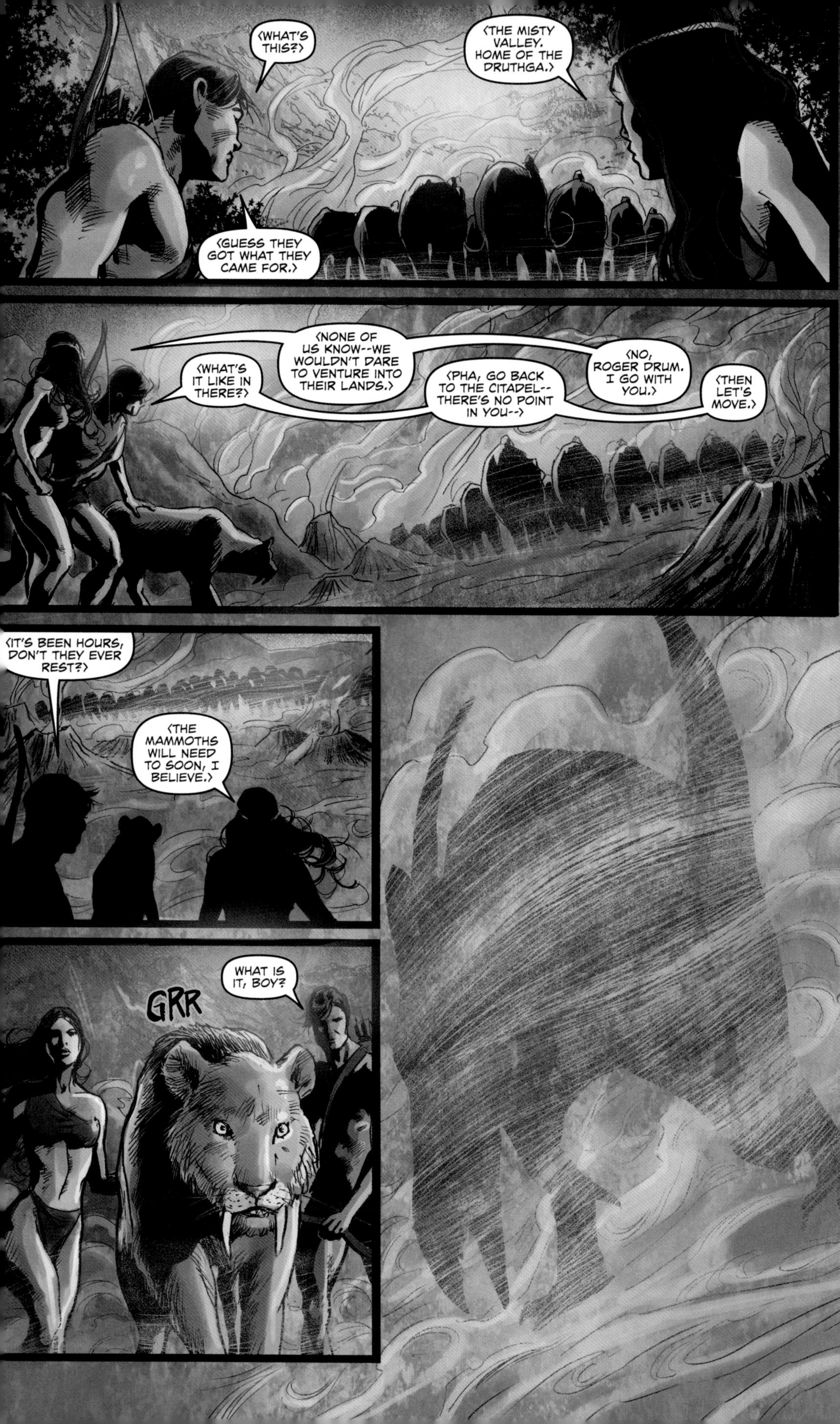

‹WHAT'S THIS?›
‹THE MISTY VALLEY. HOME OF THE DRUTHGA.›
‹GUESS THEY GOT WHAT THEY CAME FOR.›
‹WHAT'S IT LIKE IN THERE?›
‹NONE OF US KNOW--WE WOULDN'T DARE TO VENTURE INTO THEIR LANDS.›
‹PHA, GO BACK TO THE CITADEL--THERE'S NO POINT IN YOU--›
‹NO, ROGER DRUM. I GO WITH YOU.›
‹THEN LET'S MOVE.›
‹IT'S BEEN HOURS, DON'T THEY EVER REST?›
‹THE MAMMOTHS WILL NEED TO SOON, I BELIEVE.›
GRR
WHAT IS IT, BOY?

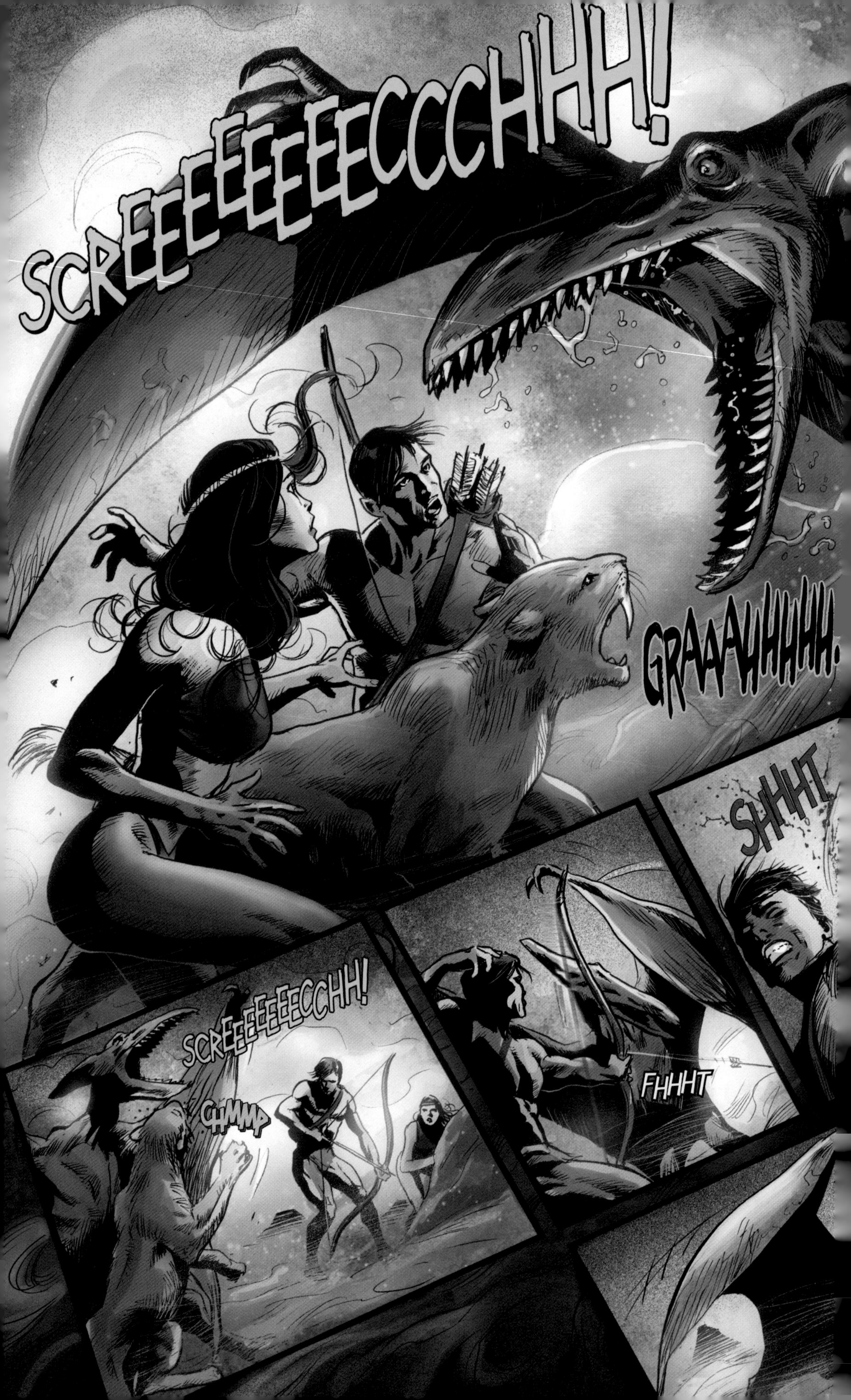
SCREEEEEEEEECCCHHH!
GRAAAHHHHH.
SCREEEEEEEECCHH!
CHMMP
FHHHT
SHHHT

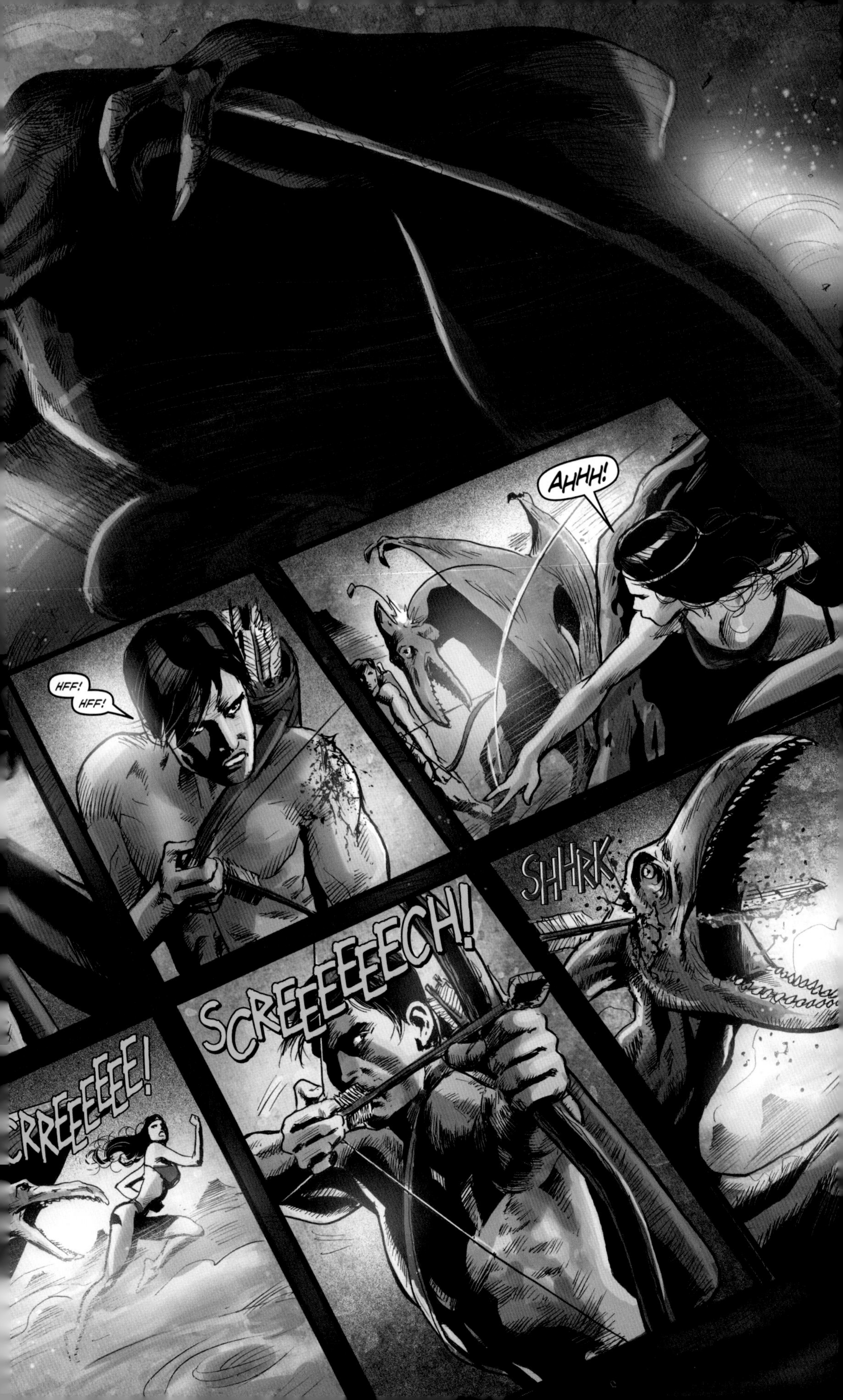
HFF! HFF!
AHHH!
SHHRK
SCREEEEEEECH!
CRREEEEEEE!

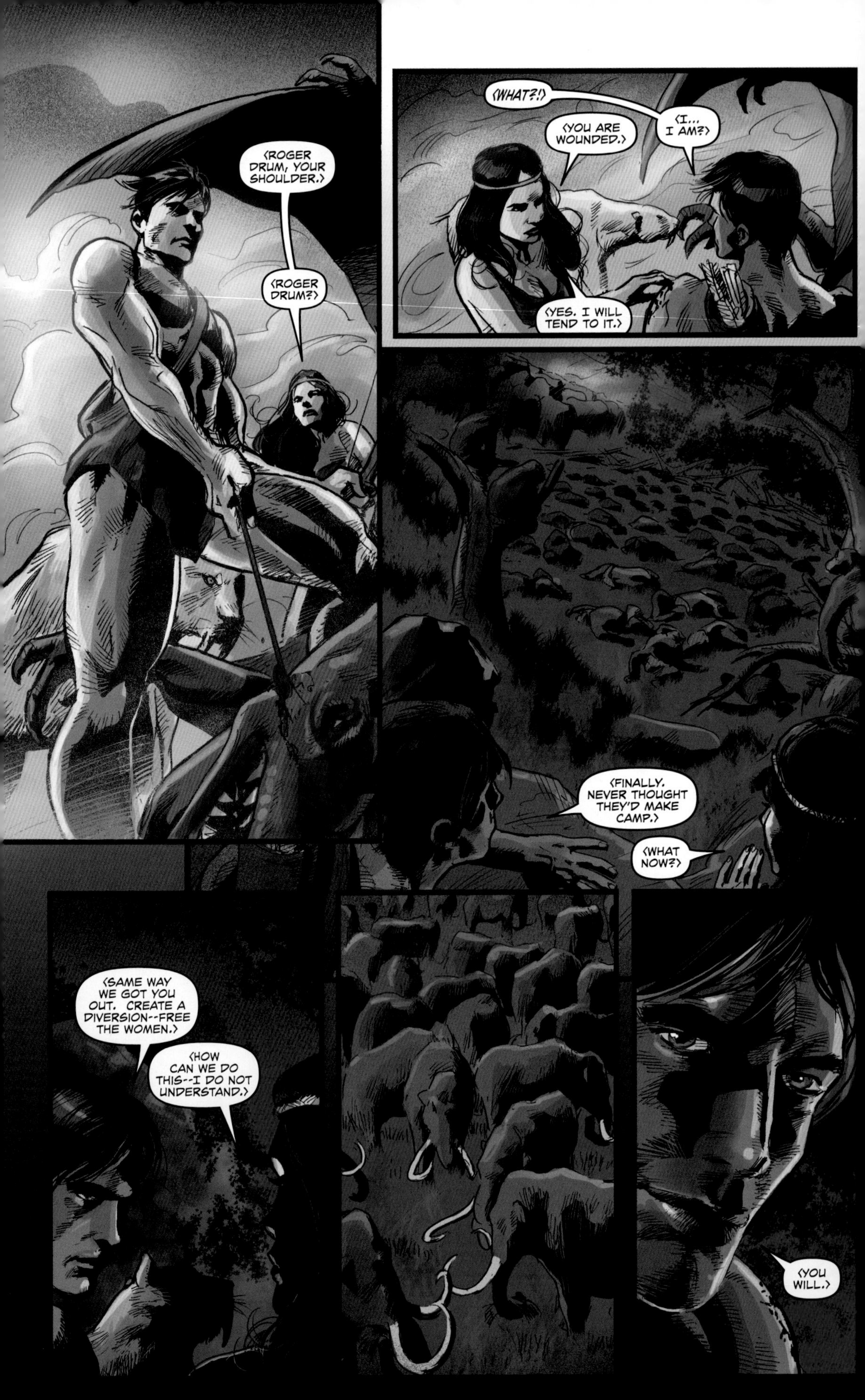

‹ROGER DRUM, YOUR SHOULDER.›
‹ROGER DRUM?›
‹WHAT?!›
‹YOU ARE WOUNDED.›
‹I... I AM?›
‹YES. I WILL TEND TO IT.›
‹FINALLY. NEVER THOUGHT THEY'D MAKE CAMP.›
‹WHAT NOW?›
‹SAME WAY WE GOT YOU OUT. CREATE A DIVERSION--FREE THE WOMEN.›
‹HOW CAN WE DO THIS--I DO NOT UNDERSTAND.›
‹YOU WILL.›

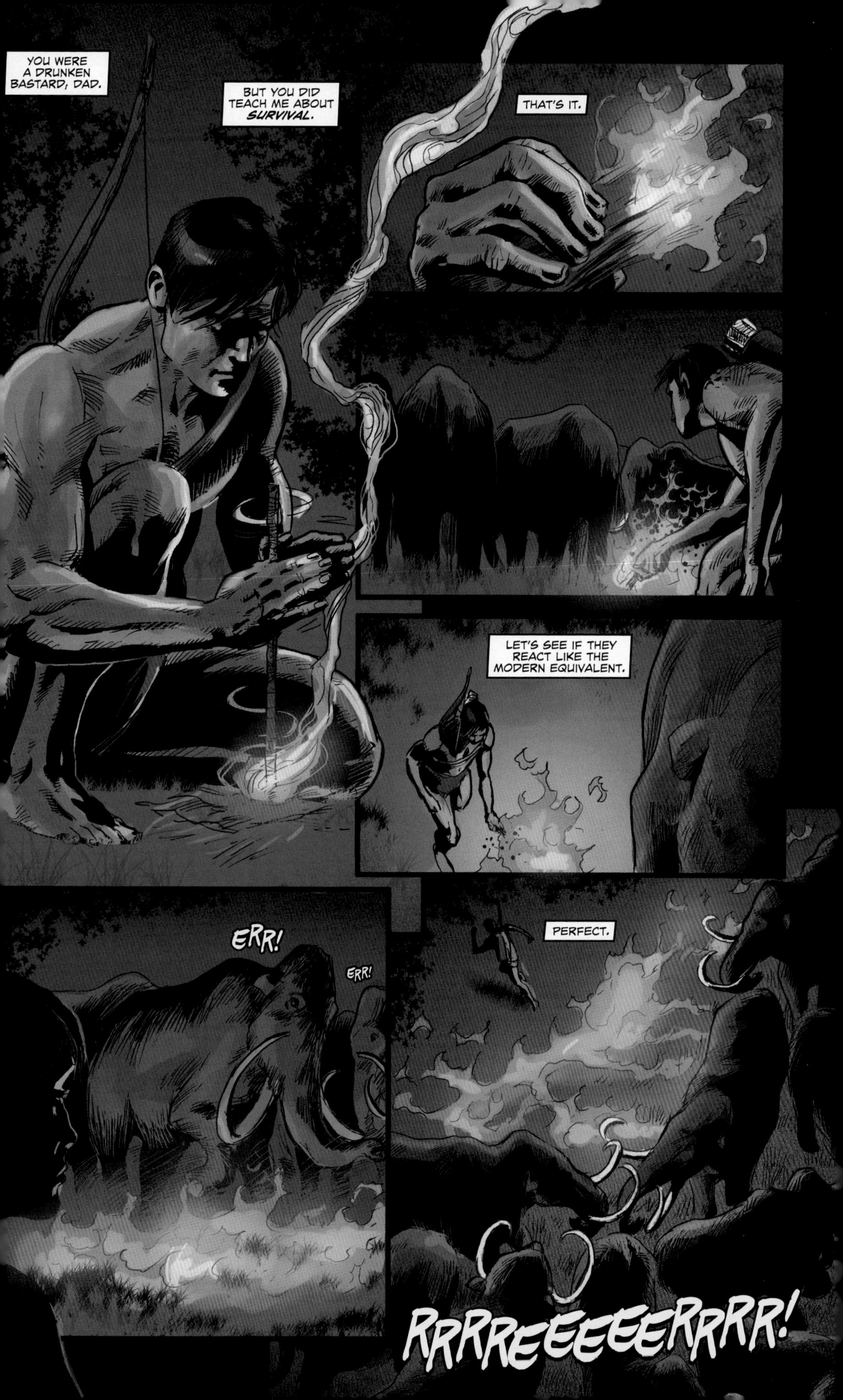
YOU WERE A DRUNKEN BASTARD, DAD.
BUT YOU DID TEACH ME ABOUT *SURVIVAL*.
THAT'S IT.
LET'S SEE IF THEY REACT LIKE THE MODERN EQUIVALENT.
ERR!
ERR!
PERFECT.
RRRREEEEEERRRR!

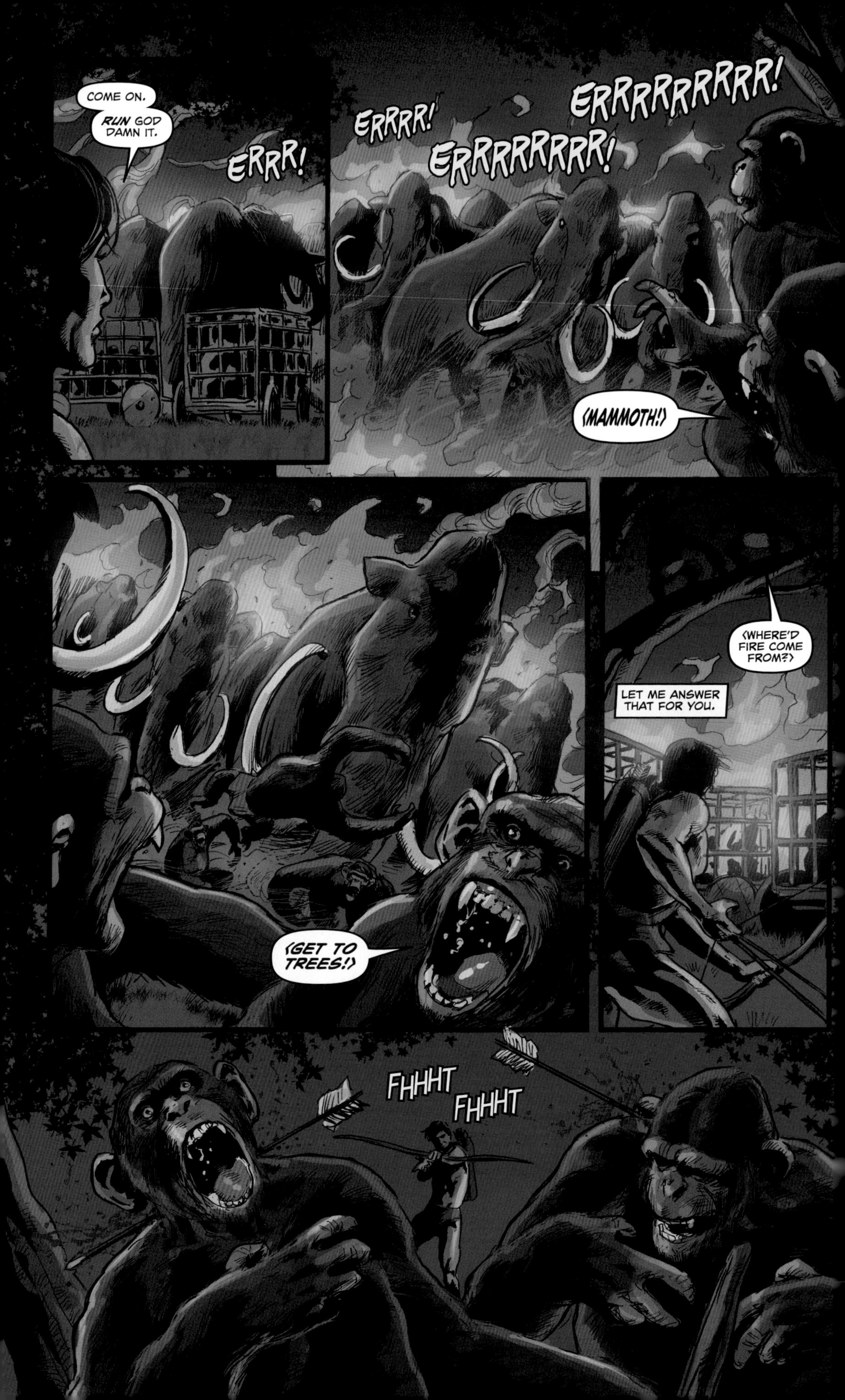
COME ON. RUN GOD DAMN IT.
ERRR!
ERRRR!
ERRRRRRRRR!
ERRRRRRRRRR!
‹MAMMOTH!›
‹GET TO TREES!›
‹WHERE'D FIRE COME FROM?›
LET ME ANSWER THAT FOR YOU.
FHHHT
FHHHT

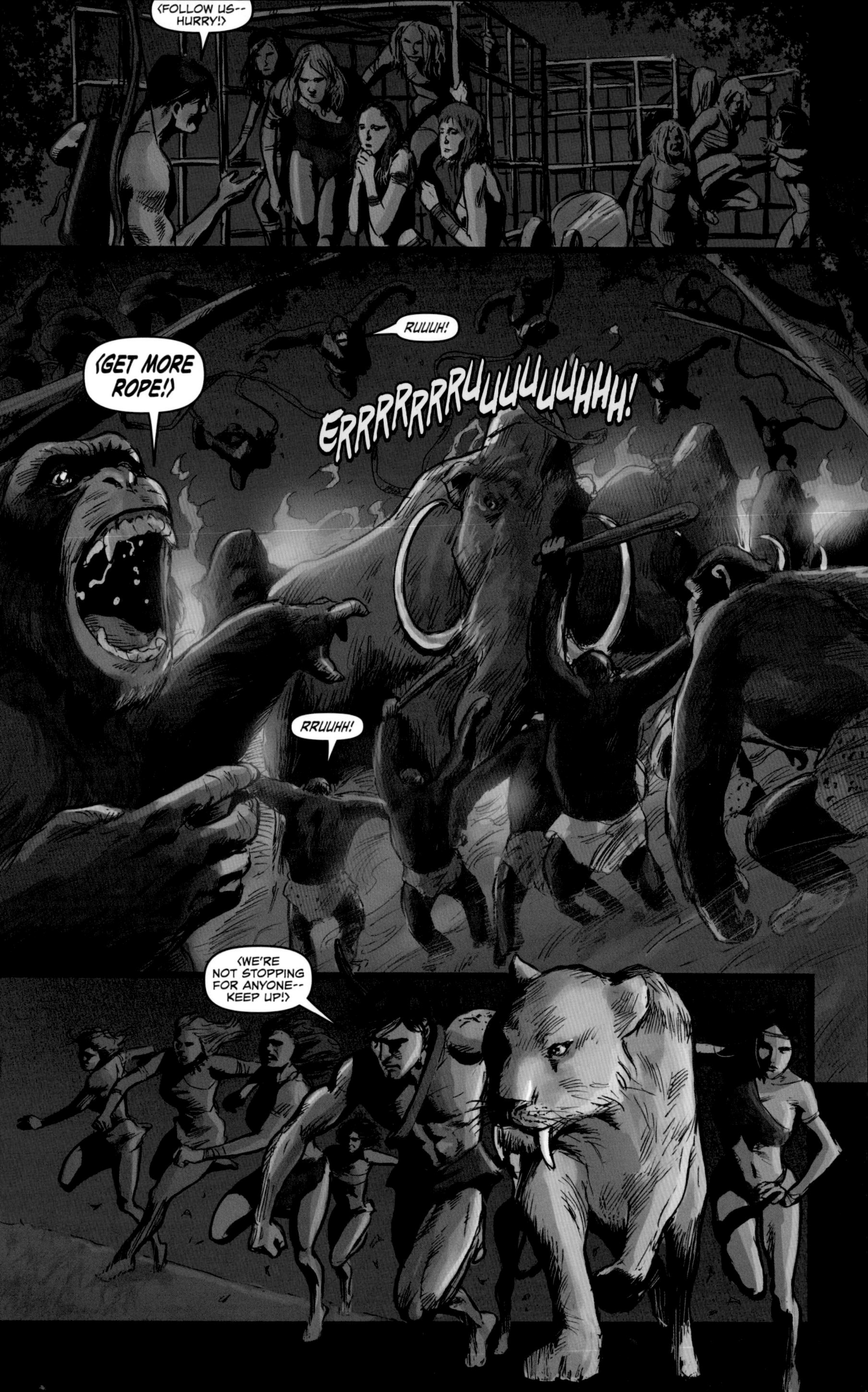
‹FOLLOW US--
HURRY!›
RUUUH!
‹GET MORE ROPE!›
ERRRRRRRUUUUUUUHH!
RRUUHH!
‹WE'RE NOT STOPPING FOR ANYONE-- KEEP UP!›

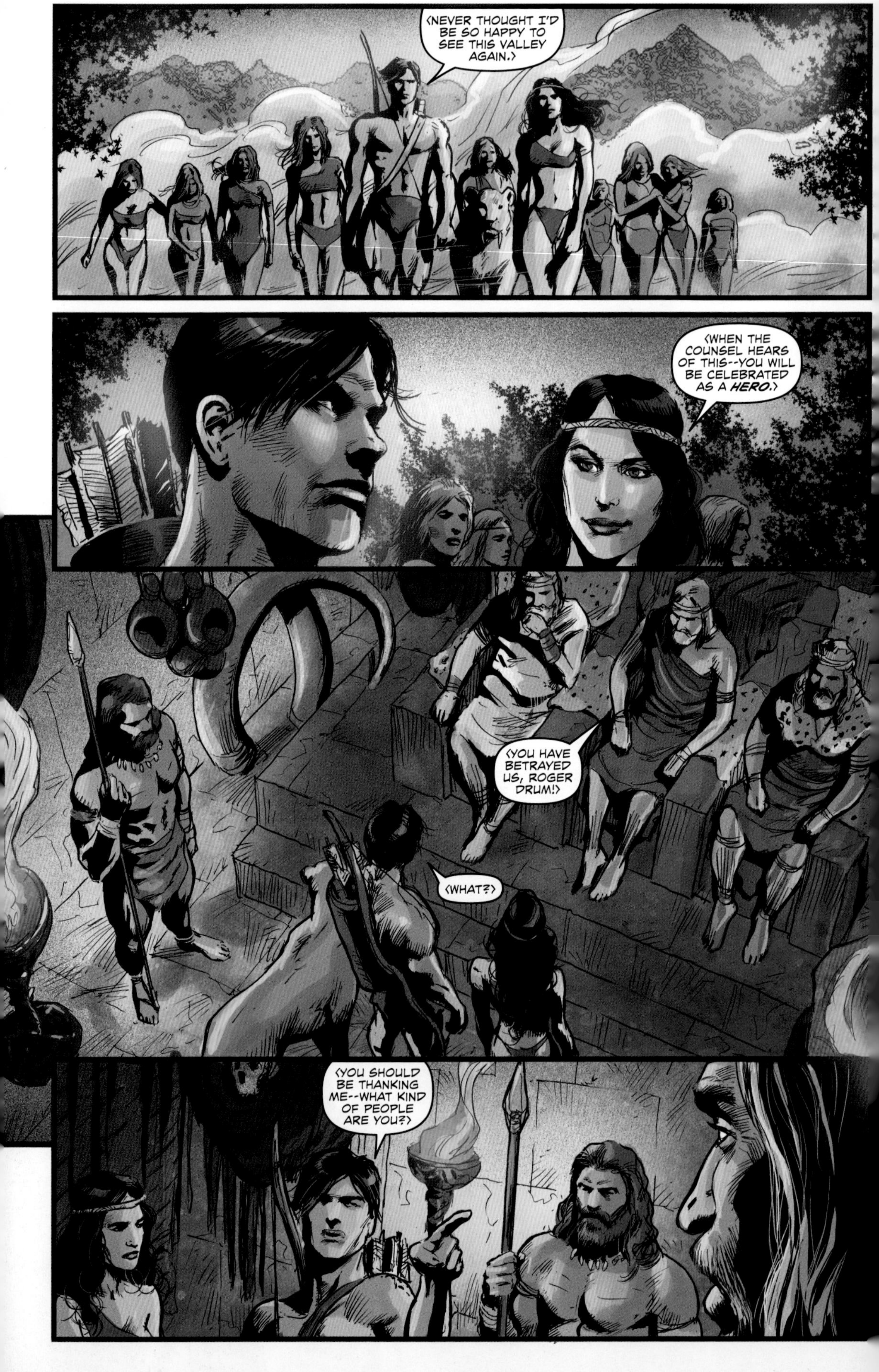

‹NEVER THOUGHT I'D BE SO HAPPY TO SEE THIS VALLEY AGAIN.›
‹WHEN THE COUNSEL HEARS OF THIS--YOU WILL BE CELEBRATED AS A *HERO*.›
‹YOU HAVE BETRAYED US, ROGER DRUM!›
‹WHAT?›
‹YOU SHOULD BE THANKING ME--WHAT KIND OF PEOPLE ARE YOU?›

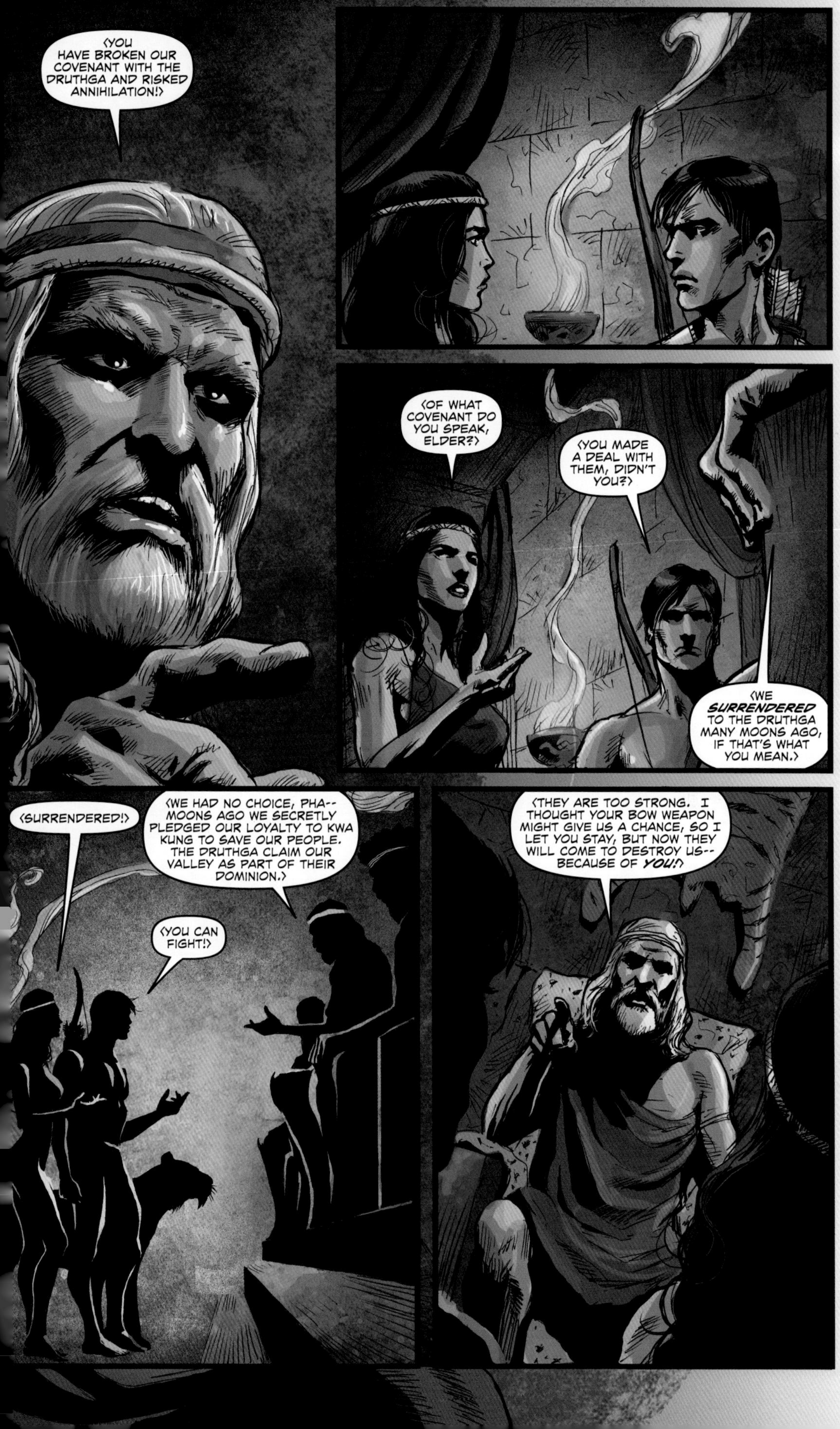
‹YOU HAVE BROKEN OUR COVENANT WITH THE DRUTHGA AND RISKED ANNIHILATION!›
‹OF WHAT COVENANT DO YOU SPEAK, ELDER?›
‹YOU MADE A DEAL WITH THEM, DIDN'T YOU?›
‹WE *SURRENDERED* TO THE DRUTHGA MANY MOONS AGO, IF THAT'S WHAT YOU MEAN.›
‹SURRENDERED!›
‹WE HAD NO CHOICE, PHA--MOONS AGO WE SECRETLY PLEDGED OUR LOYALTY TO KWA KUNG TO SAVE OUR PEOPLE. THE DRUTHGA CLAIM OUR VALLEY AS PART OF THEIR DOMINION.›
‹YOU CAN FIGHT!›
‹THEY ARE TOO STRONG. I THOUGHT YOUR BOW WEAPON MIGHT GIVE US A CHANCE, SO I LET YOU STAY, BUT NOW THEY WILL COME TO DESTROY US--BECAUSE OF *YOU!*›

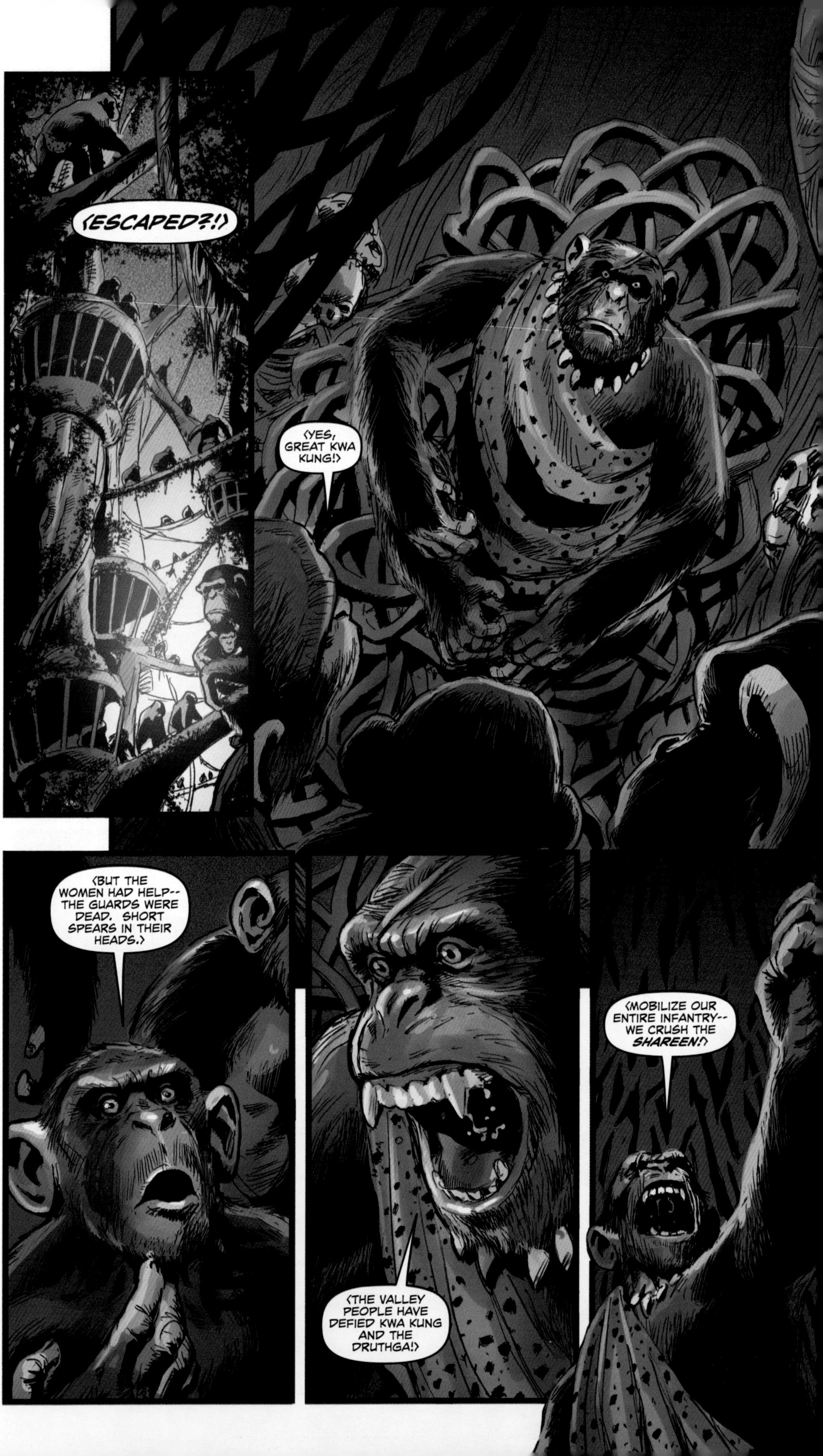

‹ESCAPED?!›
‹YES, GREAT KWA KUNG!›
‹BUT THE WOMEN HAD HELP-- THE GUARDS WERE DEAD. SHORT SPEARS IN THEIR HEADS.›
‹THE VALLEY PEOPLE HAVE DEFIED KWA KUNG AND THE DRUTHGA!›
‹MOBILIZE OUR ENTIRE INFANTRY-- WE CRUSH THE SHAREEN!›

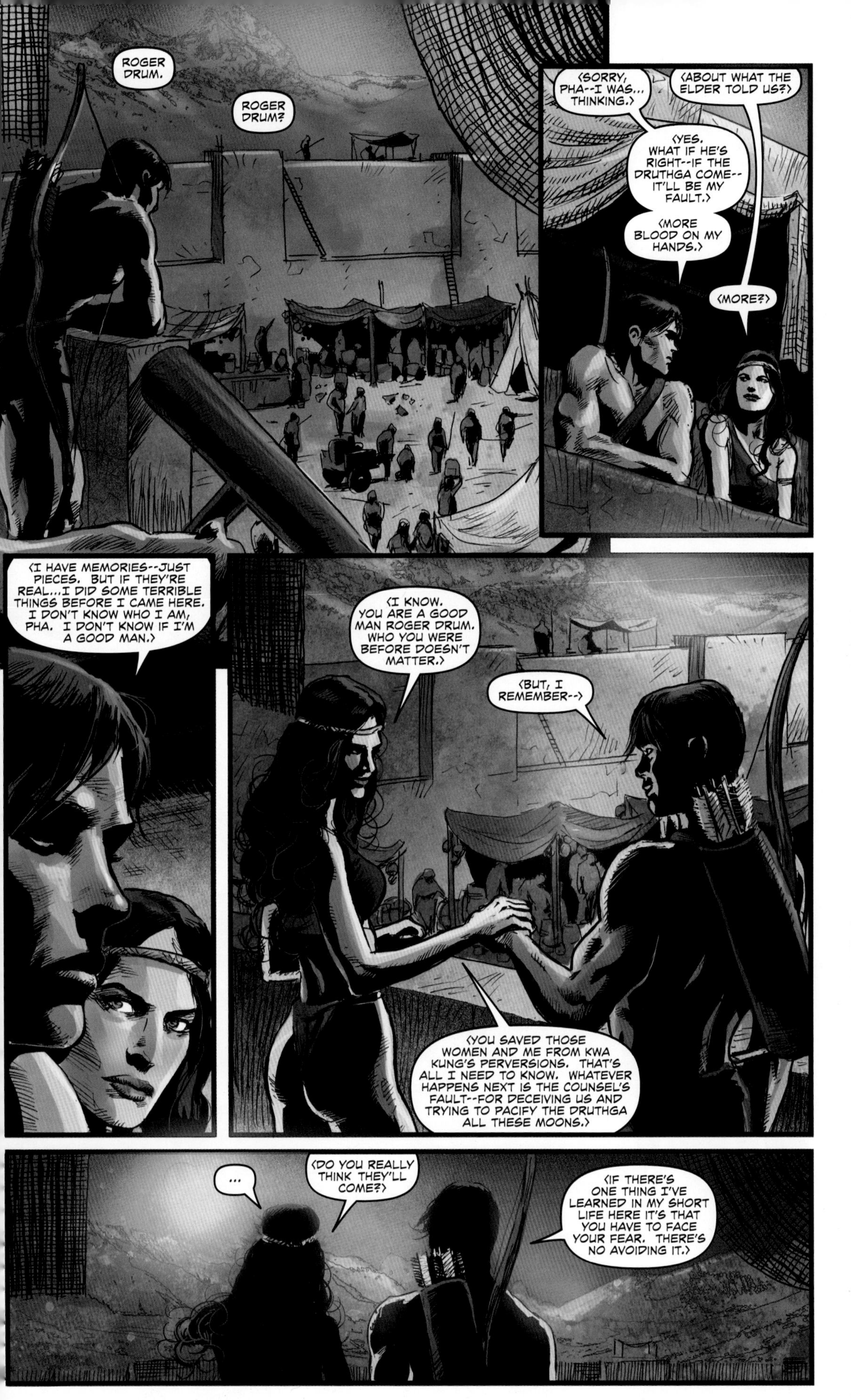
ROGER DRUM.
ROGER DRUM?
<SORRY, PHA--I WAS... THINKING.>
<ABOUT WHAT THE ELDER TOLD US?>
<YES. WHAT IF HE'S RIGHT--IF THE DRUTHGA COME--IT'LL BE MY FAULT.>
<MORE BLOOD ON MY HANDS.>
<MORE?>
<I HAVE MEMORIES--JUST PIECES. BUT IF THEY'RE REAL...I DID SOME TERRIBLE THINGS BEFORE I CAME HERE. I DON'T KNOW WHO I AM, PHA. I DON'T KNOW IF I'M A GOOD MAN.>
<I KNOW. YOU ARE A GOOD MAN ROGER DRUM. WHO YOU WERE BEFORE DOESN'T MATTER.>
<BUT, I REMEMBER-->
<YOU SAVED THOSE WOMEN AND ME FROM KWA KUNG'S PERVERSIONS. THAT'S ALL I NEED TO KNOW. WHATEVER HAPPENS NEXT IS THE COUNSEL'S FAULT--FOR DECEIVING US AND TRYING TO PACIFY THE DRUTHGA ALL THESE MOONS.>
...
<DO YOU REALLY THINK THEY'LL COME?>
<IF THERE'S ONE THING I'VE LEARNED IN MY SHORT LIFE HERE IT'S THAT YOU HAVE TO FACE YOUR FEAR. THERE'S NO AVOIDING IT.>

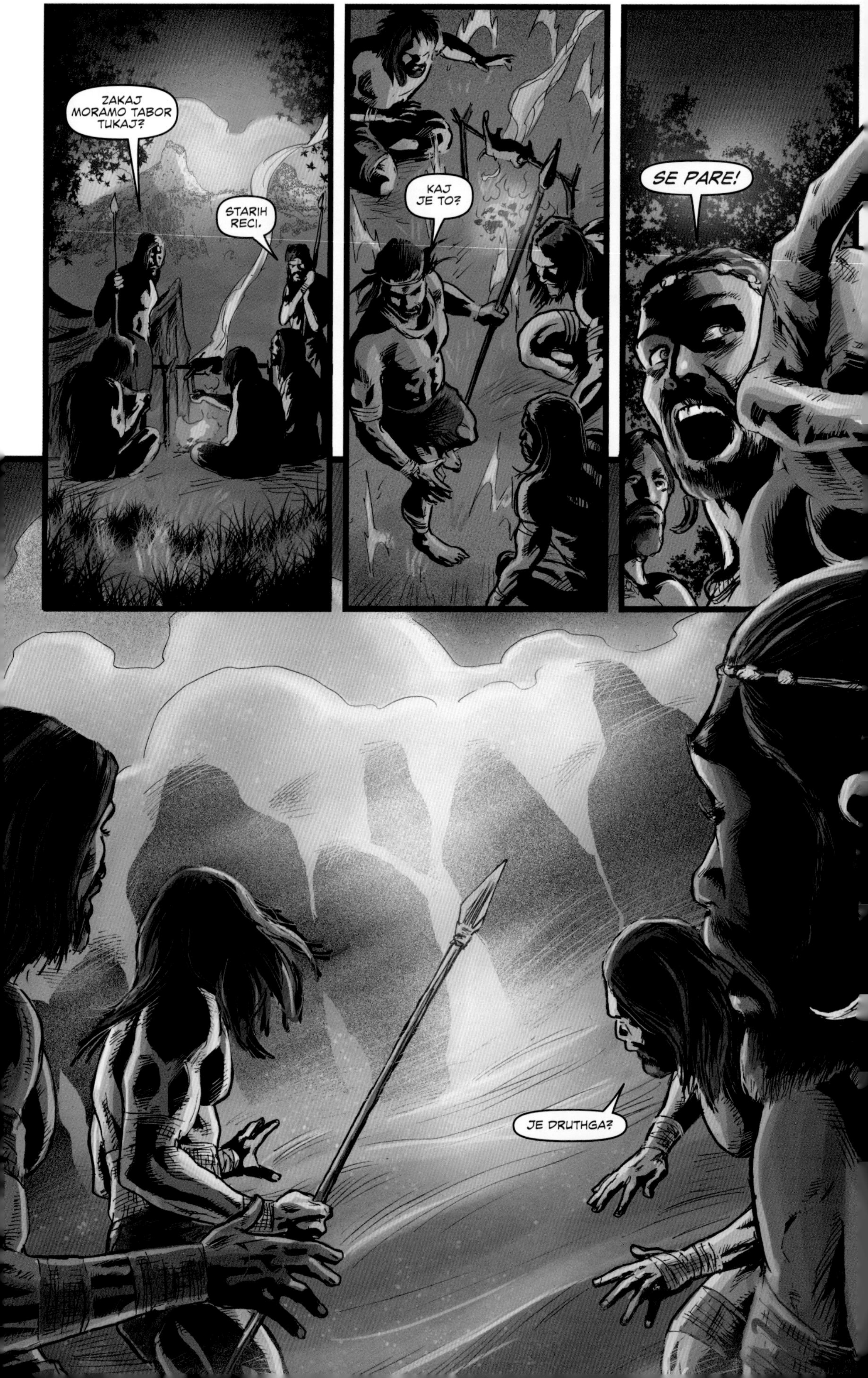
ZAKAJ MORAMO TABOR TUKAJ?
STARIH RECI.
KAJ JE TO?
SE PARE!
JE DRUTHGA?

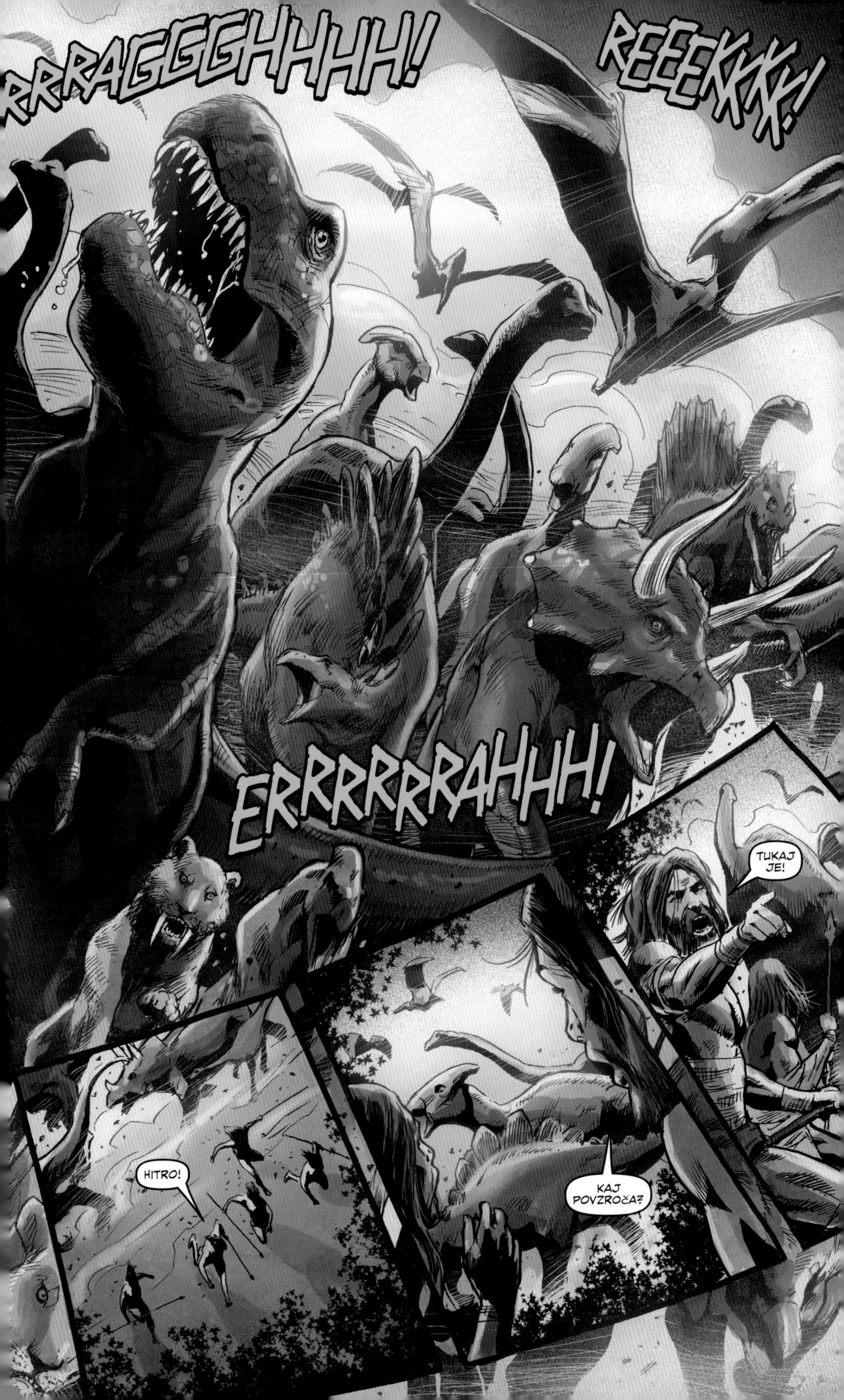
RRRAGGGHHHH!
REEEKKKK!
ERRRRRRAHHH!
TUKAJ JE!
KAJ POVZROČA?
HITRO!

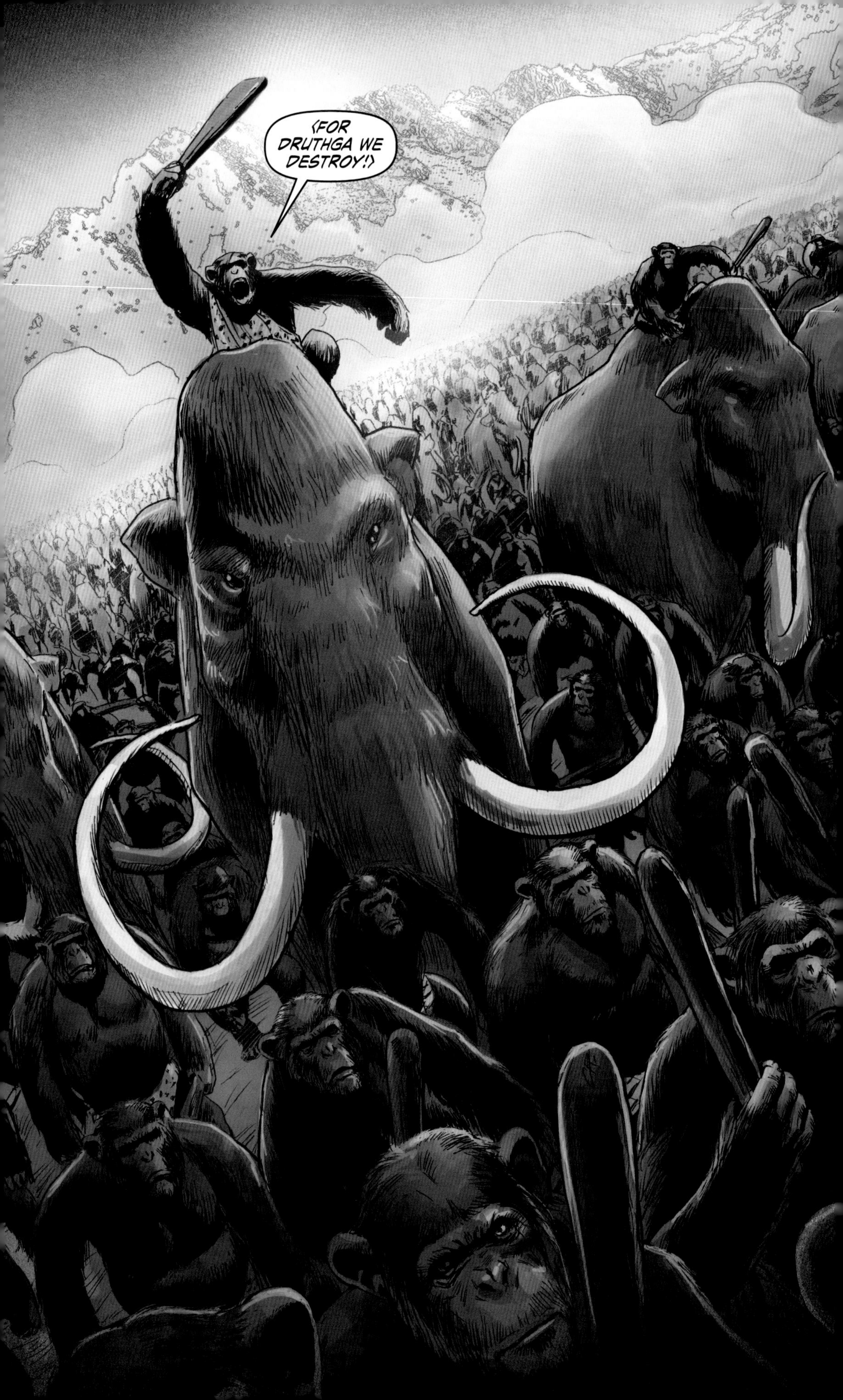
⟨FOR DRUTHGA WE DESTROY!⟩

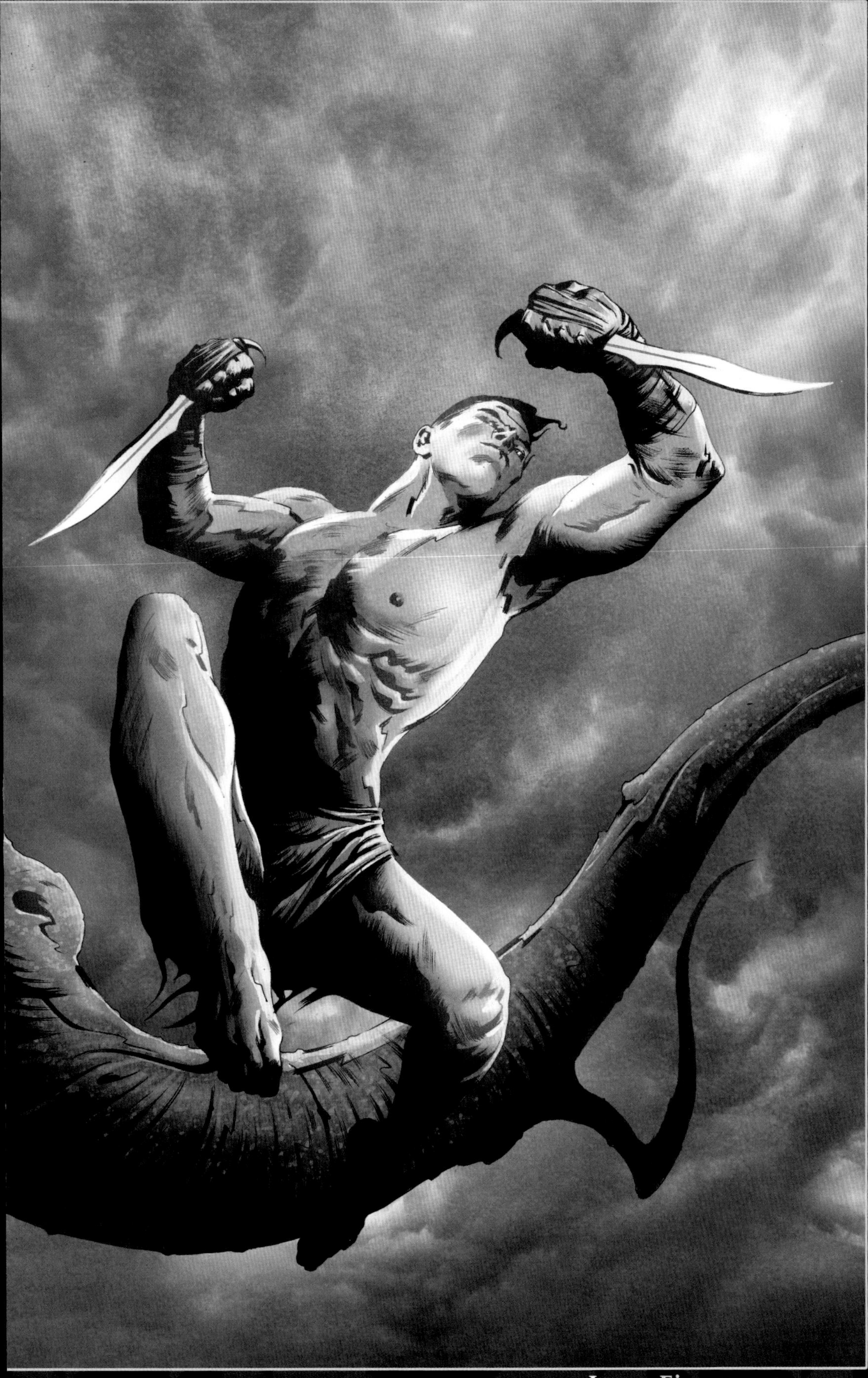

Issue Five Cover by Jae Lee

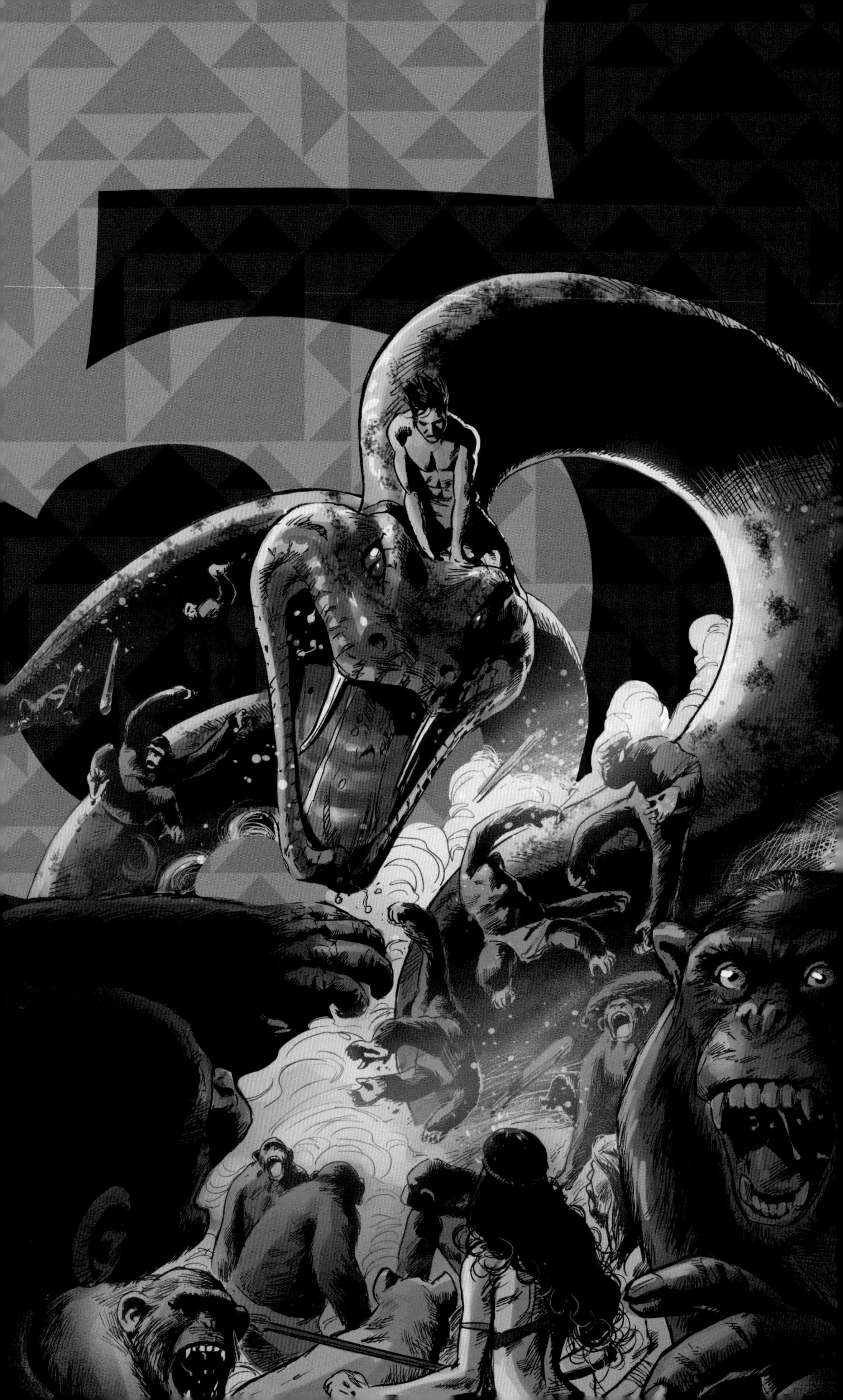

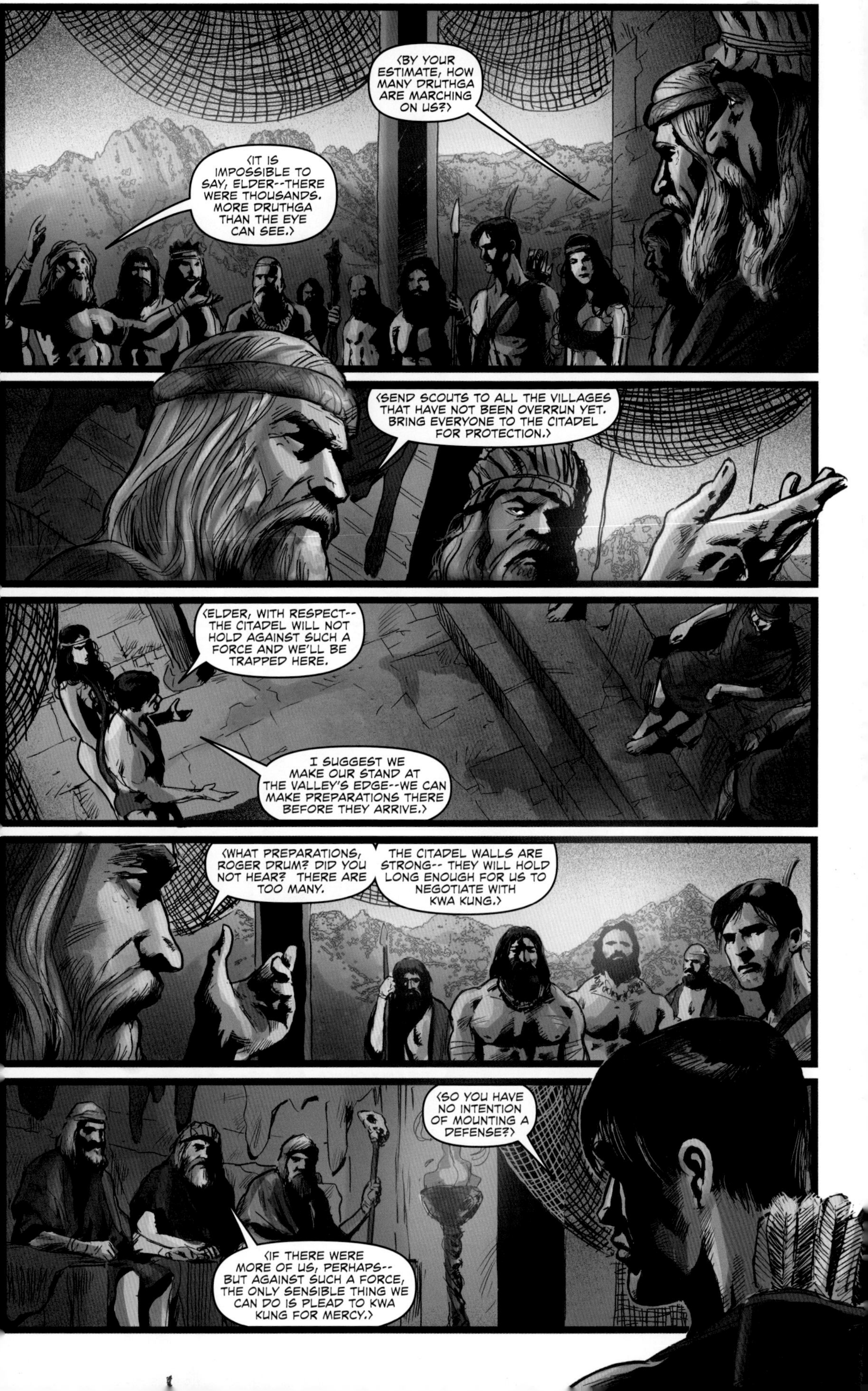

‹BY YOUR ESTIMATE, HOW MANY DRUTHGA ARE MARCHING ON US?›
‹IT IS IMPOSSIBLE TO SAY, ELDER--THERE WERE THOUSANDS. MORE DRUTHGA THAN THE EYE CAN SEE.›
‹SEND SCOUTS TO ALL THE VILLAGES THAT HAVE NOT BEEN OVERRUN YET. BRING EVERYONE TO THE CITADEL FOR PROTECTION.›
‹ELDER, WITH RESPECT--THE CITADEL WILL NOT HOLD AGAINST SUCH A FORCE AND WE'LL BE TRAPPED HERE.
I SUGGEST WE MAKE OUR STAND AT THE VALLEY'S EDGE--WE CAN MAKE PREPARATIONS THERE BEFORE THEY ARRIVE.›
‹WHAT PREPARATIONS, ROGER DRUM? DID YOU NOT HEAR? THERE ARE TOO MANY.
THE CITADEL WALLS ARE STRONG-- THEY WILL HOLD LONG ENOUGH FOR US TO NEGOTIATE WITH KWA KUNG.›
‹SO YOU HAVE NO INTENTION OF MOUNTING A DEFENSE?›
‹IF THERE WERE MORE OF US, PERHAPS--BUT AGAINST SUCH A FORCE, THE ONLY SENSIBLE THING WE CAN DO IS PLEAD TO KWA KUNG FOR MERCY.›

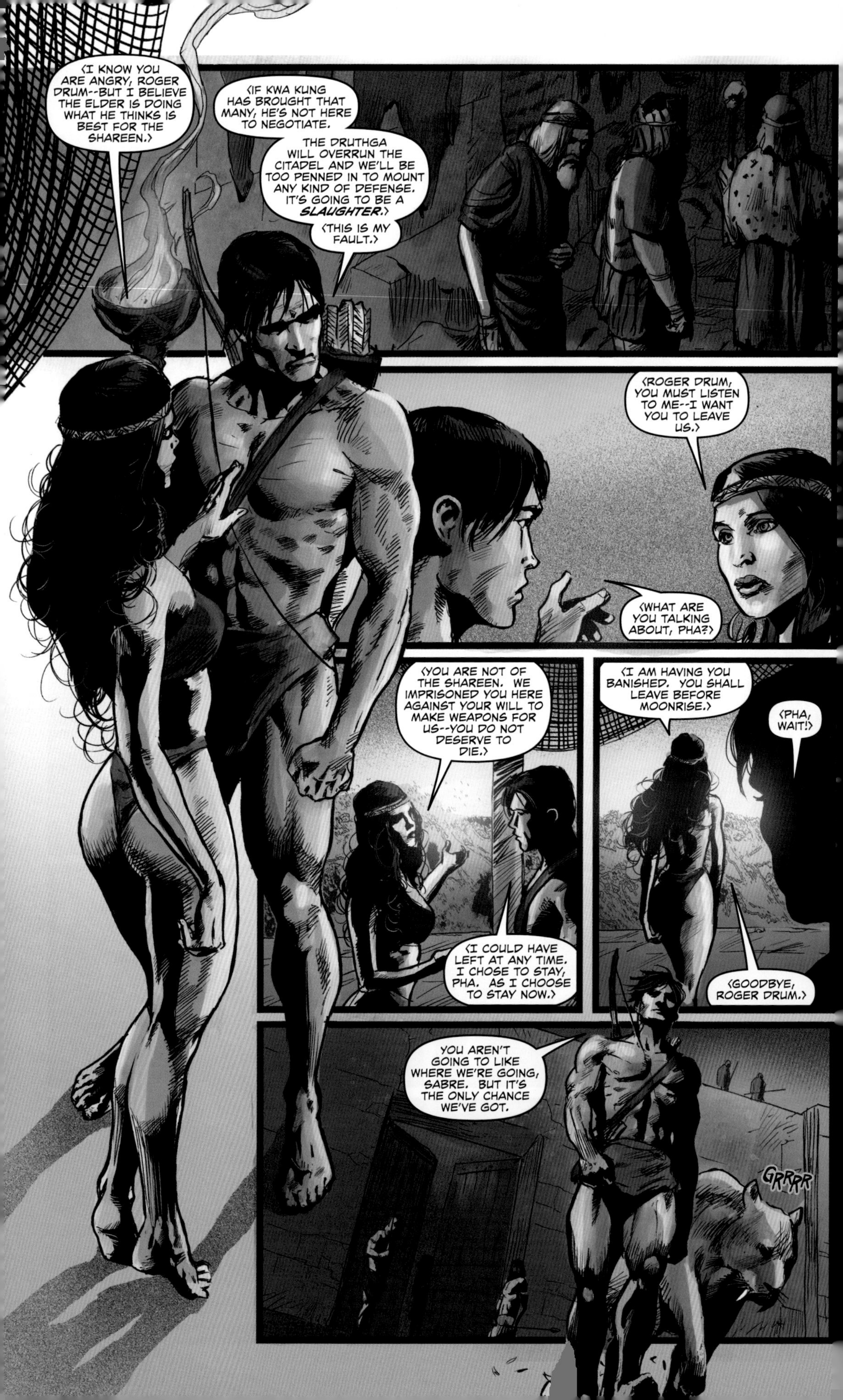

‹I KNOW YOU ARE ANGRY, ROGER DRUM--BUT I BELIEVE THE ELDER IS DOING WHAT HE THINKS IS BEST FOR THE SHAREEN.›
‹IF KWA KUNG HAS BROUGHT THAT MANY, HE'S NOT HERE TO NEGOTIATE.
THE DRUTHGA WILL OVERRUN THE CITADEL AND WE'LL BE TOO PENNED IN TO MOUNT ANY KIND OF DEFENSE. IT'S GOING TO BE A ***SLAUGHTER***.›
‹THIS IS MY FAULT.›
‹ROGER DRUM, YOU MUST LISTEN TO ME--I WANT YOU TO LEAVE US.›
‹WHAT ARE YOU TALKING ABOUT, PHA?›
‹YOU ARE NOT OF THE SHAREEN. WE IMPRISONED YOU HERE AGAINST YOUR WILL TO MAKE WEAPONS FOR US--YOU DO NOT DESERVE TO DIE.›
‹I COULD HAVE LEFT AT ANY TIME. I CHOSE TO STAY, PHA. AS I CHOOSE TO STAY NOW.›
‹I AM HAVING YOU BANISHED. YOU SHALL LEAVE BEFORE MOONRISE.›
‹PHA, WAIT!›
‹GOODBYE, ROGER DRUM.›
YOU AREN'T GOING TO LIKE WHERE WE'RE GOING, SABRE. BUT IT'S THE ONLY CHANCE WE'VE GOT.
GRRRR

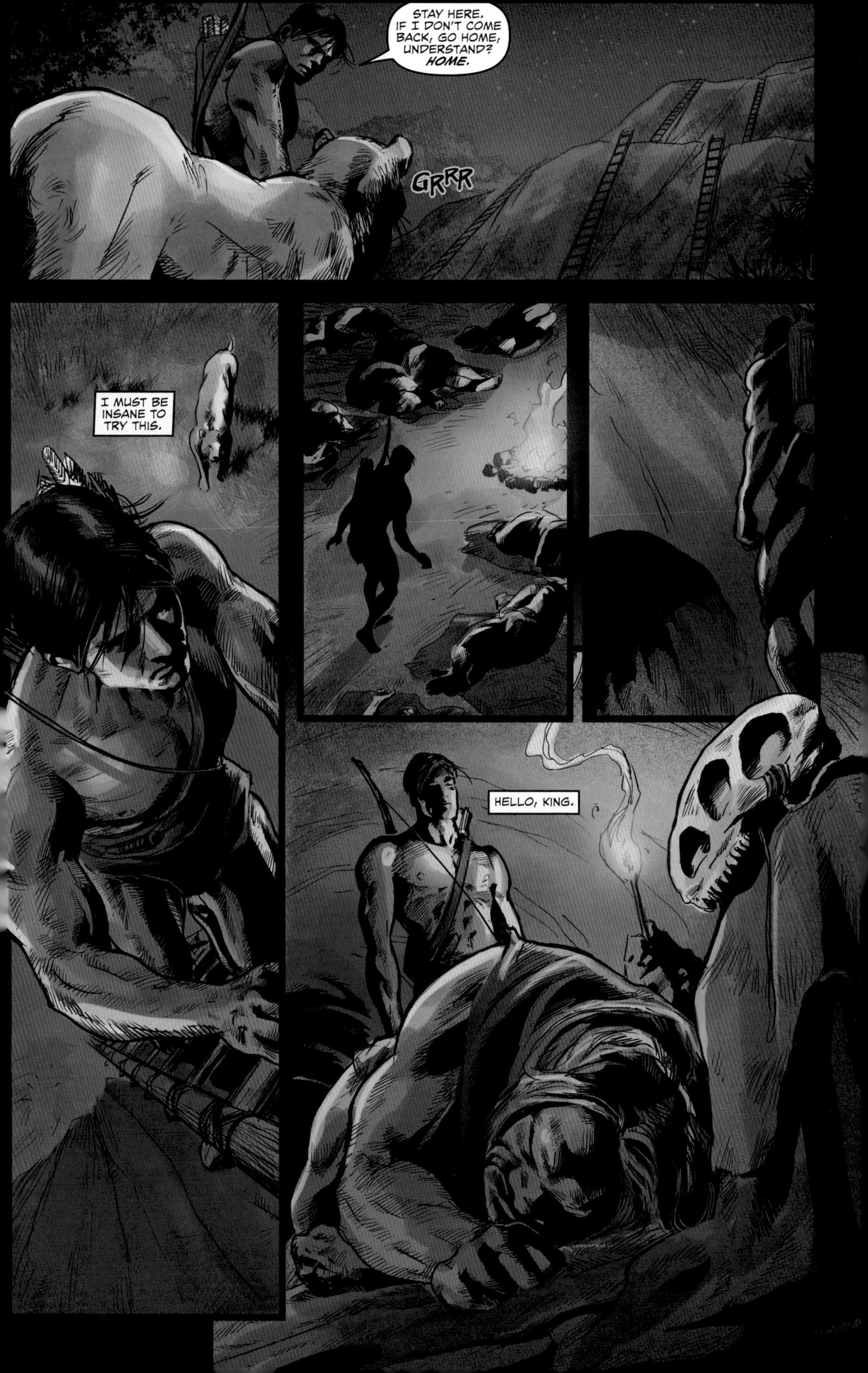
STAY HERE. IF I DON'T COME BACK, GO HOME, UNDERSTAND? HOME.
GRRR
I MUST BE INSANE TO TRY THIS.
HELLO, KING.

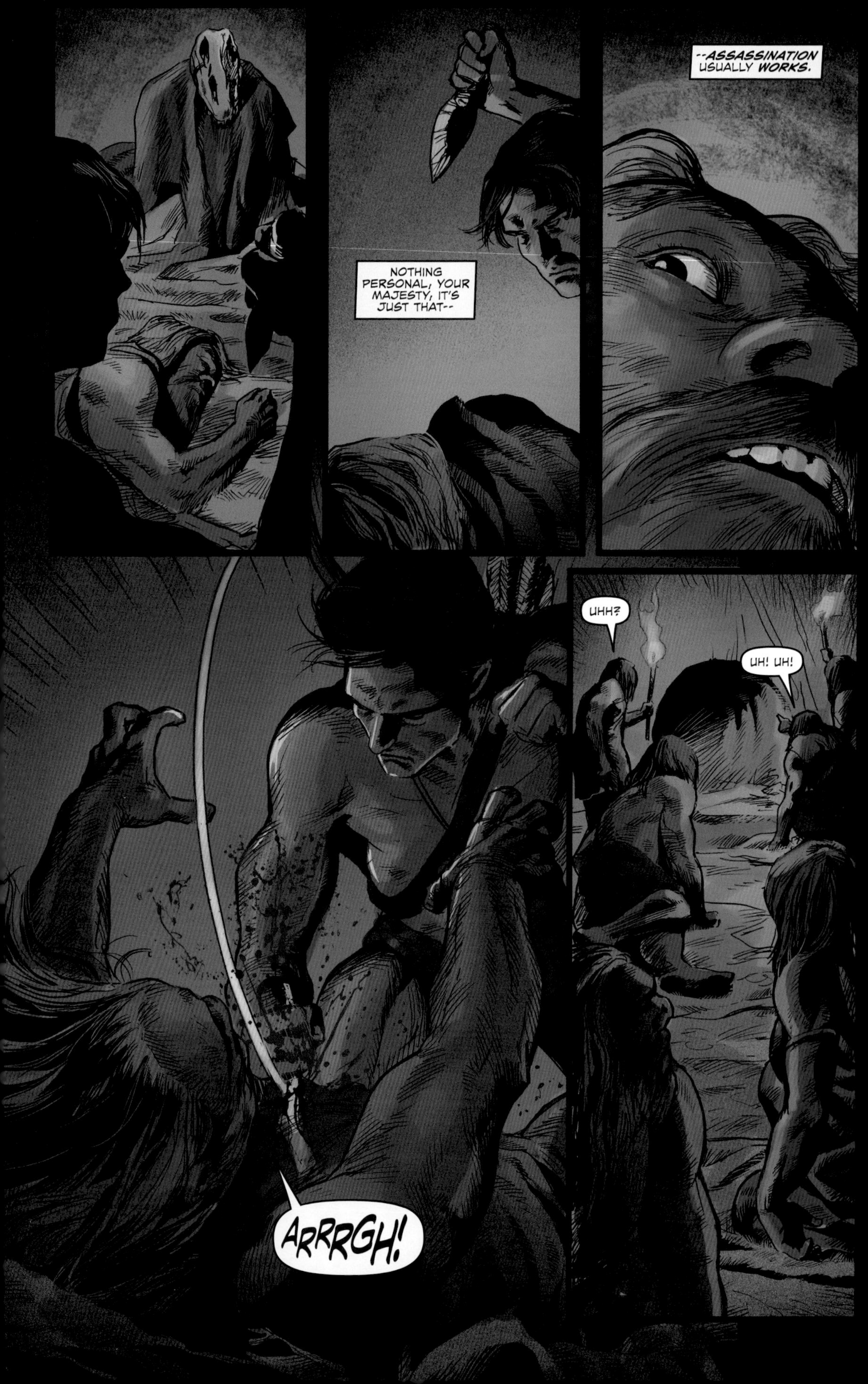
NOTHING PERSONAL, YOUR MAJESTY, IT'S JUST THAT--
--ASSASSINATION USUALLY WORKS.
ARRRGH!
UHH?
UH! UH!

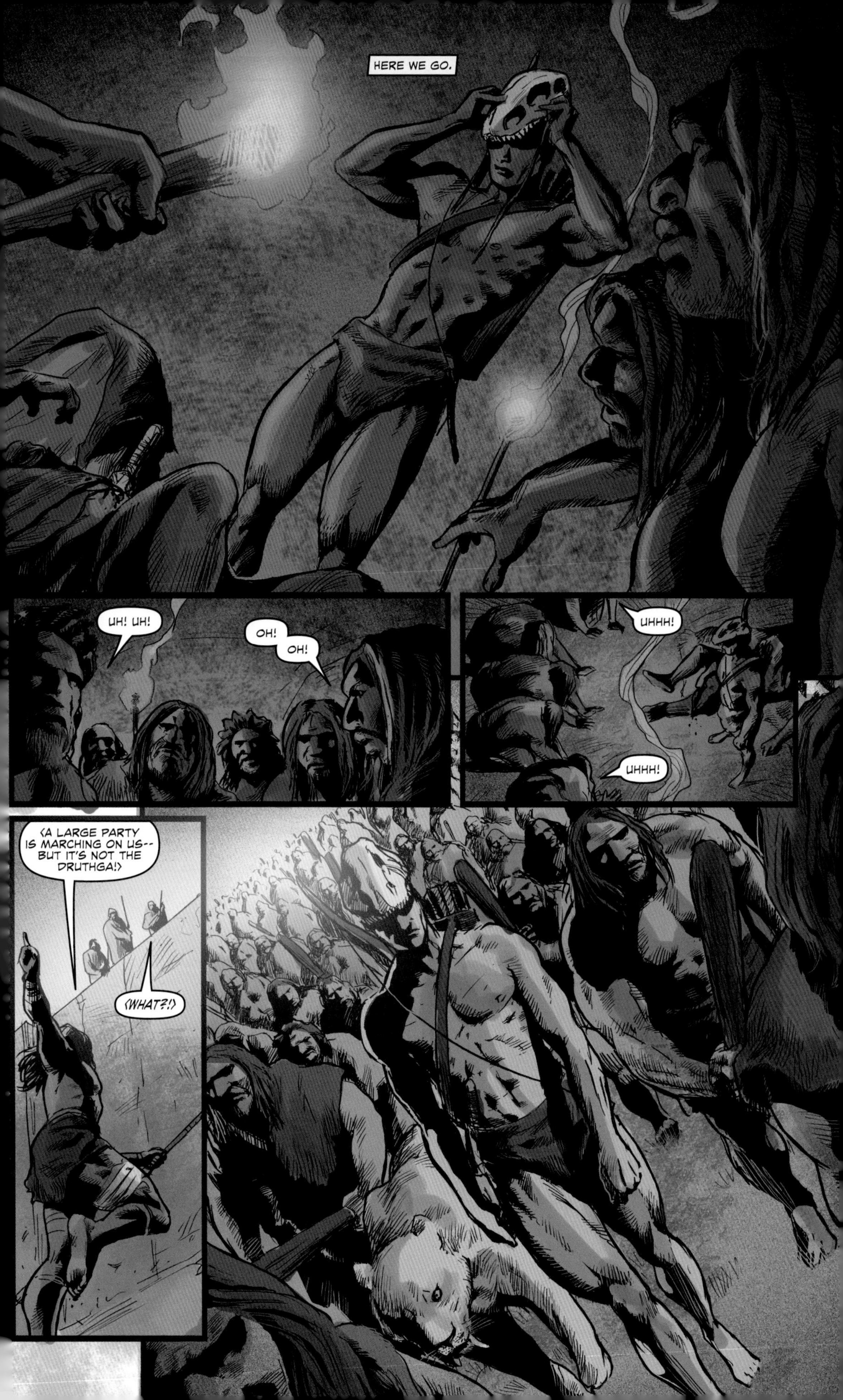
HERE WE GO.
UH! UH!
OH!
OH!
UHHH!
UHHH!
‹A LARGE PARTY IS MARCHING ON US-- BUT IT'S NOT THE DRUTHGA!›
‹WHAT?!›

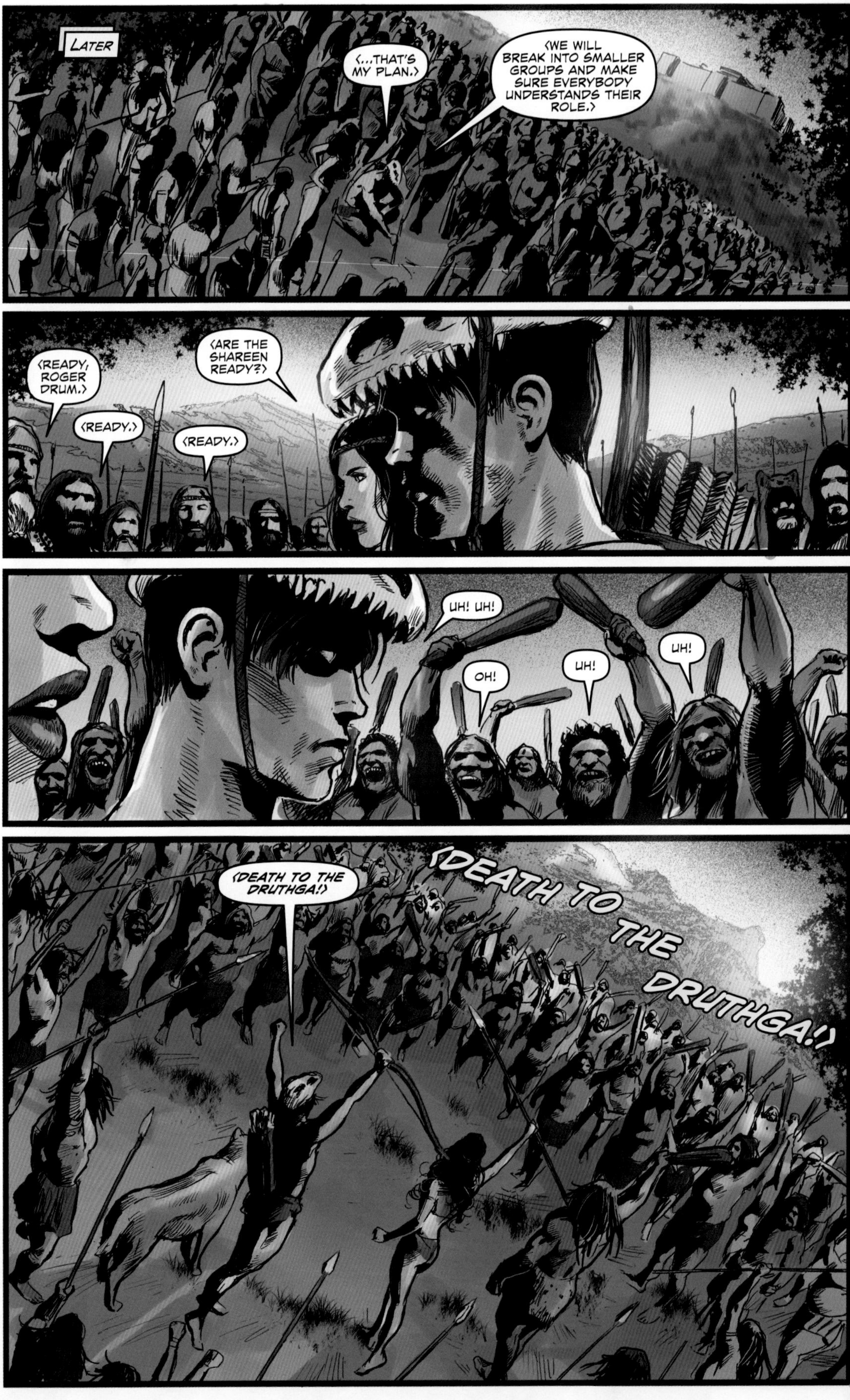
LATER
‹...THAT'S MY PLAN.›
‹WE WILL BREAK INTO SMALLER GROUPS AND MAKE SURE EVERYBODY UNDERSTANDS THEIR ROLE.›
‹ARE THE SHAREEN READY?›
‹READY, ROGER DRUM.›
‹READY.›
‹READY.›
UH! UH!
OH!
UH!
UH!
‹DEATH TO THE DRUTHGA!›
‹DEATH TO THE DRUTHGA!›

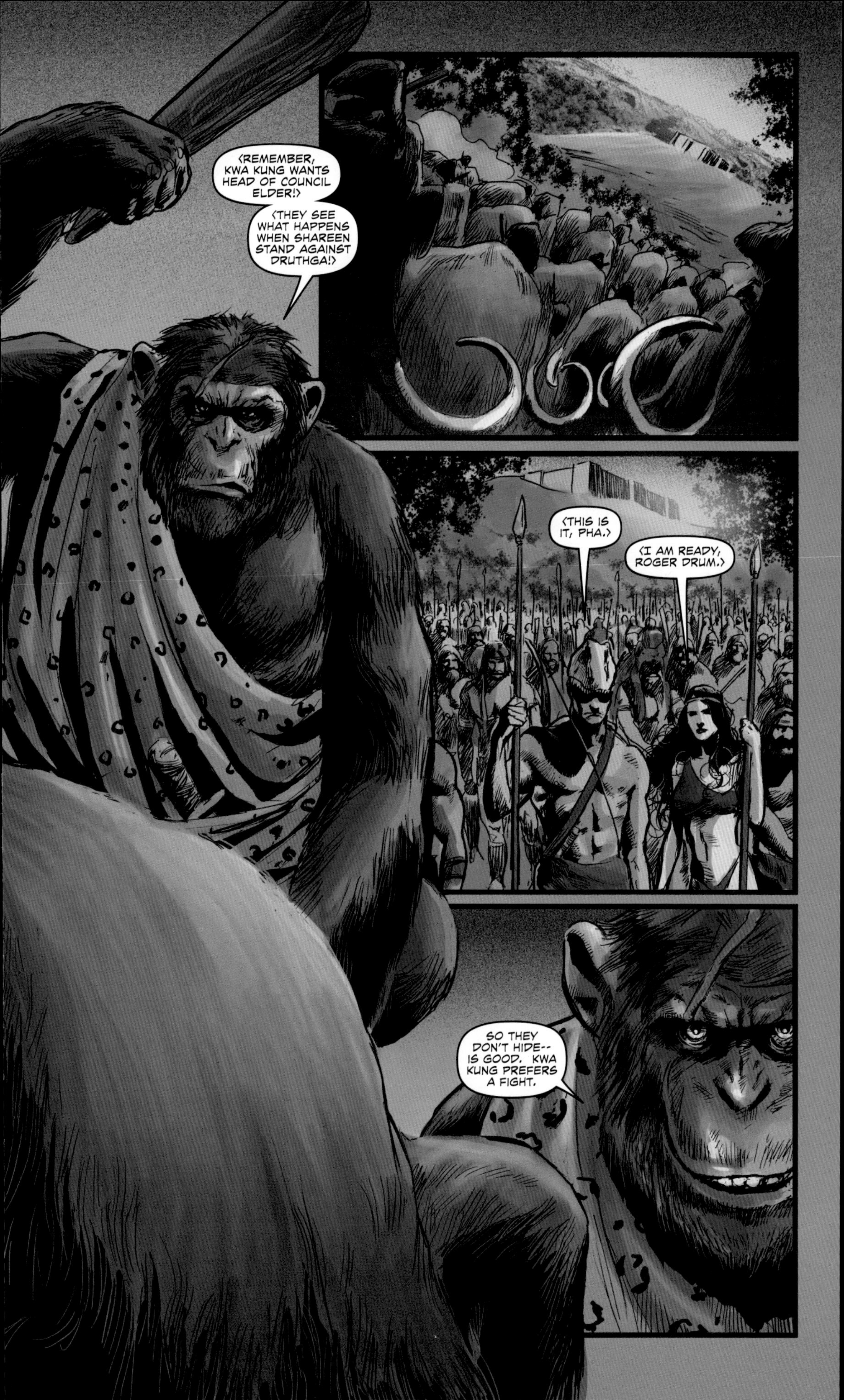
<REMEMBER, KWA KUNG WANTS HEAD OF COUNCIL ELDER!>
<THEY SEE WHAT HAPPENS WHEN SHAREEN STAND AGAINST DRUTHGA!>
<THIS IS IT, PHA.>
<I AM READY, ROGER DRUM.>
SO THEY DON'T HIDE--IS GOOD. KWA KUNG PREFERS A FIGHT.

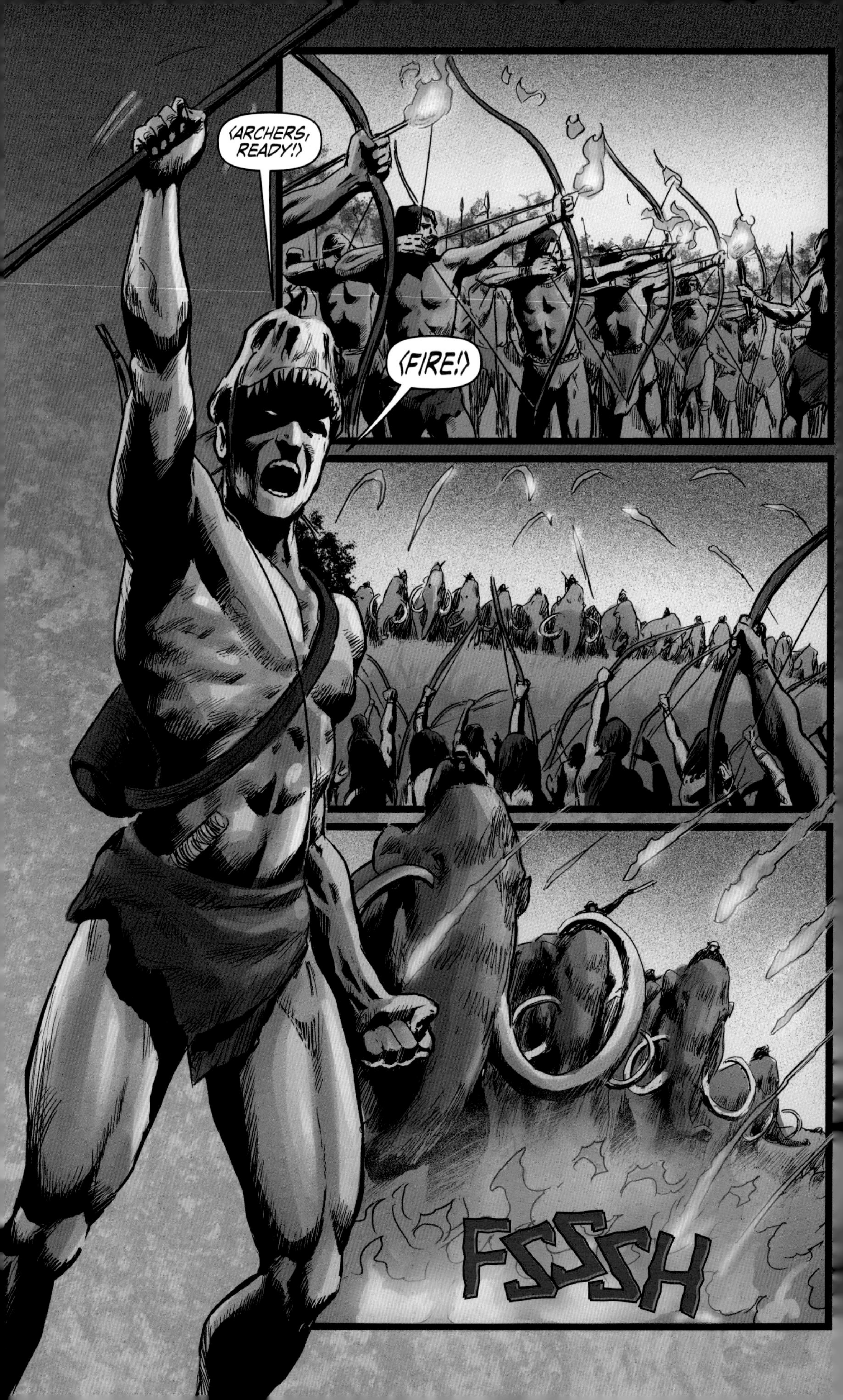

⟨ARCHERS, READY!⟩
⟨FIRE!⟩
FSSSH

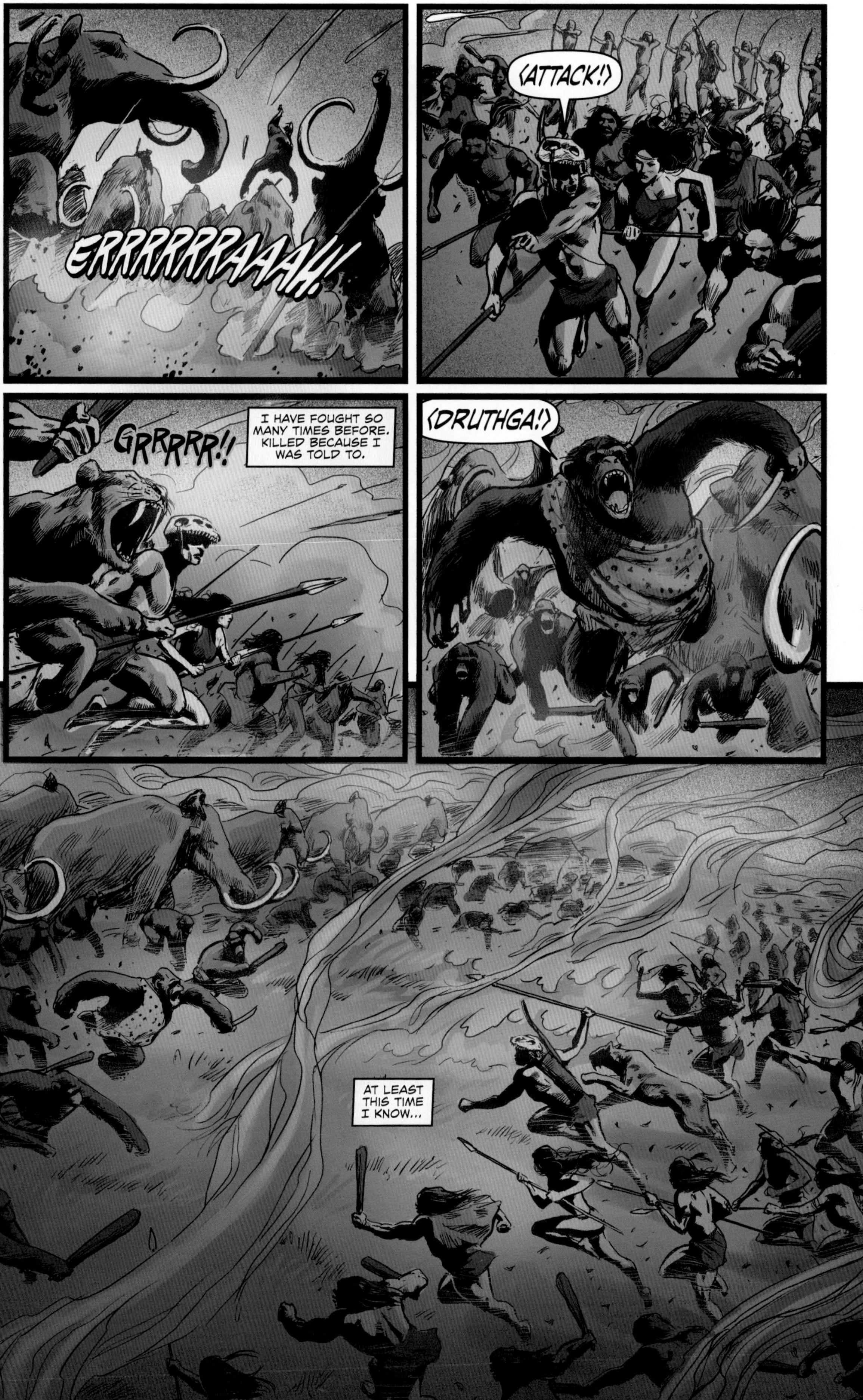
ERRRRRRAAAH!!
‹ATTACK!›
GRRRRR!!
I HAVE FOUGHT SO MANY TIMES BEFORE. KILLED BECAUSE I WAS TOLD TO.
‹DRUTHGA!›
AT LEAST THIS TIME I KNOW...

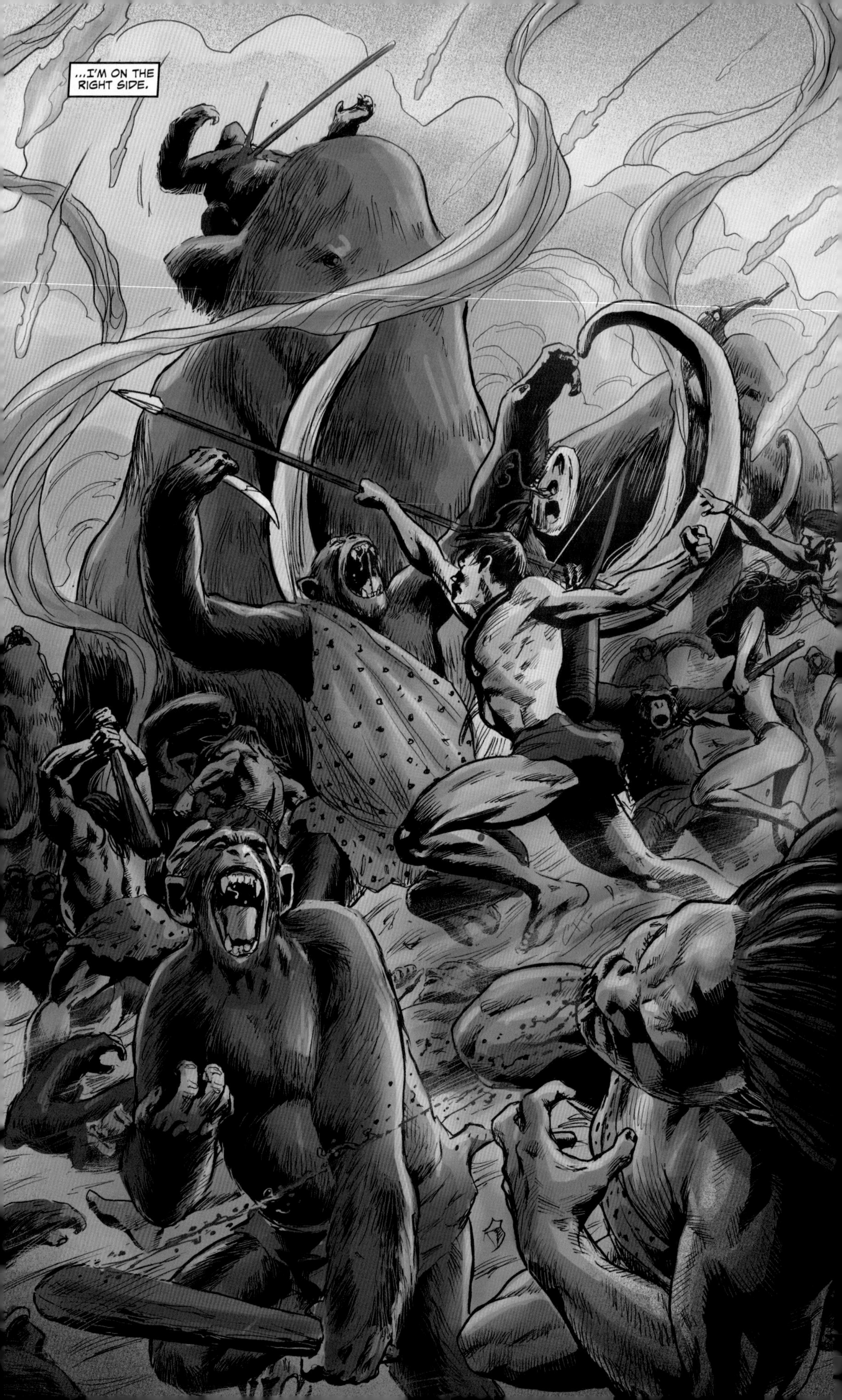
...I'M ON THE RIGHT SIDE.

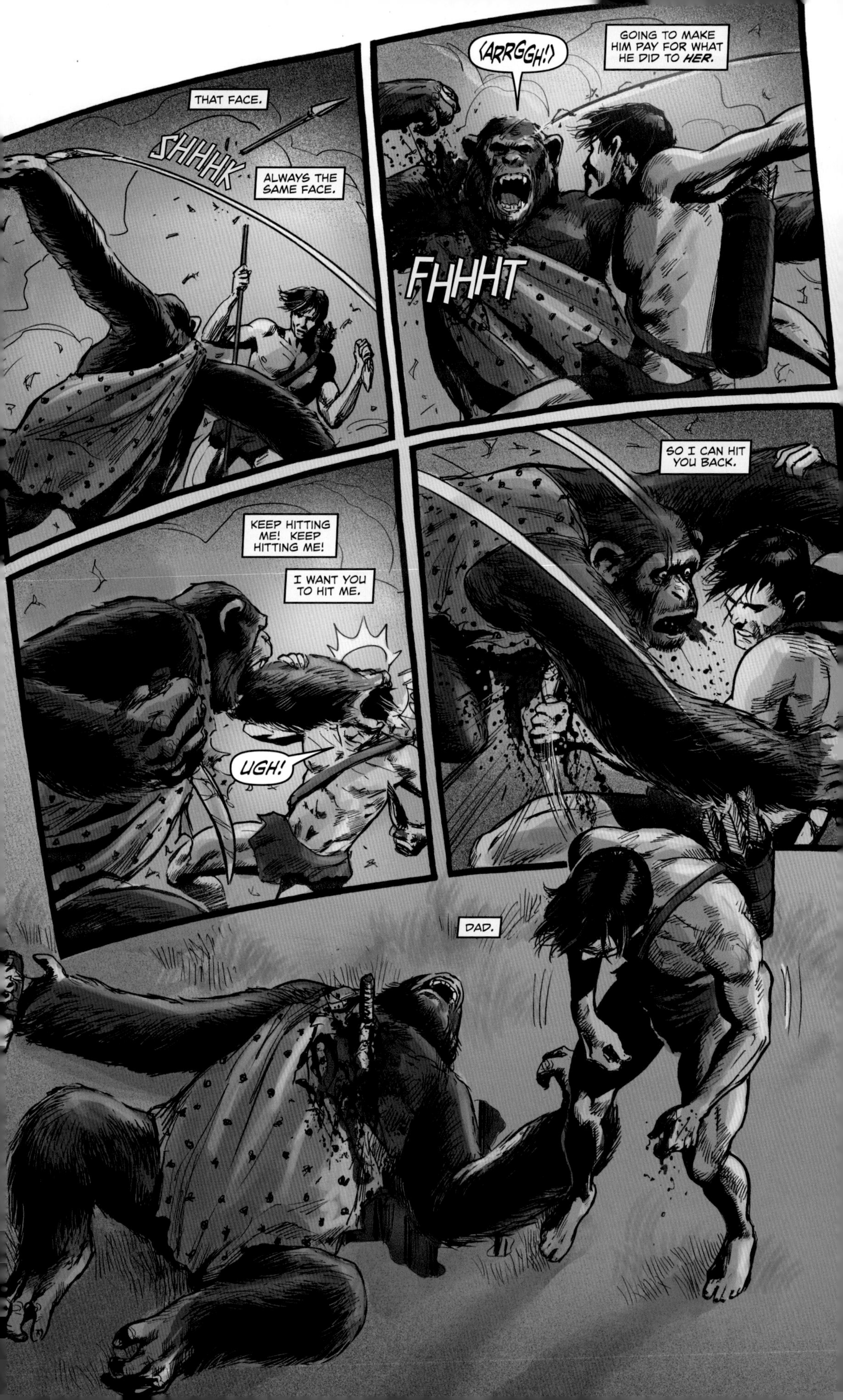
THAT FACE.
SHHHK
ALWAYS THE SAME FACE.
‹ARRGGH!›
GOING TO MAKE HIM PAY FOR WHAT HE DID TO HER.
FHHHT
KEEP HITTING ME! KEEP HITTING ME!
I WANT YOU TO HIT ME.
UGH!
SO I CAN HIT YOU BACK.
DAD.

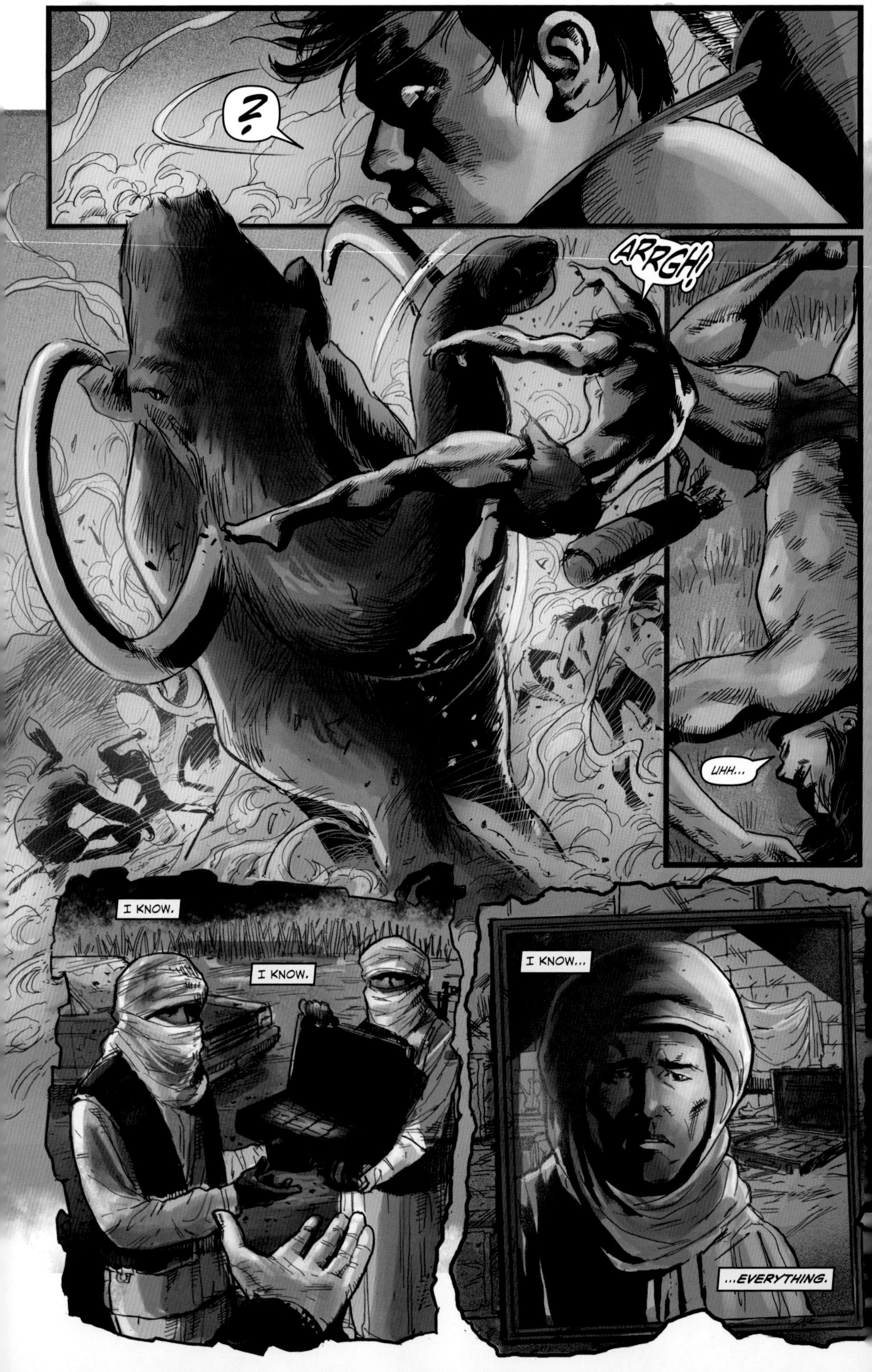

?
ARRGH!
UHH...
I KNOW.
I KNOW.
I KNOW...
...EVERYTHING.

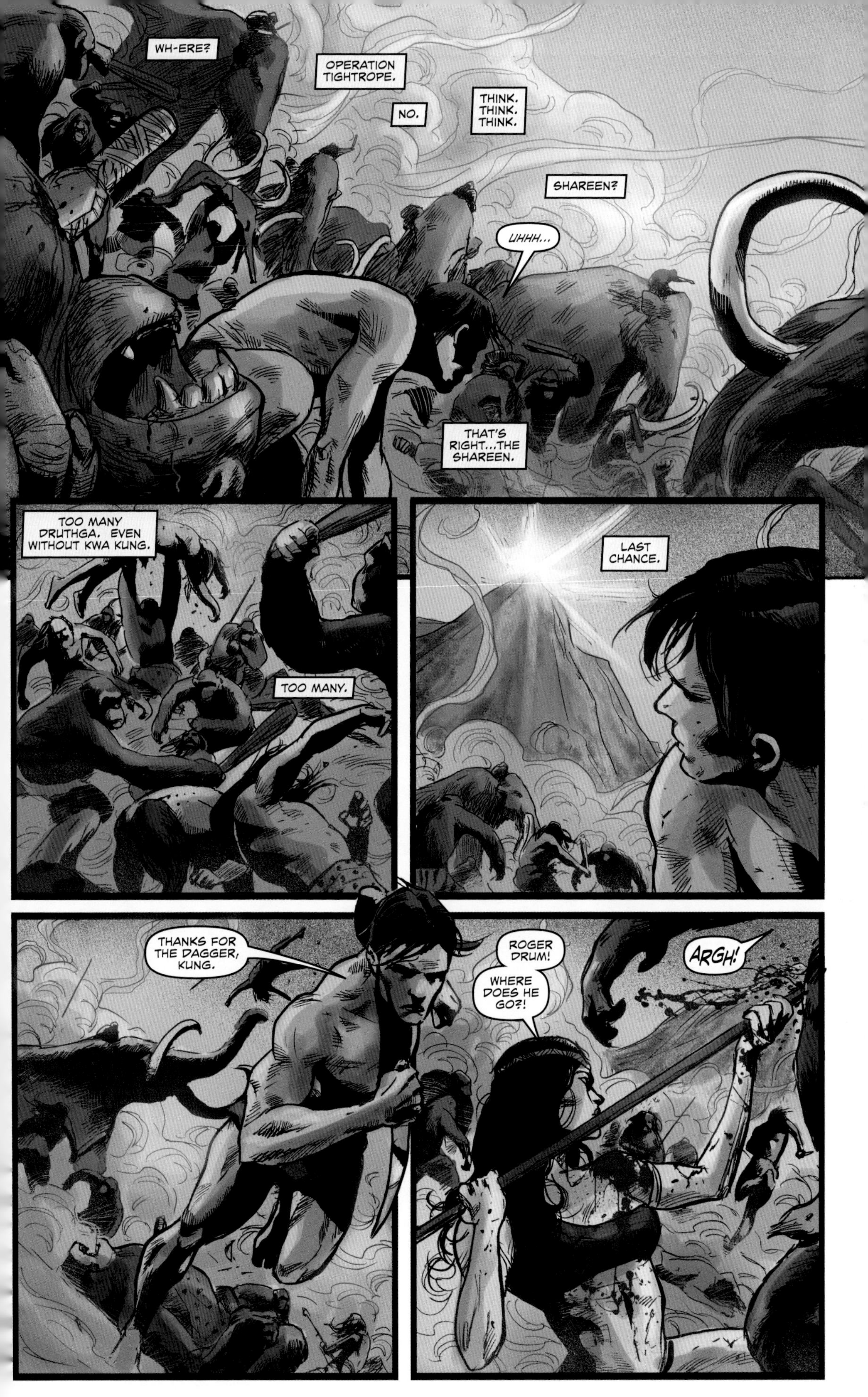
WH-ERE?
OPERATION TIGHTROPE.
NO.
THINK. THINK. THINK.
SHAREEN?
UHHH...
THAT'S RIGHT...THE SHAREEN.
TOO MANY DRUTHGA. EVEN WITHOUT KWA KUNG.
TOO MANY.
LAST CHANCE.
THANKS FOR THE DAGGER, KUNG.
ROGER DRUM!
WHERE DOES HE GO?!
ARGH!

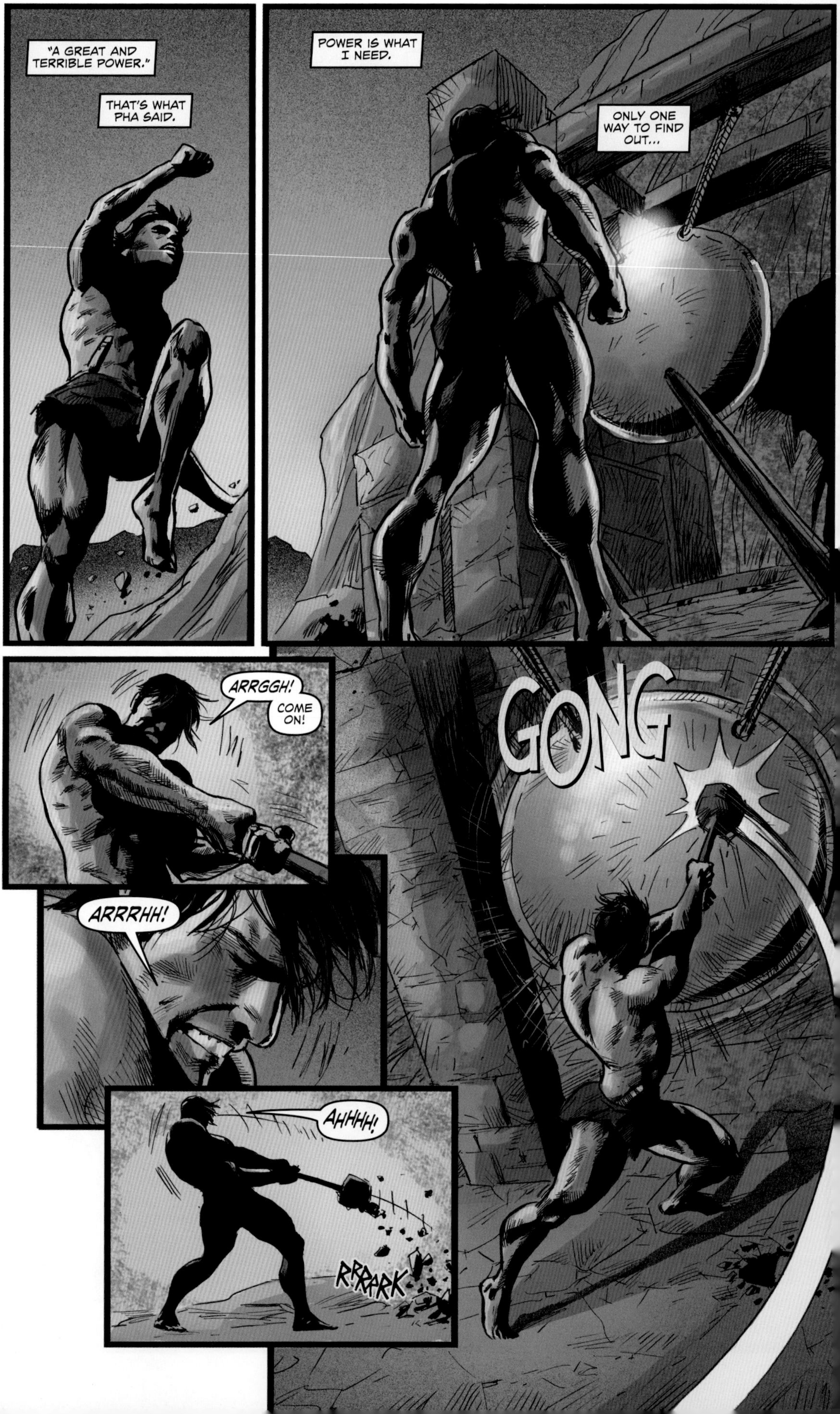
"A GREAT AND TERRIBLE POWER."
THAT'S WHAT PHA SAID.
POWER IS WHAT I NEED.
ONLY ONE WAY TO FIND OUT...
ARRGGH!
COME ON!
ARRRHH!
AHHHH!
RRRARK
GONG

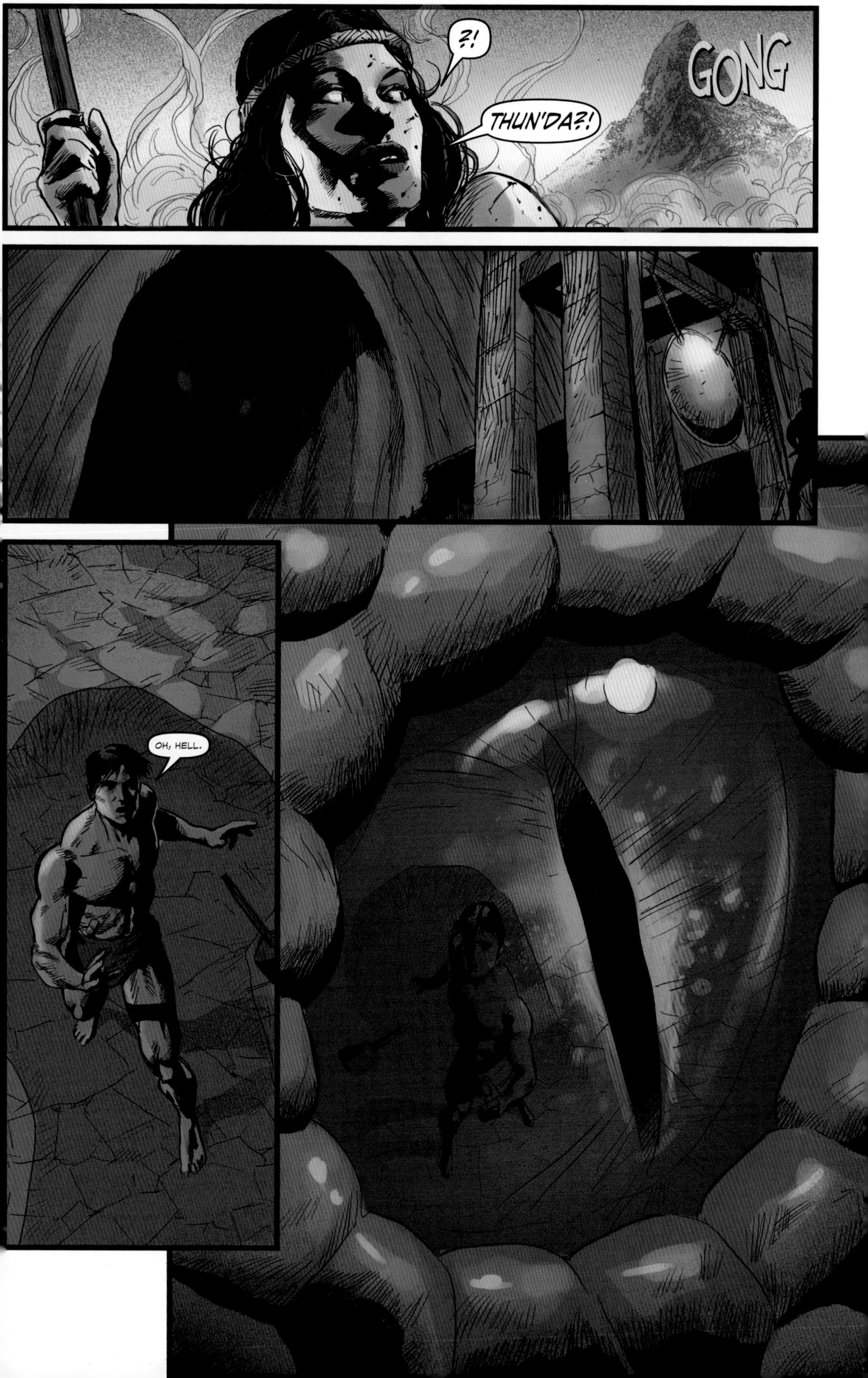
?!
THUN'DA?!
GONG
OH, HELL.

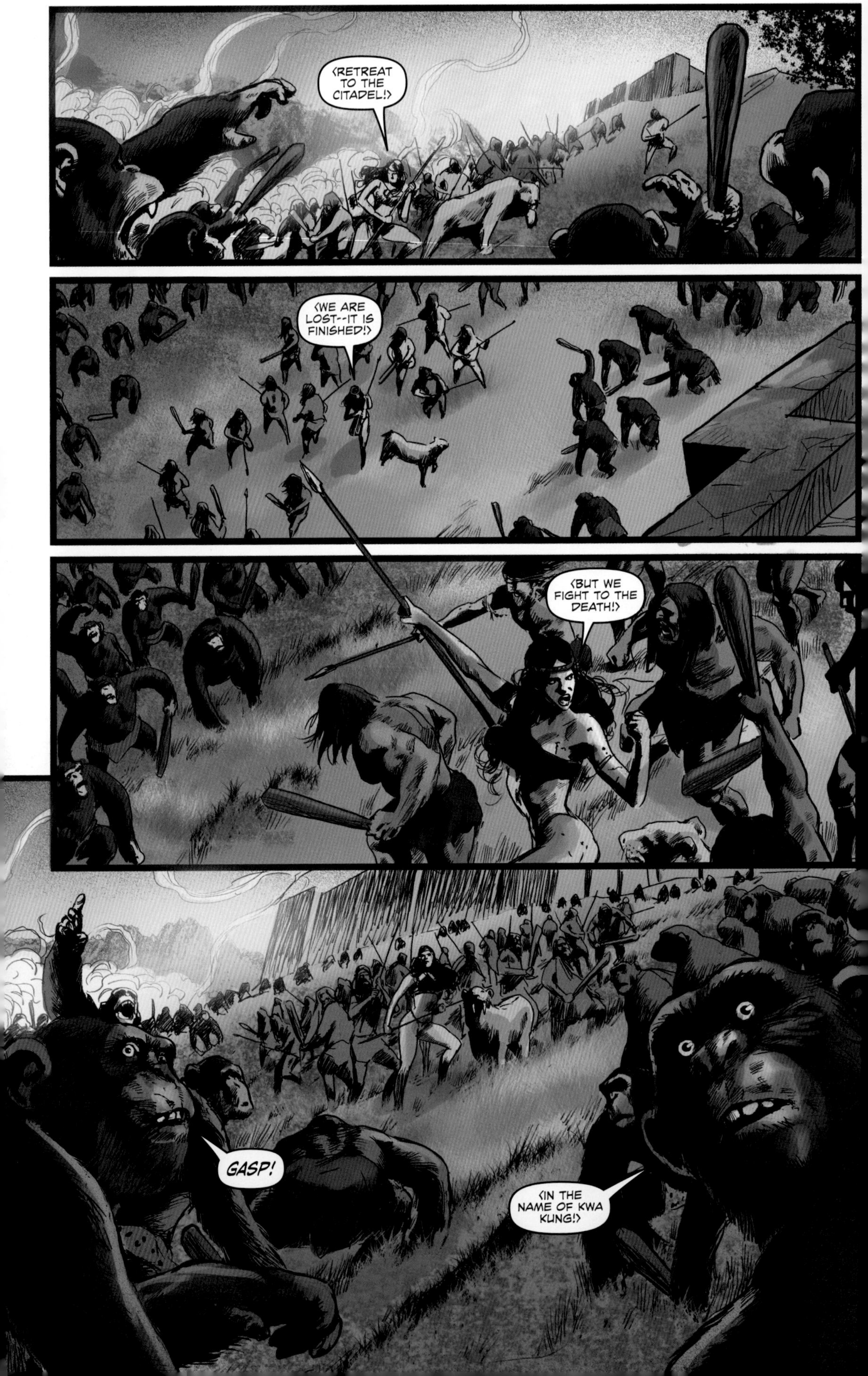

‹RETREAT TO THE CITADEL!›
‹WE ARE LOST--IT IS FINISHED!›
‹BUT WE FIGHT TO THE DEATH!›
GASP!
‹IN THE NAME OF KWA KUNG!›

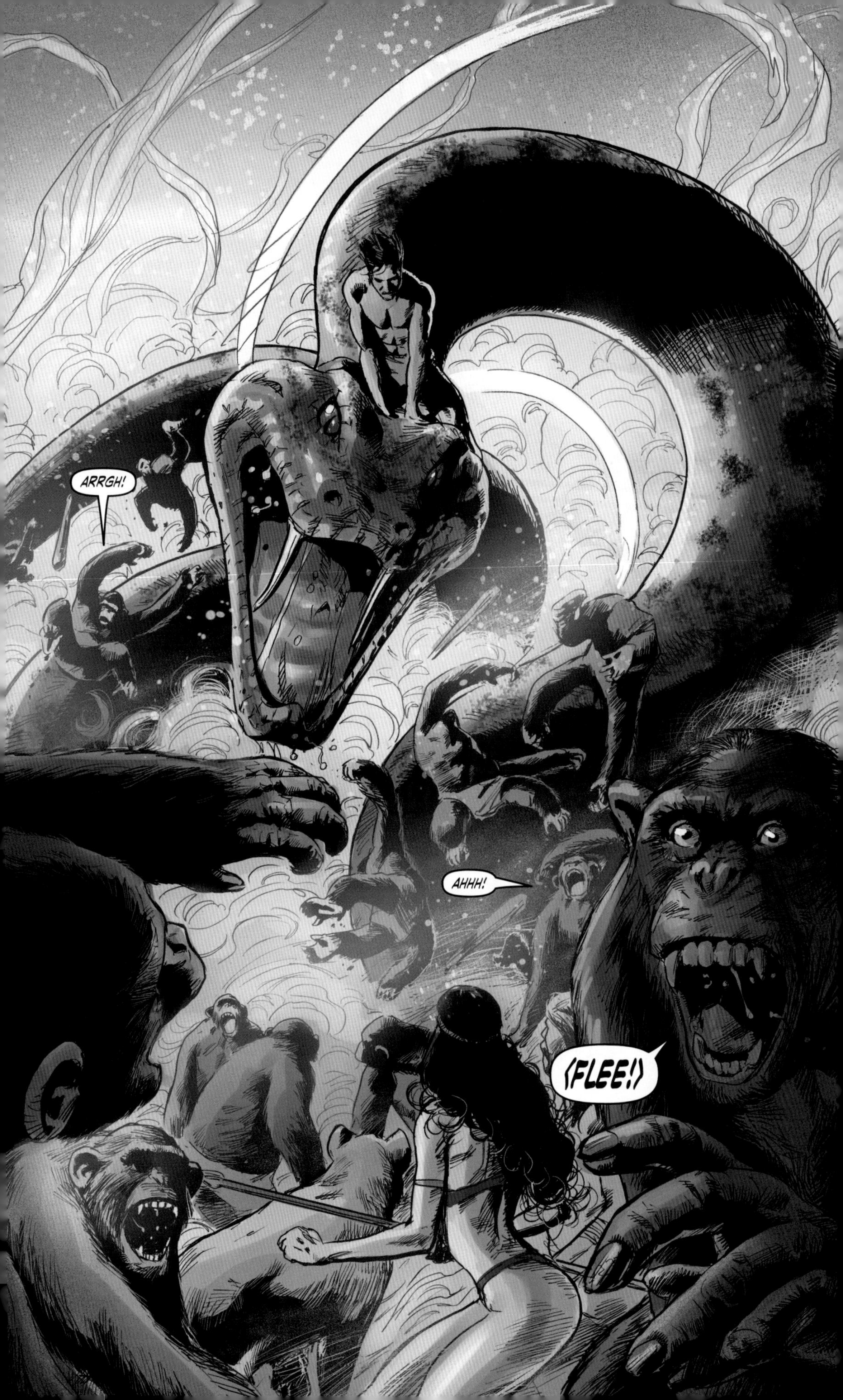
ARRGH!
AHHH!
⟨FLEE!⟩

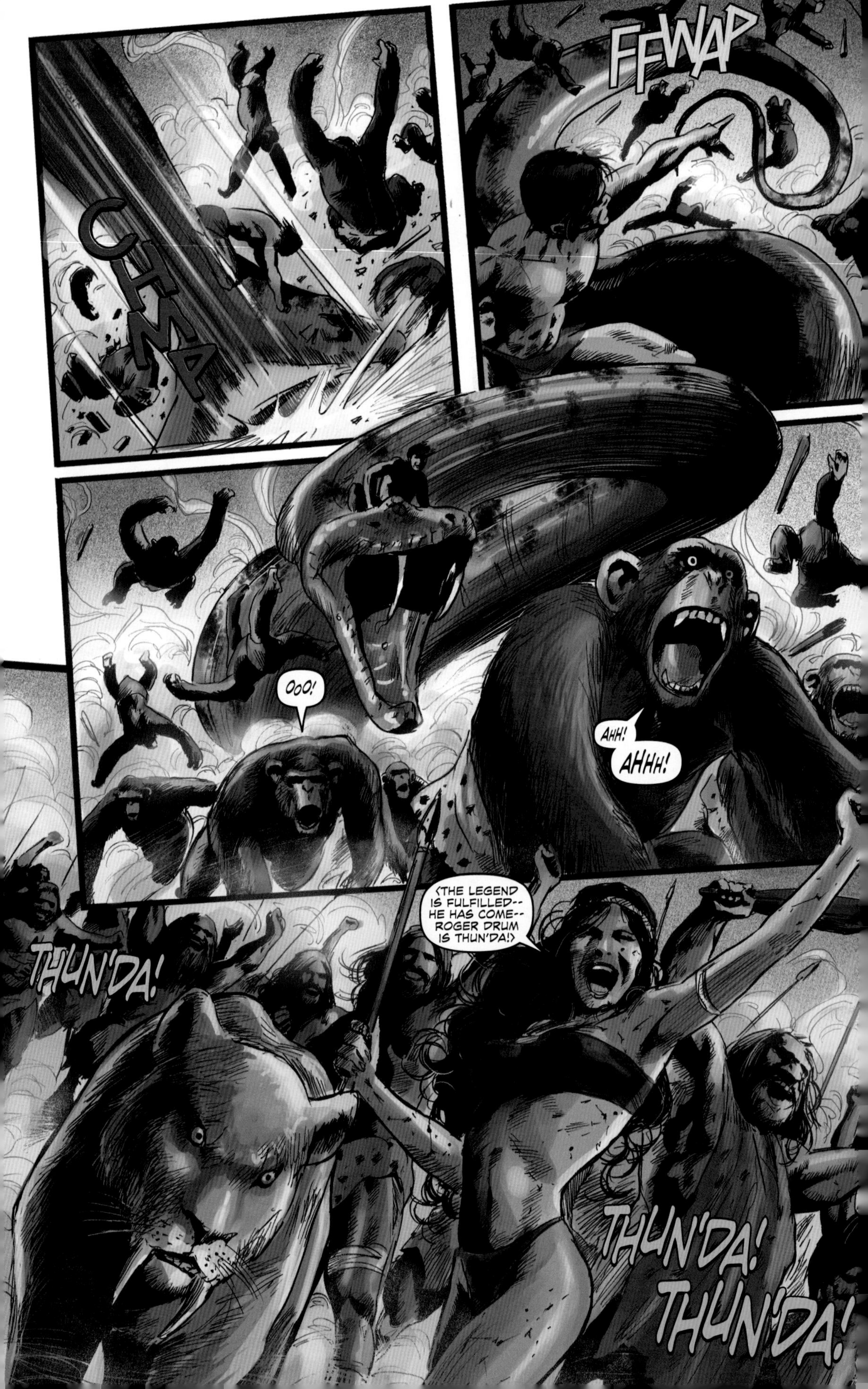
CHMP
FFWAP
OOO!
AHH! AHHH!
<THE LEGEND IS FULFILLED-- HE HAS COME-- ROGER DRUM IS THUN'DA!>
THUN'DA!
THUN'DA! THUN'DA!

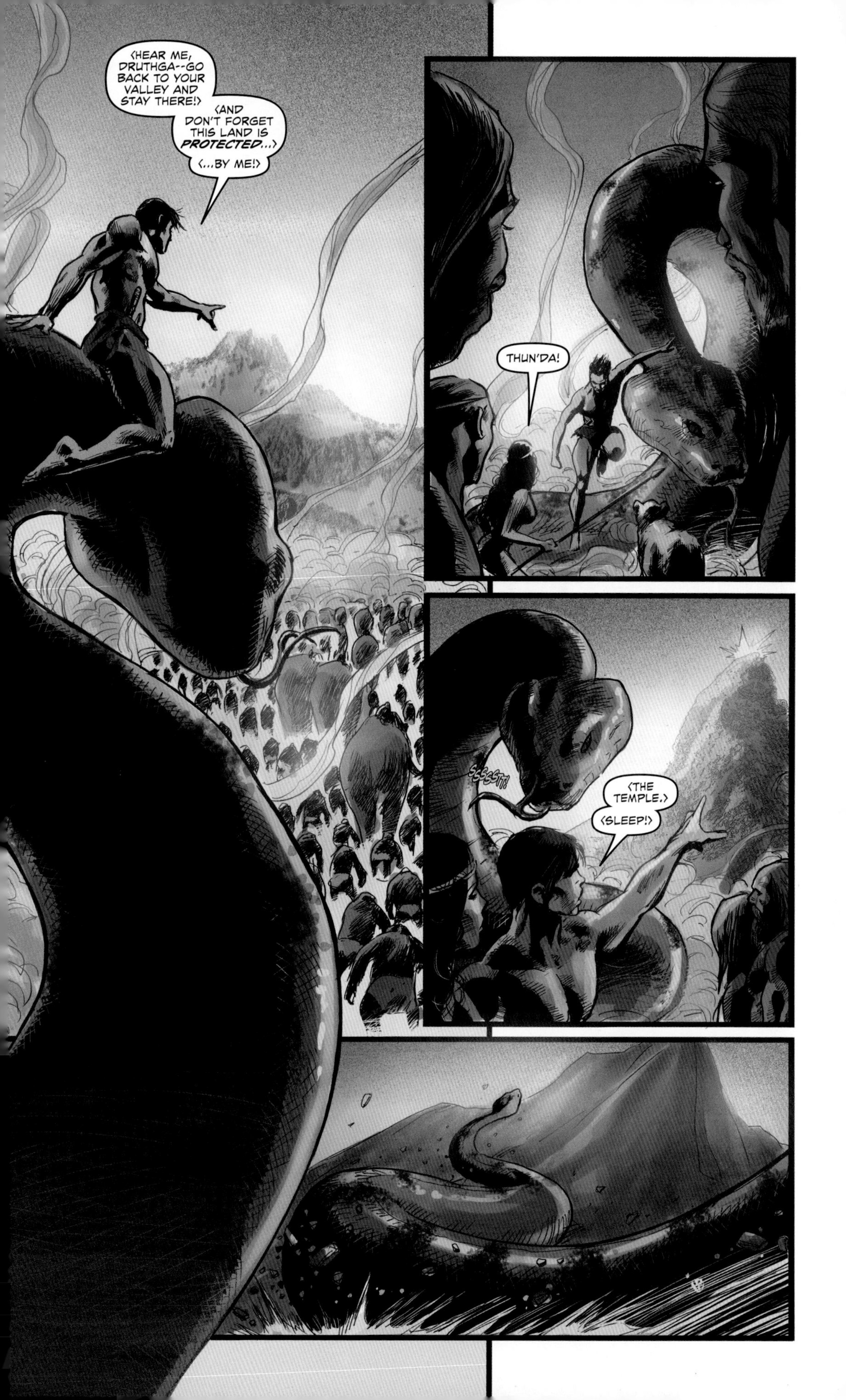
‹HEAR ME, DRUTHGA--GO BACK TO YOUR VALLEY AND STAY THERE!›
‹AND DON'T FORGET THIS LAND IS *PROTECTED*...›
‹...BY ME!›
THUN'DA!
SSSSSTT!
‹THE TEMPLE.›
‹SLEEP!›

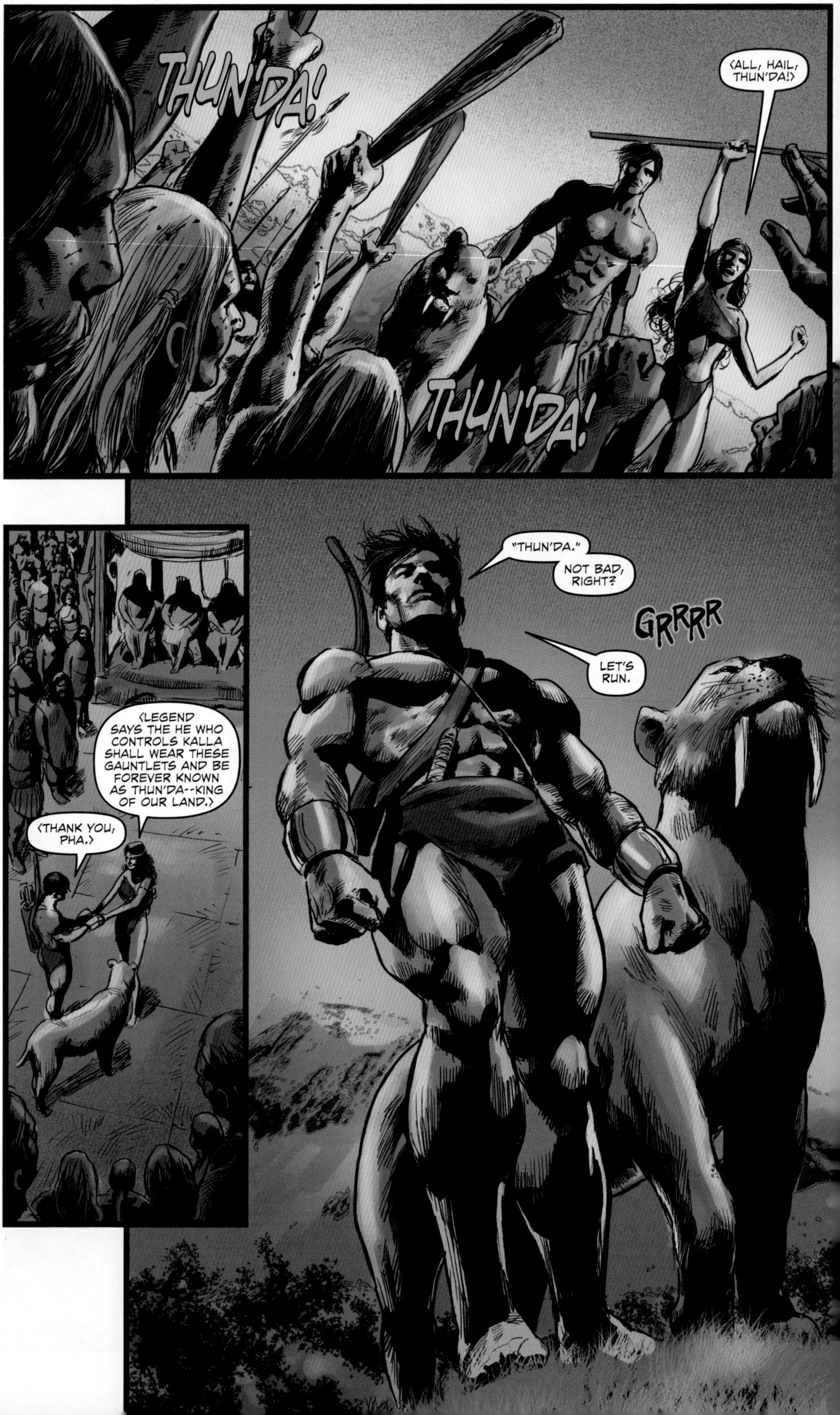
THUN'DA!
‹ALL, HAIL, THUN'DA!›
THUN'DA!
‹LEGEND SAYS THE HE WHO CONTROLS KALLA SHALL WEAR THESE GAUNTLETS AND BE FOREVER KNOWN AS THUN'DA--KING OF OUR LAND.›
‹THANK YOU, PHA.›
"THUN'DA."
NOT BAD, RIGHT?
GRRRR
LET'S RUN.

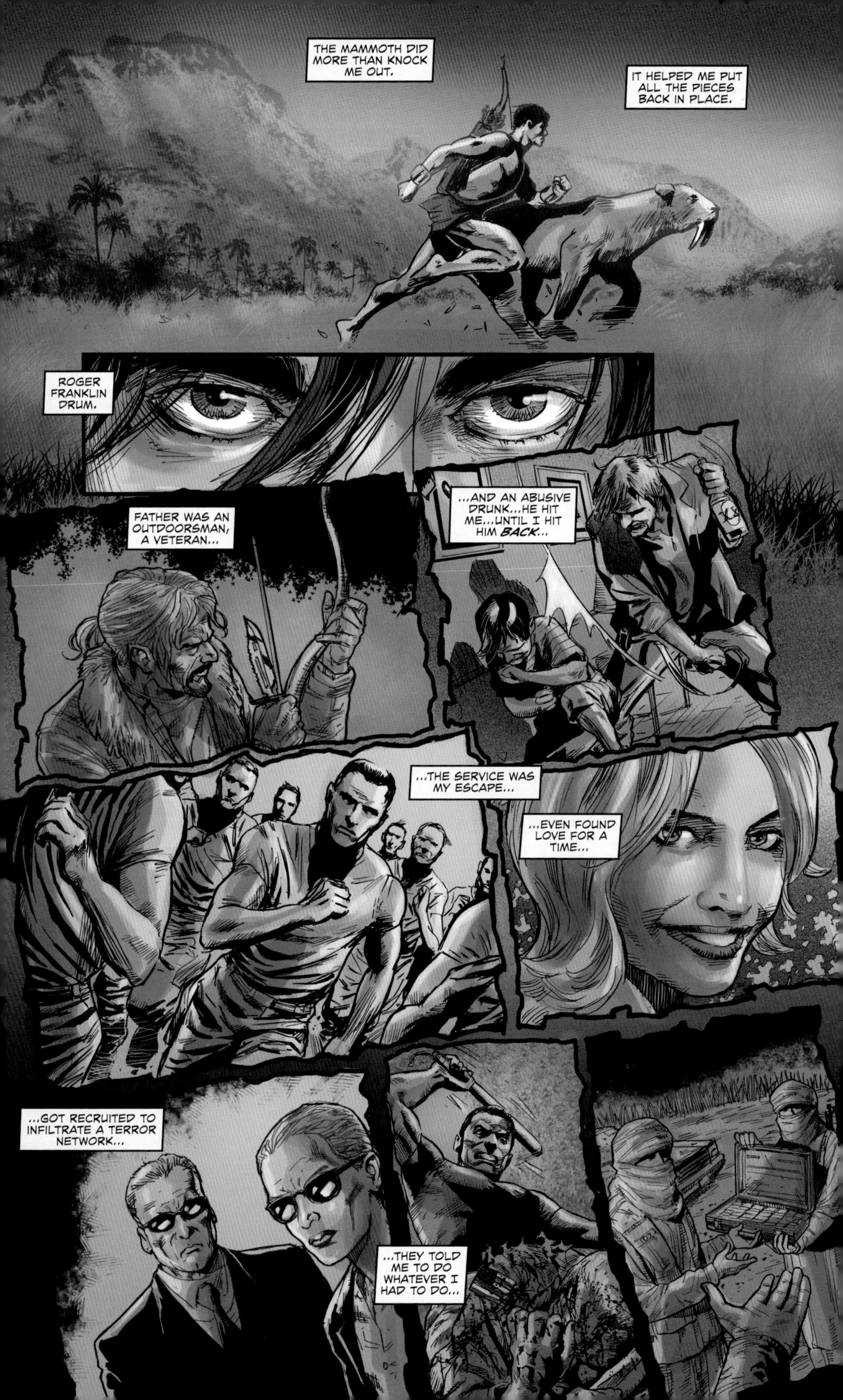
THE MAMMOTH DID MORE THAN KNOCK ME OUT.
IT HELPED ME PUT ALL THE PIECES BACK IN PLACE.
ROGER FRANKLIN DRUM.
FATHER WAS AN OUTDOORSMAN, A VETERAN...
...AND AN ABUSIVE DRUNK...HE HIT ME...UNTIL I HIT HIM *BACK*...
...THE SERVICE WAS MY ESCAPE...
...EVEN FOUND LOVE FOR A TIME...
...GOT RECRUITED TO INFILTRATE A TERROR NETWORK...
...THEY TOLD ME TO DO WHATEVER I HAD TO DO...

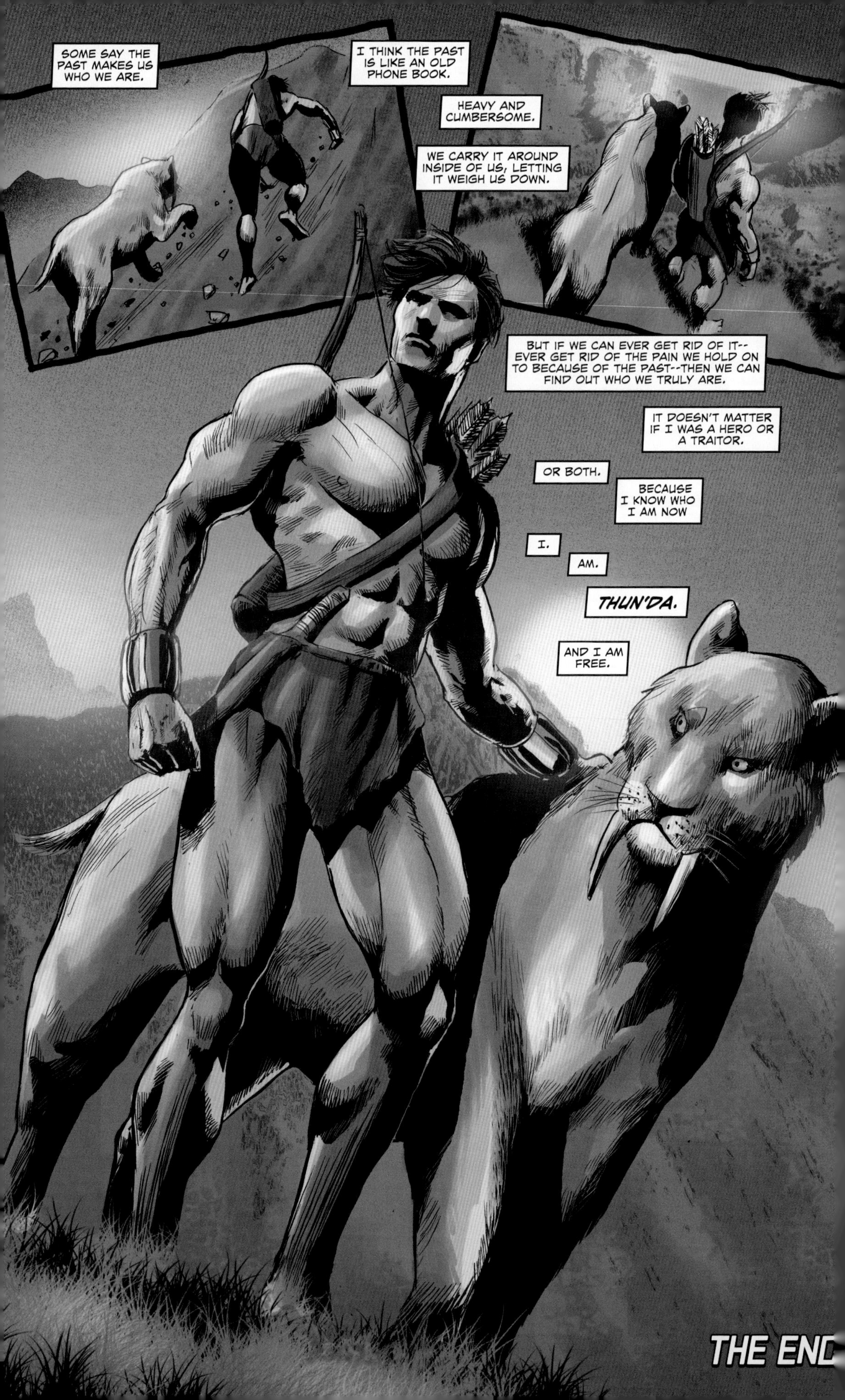
SOME SAY THE PAST MAKES US WHO WE ARE.
I THINK THE PAST IS LIKE AN OLD PHONE BOOK.
HEAVY AND CUMBERSOME.
WE CARRY IT AROUND INSIDE OF US, LETTING IT WEIGH US DOWN.
BUT IF WE CAN EVER GET RID OF IT-- EVER GET RID OF THE PAIN WE HOLD ON TO BECAUSE OF THE PAST--THEN WE CAN FIND OUT WHO WE TRULY ARE.
IT DOESN'T MATTER IF I WAS A HERO OR A TRAITOR.
OR BOTH.
BECAUSE I KNOW WHO I AM NOW
I.
AM.
THUN'DA.
AND I AM FREE.
THE END

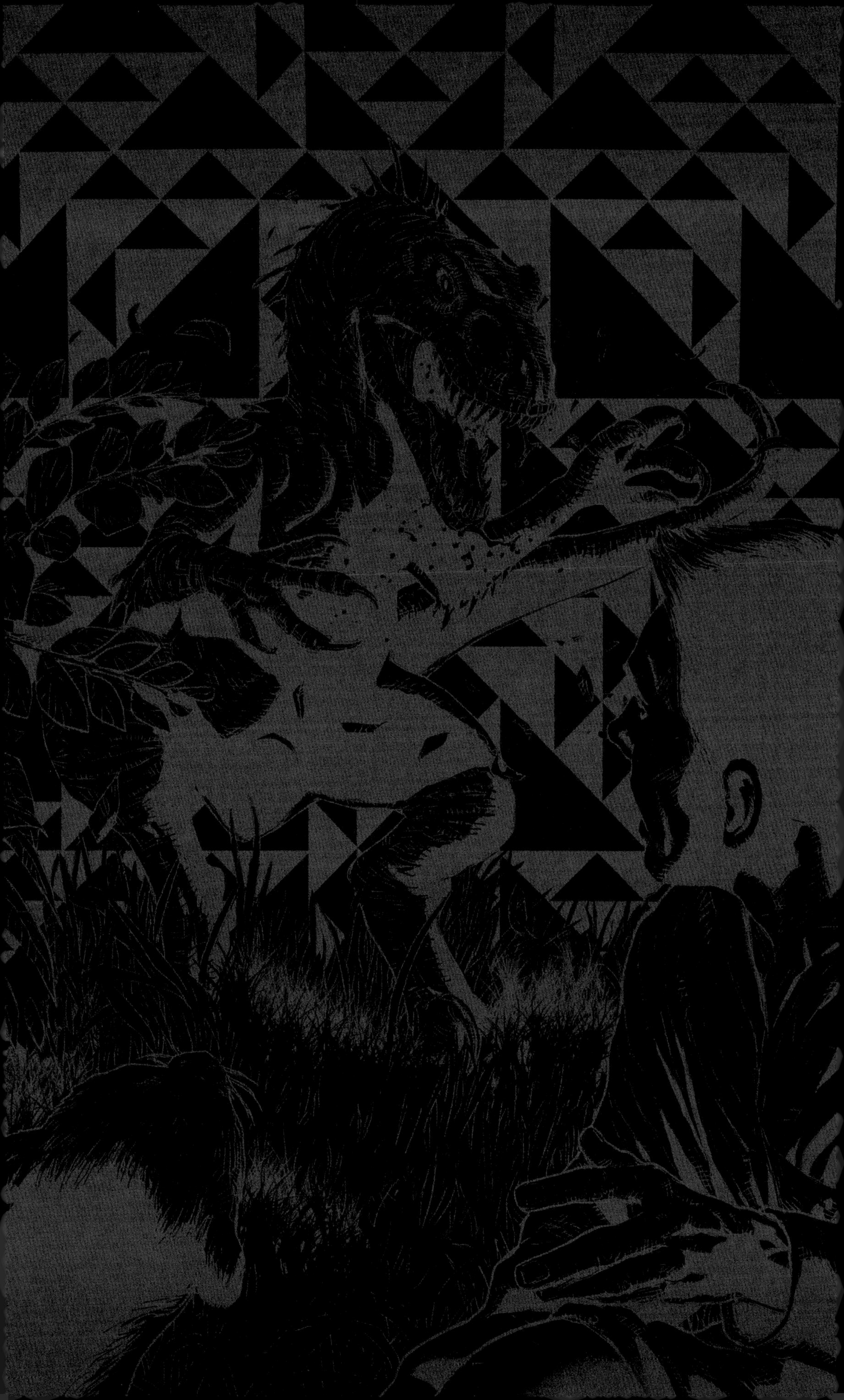

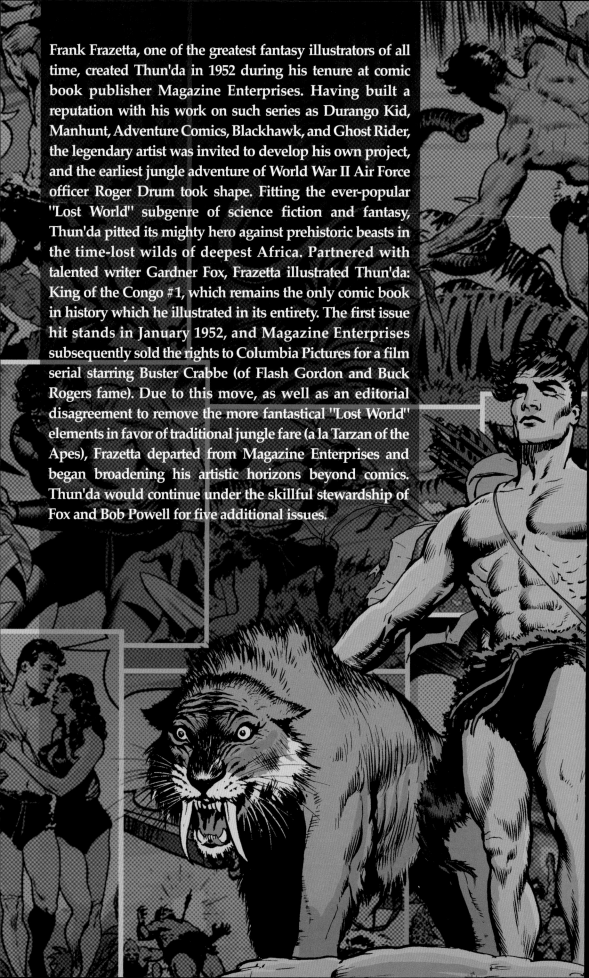

Frank Frazetta, one of the greatest fantasy illustrators of all time, created Thun'da in 1952 during his tenure at comic book publisher Magazine Enterprises. Having built a reputation with his work on such series as Durango Kid, Manhunt, Adventure Comics, Blackhawk, and Ghost Rider, the legendary artist was invited to develop his own project, and the earliest jungle adventure of World War II Air Force officer Roger Drum took shape. Fitting the ever-popular "Lost World" subgenre of science fiction and fantasy, Thun'da pitted its mighty hero against prehistoric beasts in the time-lost wilds of deepest Africa. Partnered with talented writer Gardner Fox, Frazetta illustrated Thun'da: King of the Congo #1, which remains the only comic book in history which he illustrated in its entirety. The first issue hit stands in January 1952, and Magazine Enterprises subsequently sold the rights to Columbia Pictures for a film serial starring Buster Crabbe (of Flash Gordon and Buck Rogers fame). Due to this move, as well as an editorial disagreement to remove the more fantastical "Lost World" elements in favor of traditional jungle fare (a la Tarzan of the Apes), Frazetta departed from Magazine Enterprises and began broadening his artistic horizons beyond comics. Thun'da would continue under the skillful stewardship of Fox and Bob Powell for five additional issues.

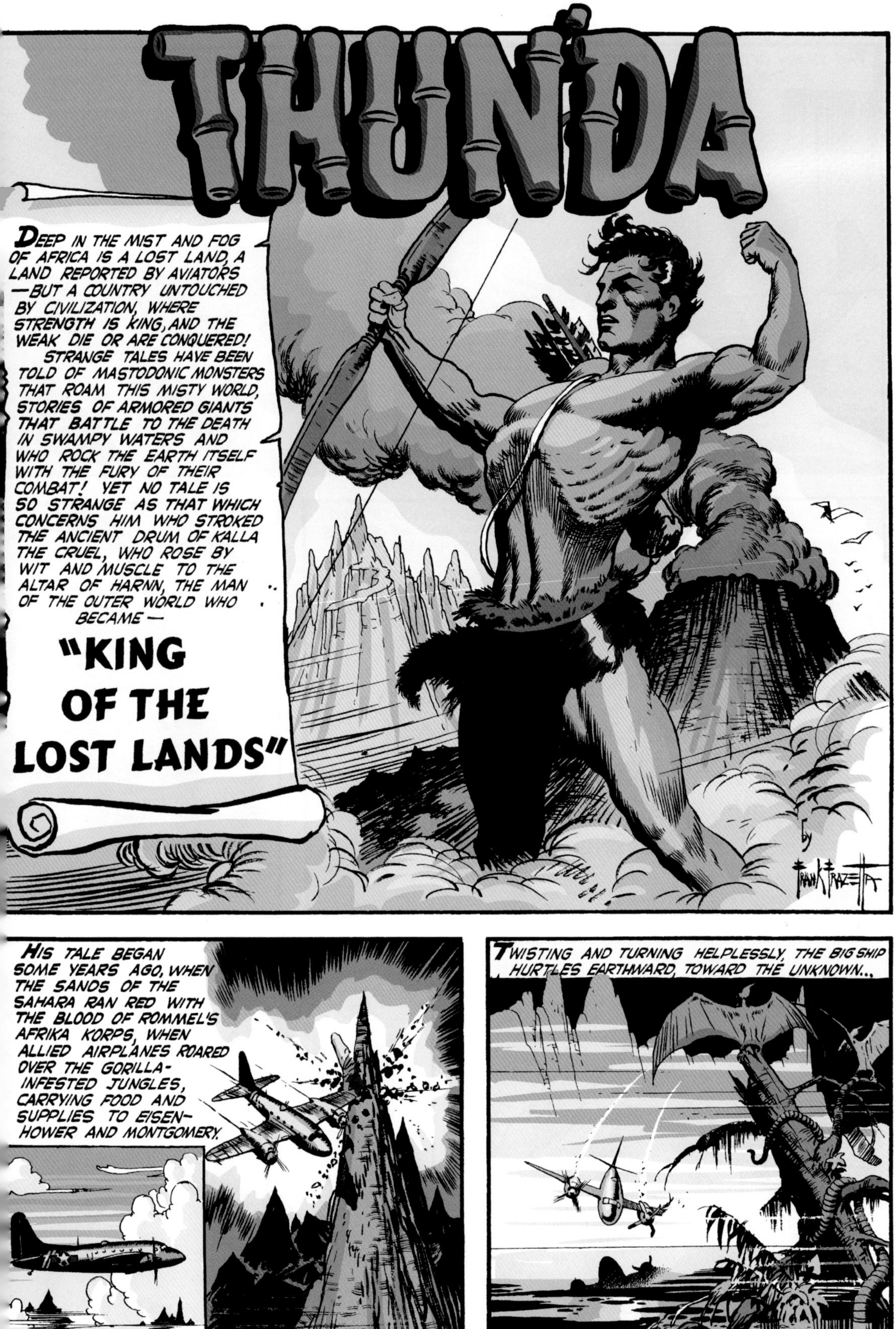
THUN'DA
DEEP IN THE MIST AND FOG OF AFRICA IS A LOST LAND, A LAND REPORTED BY AVIATORS —BUT A COUNTRY UNTOUCHED BY CIVILIZATION, WHERE STRENGTH IS KING, AND THE WEAK DIE OR ARE CONQUERED! STRANGE TALES HAVE BEEN TOLD OF MASTODONIC MONSTERS THAT ROAM THIS MISTY WORLD, STORIES OF ARMORED GIANTS THAT BATTLE TO THE DEATH IN SWAMPY WATERS AND WHO ROCK THE EARTH ITSELF WITH THE FURY OF THEIR COMBAT! YET NO TALE IS SO STRANGE AS THAT WHICH CONCERNS HIM WHO STROKED THE ANCIENT DRUM OF KALLA THE CRUEL, WHO ROSE BY WIT AND MUSCLE TO THE ALTAR OF HARNN, THE MAN OF THE OUTER WORLD WHO BECAME —
"KING OF THE LOST LANDS"
by FRANK FRAZETTA
HIS TALE BEGAN SOME YEARS AGO, WHEN THE SANDS OF THE SAHARA RAN RED WITH THE BLOOD OF ROMMEL'S AFRIKA KORPS, WHEN ALLIED AIRPLANES ROARED OVER THE GORILLA-INFESTED JUNGLES, CARRYING FOOD AND SUPPLIES TO EISENHOWER AND MONTGOMERY.
TWISTING AND TURNING HELPLESSLY, THE BIG SHIP HURTLES EARTHWARD, TOWARD THE UNKNOWN...

Writer: **GARDNER FOX** • Artist: **FRANK FRAZETTA**
Re-mastering and colors by: **MIKE KELLEHER**

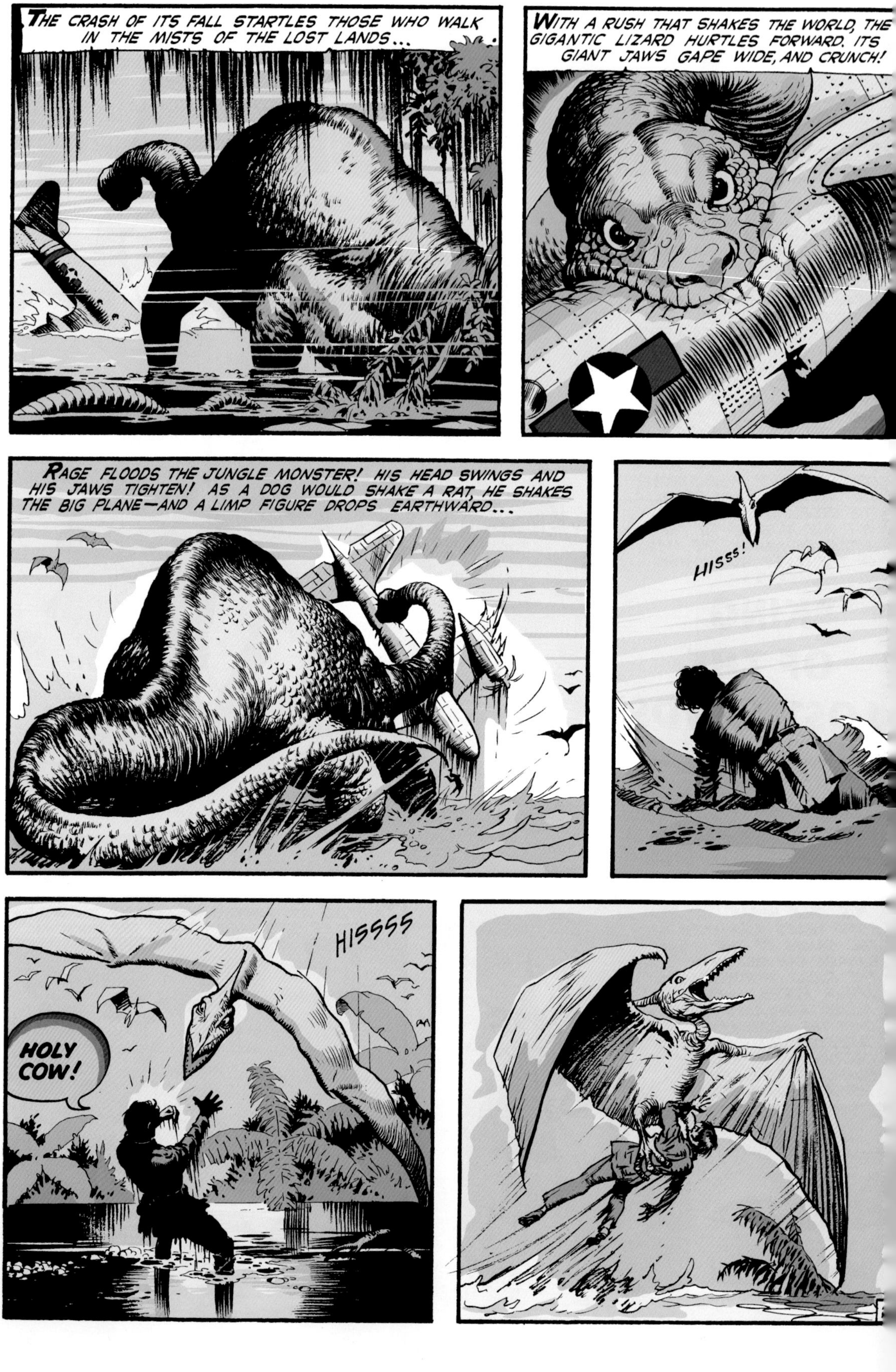
THE CRASH OF ITS FALL STARTLES THOSE WHO WALK IN THE MISTS OF THE LOST LANDS...
WITH A RUSH THAT SHAKES THE WORLD, THE GIGANTIC LIZARD HURTLES FORWARD. ITS GIANT JAWS GAPE WIDE, AND CRUNCH!
RAGE FLOODS THE JUNGLE MONSTER! HIS HEAD SWINGS AND HIS JAWS TIGHTEN! AS A DOG WOULD SHAKE A RAT, HE SHAKES THE BIG PLANE—AND A LIMP FIGURE DROPS EARTHWARD...
HISSS!
HISSSS
HOLY COW!

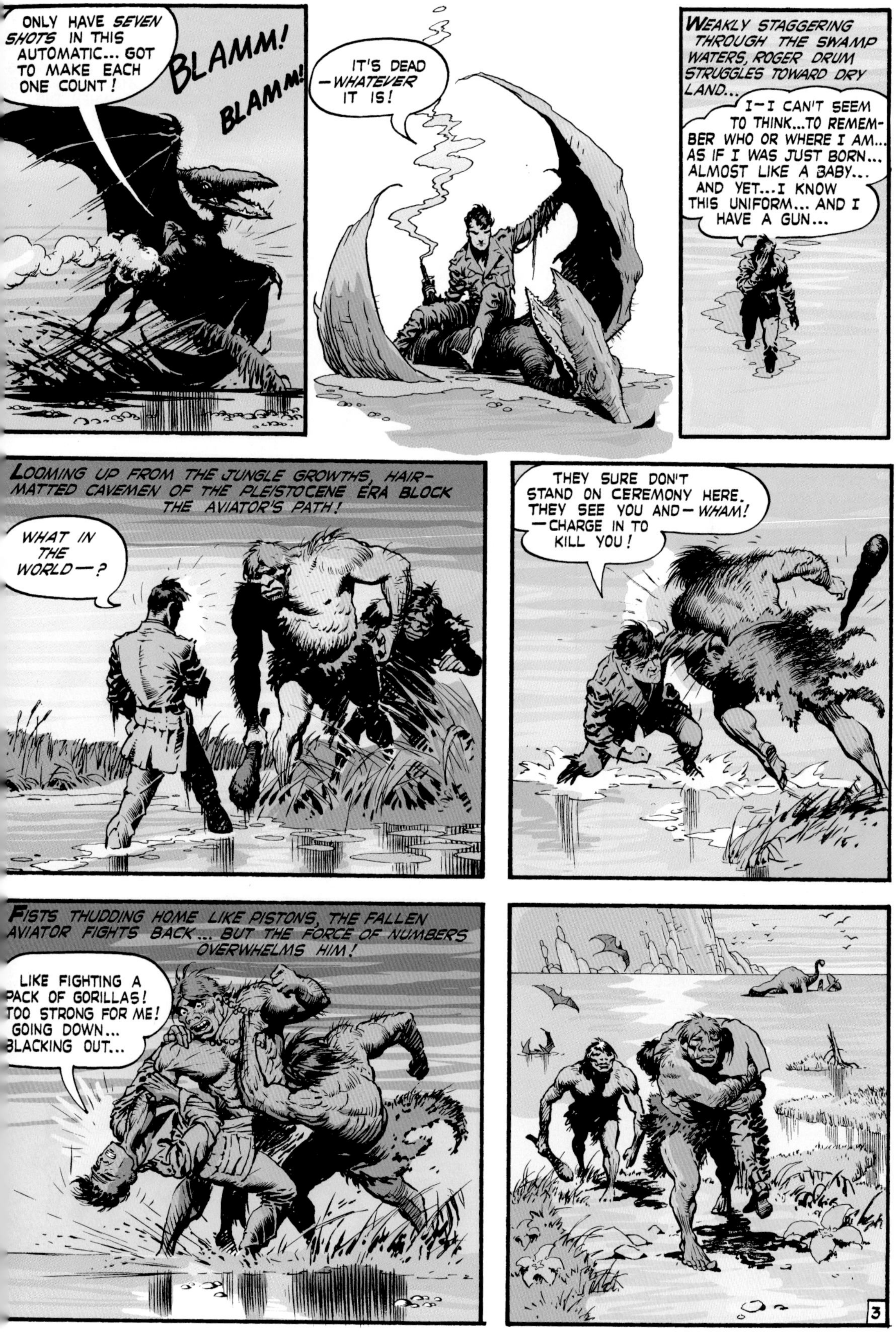
ONLY HAVE SEVEN SHOTS IN THIS AUTOMATIC... GOT TO MAKE EACH ONE COUNT!
BLAMM!
BLAMM!
IT'S DEAD —WHATEVER IT IS!
WEAKLY STAGGERING THROUGH THE SWAMP WATERS, ROGER DRUM STRUGGLES TOWARD DRY LAND...
I—I CAN'T SEEM TO THINK...TO REMEMBER WHO OR WHERE I AM... AS IF I WAS JUST BORN... ALMOST LIKE A BABY... AND YET...I KNOW THIS UNIFORM... AND I HAVE A GUN...
LOOMING UP FROM THE JUNGLE GROWTHS, HAIR-MATTED CAVEMEN OF THE PLEISTOCENE ERA BLOCK THE AVIATOR'S PATH!
WHAT IN THE WORLD—?
THEY SURE DON'T STAND ON CEREMONY HERE. THEY SEE YOU AND—WHAM! —CHARGE IN TO KILL YOU!
FISTS THUDDING HOME LIKE PISTONS, THE FALLEN AVIATOR FIGHTS BACK... BUT THE FORCE OF NUMBERS OVERWHELMS HIM!
LIKE FIGHTING A PACK OF GORILLAS! TOO STRONG FOR ME! GOING DOWN... BLACKING OUT...
3

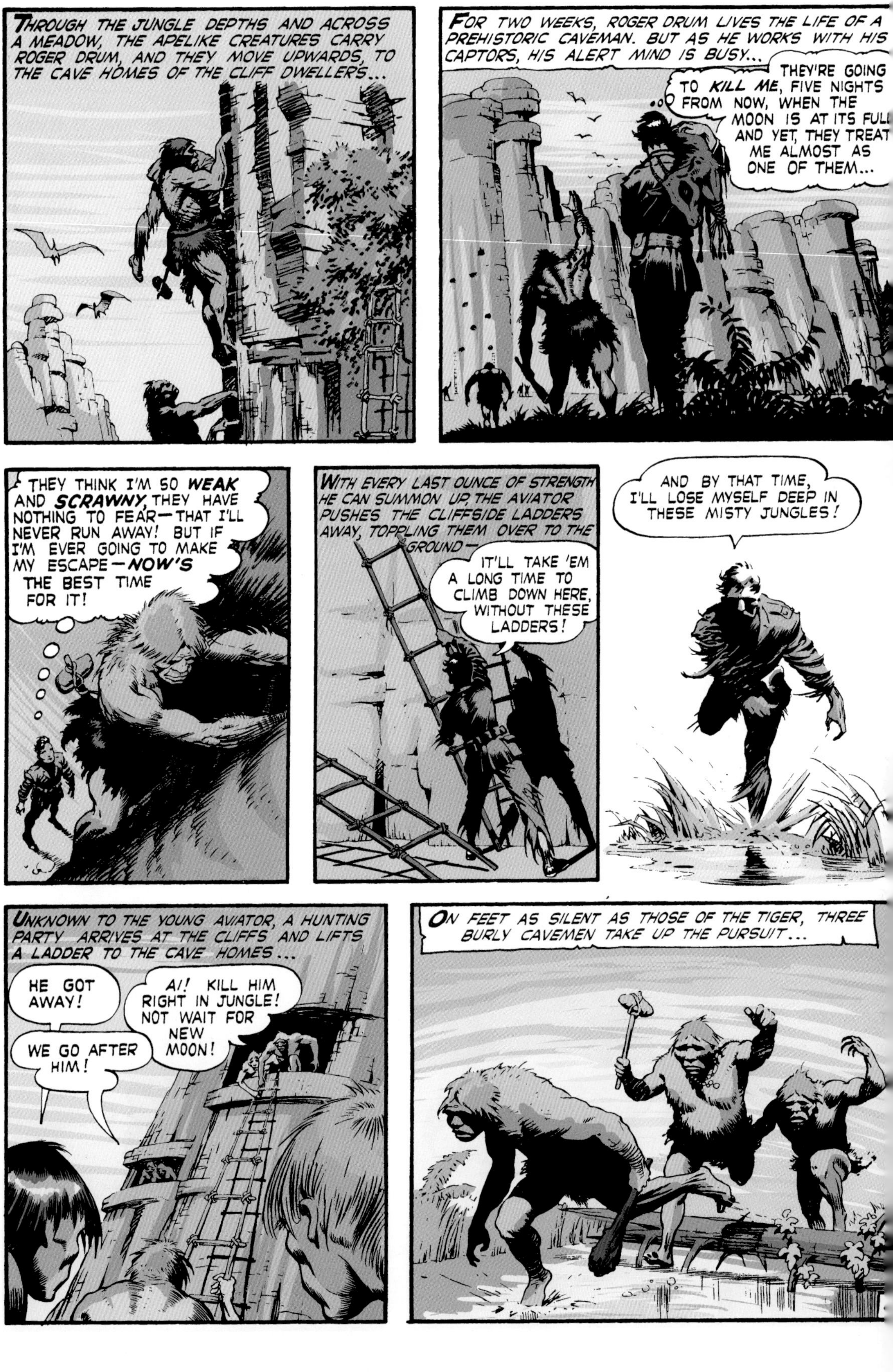
THROUGH THE JUNGLE DEPTHS AND ACROSS A MEADOW, THE APELIKE CREATURES CARRY ROGER DRUM, AND THEY MOVE UPWARDS, TO THE CAVE HOMES OF THE CLIFF DWELLERS...
FOR TWO WEEKS, ROGER DRUM LIVES THE LIFE OF A PREHISTORIC CAVEMAN. BUT AS HE WORKS WITH HIS CAPTORS, HIS ALERT MIND IS BUSY...
THEY'RE GOING TO KILL ME, FIVE NIGHTS FROM NOW, WHEN THE MOON IS AT ITS FULL AND YET, THEY TREAT ME ALMOST AS ONE OF THEM...
THEY THINK I'M SO WEAK AND SCRAWNY, THEY HAVE NOTHING TO FEAR—THAT I'LL NEVER RUN AWAY! BUT IF I'M EVER GOING TO MAKE MY ESCAPE—NOW'S THE BEST TIME FOR IT!
WITH EVERY LAST OUNCE OF STRENGTH HE CAN SUMMON UP, THE AVIATOR PUSHES THE CLIFFSIDE LADDERS AWAY, TOPPLING THEM OVER TO THE GROUND—
IT'LL TAKE 'EM A LONG TIME TO CLIMB DOWN HERE, WITHOUT THESE LADDERS!
AND BY THAT TIME, I'LL LOSE MYSELF DEEP IN THESE MISTY JUNGLES!
UNKNOWN TO THE YOUNG AVIATOR, A HUNTING PARTY ARRIVES AT THE CLIFFS AND LIFTS A LADDER TO THE CAVE HOMES...
HE GOT AWAY!
AI! KILL HIM RIGHT IN JUNGLE! NOT WAIT FOR NEW MOON!
WE GO AFTER HIM!
ON FEET AS SILENT AS THOSE OF THE TIGER, THREE BURLY CAVEMEN TAKE UP THE PURSUIT...

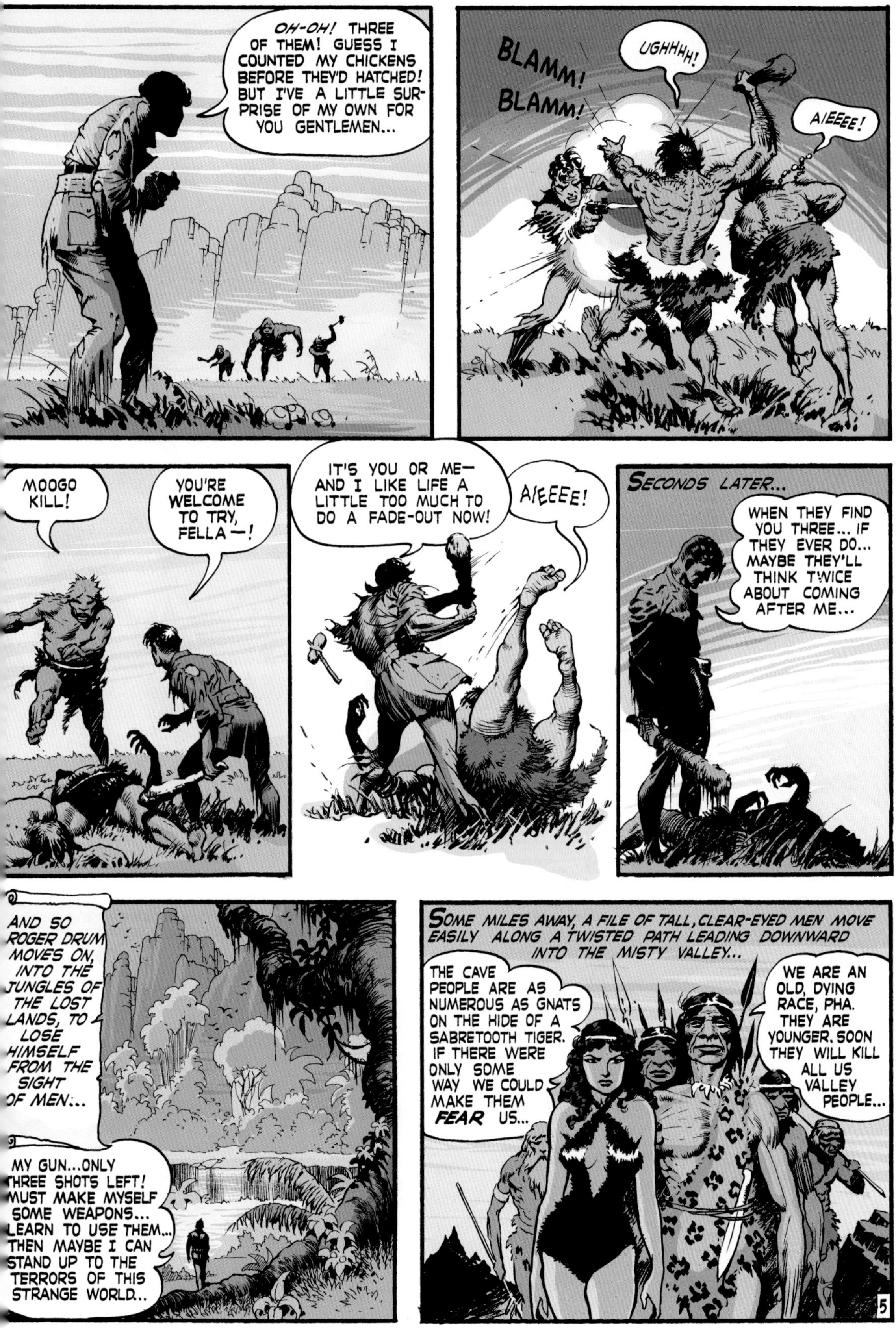

OH-OH! THREE OF THEM! GUESS I COUNTED MY CHICKENS BEFORE THEY'D HATCHED! BUT I'VE A LITTLE SURPRISE OF MY OWN FOR YOU GENTLEMEN...
BLAMM! BLAMM!
UGHHHH!
AIEEEE!
MOOGO KILL!
YOU'RE WELCOME TO TRY, FELLA—!
IT'S YOU OR ME— AND I LIKE LIFE A LITTLE TOO MUCH TO DO A FADE-OUT NOW!
AIEEEE!
SECONDS LATER...
WHEN THEY FIND YOU THREE... IF THEY EVER DO... MAYBE THEY'LL THINK TWICE ABOUT COMING AFTER ME...
AND SO ROGER DRUM MOVES ON, INTO THE JUNGLES OF THE LOST LANDS, TO LOSE HIMSELF FROM THE SIGHT OF MEN...
MY GUN...ONLY THREE SHOTS LEFT! MUST MAKE MYSELF SOME WEAPONS... LEARN TO USE THEM... THEN MAYBE I CAN STAND UP TO THE TERRORS OF THIS STRANGE WORLD...
SOME MILES AWAY, A FILE OF TALL, CLEAR-EYED MEN MOVE EASILY ALONG A TWISTED PATH LEADING DOWNWARD INTO THE MISTY VALLEY...
THE CAVE PEOPLE ARE AS NUMEROUS AS GNATS ON THE HIDE OF A SABRETOOTH TIGER. IF THERE WERE ONLY SOME WAY WE COULD MAKE THEM FEAR US...
WE ARE AN OLD, DYING RACE, PHA. THEY ARE YOUNGER. SOON THEY WILL KILL ALL US VALLEY PEOPLE...

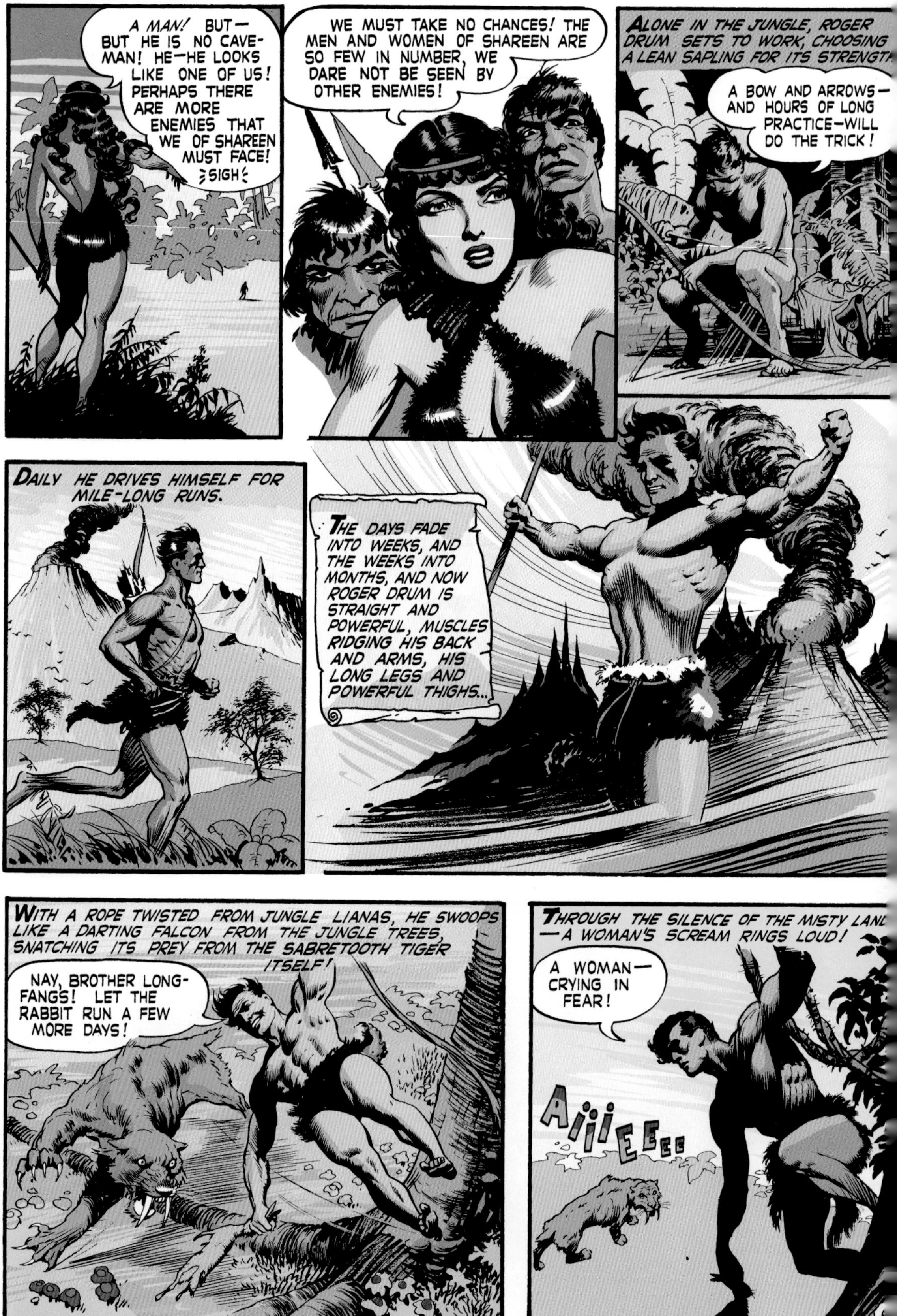

A MAN! BUT—BUT HE IS NO CAVE-MAN! HE—HE LOOKS LIKE ONE OF US! PERHAPS THERE ARE MORE ENEMIES THAT WE OF SHAREEN MUST FACE! SIGH
WE MUST TAKE NO CHANCES! THE MEN AND WOMEN OF SHAREEN ARE SO FEW IN NUMBER, WE DARE NOT BE SEEN BY OTHER ENEMIES!
ALONE IN THE JUNGLE, ROGER DRUM SETS TO WORK, CHOOSING A LEAN SAPLING FOR ITS STRENGTH
A BOW AND ARROWS—AND HOURS OF LONG PRACTICE—WILL DO THE TRICK!
DAILY HE DRIVES HIMSELF FOR MILE-LONG RUNS.
THE DAYS FADE INTO WEEKS, AND THE WEEKS INTO MONTHS, AND NOW ROGER DRUM IS STRAIGHT AND POWERFUL, MUSCLES RIDGING HIS BACK AND ARMS, HIS LONG LEGS AND POWERFUL THIGHS...
WITH A ROPE TWISTED FROM JUNGLE LIANAS, HE SWOOPS LIKE A DARTING FALCON FROM THE JUNGLE TREES, SNATCHING ITS PREY FROM THE SABRETOOTH TIGER ITSELF!
NAY, BROTHER LONG-FANGS! LET THE RABBIT RUN A FEW MORE DAYS!
THROUGH THE SILENCE OF THE MISTY LAND—A WOMAN'S SCREAM RINGS LOUD!
A WOMAN—CRYING IN FEAR!
AIIIEEEE

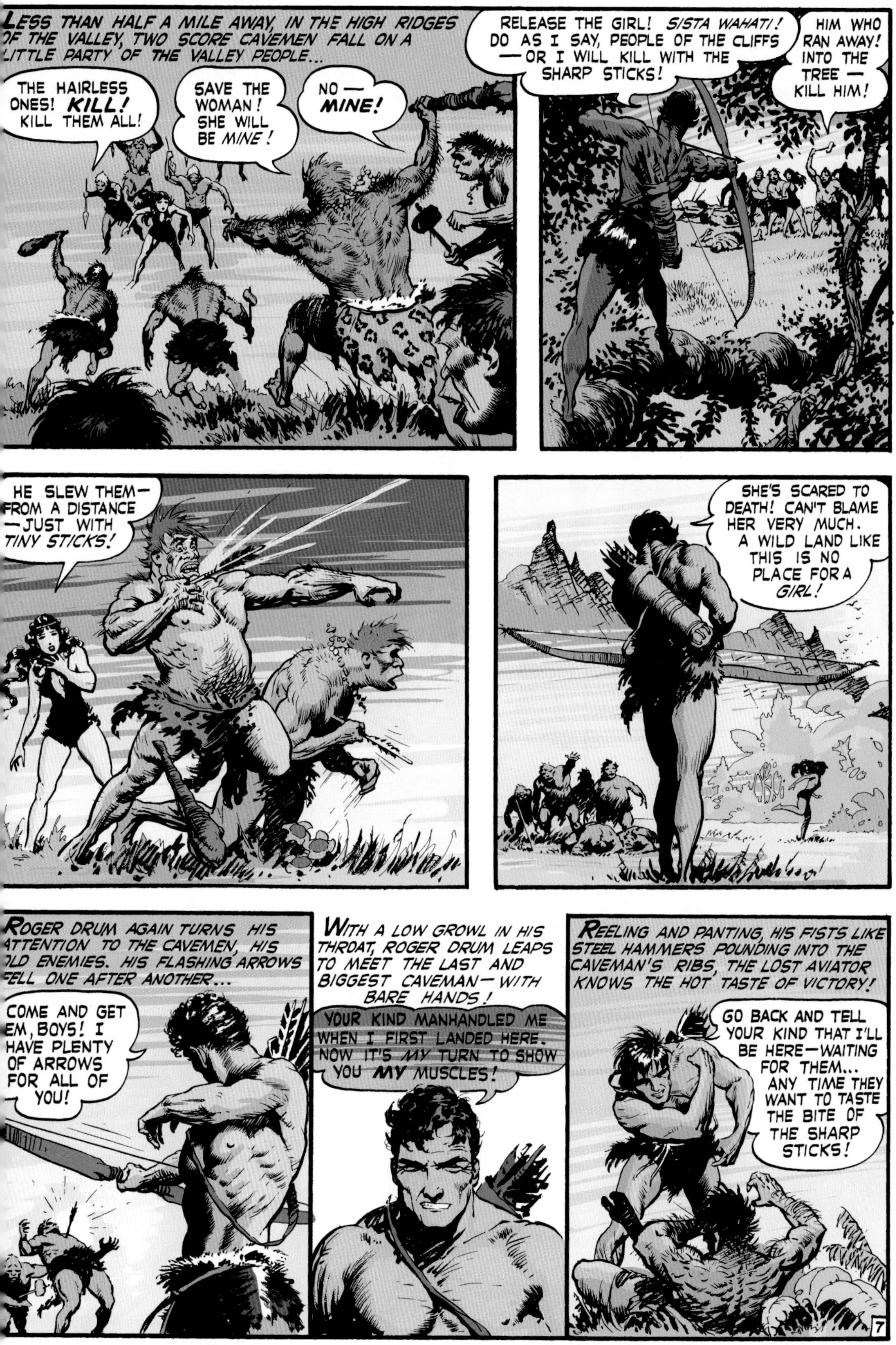

LESS THAN HALF A MILE AWAY, IN THE HIGH RIDGES OF THE VALLEY, TWO SCORE CAVEMEN FALL ON A LITTLE PARTY OF THE VALLEY PEOPLE...
THE HAIRLESS ONES! KILL! KILL THEM ALL!
SAVE THE WOMAN! SHE WILL BE MINE!
NO — MINE!
RELEASE THE GIRL! SISTA WAHATI! DO AS I SAY, PEOPLE OF THE CLIFFS — OR I WILL KILL WITH THE SHARP STICKS!
HIM WHO RAN AWAY! INTO THE TREE — KILL HIM!
HE SLEW THEM — FROM A DISTANCE — JUST WITH TINY STICKS!
SHE'S SCARED TO DEATH! CAN'T BLAME HER VERY MUCH. A WILD LAND LIKE THIS IS NO PLACE FOR A GIRL!
ROGER DRUM AGAIN TURNS HIS ATTENTION TO THE CAVEMEN, HIS OLD ENEMIES. HIS FLASHING ARROWS FELL ONE AFTER ANOTHER...
COME AND GET 'EM, BOYS! I HAVE PLENTY OF ARROWS FOR ALL OF YOU!
WITH A LOW GROWL IN HIS THROAT, ROGER DRUM LEAPS TO MEET THE LAST AND BIGGEST CAVEMAN — WITH BARE HANDS!
YOUR KIND MANHANDLED ME WHEN I FIRST LANDED HERE. NOW IT'S MY TURN TO SHOW YOU MY MUSCLES!
REELING AND PANTING, HIS FISTS LIKE STEEL HAMMERS POUNDING INTO THE CAVEMAN'S RIBS, THE LOST AVIATOR KNOWS THE HOT TASTE OF VICTORY!
GO BACK AND TELL YOUR KIND THAT I'LL BE HERE — WAITING FOR THEM... ANY TIME THEY WANT TO TASTE THE BITE OF THE SHARP STICKS!

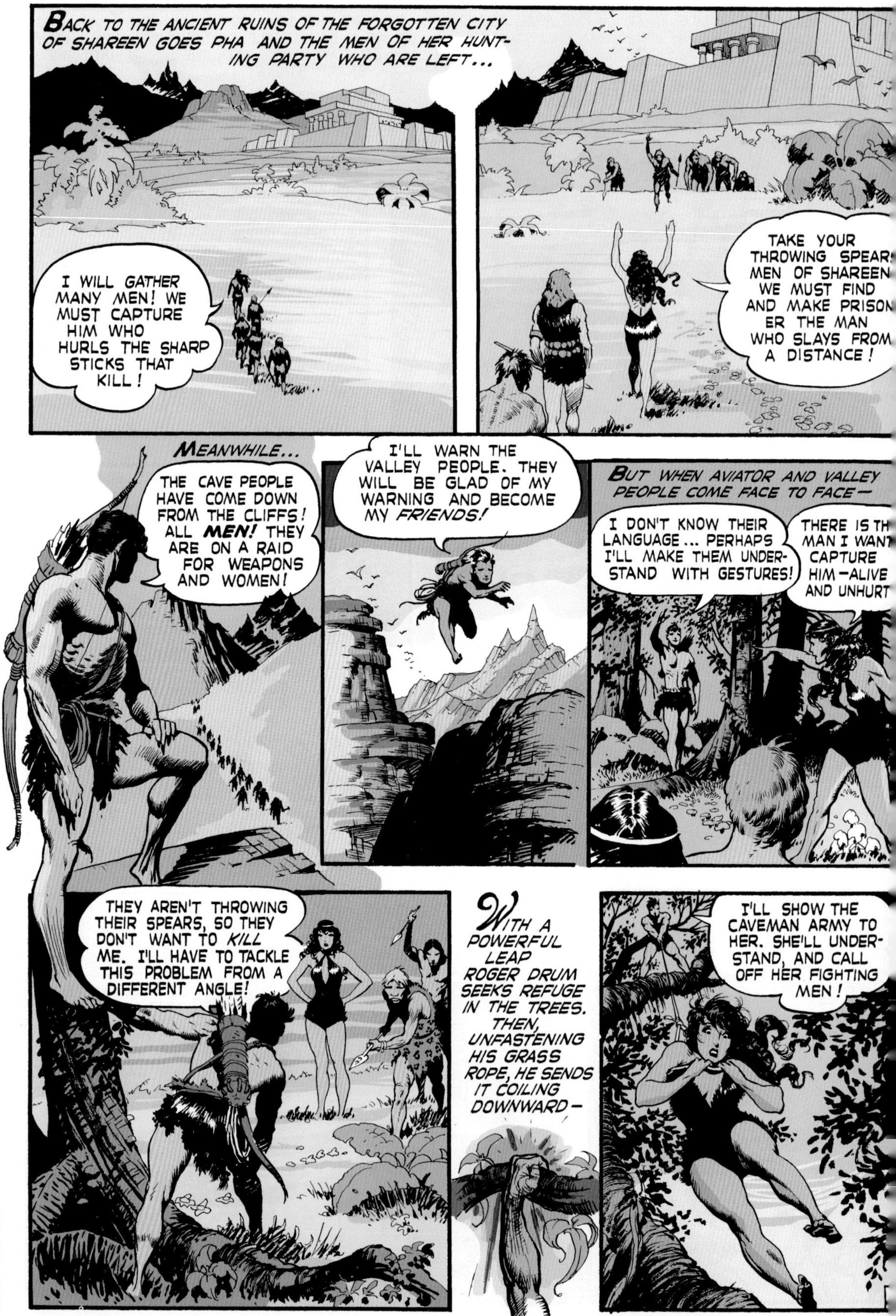
BACK TO THE ANCIENT RUINS OF THE FORGOTTEN CITY OF SHAREEN GOES PHA AND THE MEN OF HER HUNTING PARTY WHO ARE LEFT...
I WILL GATHER MANY MEN! WE MUST CAPTURE HIM WHO HURLS THE SHARP STICKS THAT KILL!
TAKE YOUR THROWING SPEAR MEN OF SHAREEN WE MUST FIND AND MAKE PRISON ER THE MAN WHO SLAYS FROM A DISTANCE!
MEANWHILE...
THE CAVE PEOPLE HAVE COME DOWN FROM THE CLIFFS! ALL MEN! THEY ARE ON A RAID FOR WEAPONS AND WOMEN!
I'LL WARN THE VALLEY PEOPLE. THEY WILL BE GLAD OF MY WARNING AND BECOME MY FRIENDS!
BUT WHEN AVIATOR AND VALLEY PEOPLE COME FACE TO FACE—
I DON'T KNOW THEIR LANGUAGE... PERHAPS I'LL MAKE THEM UNDERSTAND WITH GESTURES!
THERE IS TH MAN I WANT CAPTURE HIM—ALIVE AND UNHURT
THEY AREN'T THROWING THEIR SPEARS, SO THEY DON'T WANT TO KILL ME. I'LL HAVE TO TACKLE THIS PROBLEM FROM A DIFFERENT ANGLE!
WITH A POWERFUL LEAP ROGER DRUM SEEKS REFUGE IN THE TREES. THEN, UNFASTENING HIS GRASS ROPE, HE SENDS IT COILING DOWNWARD—
I'LL SHOW THE CAVEMAN ARMY TO HER. SHE'LL UNDERSTAND, AND CALL OFF HER FIGHTING MEN!

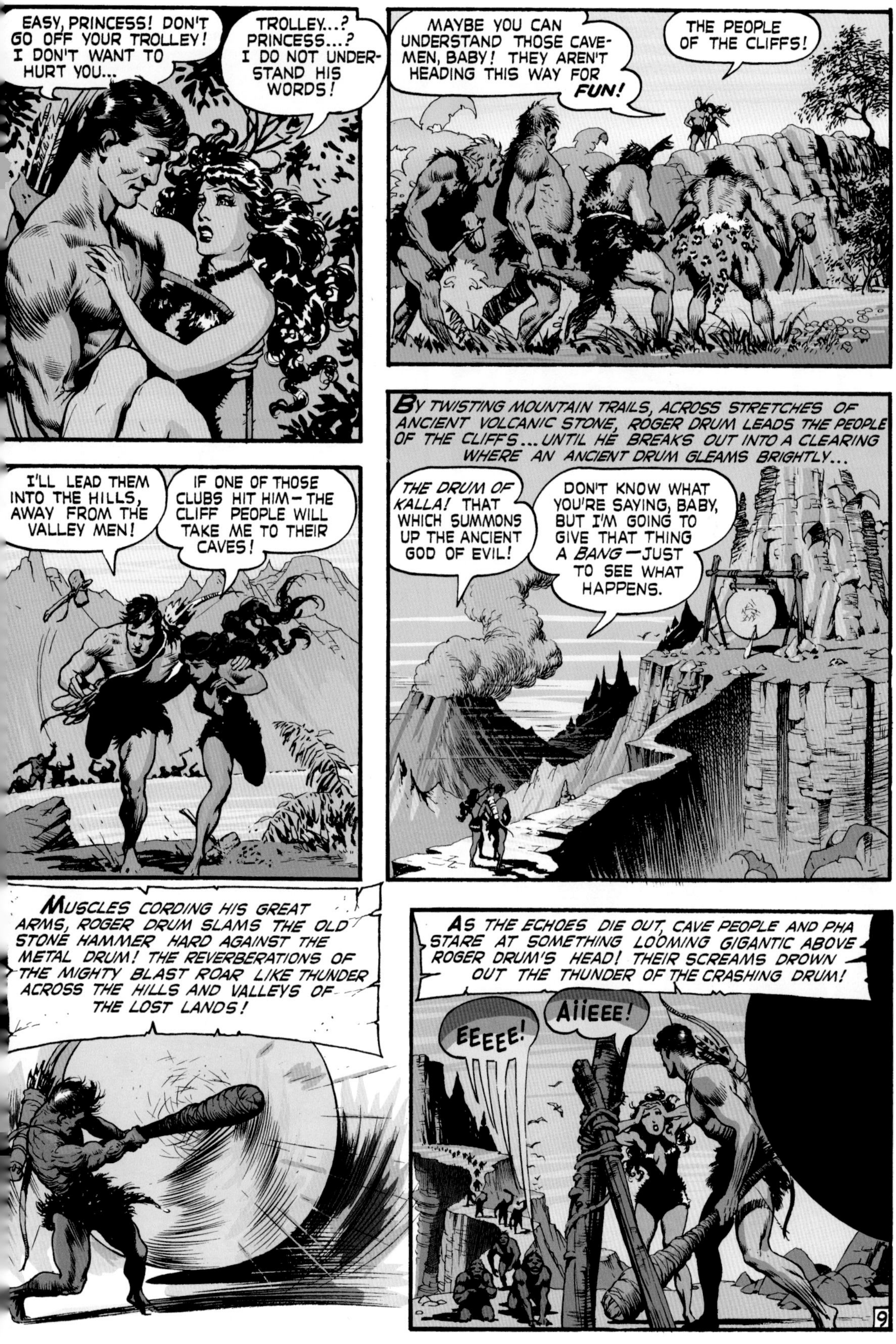

EASY, PRINCESS! DON'T GO OFF YOUR TROLLEY! I DON'T WANT TO HURT YOU...
TROLLEY...? PRINCESS...? I DO NOT UNDERSTAND HIS WORDS!
MAYBE YOU CAN UNDERSTAND THOSE CAVE-MEN, BABY! THEY AREN'T HEADING THIS WAY FOR FUN!
THE PEOPLE OF THE CLIFFS!
I'LL LEAD THEM INTO THE HILLS, AWAY FROM THE VALLEY MEN!
IF ONE OF THOSE CLUBS HIT HIM—THE CLIFF PEOPLE WILL TAKE ME TO THEIR CAVES!
BY TWISTING MOUNTAIN TRAILS, ACROSS STRETCHES OF ANCIENT VOLCANIC STONE, ROGER DRUM LEADS THE PEOPLE OF THE CLIFFS... UNTIL HE BREAKS OUT INTO A CLEARING WHERE AN ANCIENT DRUM GLEAMS BRIGHTLY...
THE DRUM OF KALLA! THAT WHICH SUMMONS UP THE ANCIENT GOD OF EVIL!
DON'T KNOW WHAT YOU'RE SAYING, BABY, BUT I'M GOING TO GIVE THAT THING A BANG—JUST TO SEE WHAT HAPPENS.
MUSCLES CORDING HIS GREAT ARMS, ROGER DRUM SLAMS THE OLD STONE HAMMER HARD AGAINST THE METAL DRUM! THE REVERBERATIONS OF THE MIGHTY BLAST ROAR LIKE THUNDER ACROSS THE HILLS AND VALLEYS OF THE LOST LANDS!
AS THE ECHOES DIE OUT, CAVE PEOPLE AND PHA STARE AT SOMETHING LOOMING GIGANTIC ABOVE ROGER DRUM'S HEAD! THEIR SCREAMS DROWN OUT THE THUNDER OF THE CRASHING DRUM!
EEEEE!
AiiEEE!
9

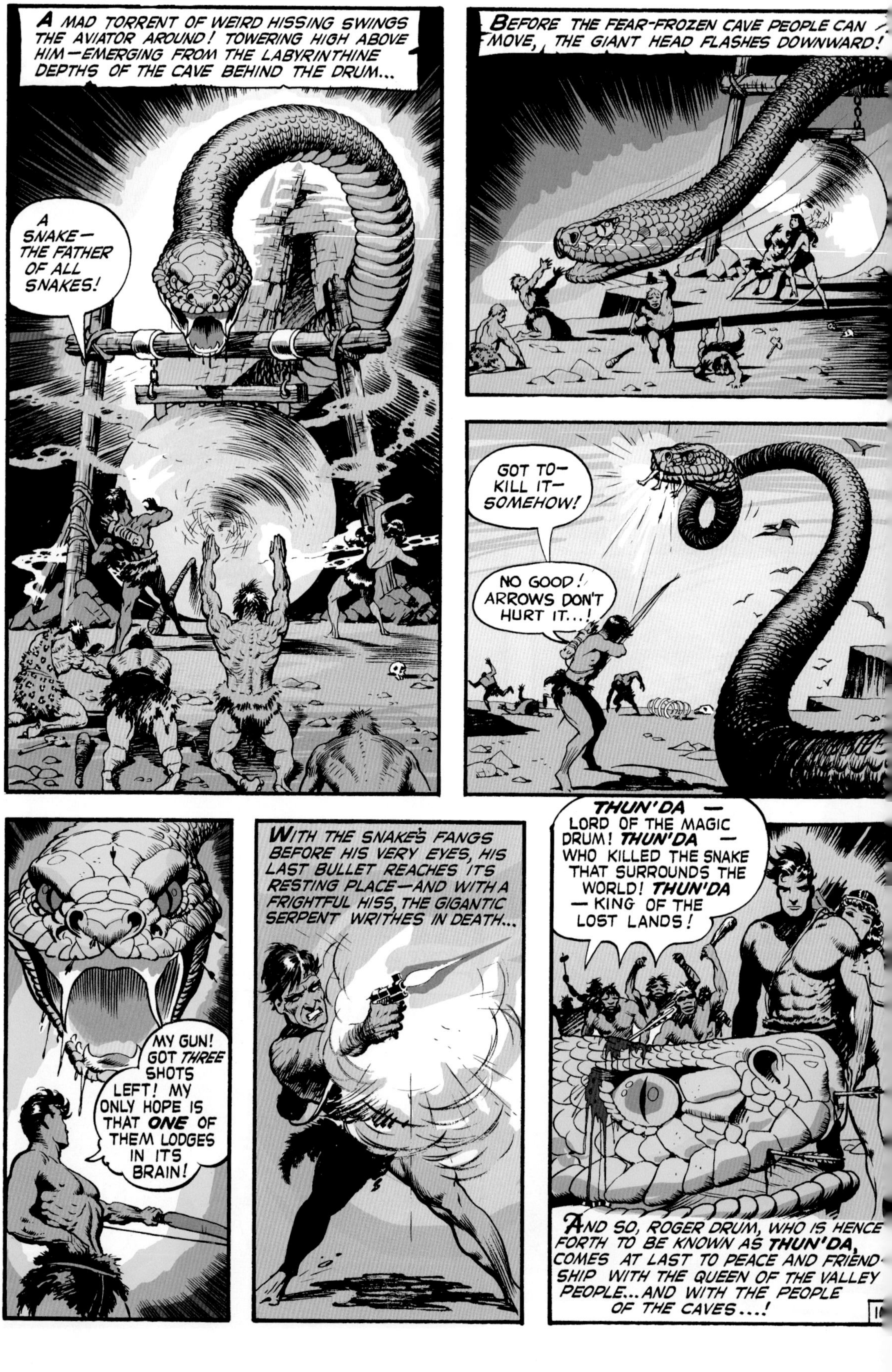
A MAD TORRENT OF WEIRD HISSING SWINGS THE AVIATOR AROUND! TOWERING HIGH ABOVE HIM—EMERGING FROM THE LABYRINTHINE DEPTHS OF THE CAVE BEHIND THE DRUM...
A SNAKE— THE FATHER OF ALL SNAKES!
BEFORE THE FEAR-FROZEN CAVE PEOPLE CAN MOVE, THE GIANT HEAD FLASHES DOWNWARD!
GOT TO— KILL IT— SOMEHOW!
NO GOOD! ARROWS DON'T HURT IT...!
MY GUN! GOT THREE SHOTS LEFT! MY ONLY HOPE IS THAT ONE OF THEM LODGES IN ITS BRAIN!
WITH THE SNAKE'S FANGS BEFORE HIS VERY EYES, HIS LAST BULLET REACHES ITS RESTING PLACE—AND WITH A FRIGHTFUL HISS, THE GIGANTIC SERPENT WRITHES IN DEATH...
THUN'DA — LORD OF THE MAGIC DRUM! THUN'DA — WHO KILLED THE SNAKE THAT SURROUNDS THE WORLD! THUN'DA — KING OF THE LOST LANDS!
AND SO, ROGER DRUM, WHO IS HENCEFORTH TO BE KNOWN AS THUN'DA, COMES AT LAST TO PEACE AND FRIENDSHIP WITH THE QUEEN OF THE VALLEY PEOPLE...AND WITH THE PEOPLE OF THE CAVES...!

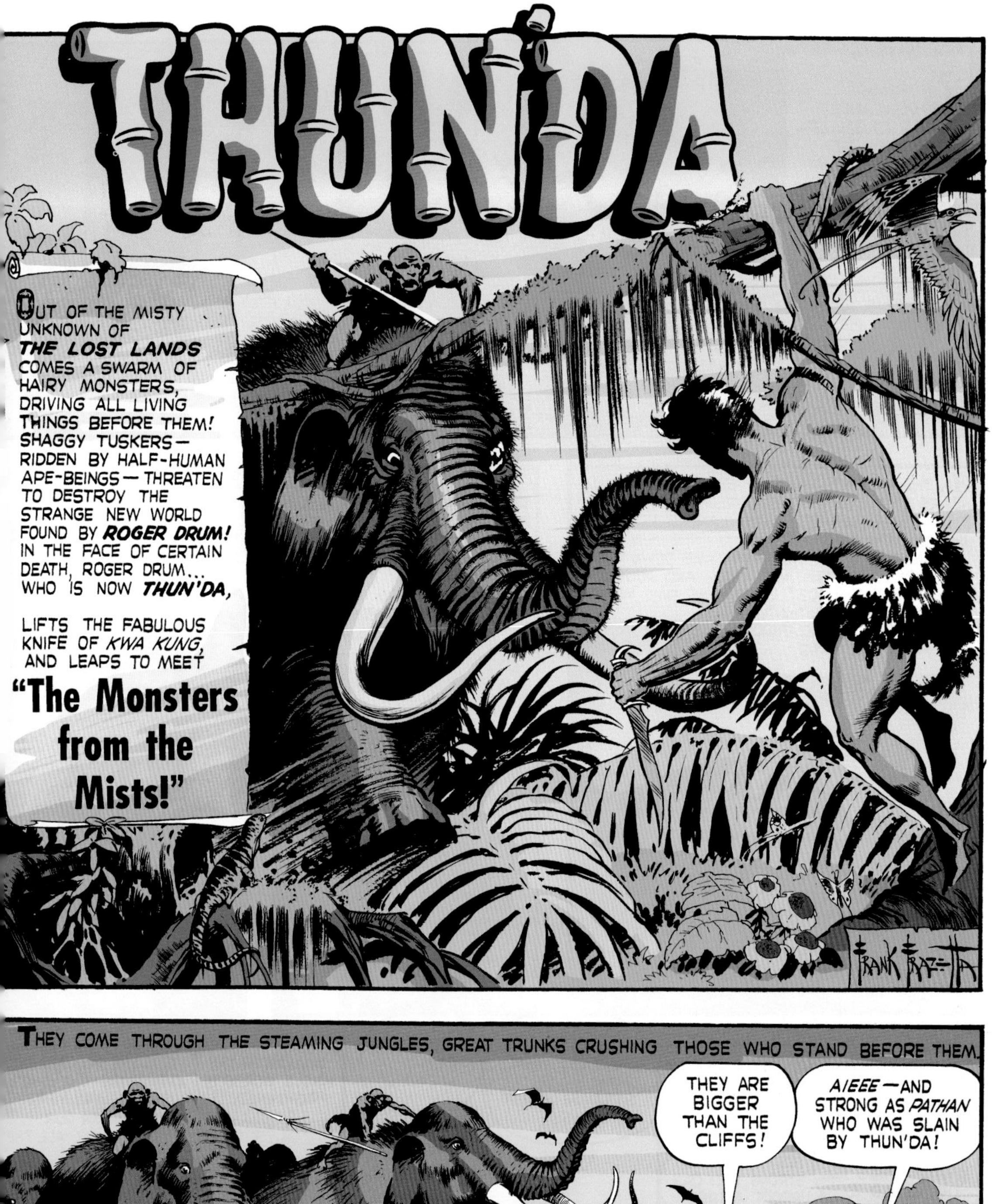
THUN'DA
OUT OF THE MISTY UNKNOWN OF THE LOST LANDS COMES A SWARM OF HAIRY MONSTERS, DRIVING ALL LIVING THINGS BEFORE THEM! SHAGGY TUSKERS— RIDDEN BY HALF-HUMAN APE-BEINGS— THREATEN TO DESTROY THE STRANGE NEW WORLD FOUND BY ROGER DRUM! IN THE FACE OF CERTAIN DEATH, ROGER DRUM... WHO IS NOW THUN'DA,
LIFTS THE FABULOUS KNIFE OF KWA KUNG, AND LEAPS TO MEET
"The Monsters from the Mists!"
FRANK FRAZETTA

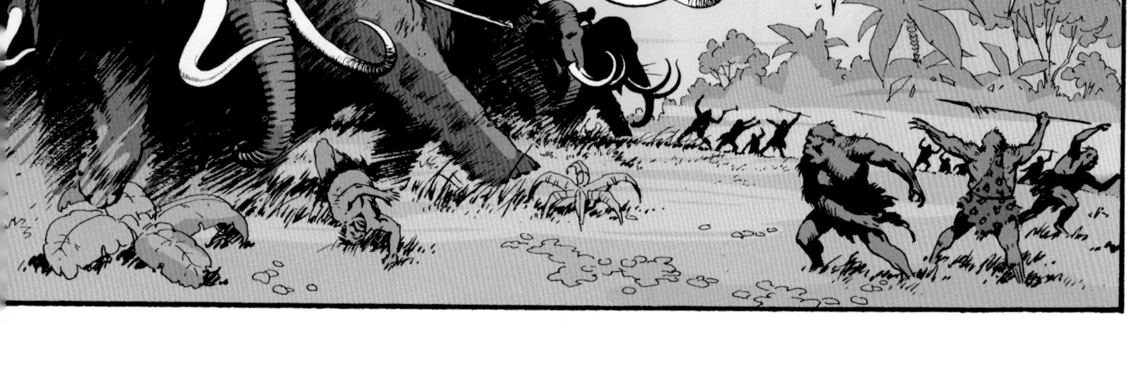
THEY COME THROUGH THE STEAMING JUNGLES, GREAT TRUNKS CRUSHING THOSE WHO STAND BEFORE THEM.
THEY ARE BIGGER THAN THE CLIFFS!
AIEEE—AND STRONG AS PATHAN WHO WAS SLAIN BY THUN'DA!

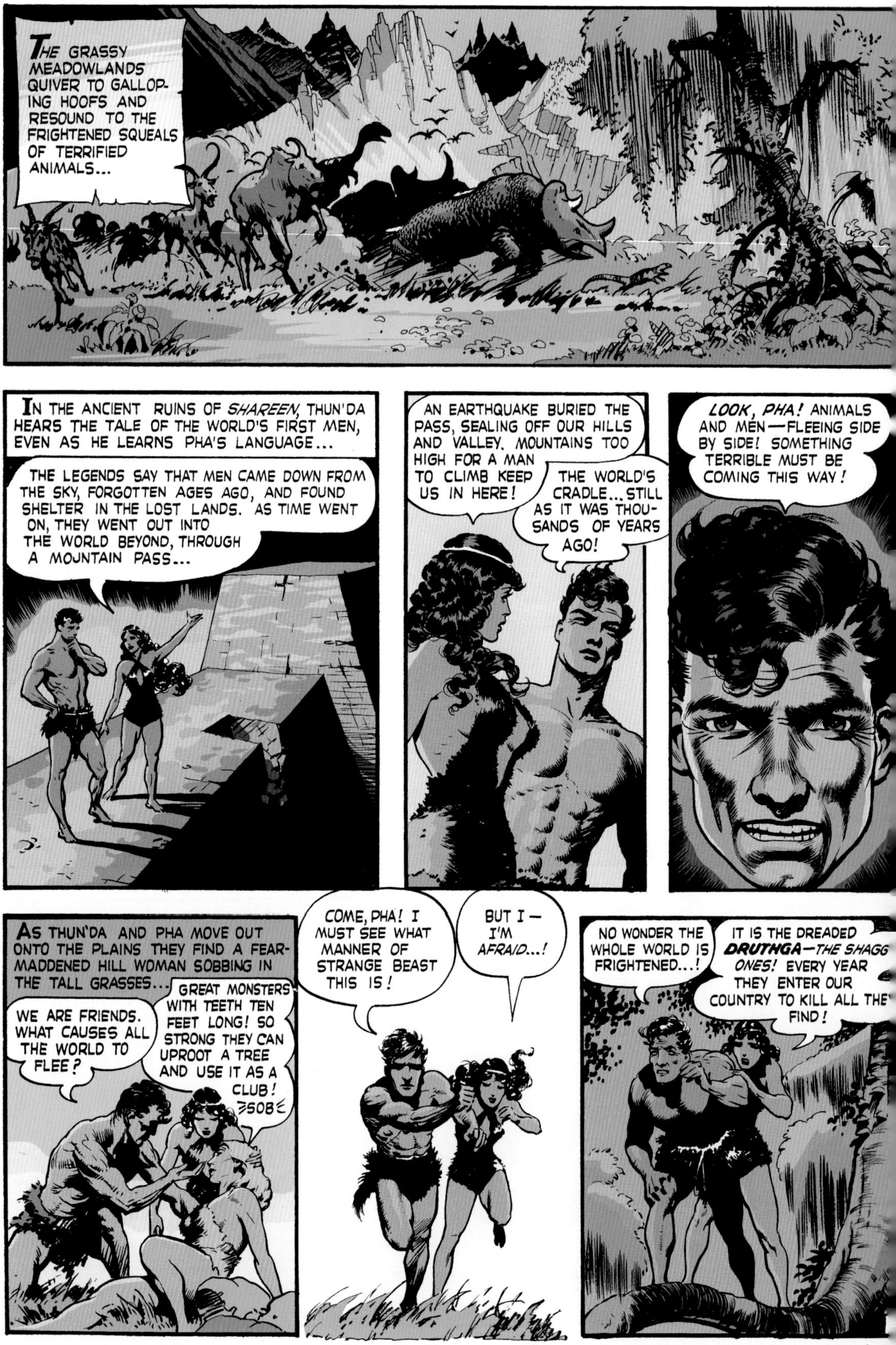
THE GRASSY MEADOWLANDS QUIVER TO GALLOPING HOOFS AND RESOUND TO THE FRIGHTENED SQUEALS OF TERRIFIED ANIMALS...
IN THE ANCIENT RUINS OF SHAREEN, THUN'DA HEARS THE TALE OF THE WORLD'S FIRST MEN, EVEN AS HE LEARNS PHA'S LANGUAGE...
THE LEGENDS SAY THAT MEN CAME DOWN FROM THE SKY, FORGOTTEN AGES AGO, AND FOUND SHELTER IN THE LOST LANDS. AS TIME WENT ON, THEY WENT OUT INTO THE WORLD BEYOND, THROUGH A MOUNTAIN PASS...
AN EARTHQUAKE BURIED THE PASS, SEALING OFF OUR HILLS AND VALLEY. MOUNTAINS TOO HIGH FOR A MAN TO CLIMB KEEP US IN HERE!
THE WORLD'S CRADLE... STILL AS IT WAS THOUSANDS OF YEARS AGO!
LOOK, PHA! ANIMALS AND MEN—FLEEING SIDE BY SIDE! SOMETHING TERRIBLE MUST BE COMING THIS WAY!
AS THUN'DA AND PHA MOVE OUT ONTO THE PLAINS THEY FIND A FEAR-MADDENED HILL WOMAN SOBBING IN THE TALL GRASSES...
WE ARE FRIENDS. WHAT CAUSES ALL THE WORLD TO FLEE?
GREAT MONSTERS WITH TEETH TEN FEET LONG! SO STRONG THEY CAN UPROOT A TREE AND USE IT AS A CLUB!
SOB
COME, PHA! I MUST SEE WHAT MANNER OF STRANGE BEAST THIS IS!
BUT I— I'M AFRAID...!
NO WONDER THE WHOLE WORLD IS FRIGHTENED...!
IT IS THE DREADED DRUTHGA—THE SHAGG ONES! EVERY YEAR THEY ENTER OUR COUNTRY TO KILL ALL THE FIND!

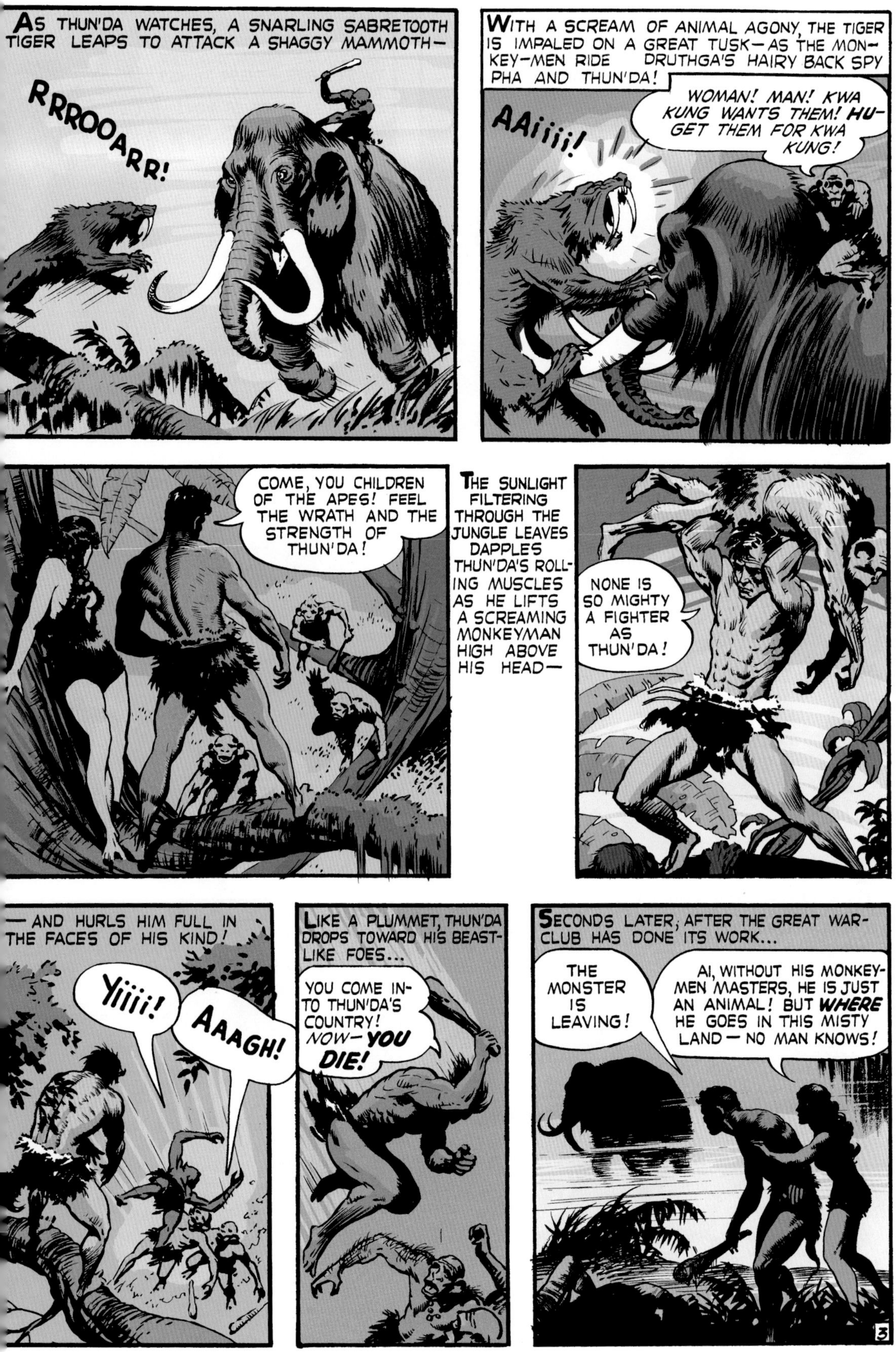

AS THUN'DA WATCHES, A SNARLING SABRETOOTH TIGER LEAPS TO ATTACK A SHAGGY MAMMOTH—
RRROOARR!
WITH A SCREAM OF ANIMAL AGONY, THE TIGER IS IMPALED ON A GREAT TUSK—AS THE MONKEY-MEN RIDE DRUTHGA'S HAIRY BACK SPY PHA AND THUN'DA!
AAiiiii!
WOMAN! MAN! KWA KUNG WANTS THEM! HU-GET THEM FOR KWA KUNG!
COME, YOU CHILDREN OF THE APES! FEEL THE WRATH AND THE STRENGTH OF THUN'DA!
THE SUNLIGHT FILTERING THROUGH THE JUNGLE LEAVES DAPPLES THUN'DA'S ROLLING MUSCLES AS HE LIFTS A SCREAMING MONKEYMAN HIGH ABOVE HIS HEAD—
NONE IS SO MIGHTY A FIGHTER AS THUN'DA!
— AND HURLS HIM FULL IN THE FACES OF HIS KIND!
Yiiii!
AAAGH!
LIKE A PLUMMET, THUN'DA DROPS TOWARD HIS BEAST-LIKE FOES...
YOU COME INTO THUN'DA'S COUNTRY! NOW—YOU DIE!
SECONDS LATER, AFTER THE GREAT WAR-CLUB HAS DONE ITS WORK...
THE MONSTER IS LEAVING!
AI, WITHOUT HIS MONKEY-MEN MASTERS, HE IS JUST AN ANIMAL! BUT WHERE HE GOES IN THIS MISTY LAND — NO MAN KNOWS!
3

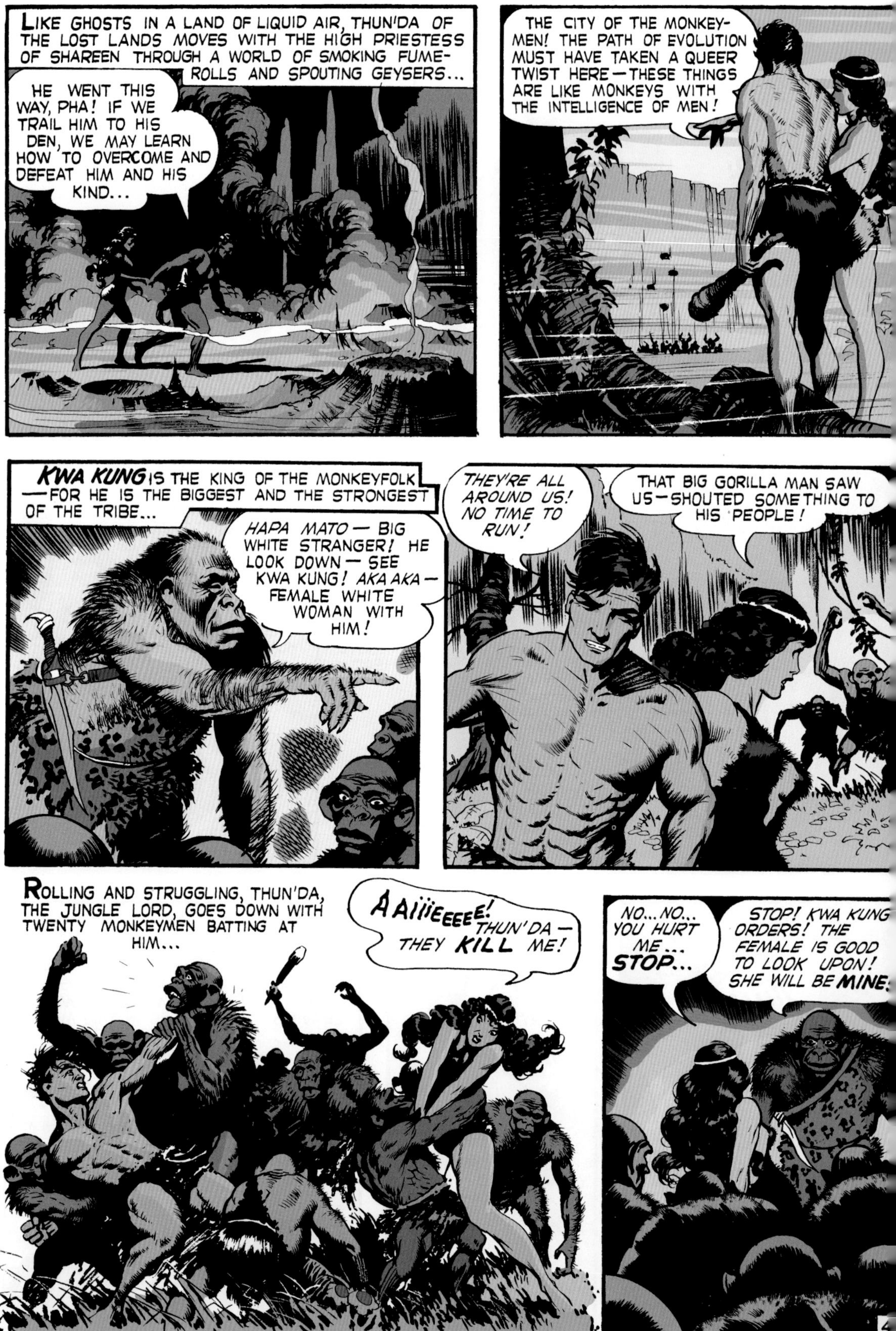

LIKE GHOSTS IN A LAND OF LIQUID AIR, THUN'DA OF THE LOST LANDS MOVES WITH THE HIGH PRIESTESS OF SHAREEN THROUGH A WORLD OF SMOKING FUME-ROLLS AND SPOUTING GEYSERS...
HE WENT THIS WAY, PHA! IF WE TRAIL HIM TO HIS DEN, WE MAY LEARN HOW TO OVERCOME AND DEFEAT HIM AND HIS KIND...
THE CITY OF THE MONKEY-MEN! THE PATH OF EVOLUTION MUST HAVE TAKEN A QUEER TWIST HERE—THESE THINGS ARE LIKE MONKEYS WITH THE INTELLIGENCE OF MEN!
KWA KUNG IS THE KING OF THE MONKEYFOLK—FOR HE IS THE BIGGEST AND THE STRONGEST OF THE TRIBE...
HAPA MATO—BIG WHITE STRANGER! HE LOOK DOWN—SEE KWA KUNG! AKA AKA—FEMALE WHITE WOMAN WITH HIM!
THEY'RE ALL AROUND US! NO TIME TO RUN!
THAT BIG GORILLA MAN SAW US—SHOUTED SOMETHING TO HIS PEOPLE!
ROLLING AND STRUGGLING, THUN'DA, THE JUNGLE LORD, GOES DOWN WITH TWENTY MONKEYMEN BATTING AT HIM...
AAIIIEEEEE! THUN'DA—THEY KILL ME!
NO...NO... YOU HURT ME... STOP...
STOP! KWA KUNG ORDERS! THE FEMALE IS GOOD TO LOOK UPON! SHE WILL BE MINE!

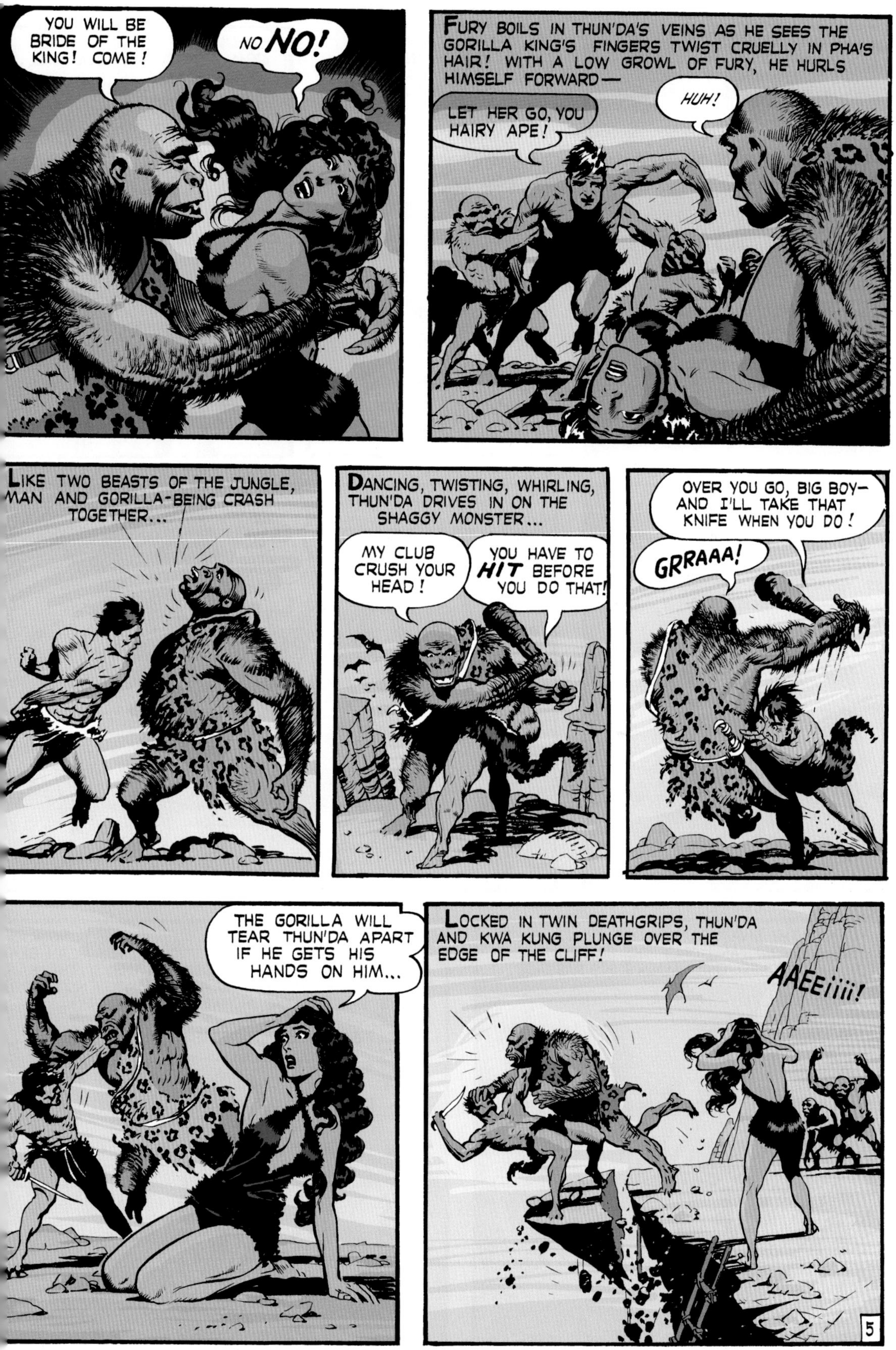
YOU WILL BE BRIDE OF THE KING! COME!
NO NO!
FURY BOILS IN THUN'DA'S VEINS AS HE SEES THE GORILLA KING'S FINGERS TWIST CRUELLY IN PHA'S HAIR! WITH A LOW GROWL OF FURY, HE HURLS HIMSELF FORWARD—
LET HER GO, YOU HAIRY APE!
HUH!
LIKE TWO BEASTS OF THE JUNGLE, MAN AND GORILLA-BEING CRASH TOGETHER...
DANCING, TWISTING, WHIRLING, THUN'DA DRIVES IN ON THE SHAGGY MONSTER...
MY CLUB CRUSH YOUR HEAD!
YOU HAVE TO HIT BEFORE YOU DO THAT!
OVER YOU GO, BIG BOY— AND I'LL TAKE THAT KNIFE WHEN YOU DO!
GRRAAA!
THE GORILLA WILL TEAR THUN'DA APART IF HE GETS HIS HANDS ON HIM...
LOCKED IN TWIN DEATHGRIPS, THUN'DA AND KWA KUNG PLUNGE OVER THE EDGE OF THE CLIFF!
AAEEiiii!
5

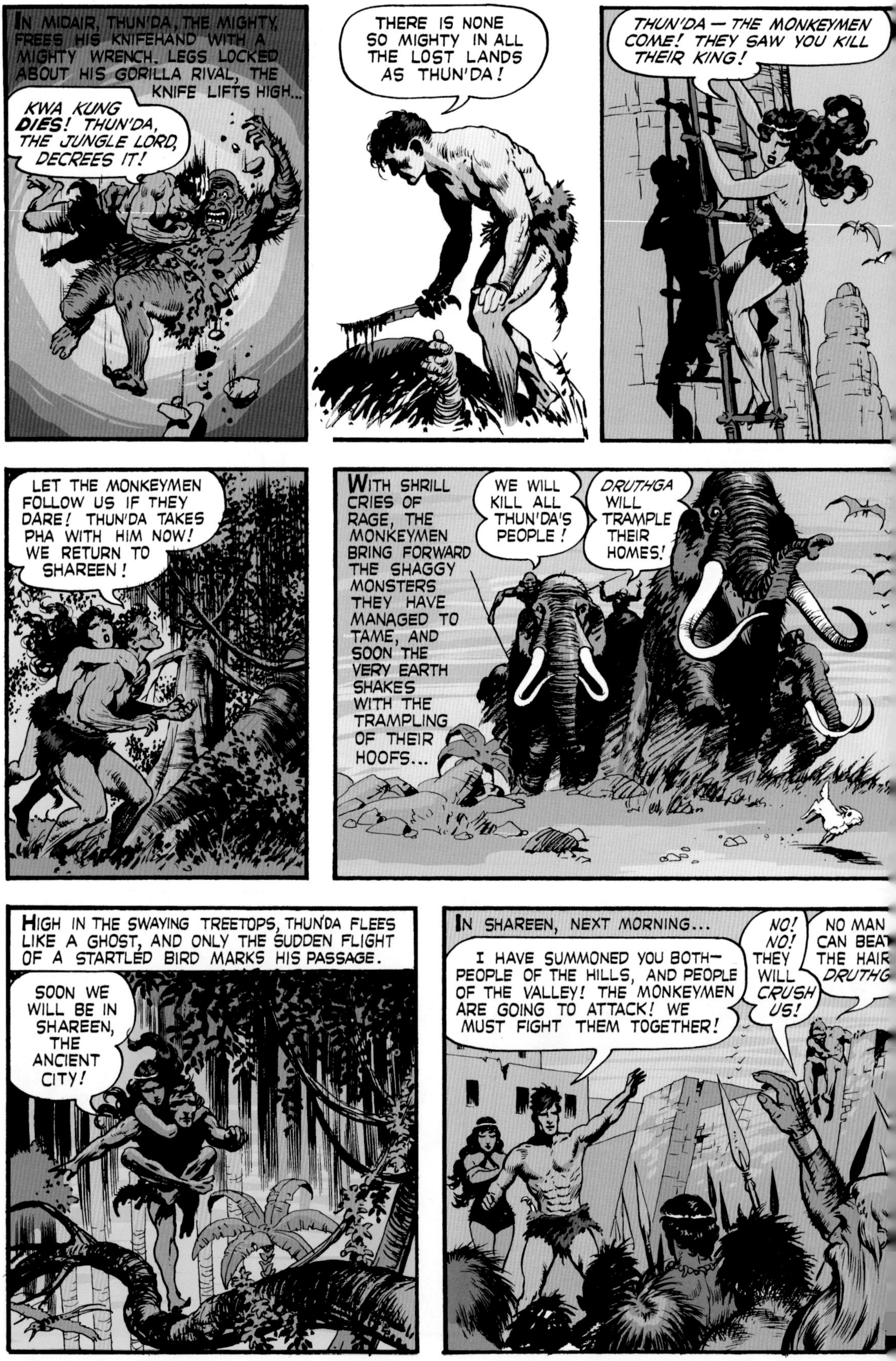

IN MIDAIR, THUN'DA, THE MIGHTY, FREES HIS KNIFEHAND WITH A MIGHTY WRENCH. LEGS LOCKED ABOUT HIS GORILLA RIVAL, THE KNIFE LIFTS HIGH...
KWA KUNG DIES! THUN'DA, THE JUNGLE LORD, DECREES IT!
THERE IS NONE SO MIGHTY IN ALL THE LOST LANDS AS THUN'DA!
THUN'DA — THE MONKEYMEN COME! THEY SAW YOU KILL THEIR KING!
LET THE MONKEYMEN FOLLOW US IF THEY DARE! THUN'DA TAKES PHA WITH HIM NOW! WE RETURN TO SHAREEN!
WITH SHRILL CRIES OF RAGE, THE MONKEYMEN BRING FORWARD THE SHAGGY MONSTERS THEY HAVE MANAGED TO TAME, AND SOON THE VERY EARTH SHAKES WITH THE TRAMPLING OF THEIR HOOFS...
WE WILL KILL ALL THUN'DA'S PEOPLE!
DRUTHGA WILL TRAMPLE THEIR HOMES!
HIGH IN THE SWAYING TREETOPS, THUN'DA FLEES LIKE A GHOST, AND ONLY THE SUDDEN FLIGHT OF A STARTLED BIRD MARKS HIS PASSAGE.
SOON WE WILL BE IN SHAREEN, THE ANCIENT CITY!
IN SHAREEN, NEXT MORNING...
I HAVE SUMMONED YOU BOTH— PEOPLE OF THE HILLS, AND PEOPLE OF THE VALLEY! THE MONKEYMEN ARE GOING TO ATTACK! WE MUST FIGHT THEM TOGETHER!
NO! NO! THEY WILL CRUSH US!
NO MAN CAN BEAT THE HAIR DRUTHG

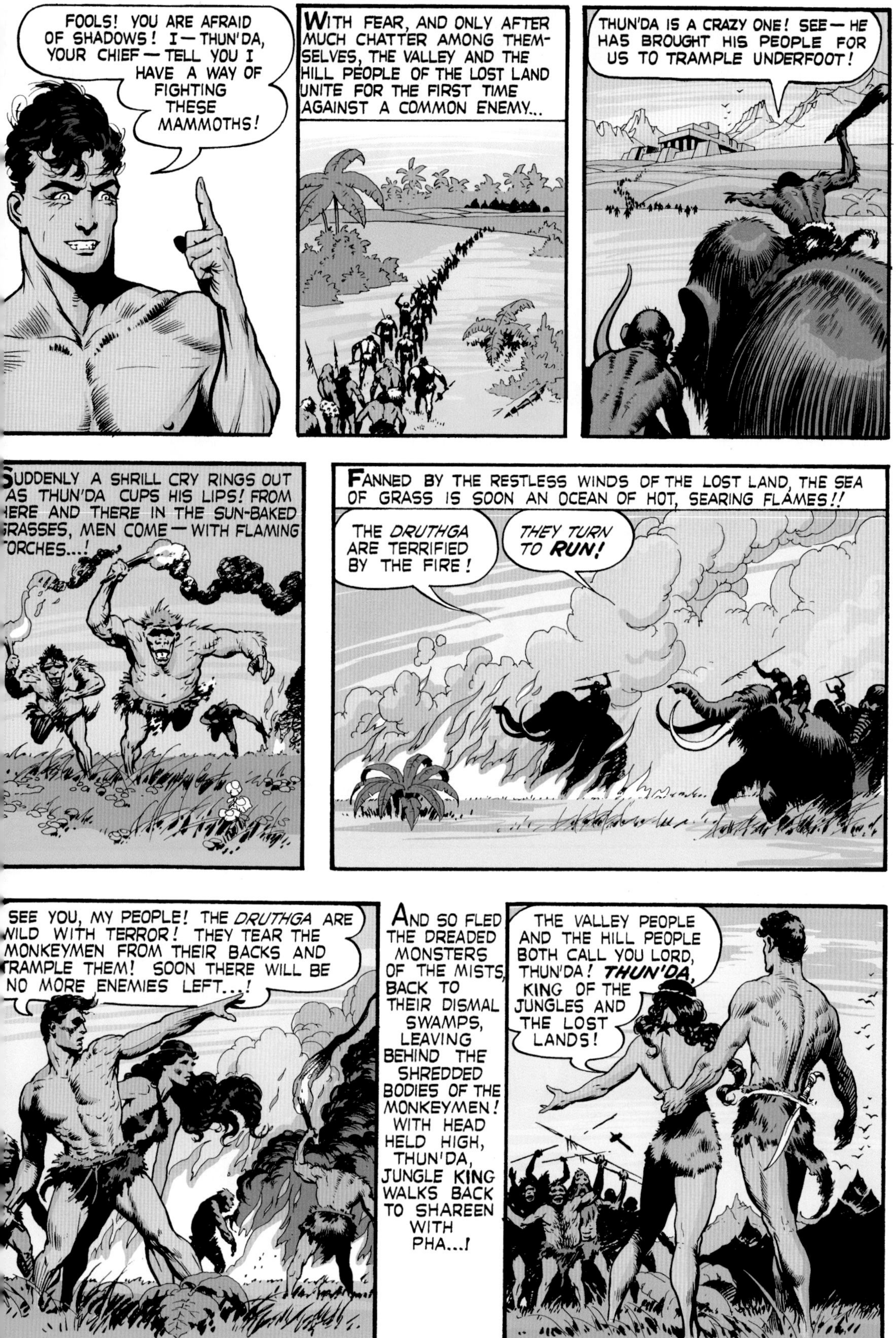
FOOLS! YOU ARE AFRAID OF SHADOWS! I — THUN'DA, YOUR CHIEF — TELL YOU I HAVE A WAY OF FIGHTING THESE MAMMOTHS!
WITH FEAR, AND ONLY AFTER MUCH CHATTER AMONG THEMSELVES, THE VALLEY AND THE HILL PEOPLE OF THE LOST LAND UNITE FOR THE FIRST TIME AGAINST A COMMON ENEMY...
THUN'DA IS A CRAZY ONE! SEE — HE HAS BROUGHT HIS PEOPLE FOR US TO TRAMPLE UNDERFOOT!
SUDDENLY A SHRILL CRY RINGS OUT AS THUN'DA CUPS HIS LIPS! FROM HERE AND THERE IN THE SUN-BAKED GRASSES, MEN COME — WITH FLAMING TORCHES...!
FANNED BY THE RESTLESS WINDS OF THE LOST LAND, THE SEA OF GRASS IS SOON AN OCEAN OF HOT, SEARING FLAMES!!
THE DRUTHGA ARE TERRIFIED BY THE FIRE!
THEY TURN TO RUN!
SEE YOU, MY PEOPLE! THE DRUTHGA ARE WILD WITH TERROR! THEY TEAR THE MONKEYMEN FROM THEIR BACKS AND TRAMPLE THEM! SOON THERE WILL BE NO MORE ENEMIES LEFT...!
AND SO FLED THE DREADED MONSTERS OF THE MISTS, BACK TO THEIR DISMAL SWAMPS, LEAVING BEHIND THE SHREDDED BODIES OF THE MONKEYMEN! WITH HEAD HELD HIGH, THUN'DA, JUNGLE KING WALKS BACK TO SHAREEN WITH PHA...!
THE VALLEY PEOPLE AND THE HILL PEOPLE BOTH CALL YOU LORD, THUN'DA! THUN'DA, KING OF THE JUNGLES AND THE LOST LANDS!

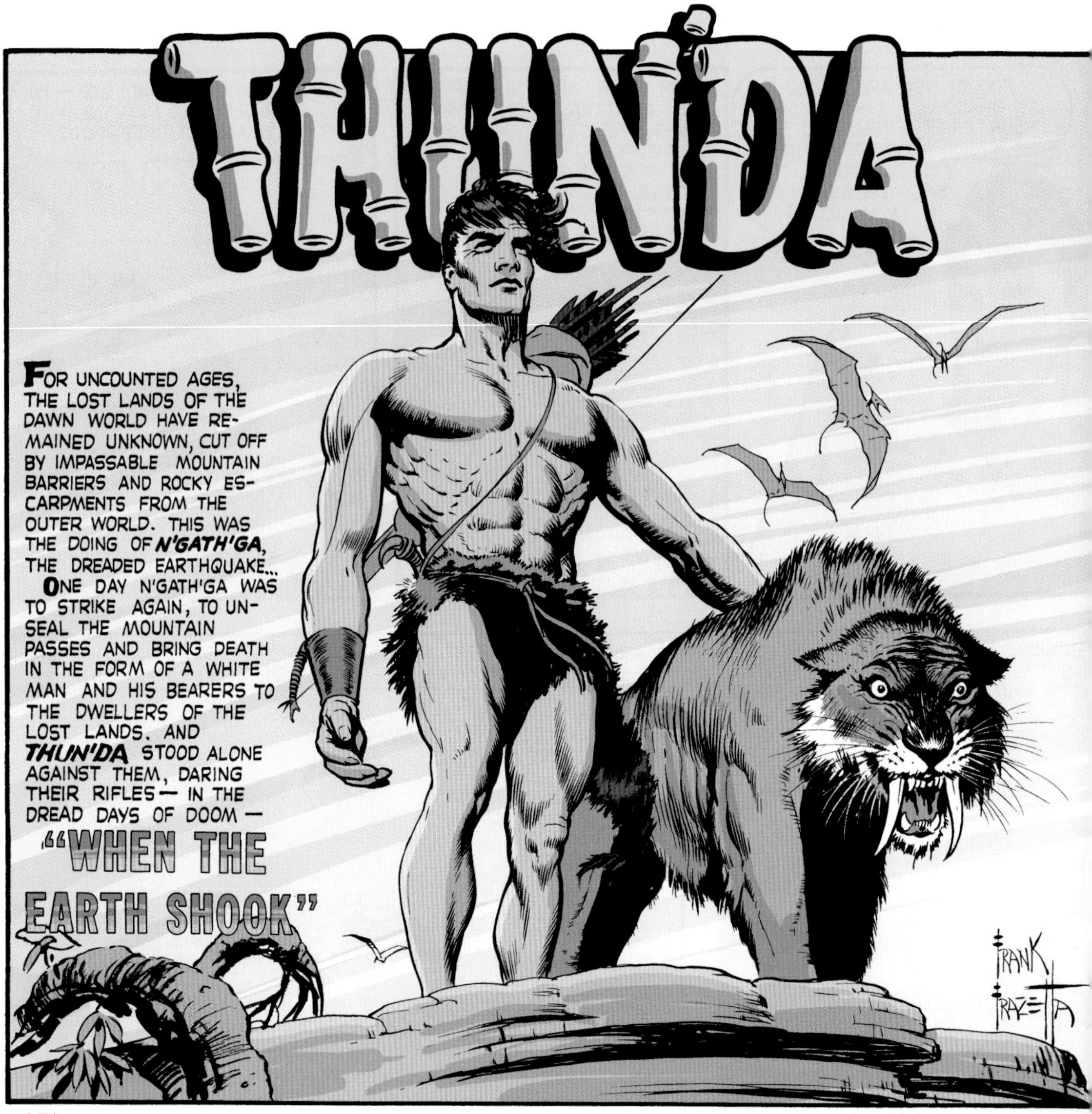
THUN'DA
FOR UNCOUNTED AGES, THE LOST LANDS OF THE DAWN WORLD HAVE REMAINED UNKNOWN, CUT OFF BY IMPASSABLE MOUNTAIN BARRIERS AND ROCKY ESCARPMENTS FROM THE OUTER WORLD. THIS WAS THE DOING OF N'GATH'GA, THE DREADED EARTHQUAKE...
ONE DAY N'GATH'GA WAS TO STRIKE AGAIN, TO UNSEAL THE MOUNTAIN PASSES AND BRING DEATH IN THE FORM OF A WHITE MAN AND HIS BEARERS TO THE DWELLERS OF THE LOST LANDS. AND THUN'DA STOOD ALONE AGAINST THEM, DARING THEIR RIFLES— IN THE DREAD DAYS OF DOOM —
"WHEN THE EARTH SHOOK"
FRANK FRAZETTA

THUN'DA HUNTS IN THE DAWN WORLD, HIS BOW A LIVING THING THAT CATAPULTS AN ARROW WITH THE FORCE OF A BULLET...

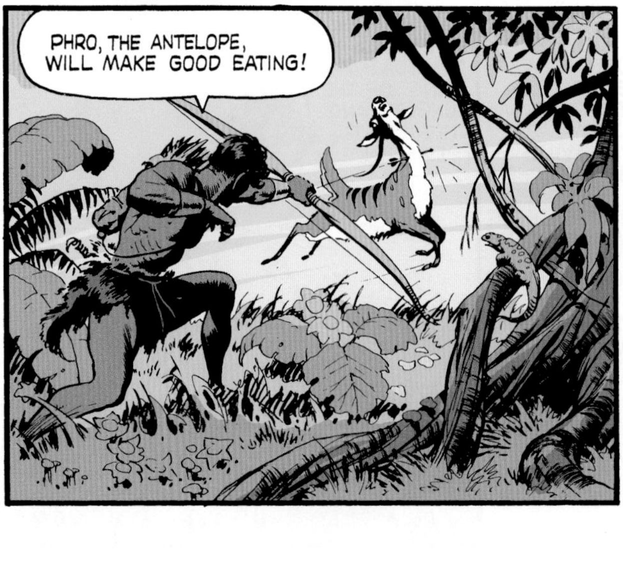
PHRO, THE ANTELOPE, WILL MAKE GOOD EATING!

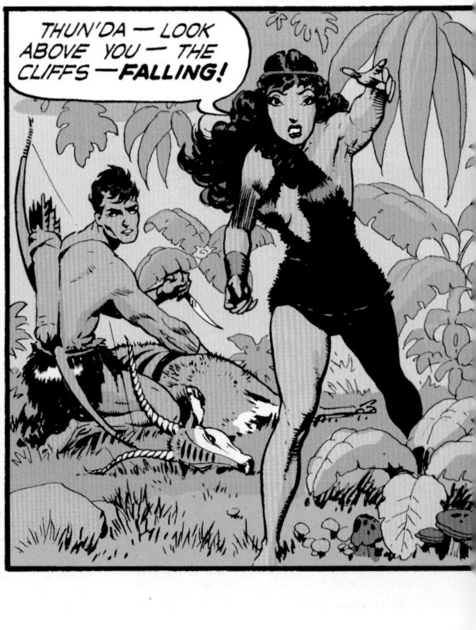
THUN'DA — LOOK ABOVE YOU — THE CLIFFS — FALLING!

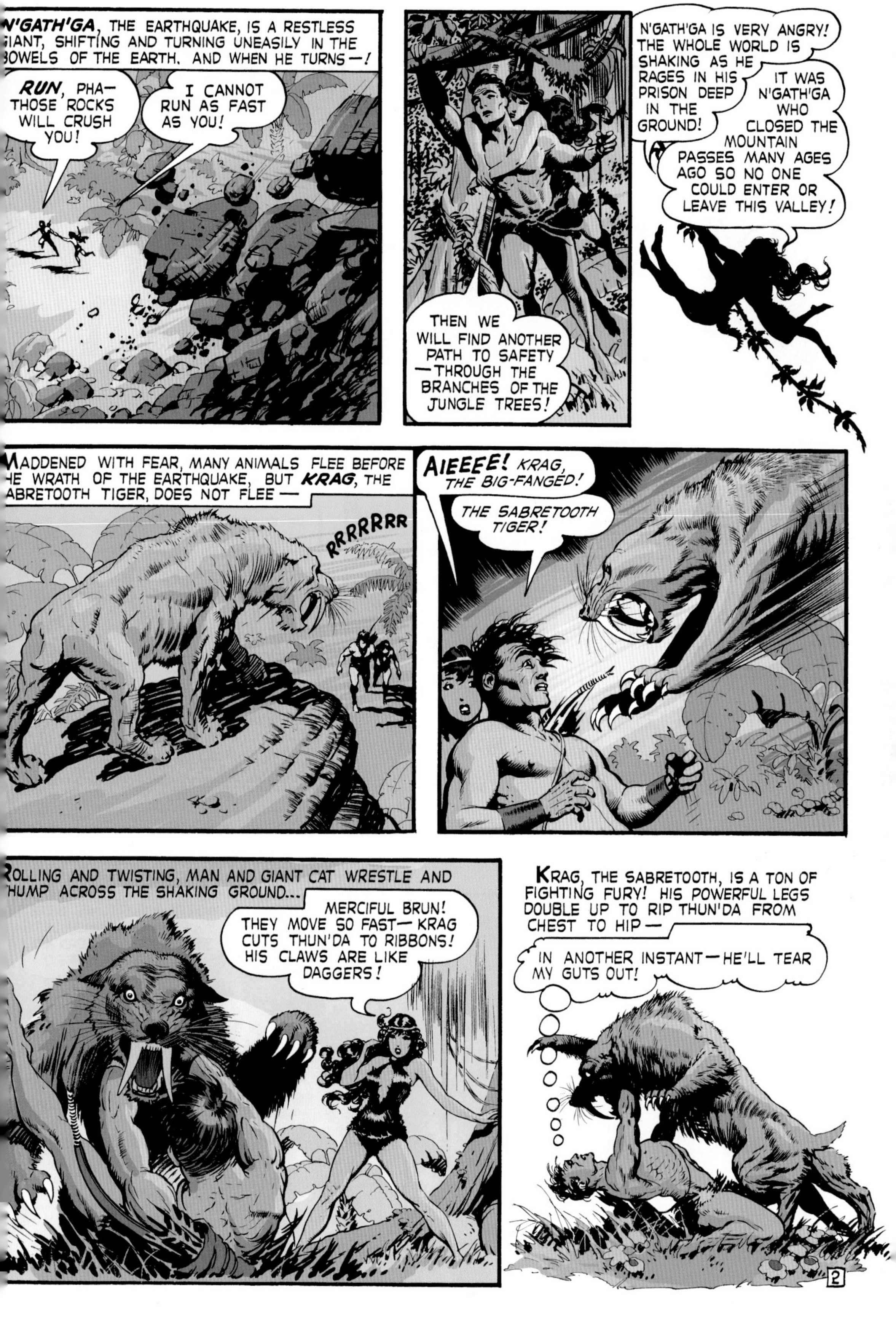

N'GATH'GA, THE EARTHQUAKE, IS A RESTLESS GIANT, SHIFTING AND TURNING UNEASILY IN THE BOWELS OF THE EARTH. AND WHEN HE TURNS—!
RUN, PHA—THOSE ROCKS WILL CRUSH YOU!
I CANNOT RUN AS FAST AS YOU!
THEN WE WILL FIND ANOTHER PATH TO SAFETY —THROUGH THE BRANCHES OF THE JUNGLE TREES!
N'GATH'GA IS VERY ANGRY! THE WHOLE WORLD IS SHAKING AS HE RAGES IN HIS PRISON DEEP IN THE GROUND!
IT WAS N'GATH'GA WHO CLOSED THE MOUNTAIN PASSES MANY AGES AGO SO NO ONE COULD ENTER OR LEAVE THIS VALLEY!
MADDENED WITH FEAR, MANY ANIMALS FLEE BEFORE THE WRATH OF THE EARTHQUAKE, BUT KRAG, THE SABRETOOTH TIGER, DOES NOT FLEE—
RRRRRRR
AIEEEE! KRAG, THE BIG-FANGED!
THE SABRETOOTH TIGER!
ROLLING AND TWISTING, MAN AND GIANT CAT WRESTLE AND THUMP ACROSS THE SHAKING GROUND...
MERCIFUL BRUN! THEY MOVE SO FAST—KRAG CUTS THUN'DA TO RIBBONS! HIS CLAWS ARE LIKE DAGGERS!
KRAG, THE SABRETOOTH, IS A TON OF FIGHTING FURY! HIS POWERFUL LEGS DOUBLE UP TO RIP THUN'DA FROM CHEST TO HIP—
IN ANOTHER INSTANT—HE'LL TEAR MY GUTS OUT!

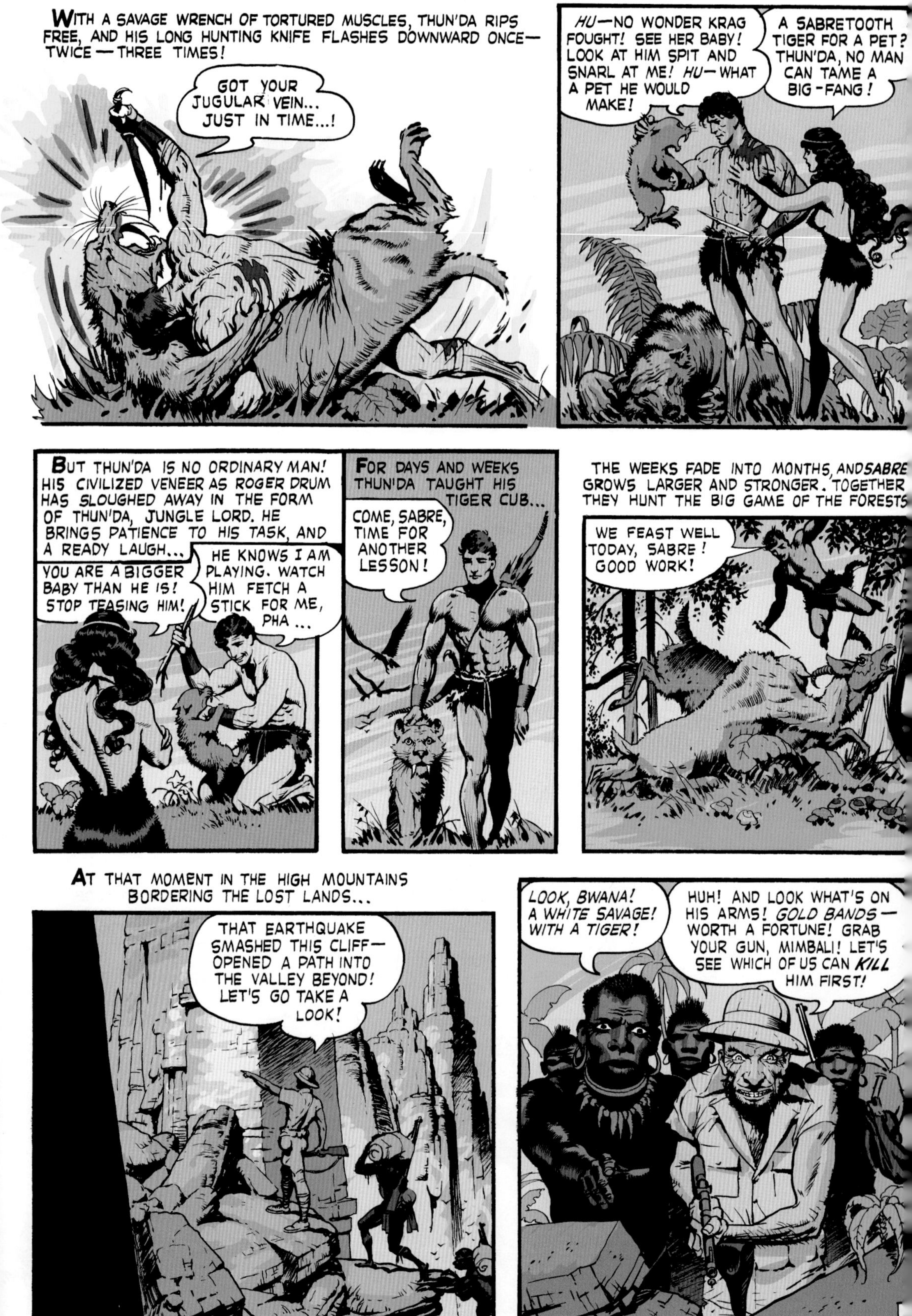
WITH A SAVAGE WRENCH OF TORTURED MUSCLES, THUN'DA RIPS FREE, AND HIS LONG HUNTING KNIFE FLASHES DOWNWARD ONCE— TWICE — THREE TIMES!
GOT YOUR JUGULAR VEIN... JUST IN TIME...!
HU—NO WONDER KRAG FOUGHT! SEE HER BABY! LOOK AT HIM SPIT AND SNARL AT ME! HU—WHAT A PET HE WOULD MAKE!
A SABRETOOTH TIGER FOR A PET? THUN'DA, NO MAN CAN TAME A BIG-FANG!
BUT THUN'DA IS NO ORDINARY MAN! HIS CIVILIZED VENEER AS ROGER DRUM HAS SLOUGHED AWAY IN THE FORM OF THUN'DA, JUNGLE LORD. HE BRINGS PATIENCE TO HIS TASK, AND A READY LAUGH...
YOU ARE A BIGGER BABY THAN HE IS! STOP TEASING HIM!
HE KNOWS I AM PLAYING. WATCH HIM FETCH A STICK FOR ME, PHA ...
FOR DAYS AND WEEKS THUN'DA TAUGHT HIS TIGER CUB...
COME, SABRE, TIME FOR ANOTHER LESSON!
THE WEEKS FADE INTO MONTHS, AND SABRE GROWS LARGER AND STRONGER. TOGETHER THEY HUNT THE BIG GAME OF THE FORESTS
WE FEAST WELL TODAY, SABRE! GOOD WORK!
AT THAT MOMENT IN THE HIGH MOUNTAINS BORDERING THE LOST LANDS...
THAT EARTHQUAKE SMASHED THIS CLIFF— OPENED A PATH INTO THE VALLEY BEYOND! LET'S GO TAKE A LOOK!
LOOK, BWANA! A WHITE SAVAGE! WITH A TIGER!
HUH! AND LOOK WHAT'S ON HIS ARMS! GOLD BANDS— WORTH A FORTUNE! GRAB YOUR GUN, MIMBALI! LET'S SEE WHICH OF US CAN KILL HIM FIRST!

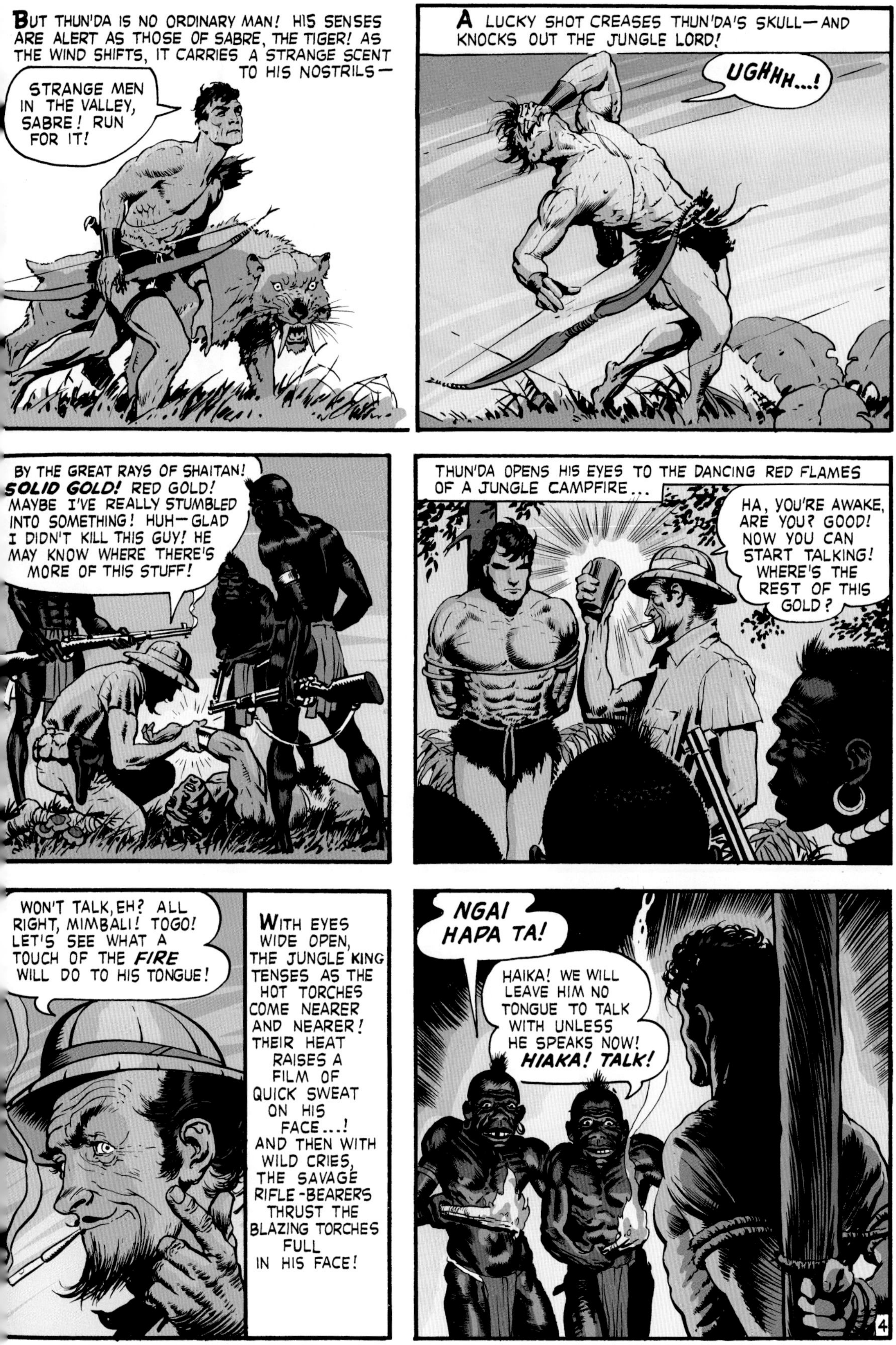
BUT THUN'DA IS NO ORDINARY MAN! HIS SENSES ARE ALERT AS THOSE OF SABRE, THE TIGER! AS THE WIND SHIFTS, IT CARRIES A STRANGE SCENT TO HIS NOSTRILS—
STRANGE MEN IN THE VALLEY, SABRE! RUN FOR IT!
A LUCKY SHOT CREASES THUN'DA'S SKULL—AND KNOCKS OUT THE JUNGLE LORD!
UGHHH...!
BY THE GREAT RAYS OF SHAITAN! SOLID GOLD! RED GOLD! MAYBE I'VE REALLY STUMBLED INTO SOMETHING! HUH—GLAD I DIDN'T KILL THIS GUY! HE MAY KNOW WHERE THERE'S MORE OF THIS STUFF!
THUN'DA OPENS HIS EYES TO THE DANCING RED FLAMES OF A JUNGLE CAMPFIRE...
HA, YOU'RE AWAKE, ARE YOU? GOOD! NOW YOU CAN START TALKING! WHERE'S THE REST OF THIS GOLD?
WON'T TALK, EH? ALL RIGHT, MIMBALI! TOGO! LET'S SEE WHAT A TOUCH OF THE FIRE WILL DO TO HIS TONGUE!
WITH EYES WIDE OPEN, THE JUNGLE KING TENSES AS THE HOT TORCHES COME NEARER AND NEARER! THEIR HEAT RAISES A FILM OF QUICK SWEAT ON HIS FACE...! AND THEN WITH WILD CRIES, THE SAVAGE RIFLE-BEARERS THRUST THE BLAZING TORCHES FULL IN HIS FACE!
NGAI HAPA TA!
HAIKA! WE WILL LEAVE HIM NO TONGUE TO TALK WITH UNLESS HE SPEAKS NOW! HIAKA! TALK!
4

A LOW RUMBLE OF FURY ERUPTS FROM SABRE'S SHAGGY THROAT! LIKE A LIVING LIGHTNING BOLT, HE LEAPS FROM THE JUNGLE TO SAVE HIS YOUNG MASTER —

AIEEEE!

SHIV ISLIP IS PARALYZED WITH AMAZEMENT FOR A LONG MOMENT...

A SABRETOOTH TIGER! WHAT KIND OF A LAND IS THIS?

I'M NOT GOING TO KILL YOU, YOU CRAZY CAVEMAN! BUT I SURE WILL **CRIPPLE** YOU!

HAGAKA! SABRE! INTO THE TREES!

THE BRANCHES AND THE LEAVES WILL HIDE ME FROM HIM! I CAN MOVE SWIFTLY YET SILENTLY AND INVISIBLY IN THE JUNGLE TREES. NO MAN CAN FIND THUN'DA HERE...

HOURS LATER, THE JUNGLE GIANT STANDS BY THE ENTRANCE TO THE CAVE OF THE DRUM. IN HIS HANDS, THE HAMMER SMASHES THE ANCIENT TAMBOURINE...

FROM FIELDS AND GOLD MINES, THE HUNT, AND THE CHASE, COME THE VALLEY AND HILL PEOPLE...

WITH SPEAR AND ARROW THEY CHARGE DOWN ON SHIV ISLIP AND HIS GOLD-HUNGRY NATIVES. COOLLY, THE WHITE HUNTER DIRECTS HIS RIFLE FIRE...

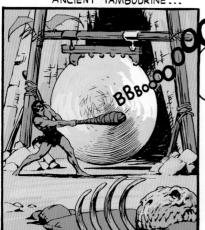

BBBoooooOOOMMMMMMMM!

THE DRUM OF THE JUNGLE LORD!

THUN'DA WARNS US OF DANGER!

AIEEE! WE WILL FIGHT TO THE DEATH!

THEY'LL NEVER STAND IN THE FACE OF HOT LEAD **SHOOT TO KILL!**

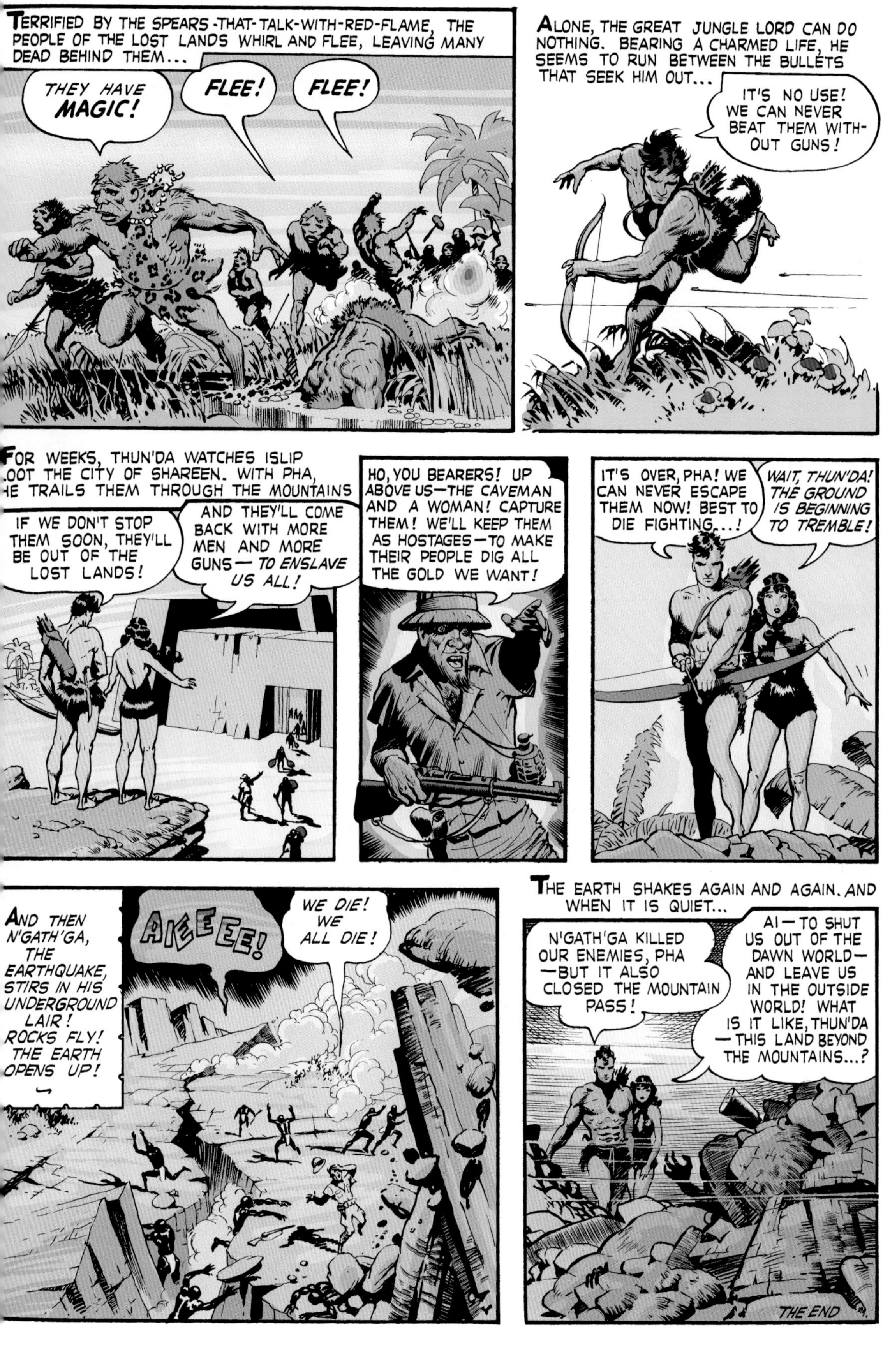
TERRIFIED BY THE SPEARS-THAT-TALK-WITH-RED-FLAME, THE PEOPLE OF THE LOST LANDS WHIRL AND FLEE, LEAVING MANY DEAD BEHIND THEM...
THEY HAVE MAGIC!
FLEE!
FLEE!
ALONE, THE GREAT JUNGLE LORD CAN DO NOTHING. BEARING A CHARMED LIFE, HE SEEMS TO RUN BETWEEN THE BULLETS THAT SEEK HIM OUT...
IT'S NO USE! WE CAN NEVER BEAT THEM WITH-OUT GUNS!
FOR WEEKS, THUN'DA WATCHES ISLIP LOOT THE CITY OF SHAREEN. WITH PHA, HE TRAILS THEM THROUGH THE MOUNTAINS
IF WE DON'T STOP THEM SOON, THEY'LL BE OUT OF THE LOST LANDS!
AND THEY'LL COME BACK WITH MORE MEN AND MORE GUNS — TO ENSLAVE US ALL!
HO, YOU BEARERS! UP ABOVE US—THE CAVEMAN AND A WOMAN! CAPTURE THEM! WE'LL KEEP THEM AS HOSTAGES—TO MAKE THEIR PEOPLE DIG ALL THE GOLD WE WANT!
IT'S OVER, PHA! WE CAN NEVER ESCAPE THEM NOW! BEST TO DIE FIGHTING...!
WAIT, THUN'DA! THE GROUND IS BEGINNING TO TREMBLE!
AND THEN N'GATH'GA, THE EARTHQUAKE, STIRS IN HIS UNDERGROUND LAIR! ROCKS FLY! THE EARTH OPENS UP!
AIEEEEE!
WE DIE! WE ALL DIE!
THE EARTH SHAKES AGAIN AND AGAIN. AND WHEN IT IS QUIET...
N'GATH'GA KILLED OUR ENEMIES, PHA —BUT IT ALSO CLOSED THE MOUNTAIN PASS!
AI— TO SHUT US OUT OF THE DAWN WORLD— AND LEAVE US IN THE OUTSIDE WORLD! WHAT IS IT LIKE, THUN'DA — THIS LAND BEYOND THE MOUNTAINS...?
THE END

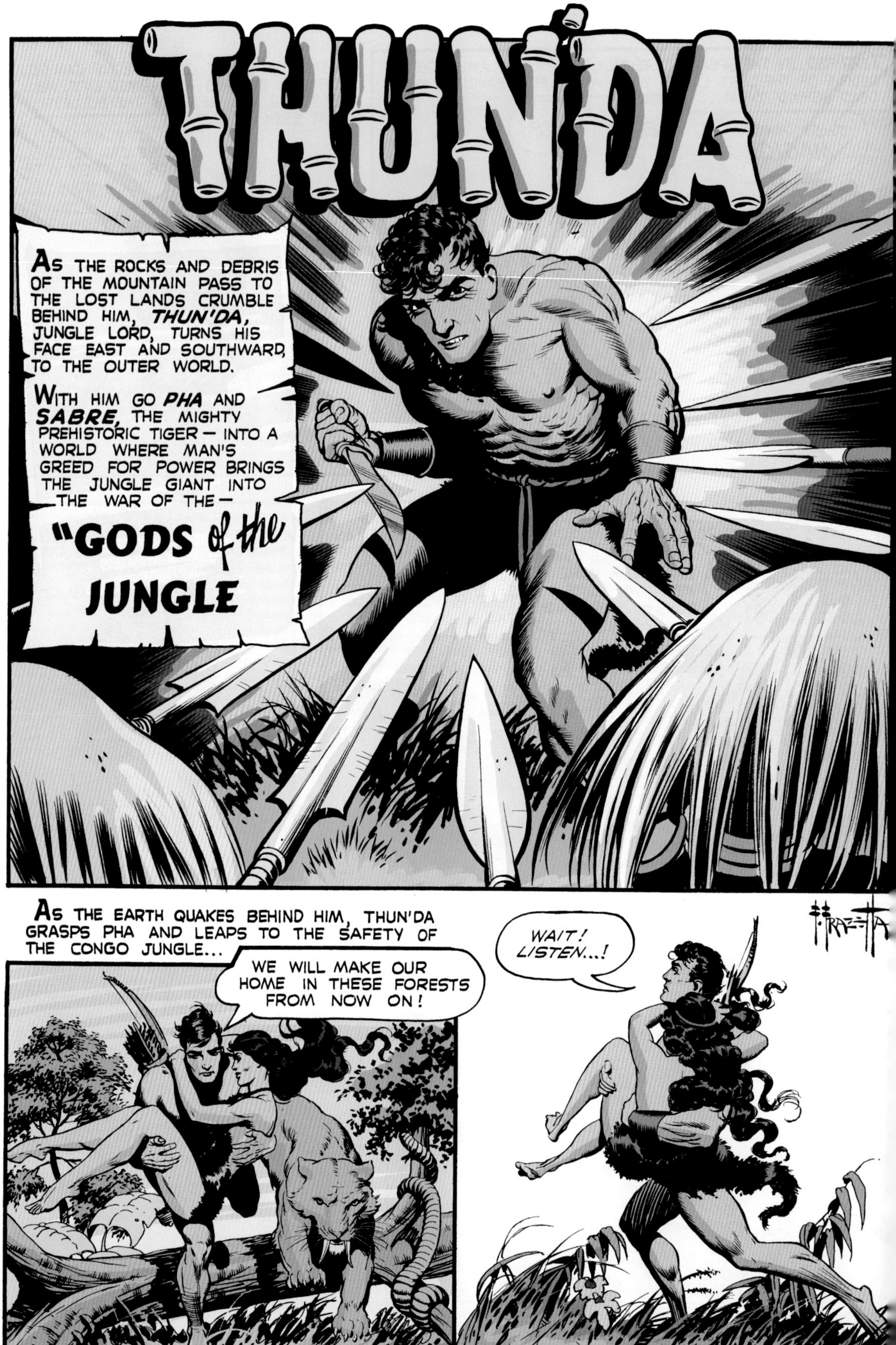
THUN'DA
AS THE ROCKS AND DEBRIS OF THE MOUNTAIN PASS TO THE LOST LANDS CRUMBLE BEHIND HIM, THUN'DA, JUNGLE LORD, TURNS HIS FACE EAST AND SOUTHWARD, TO THE OUTER WORLD.
WITH HIM GO PHA AND SABRE, THE MIGHTY PREHISTORIC TIGER — INTO A WORLD WHERE MAN'S GREED FOR POWER BRINGS THE JUNGLE GIANT INTO THE WAR OF THE —
"GODS of the JUNGLE
AS THE EARTH QUAKES BEHIND HIM, THUN'DA GRASPS PHA AND LEAPS TO THE SAFETY OF THE CONGO JUNGLE...
WE WILL MAKE OUR HOME IN THESE FORESTS FROM NOW ON!
WAIT! LISTEN...!

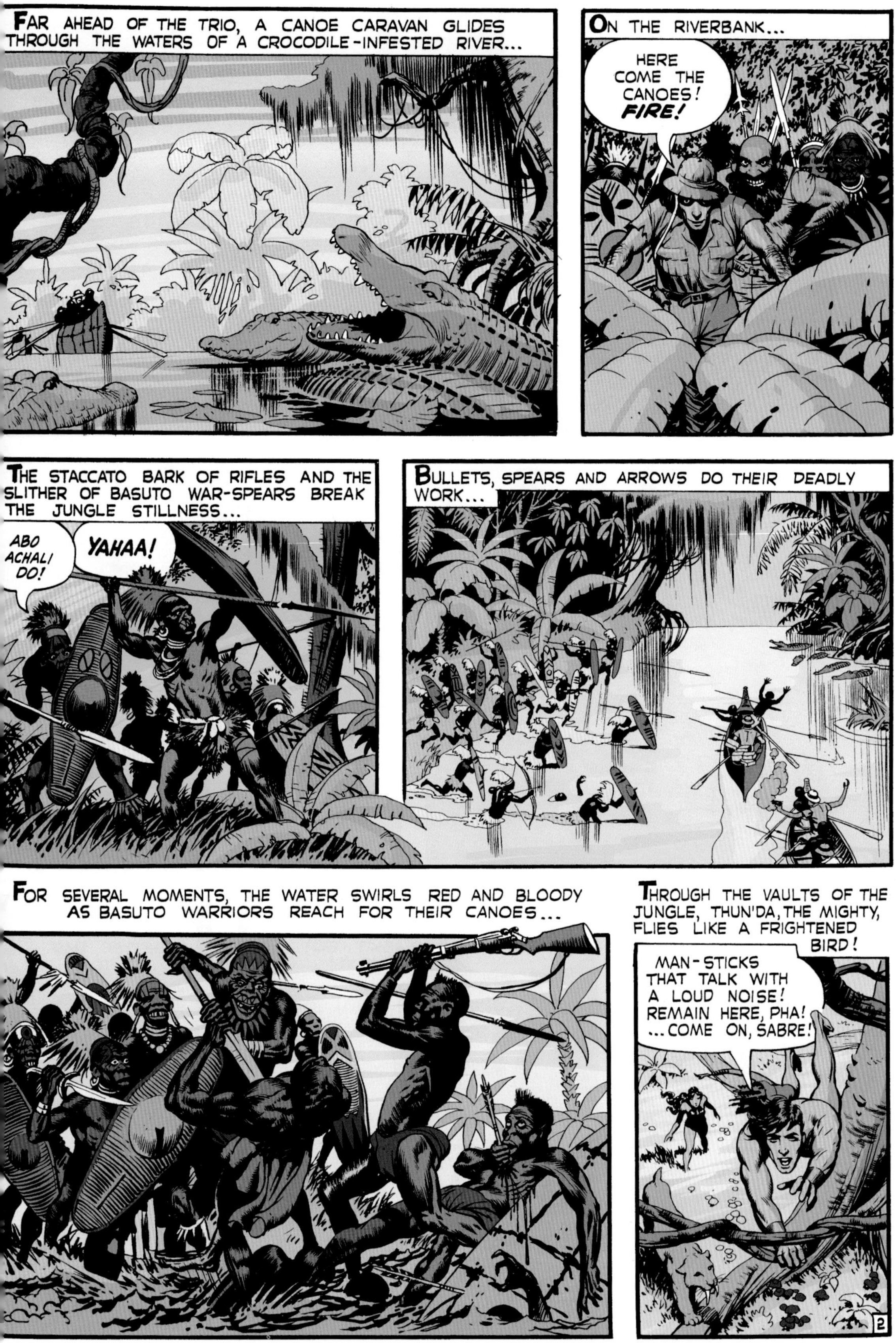
FAR AHEAD OF THE TRIO, A CANOE CARAVAN GLIDES THROUGH THE WATERS OF A CROCODILE-INFESTED RIVER...
ON THE RIVERBANK...
HERE COME THE CANOES! FIRE!
THE STACCATO BARK OF RIFLES AND THE SLITHER OF BASUTO WAR-SPEARS BREAK THE JUNGLE STILLNESS...
ABO ACHALI DO!
YAHAA!
BULLETS, SPEARS AND ARROWS DO THEIR DEADLY WORK...
FOR SEVERAL MOMENTS, THE WATER SWIRLS RED AND BLOODY AS BASUTO WARRIORS REACH FOR THEIR CANOES...
THROUGH THE VAULTS OF THE JUNGLE, THUN'DA, THE MIGHTY, FLIES LIKE A FRIGHTENED BIRD!
MAN-STICKS THAT TALK WITH A LOUD NOISE! REMAIN HERE, PHA! ...COME ON, SABRE!
2

SOON AFTER... WHITE MEN LIKE MYSELF... BEING ATTACKED IN CANOES! I DON'T LIKE THOSE ODDS, SABRE!

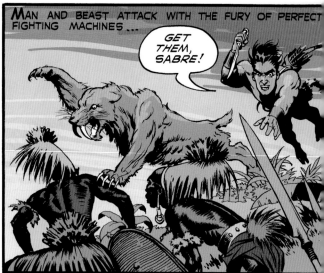

MAN AND BEAST ATTACK WITH THE FURY OF PERFECT FIGHTING MACHINES...

GET THEM, SABRE!

BACK TO YOUR KENNELS, JUNGLE DOGS!

YOU FACE THUN'DA— MIGHTY FIGHTER!

TERRIFIED AT SIGHT OF THE POWERFULLY-MUSCLED JUNGLE GIANT, THE BASUTOS TURN WITH FRIGHT-FOAM ON THEIR LIPS...

GET BACK THERE, YOU FOOLS!

IT'S ONLY ONE MAN— AND HE HASN'T GOT A GUN!

GULP! PERHAPS IT IS BETTER WE GO, TOO!

ZIP!

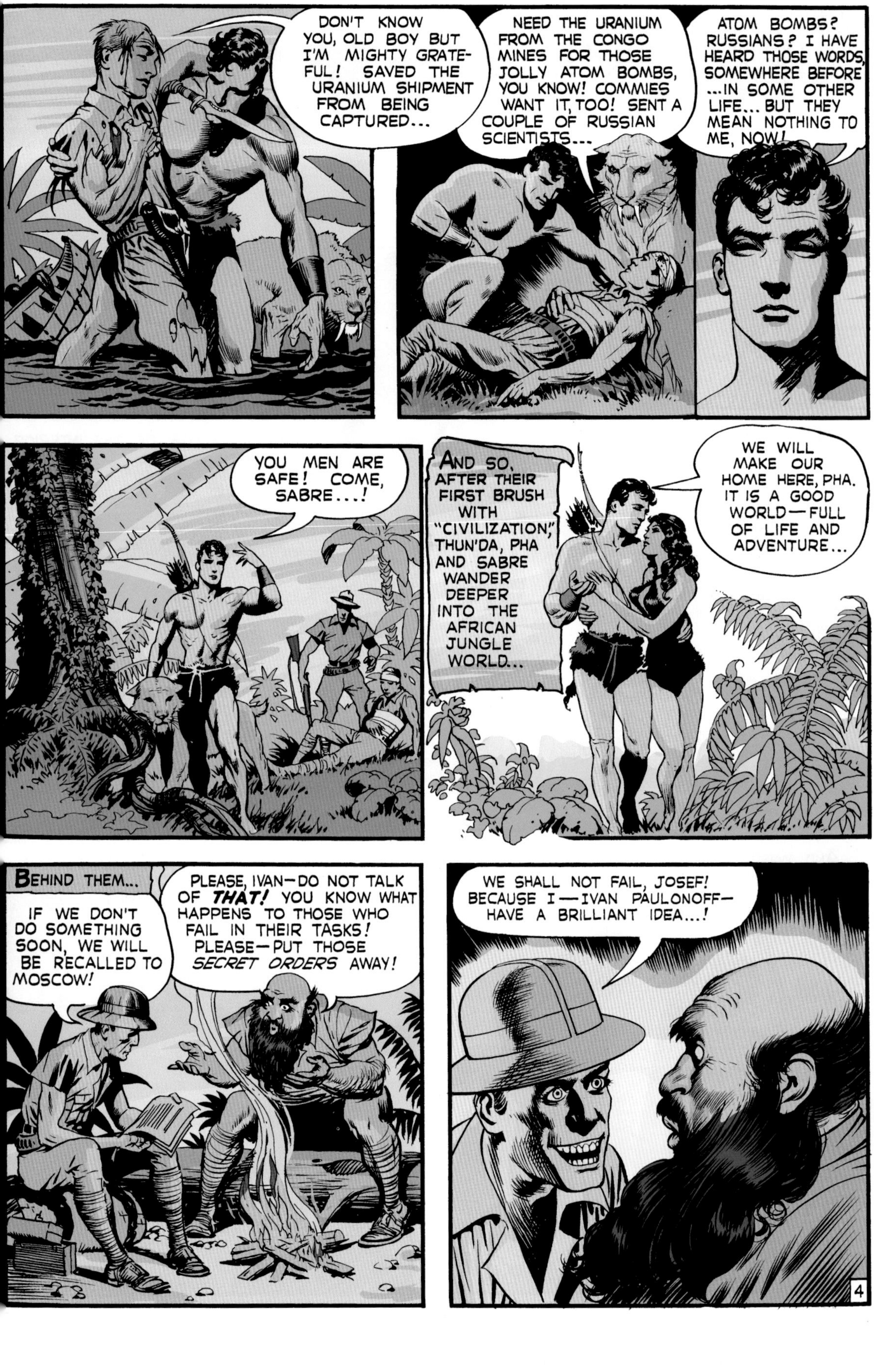

DON'T KNOW YOU, OLD BOY BUT I'M MIGHTY GRATEFUL! SAVED THE URANIUM SHIPMENT FROM BEING CAPTURED...
NEED THE URANIUM FROM THE CONGO MINES FOR THOSE JOLLY ATOM BOMBS, YOU KNOW! COMMIES WANT IT, TOO! SENT A COUPLE OF RUSSIAN SCIENTISTS...
ATOM BOMBS? RUSSIANS? I HAVE HEARD THOSE WORDS, SOMEWHERE BEFORE ...IN SOME OTHER LIFE... BUT THEY MEAN NOTHING TO ME, NOW!
YOU MEN ARE SAFE! COME, SABRE...!
AND SO, AFTER THEIR FIRST BRUSH WITH "CIVILIZATION," THUN'DA, PHA AND SABRE WANDER DEEPER INTO THE AFRICAN JUNGLE WORLD...
WE WILL MAKE OUR HOME HERE, PHA. IT IS A GOOD WORLD—FULL OF LIFE AND ADVENTURE...
BEHIND THEM...
IF WE DON'T DO SOMETHING SOON, WE WILL BE RECALLED TO MOSCOW!
PLEASE, IVAN—DO NOT TALK OF THAT! YOU KNOW WHAT HAPPENS TO THOSE WHO FAIL IN THEIR TASKS! PLEASE—PUT THOSE SECRET ORDERS AWAY!
WE SHALL NOT FAIL, JOSEF! BECAUSE I—IVAN PAULONOFF—HAVE A BRILLIANT IDEA...!

THE NATIVES TALKED OF A JUNGLE GOD CALLED *THUN'DA!* THEY FEAR HIM! WELL, WE'LL GIVE THEM A JUNGLE GOD THAT THEY WILL FEAR —AND *OBEY!*

I SEE WHAT YOU MEAN, IVAN! CLEVER — VERY CLEVER!

THEREAFTER, THE HILLS AND FORESTS THROB WITH THE STEADY BEAT OF RHINOCEROUS HIDE DRUMS. THEY TELL OF A GROTESQUE THING WITH A SCALY FACE . . .

INTO THE HILL VILLAGES OF THE WARLIKE KASIMBA COMES THE MASKED HORROR...

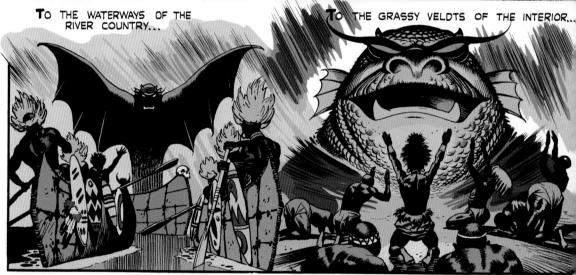

TO THE WATERWAYS OF THE RIVER COUNTRY...

TO THE GRASSY VELDTS OF THE INTERIOR...

AND WHERE THE JUNGLE GOD WALKS, NATIVE FIGHTING MEN HEFT THEIR WAR SPEARS AND MARCH...

WHILE THE RUSSIANS RUB THEIR HANDS AND CHUCKLE IN GLEE...

YOU WERE A GOOD JUNGLE GOD, JOSEF! SO, WE HAVE OBEYED OUR ORDERS! WE HAVE ROUSED UP THE JUNGLE TRIBES! WE ARE READY TO *STRIKE!*

5

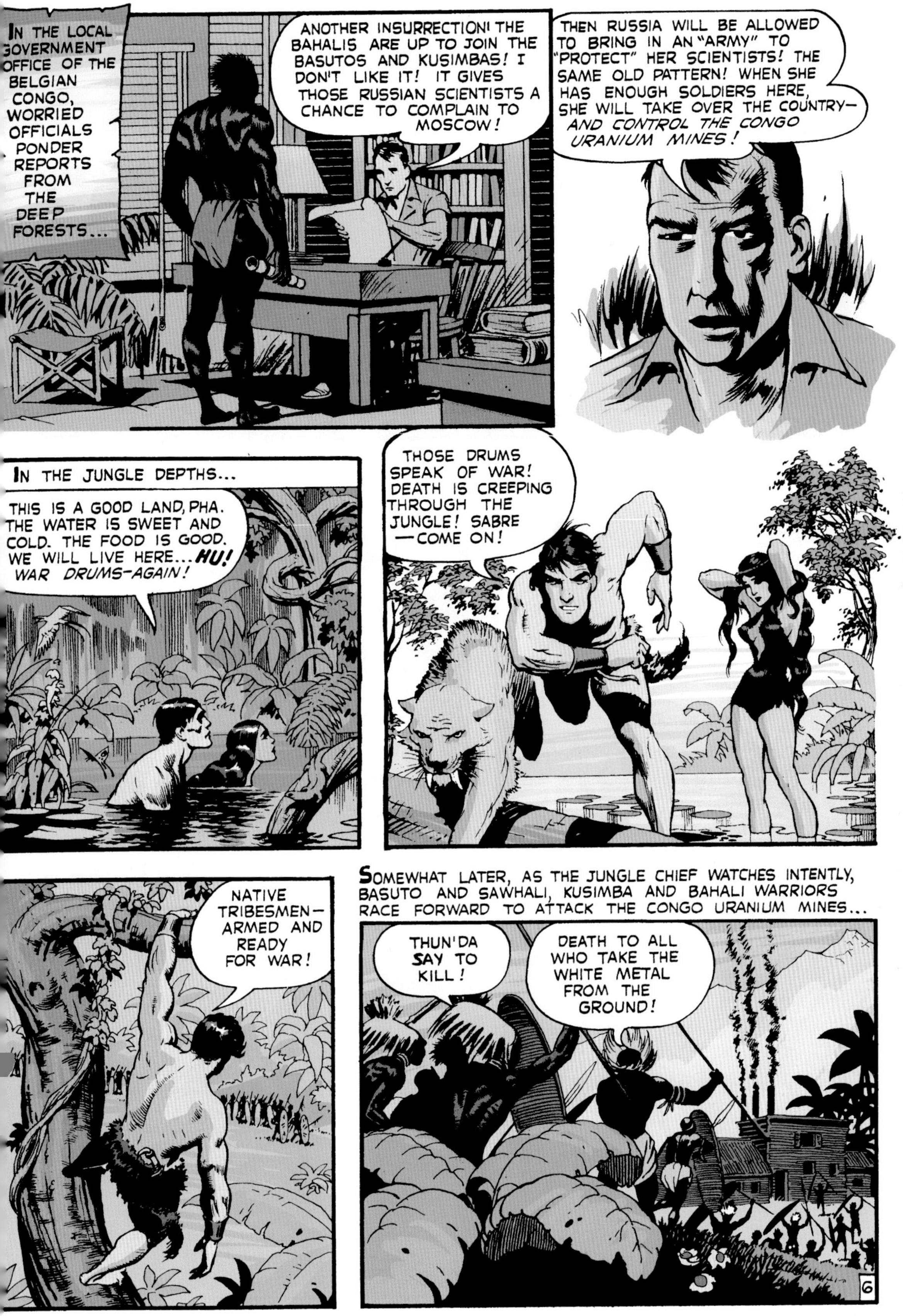
IN THE LOCAL GOVERNMENT OFFICE OF THE BELGIAN CONGO, WORRIED OFFICIALS PONDER REPORTS FROM THE DEEP FORESTS...
ANOTHER INSURRECTION! THE BAHALIS ARE UP TO JOIN THE BASUTOS AND KUSIMBAS! I DON'T LIKE IT! IT GIVES THOSE RUSSIAN SCIENTISTS A CHANCE TO COMPLAIN TO MOSCOW!
THEN RUSSIA WILL BE ALLOWED TO BRING IN AN "ARMY" TO "PROTECT" HER SCIENTISTS! THE SAME OLD PATTERN! WHEN SHE HAS ENOUGH SOLDIERS HERE, SHE WILL TAKE OVER THE COUNTRY— AND CONTROL THE CONGO URANIUM MINES!
IN THE JUNGLE DEPTHS...
THIS IS A GOOD LAND, PHA. THE WATER IS SWEET AND COLD. THE FOOD IS GOOD. WE WILL LIVE HERE... HU! WAR DRUMS-AGAIN!
THOSE DRUMS SPEAK OF WAR! DEATH IS CREEPING THROUGH THE JUNGLE! SABRE —COME ON!
NATIVE TRIBESMEN— ARMED AND READY FOR WAR!
SOMEWHAT LATER, AS THE JUNGLE CHIEF WATCHES INTENTLY, BASUTO AND SAWHALI, KUSIMBA AND BAHALI WARRIORS RACE FORWARD TO ATTACK THE CONGO URANIUM MINES...
THUN'DA SAY TO KILL!
DEATH TO ALL WHO TAKE THE WHITE METAL FROM THE GROUND!
6

A RAGGED VOLLEY OF RIFLE FIRE TRIES TO BREAK THE SHIELD-WALL—AND FAILS!

THUNDA SAY —KILL!

KILL! KILL!

KILL!

THUN'DA? BUT I AM THUN'DA! THUN'DA, THE MIGHTY—LORD OF THE JUNGLE WORLD! COME ON, SABRE!

I AM THUN'DA! I AM THE JUNGLE GOD!

MAHBA AHILLA!

THE FATHER OF ALL TIGERS! AIEEEEE!

THIS MAN SPEAKS TRUTH! HE IS A JUNGLE GOD!

IN PETRIFIED FEAR AND TERROR, THE NATIVES STAND FOR ONE MOMENT AGAINST THUN'DA AND SABRE —

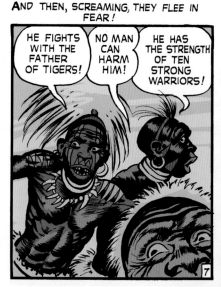

AND THEN, SCREAMING, THEY FLEE IN FEAR!

HE FIGHTS WITH THE FATHER OF TIGERS!

NO MAN CAN HARM HIM!

HE HAS THE STRENGTH OF TEN STRONG WARRIORS!

7

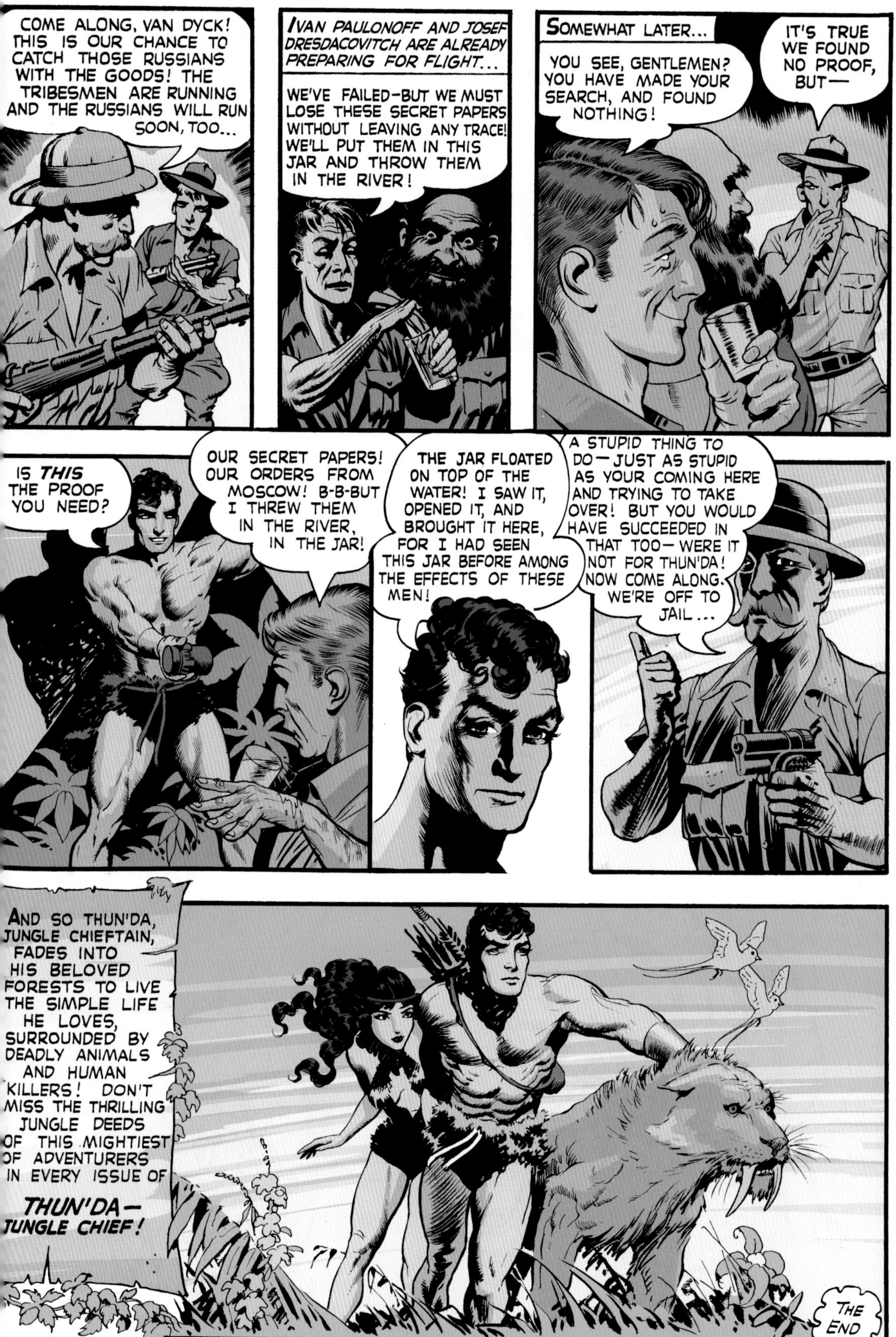
COME ALONG, VAN DYCK! THIS IS OUR CHANCE TO CATCH THOSE RUSSIANS WITH THE GOODS! THE TRIBESMEN ARE RUNNING AND THE RUSSIANS WILL RUN SOON, TOO...
IVAN PAULONOFF AND JOSEF DRESDACOVITCH ARE ALREADY PREPARING FOR FLIGHT...
WE'VE FAILED–BUT WE MUST LOSE THESE SECRET PAPERS WITHOUT LEAVING ANY TRACE! WE'LL PUT THEM IN THIS JAR AND THROW THEM IN THE RIVER!
SOMEWHAT LATER...
YOU SEE, GENTLEMEN? YOU HAVE MADE YOUR SEARCH, AND FOUND NOTHING!
IT'S TRUE WE FOUND NO PROOF, BUT—
IS THIS THE PROOF YOU NEED?
OUR SECRET PAPERS! OUR ORDERS FROM MOSCOW! B-B-BUT I THREW THEM IN THE RIVER, IN THE JAR!
THE JAR FLOATED ON TOP OF THE WATER! I SAW IT, OPENED IT, AND BROUGHT IT HERE, FOR I HAD SEEN THIS JAR BEFORE AMONG THE EFFECTS OF THESE MEN!
A STUPID THING TO DO — JUST AS STUPID AS YOUR COMING HERE AND TRYING TO TAKE OVER! BUT YOU WOULD HAVE SUCCEEDED IN THAT TOO— WERE IT NOT FOR THUN'DA! NOW COME ALONG. WE'RE OFF TO JAIL...
AND SO THUN'DA, JUNGLE CHIEFTAIN, FADES INTO HIS BELOVED FORESTS TO LIVE THE SIMPLE LIFE HE LOVES, SURROUNDED BY DEADLY ANIMALS AND HUMAN KILLERS! DON'T MISS THE THRILLING JUNGLE DEEDS OF THIS MIGHTIEST OF ADVENTURERS IN EVERY ISSUE OF THUN'DA– JUNGLE CHIEF!
THE END

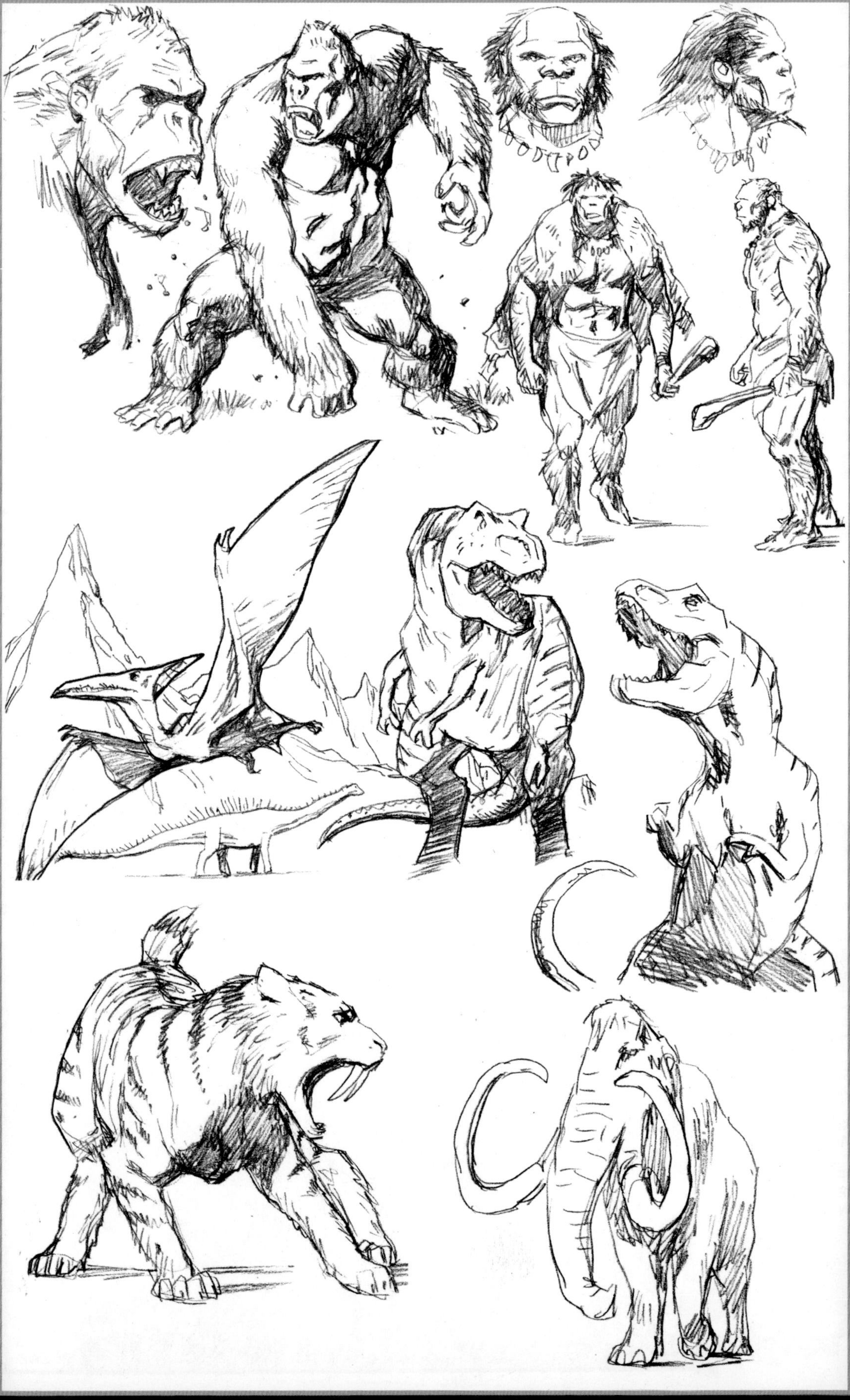

Concept Sketches by Cliff Richards

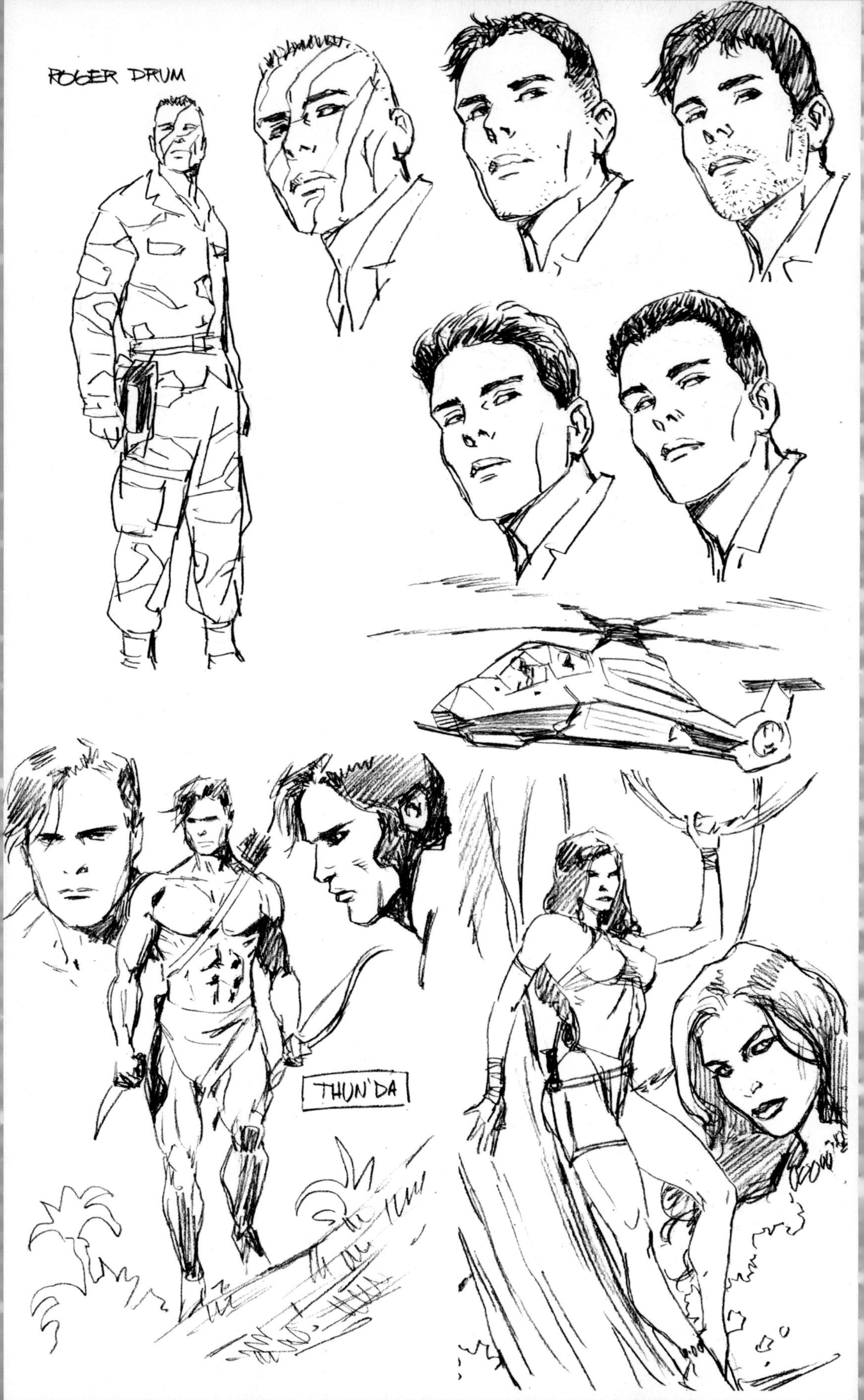
ROGER DRUM
THUN'DA

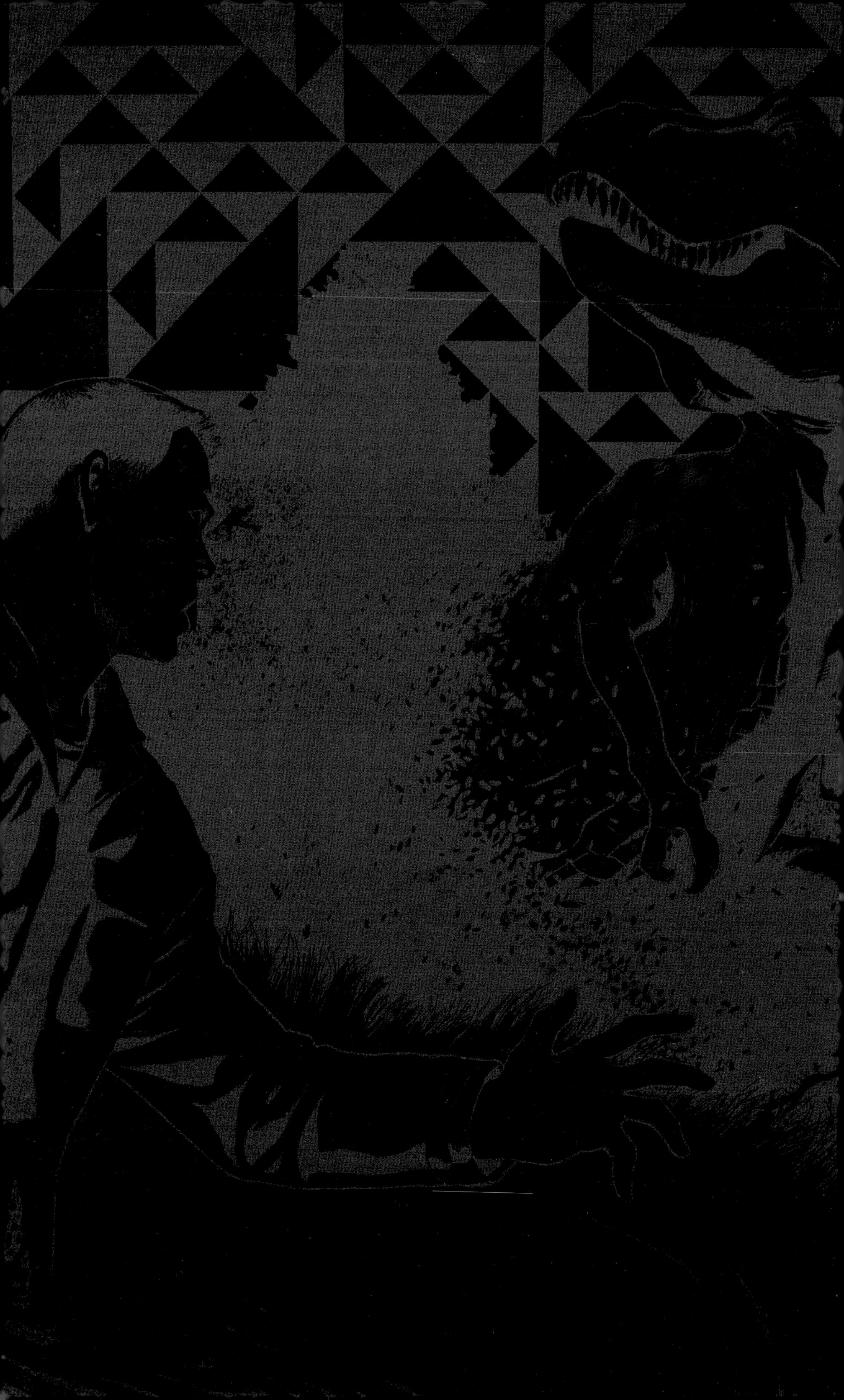